Learn Microsoft Fabric

A practical guide to performing data analytics in
the era of artificial intelligence

Arshad Ali

Bradley Schacht

‹packt›

Learn Microsoft Fabric

Copyright © 2024 Packt Publishing

Group Product Manager: Kaustubh Manglurkar

Publishing Product Manager: Deepesh Patel

Book Project Manager: Hemangi Lotlikar

Senior Editor: Rohit Singh

Technical Editor: Kavyashree K S

Copy Editor: Safis Editing

Proofreader: Safis Editing

Indexer: Subalakshmi Govindhan

Production Designer: Vijay Kamble

Developer Relations Marketing Executive: Nivedita Singh

First published: February 2024

Production reference: 1270223

Published by Packt Publishing Ltd.

Grosvenor House

11 St Paul's Square

Birmingham

B3 1RB, UK.

ISBN 978-1-83508-228-7

www.packtpub.com

This book is dedicated to my late parents, Mrs. and Mr. Md Azal Hussain, who gave me life and shaped me into who I am today. I wish they could witness this achievement, but I know they are proud of me wherever they are, and I am grateful for their love. I also dedicate this book to my wife, Shazia Arshad Ali, who has been my constant support and inspiration in everything I do, and who encouraged me to take on the challenge of writing this book; my daughter, Aidha, who is only eight years old but has been my accountability partner (keeping me in check to ensure that I finished chapters on time) and is eager to read this book; and my son, Sameed, whose smile and laughter have energized me throughout this journey.

– Arshad Ali

To my wife, Nichole, for loving me so well for the last 2,167 days.
There is no one I would rather do life with than you.

– Bradley Schacht

Contributors

About the authors

Arshad Ali is a principal product manager at Microsoft, working on the Microsoft Fabric product team in Redmond, WA. He focuses on Spark Runtime, which empowers both data engineering and data science experiences. In his previous role, he helped strategic customers and partners adopt Azure Synapse and Microsoft Fabric.

Arshad has more than 20 years of industry experience and has been with Microsoft for over 16 years. He is the co-author of the book *Big Data Analytics with Azure HDInsight* and the author of over 200 technical articles and blogs on data and analytics. Arshad holds an MBA from the Foster School of Business at the University of Washington and an MCA from India.

This book would not have been possible without the support of our colleagues at Microsoft and our friends, who have been an inspiration and have supported us in writing this book, directly or indirectly. We are truly grateful to you all for your support and the opportunity you have given us to learn and grow. Thank you, Brad, for being an amazing co-author! We would also like to thank the entire Packt team, especially Deepesh, Rohit, Hemangi, and others, for turning our proposal from a dream into a reality, and Kay Sauter for reading the entire draft of the book and providing very helpful feedback and suggestions on it.

Bradley Schacht is a principal program manager on the Microsoft Fabric product team based in Saint Augustine, Florida. Bradley is a former consultant and trainer and has co-authored five books on SQL Server and Power BI. As a member of the Microsoft Fabric product team, Bradley works directly with customers to solve some of their most complex data problems and helps shape the future of Microsoft Fabric. Bradley gives back to the community by speaking at events, such as the PASS Summit, SQL Saturday, Code Camp, and user groups across the country, including locally at the **Jacksonville SQL Server User Group** (**JSSUG**). He is a contributor on SQLServerCentral.com and blogs on his personal site, BradleySchacht.com.

I give thanks to God, for all the blessings He has given me and who I would be lost without. Thanks to my amazing, beautiful wife, Nichole, and our crazy boys, Oliver and Levi, for their unending love and support. It means more than you could possibly imagine. To Arshad, my co-author, who worked hard to make this book happen. Lastly, to Han and Chewie – you have inspired me and given me the confidence to one day build the LEGO Millennium Falcon.

About the reviewer

Kay Sauter is a senior data engineer. He has over 10 years of experience working with SQL Server and holds a Certificate of Advanced Studies in Applied Data Analytics, Machine Learning, and Customer Intelligence from HWZ University of Applied Sciences in Business Administration, Zurich, Switzerland. He has also been a Microsoft MVP for the data platform since 2022. Kay shares his knowledge and insights on his blog and his newsletter on LinkedIn. He runs the Azure Data user group **Data TGIF**, and he is a co-organizer of the online live conference **DATA BASH** and the user group **DEI Virtual Group**. He is married and is based near Zurich, Switzerland.

About the reviewer

Kay Sauter is a senior data engineer. He has over 10 years of experience working with SQL Server and holds a Certificate of Advanced Studies in Applied Data Analytics, Machine Learning, and Customer Intelligence from HWZ University of Applied Sciences in Business Administration, Zurich, Switzerland. He has also been a Microsoft MVP for the data platform since 2022. Kay shares his knowledge and insights on his blog and his newsletter on LinkedIn. He runs the Azure Data user group **Data TGIF**, and he is a co-organizer of the online live conference **DATA BASH** and the user group **DEI Virtual Group**. He is married and is based near Zurich, Switzerland.

Table of Contents

Part 2: Building End-to-End Analytics Systems

3

Building an End-to-End Analytics System – Lakehouse   63

4

Building an End-to-End Analytics System – Data Warehouse   107

Part 3: Administration and Monitoring

7

8

Part 4: Security and Developer Experience

9

10

Part 5: AI Assistance with Copilot Integration

11

Preface

Building end-to-end analytics systems has been a real challenge for organizations across the globe. While there are many services/products to cater to a specific need for the analytics system, there is no single service/product that provides complete analytics cohesively and coherently. This means customers spend a fair amount of time stitching together these services as well as managing multiple copies of their data across different data stores, rather than focusing on creating business value for their organization.

Microsoft Fabric is the first and only service/product on the market that provides a unified and complete analytics platform, built from the ground up for the era of AI. It offers an integrated experience, all the way from data integration to OneLake, data transformation, visualization, and a unified business model.

This book starts with an overview and the concepts of Microsoft Fabric and then, step by step, demonstrates building analytics systems for different types of real use cases that organizations often work with, such as lakehouses, data warehouses, real-time analytics, and data science. Finally, it talks about different manageability aspects, such as monitoring, security, DevOps, and using Copilot to supercharge developers' productivity.

Who this book is for

This book is intended for data professionals, such as data analysts, data engineers, data scientists, data warehouse developers, ETL developers, business analysts, AI/ML professionals, software developers, and chief data officers, who want to build a future-ready data analytics solution for the era of AI to drive their organization toward long-term success. For PySpark and SQL students entering the data analytics domain, the book offers a broad foundation, developing their skills to build end-to-end analytics systems for different use cases. Basic knowledge of SQL and Spark is presumed.

What this book covers

Chapter 1, Overview of Microsoft Fabric and Understanding Its Different Concepts, introduces the overall analytics landscape of Microsoft Fabric and other Microsoft offerings, and it discusses how Fabric has leaped ahead of other products/platforms available on the market with its unique differentiators.

Chapter 2, Understanding Different Workloads and Getting Started with Microsoft Fabric, sets the stage for the various workloads that are built into Microsoft Fabric, including Data Factory, Data Engineering, Data Science, Data Warehouse, Real-Time Analytics, as well as Power BI. This chapter helps you to understand each workload and correlate them to your skillsets and environment, ensuring that you understand the full environment when each workload is discussed in later chapters.

Chapter 3, Building an End-to-End Analytics System – Lakehouse, walks you through building an end-to-end lakehouse solution. This chapter works in parallel to the following data warehouse chapter, by showing you how a data engineer professional can be successful in Microsoft Fabric by leveraging Spark skillsets.

Chapter 4, Building an End-to-End Analytics System – Data Warehouse, takes you through building an end-to-end data warehouse solution. This chapter works in parallel to the previous lakehouse chapter by showing how a data warehouse professional can be successful in Microsoft Fabric.

Chapter 5, Building an End-to-End Analytics System – Real-Time Analytics, explores Fabric's real-time analytics by creating a KQL database, connecting to an eventstream that simulates data, and analyzing it using KQL. You will understand the types of sources that can be consumed, see how data is sent to OneLake for consumption by other compute engines, and be introduced to KQL.

Chapter 6, Building an End-to-End Analytics System – Data Science, shows you how to implement and operationalize machine learning and artificial intelligent models end to end, all the way from data ingesting to cleansing, preparing, visualizing for exploratory analysis, tracking, and training the model. Further, it will cover the process to operationalize the model for scoring (batch and interactive).

Chapter 7, Monitoring Overview and Monitoring Different Workloads, covers monitoring different aspects of Fabric using Monitoring hub, including Data Factory pipelines, Spark jobs for both the data science and data engineering workloads, using DMVs and query insights to monitor the data warehouse, and the KQL database activity for real-time analytics. Additionally, it covers the capacity metrics app that can be used to gain insights into the capacity unit usage.

Chapter 8, Administering Fabric, examines how to enable Fabric for a tenant, the options to overwrite the tenant-level settings at a capacity level, and how to associate a capacity with a workspace. We will also cover the different types of capacities and how tenants, capacities, and workspaces are all tied together. This information is vital to being able to administer Fabric effectively across teams and capacities.

Chapter 9, Security and Governance Overview, explores tenant-level Fabric security settings, how Entra ID is used to allow external users access to Fabric, and how to secure workspaces and items. It also demonstrates how to use Purview for data cataloging and governance, and domains for data organization.

Chapter 10, Continuous Integration and Continuous Deployment (CI/CD), covers DevOps process and teaches how to implement CI/CD to move your code items from one environment (development) to another (test or production).

Chapter 11, Overview of AI Assistance and Copilot Integration, explores how AI is used to extend the developer experience and provide deeper insights into your data with the Copilot experiences built into each workload. This includes an overview of the Copilots for data science, data engineering, Data Factory, and Power BI, as well as the tenant-level settings required to enable the capabilities in the Fabric tenant.

To get the most out of this book

Microsoft Fabric is delivered as a **Software as a Service (SaaS)** solution. As a result, all software updates and patching are handled by the service. While there are additional tools such as Visual Studio Code or Azure Data Studio that can be used to extend the developer experience, this book has been written in a way that only requires a modern web browser to complete all the tutorials.

Software/hardware covered in the book	Operating system requirements
A modern web browser (Microsoft Edge or Google Chrome)	Windows, macOS, or Linux

If you are using the digital version of this book, we advise you to type the code yourself or access the code from the book's GitHub repository (a link is available in the next section). Doing so will help you avoid any potential errors related to the copying and pasting of code.

For the most up-to-date version of the Microsoft Fabric documentation, including Spark versions and functionality not covered in this book, visit https://aka.ms/FabricDocs. To see the most current roadmap for new Fabric features, visit https://aka.ms/FabricRoadmap.

Download the example code files

You can download the example code files for this book from GitHub at https://github.com/PacktPublishing/Learn-Microsoft-Fabric. If there's an update to the code, it will be updated in the GitHub repository.

We also have other code bundles from our rich catalog of books and videos available at https://github.com/PacktPublishing/. Check them out!

Conventions used

There are a number of text conventions used throughout this book.

`Code in text`: Indicates code words in text, database table names, folder names, filenames, file extensions, pathnames, dummy URLs, user input, and Twitter handles. Here is an example: "With Fabric Spark, you can install popular Python and R libraries in-line while leveraging commands such as `pip` or `conda install`, while also installing libraries at the workspace level."

A block of code is set as follows:

```
COPY INTO [dbo].[MyTable]
FROM 'https://mystorageaccount.blob.core.windows.net/mycontainer/
curated/weather/florida_weather.parquet'
WITH (
     CREDENTIAL =
             (
             IDENTITY = 'SHARED ACCESS SIGNATURE',
             SECRET = ''
             ),
     FILE_TYPE = 'PARQUET'
);
```

Bold: Indicates a new term, an important word, or words that you see on screen. For instance, words in menus or dialog boxes appear in **bold**. Here is an example: "For that, navigate to the **Tenant settings** page in the **Admin portal** page of the tenant, expand the **Users can create Fabric items** field, toggle the switch to enable or disable it, and then hit **Apply**."

> **Tips or important notes**
> Appear like this.

Get in touch

Feedback from our readers is always welcome.

General feedback: If you have questions about any aspect of this book, email us at `customercare@packtpub.com` and mention the book title in the subject of your message.

Errata: Although we have taken every care to ensure the accuracy of our content, mistakes do happen. If you have found a mistake in this book, we would be grateful if you would report this to us. Please visit `www.packtpub.com/support/errata` and fill in the form.

Piracy: If you come across any illegal copies of our works in any form on the internet, we would be grateful if you would provide us with the location address or website name. Please contact us at copyright@packt.com with a link to the material.

If you are interested in becoming an author: If there is a topic that you have expertise in and you are interested in either writing or contributing to a book, please visit authors.packtpub.com.

Share Your Thoughts

Once you've read *Learn Microsoft Fabric*, we'd love to hear your thoughts! Scan the QR code below to go straight to the Amazon review page for this book and share your feedback.

https://packt.link/r/1-835-08228-9

Your review is important to us and the tech community and will help us make sure we're delivering excellent quality content.

Download a free PDF copy of this book

Thanks for purchasing this book!

Do you like to read on the go but are unable to carry your print books everywhere?

Is your eBook purchase not compatible with the device of your choice?

Don't worry, now with every Packt book you get a DRM-free PDF version of that book at no cost.

Read anywhere, any place, on any device. Search, copy, and paste code from your favorite technical books directly into your application.

The perks don't stop there, you can get exclusive access to discounts, newsletters, and great free content in your inbox daily

Follow these simple steps to get the benefits:

1. Scan the QR code or visit the link below

https://packt.link/free-ebook/9781835082287

2. Submit your proof of purchase
3. That's it! We'll send your free PDF and other benefits to your email directly

Part 1:
An Introduction to
Microsoft Fabric

This part of the book introduces the overall analytics landscape of Microsoft Fabric, explaining its different concepts and how Fabric has leaped ahead of other products/platforms available on the market with its unique differentiators. Further, it talks about the different types of real use cases that can be implemented quickly and easily and gets you started on your journey.

This part contains the following chapters:

- *Chapter 1, Overview of Microsoft Fabric and Understanding Its Different Concepts*
- *Chapter 2, Understanding Different Workloads and Getting Started with Microsoft Fabric*

1

Overview of Microsoft Fabric and Understanding Its Different Concepts

As data volume and complexity grow, organizations across every industry have opportunities to harness data to digitally transform themselves by exploiting its power and gaining competitive advantages. However, these organizations have to manage and stitch together different specialized and disconnected products to build their end-to-end analytics system. As a result, they end up incurring high integration costs when ensuring these products function together as one analytics system. This often results in delays in obtaining insights to the extent that the information is no longer relevant.

This chapter will introduce you to Microsoft Fabric, its core capabilities, and how it addresses the challenges of modern data analytics.

Here is what will be covered in this chapter:

- Introduction to Microsoft Fabric

- Reviewing the core capabilities of Microsoft Fabric

- An understanding of Microsoft Fabric as a complete platform for different types of workloads that are natively integrated for different, real use cases

- How the platform empowers everyone in the organization to become part of the data-driven culture and how its Copilot integration increases productivity

- An understanding of Microsoft Fabric as a unified business model with universal compute capacity

By the end of this chapter, you will have a high-level understanding of Microsoft Fabric, its core capabilities, and how it solves the long-standing challenges faced by data analytics.

Introduction to Microsoft Fabric

Microsoft Fabric is an end-to-end, all-in-one unified analytics platform that brings together all the data and analytics tools that organizations need. As a single, unified platform for data management, data lakes, data integration, data engineering, data warehousing, data science, real-time analytics, and business intelligence, it has been designed from the ground up to help organizations simplify their analytics workloads, reduce costs, and reduce the time taken to obtain insights in this era of AI. Microsoft Fabric is built on **Azure**, and it leverages the power of Azure's computing, storage, reliability, security and governance, scale, performance, and networking services.

Reviewing the core capabilities of Microsoft Fabric

Microsoft Fabric is designed for the age of AI and is delivered as a single **Software-as-a-Service (SaaS)** product that provides auto-integration, auto-optimization, common architecture, central security and governance, a unified business model, and Office-like experiences across all workloads.

There are four core pillars of Microsoft Fabric:

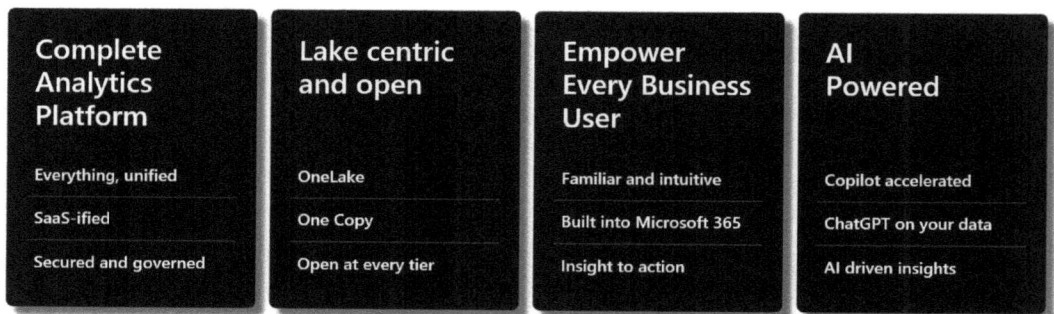

Complete Analytics Platform	Lake centric and open	Empower Every Business User	AI Powered
Everything, unified	OneLake	Familiar and intuitive	Copilot accelerated
SaaS-ified	One Copy	Built into Microsoft 365	ChatGPT on your data
Secured and governed	Open at every tier	Insight to action	AI driven insights

Figure 1.1 – Microsoft Fabric's core capability pillars

Let's review each pillar in detail in the next subsections:

- Complete Analytics Platform
- Lake-centric and open
- Empower Every Business User
- AI Powered

Complete analytics platform

While there is a standard pattern (for data warehouses or lakehouses) for typical analytics systems with well-defined components (such as ingestion, processing, and consumption), each of the components might need a different array of capabilities and might be well-served by a different class of products. Often, these products come from multiple vendors, and even if they come from a single vendor, it is too complex, expensive, time-consuming, and fragile to integrate them together because of the lack of native integration among them.

Microsoft Fabric is a single unified product that takes care of everything an organization (from departmental stores to large enterprises) needs to build an analytics system—all the way from ingesting data from different types of data sources to transforming at the correct scale using familiar utilities (SQL and Apache Spark)—serving this to business users with industry-leading Power BI, with shared security and governance that works across all the components in a cohesive manner.

Best-of-breed engines and capabilities

With Microsoft Fabric, you can use a single product with best-of-breed engines and capabilities, as shown in *Figure 1.2*. It offers a unified experience and architecture that provides all the capabilities required for an architect and developer to integrate data from different types of sources (on-premises or in the cloud), apply any necessary transformations using the tools and languages of their choice, derive insights, and present this to the business users. Moreover, by delivering the experience with SaaS as the foundation, everything is automatically integrated and optimized. This means that users can sign up for Microsoft Fabric within seconds and start getting real business value within minutes.

Microsoft Fabric empowers every team in the analytics process with the role-specific experiences they need so that data engineers, data warehousing professionals, data scientists, data analysts, and business users feel right at home as they work on the same single copy of the data and leverage the work of their colleagues.

Figure 1.2 – A complete analytics platform

As a complete platform, as shown in *Figure 1.2*, when it comes to building end-to-end analytics systems, Microsoft Fabric provides seven core workloads, which are natively integrated so that you can focus on generating business value for your organization rather than spending time on integrating different pieces together:

- **Data Factory**: You can use Data Factory in Microsoft Fabric to build your data integration component for your analytics system. It combines the scale and power of Azure Data Factory, which gives you power and control by using Power Query, giving the user an intuitive UI-based experience to build integration flow and pipelines easily and quickly. You will be able to leverage 150+ native connectors to connect to data sources on-premises and in the cloud with drag-and-drop experiences for data transformation, as well as the ability to orchestrate data pipelines with ingestion and transformation tasks. You will learn more about Data Factory in *Chapter 2, Understanding Different Workloads and Getting Started with Microsoft Fabric*, *Chapter 3, Building an End-to-End Analytics System – Lakehouse*, and *Chapter 4, Building an End-to-End Analytics System – Data Warehouse*.

- **Synapse Data Engineering**: Data Engineering provides the world-class Apache Spark platform with a great authoring experience that empowers data engineers to work and collaborate in transforming data at scale and democratizing data through lakehouses. With an instant starter pool, your Spark session gets created right away within seconds, instead of waiting for Spark to set up the nodes for you, which helps you do more with data and obtain insights as quickly as possible. Spark's integration with Data Factory in Fabric will enable notebooks and Spark jobs to be scheduled and orchestrated as part of the overall data pipelines. You will learn more about Data Engineering in *Chapter 2, Understanding Different Workloads and Getting Started with Microsoft Fabric*, and *Chapter 3, Building an End-to-End Analytics System – Lakehouse*.

- **Synapse Data Science**: Data Science enables you to build, train, deploy, and operationalize machine learning and AI models directly within the Fabric experience. It natively integrates with Azure Machine Learning to provide users with built-in experiment tracking, execution tracking, model registry, and so on. Data scientists will be empowered to work and collaborate to enrich organizational data for predictions and allow business analysts to incorporate these into Power BI reports, easily shifting insights from descriptive (analytics based on historical data) to predictive analytics (to predict patterns for future outcomes). You will learn more about Data Science in *Chapters 2–6*.

- **Synapse Data Warehousing**: Data Warehousing brings together the best of lakehouse and data warehouse experiences with the industry-leading SQL performance and scale needed for your data warehouse based on relational **Massively Parallel Processing** (**MPP**) engine. It fully separates computing from storage, both of which can be independently scaled, and unlike traditional on-premises relational database platforms, it natively stores data in the open source Delta Lake (https://delta.io/) format for greater interoperability. You will learn more about Data Warehousing in *Chapter 2, Understanding Different Workloads and Getting Started with Microsoft Fabric*, and *Chapter 4, Building an End-to-End Analytics System – Data Warehouse*.

- **Synapse Real-Time Analytics**: Real-Time Analytics enables developers to work with data streams coming in from **Internet of Things (IoT)** devices, telemetry, logs, and more, and it helps to analyze massive volumes of semi-structured data (for example, JSON and text). Streaming data often occurs at high volumes and with shifting schemas and requires high performance and low latency for processing and utilization. You will learn more about Real-Time Analytics in *Chapter 2, Understanding Different Workloads and Getting Started with Microsoft Fabric*, and *Chapter 5, Building an End-to-End Analytics System – Real-Time Analytics*.

- **Power BI**: Power BI is an industry-leading data reporting and visualization product. The native integration of Power BI with other Fabric capabilities under a single unified platform provides a **Business Intelligence (BI)** platform for data reporting and visualization, which enables business analysts and business users to gain insights from data quickly and intuitively to make better decisions. Power BI is also natively integrated into Microsoft 365 and opens up the possibility of providing relevant insights to business users when using familiar tools such as Microsoft Excel and Microsoft Teams. You will learn more about Power BI in *Chapter 2, Understanding Different Workloads and Getting Started with Microsoft Fabric, Chapter 3, Building an End-to-End Analytics System – Lakehouse*, and *Chapter 4, Building an End-to-End Analytics System – Data Warehouse*.

- **Data Activator**: Data Activator provides the real-time automated detection and monitoring of data (all the way from relatively slow-moving data in warehouses to real-time streaming data in lakehouses or from messaging queues) and can trigger notifications and required actions when it finds specified patterns in data—all within a no-code experience.

> **Important note**
> Delta Lake is an open-format storage layer that brings **Atomicity, Consistency, Isolation, and Durability (ACID)** transactions to Apache Spark and big data workloads. You can learn more about Delta Lake here: `https://learn.microsoft.com/en-us/azure/synapse-analytics/spark/apache-spark-what-is-delta-lake`.

SaaS

The architecture of Microsoft Fabric is based on a SaaS foundation, as shown in *Figure 1.3*, instead of a traditional **Platform as a Service (PaaS)** to take simplicity and integration to the next level. This doesn't mean that you have any less functionality; you will still have complete control over your data and experience, as is the case with all Azure PaaS services.

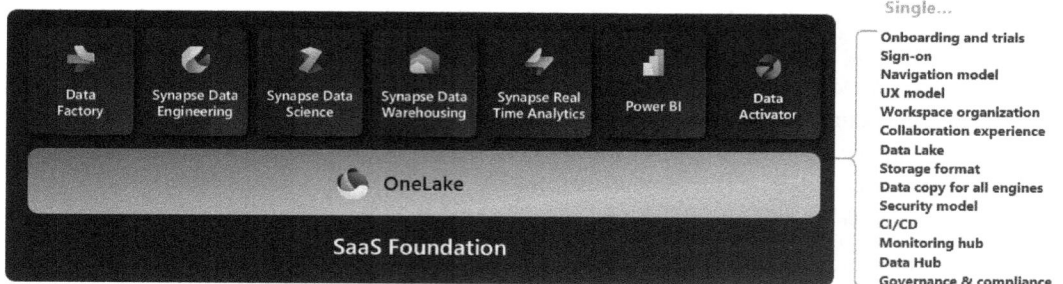

Figure 1.3 – SaaS-based intelligent data foundation

However, having this common SaaS foundation across all the previously discussed Fabric workloads means that some things change for the better, including the following:

- **Frictionless Onboarding**: This works by default and offers a smoother experience by simplifying things such as configuration overhead.

- **Simple Onboarding and Trials**: This gets you started in seconds if you just want to kick the tires:

  - Uses a single sign-on/sign-in once and works across all the workloads seamlessly.

  - Fast provisioning and automatic scaling. For example, a data warehouse takes about 10–20 seconds to spin up rather than the 10+ minutes that it takes today. Likewise, Spark pools come online in less than 15 seconds rather than 3+ minutes today in Azure Synapse.

- **Performance by Default**: It lets you focus on creating business values:

  - You have fewer knobs to tune because the best practices are implemented automatically. For example, for SQL, things such as stats are always being kept up to date, and for Spark, things such as Spark session-level configuration are auto-configured as your job progresses.

  - Fabric workloads are auto-integrated and seamlessly work when you switch contexts. For example, you can use Apache Spark as part of the Data Engineering workload to create a table. Next, you can reference the same table in the data warehouse with your SQL queries or reference the same table in Power BI for reporting without moving data.

  - All assets are easily discovered and reused by all developers across all the workloads. For example, you will be able to browse, work, and collaborate on the same coding artifacts as your colleagues.

  - A unified data lake allows customers to keep the data where they are while using any analytics tools of their choice based on their experience and preference. For example, SQL developers can continue to use SQL for data warehouses, and Spark developers can use Spark-supported languages, all while working together on a single copy of the underlying data.

- **Centralized Administration**: Offers a simplified experience:

  - For centralized administration, you have Fabric tenant-wide governance and control across all workloads.

  - With the OneSecurity feature, you can centrally define security policy once within one place, which will then be honored by all the workloads across all the engines in Fabric.

  - Centrally monitor and manage every aspect of all jobs submitted from all the workloads or engines.

  - Centrally monitor capacity metrics to understand the resource consumption used by each of the workloads and jobs submitted. This also helps you with the charge-back type scenario.

Persona-optimized experiences

Each Fabric workload targets a specific persona as part of the persona-optimized experience, as shown in *Figure 1.4* and listed here:

- Data Engineers
- Data Scientists
- Data Warehouse Developers
- Real-Time Analytics Developers
- Power BI Developers
- Data Integration (or ETL) Developers

Figure 1.4 – Persona-optimized experience

This experience reduces the noise and quickly surfaces the most relevant information for what you need to get done. Selecting an experience, such as Synapse Data Warehouse, will bring you to a screen that shows the common tasks and resources that a user working on a data warehouse would find useful; in other words, the ability to create a new warehouse, create a new data pipeline, and link these directly to get started with Data Warehouse documentation. Likewise, if you switch to Data Engineering, you will find options to create a lakehouse, create a notebook to write your Spark application, import existing notebooks, and create a Spark Job Definition, as well as a direct link to the "Getting started with Data Engineering" documentation.

Lake-centric and open

Today, in most analytics systems (if not all), data resides in silos across different systems and storage (for example, some data exist in a lakehouse, whereas other data exist in a data warehouse in its own proprietary format). This not only means you have data duplicity occurring at multiple layers, but it also adds so much complexity (with respect to time, cost, and resources) to maintaining it over time to keep it up to date.

Fabric solves this problem with **OneLake**, as shown in *Figure 1.5*. When you create a Fabric tenant, OneLake is automatically provisioned and preconfigured. This OneLake logically provides a single, unified, multi-cloud data lake for the whole organization. As an analogy, you can think of OneLake as OneDrive (which comes with Microsoft 365) but for your data.

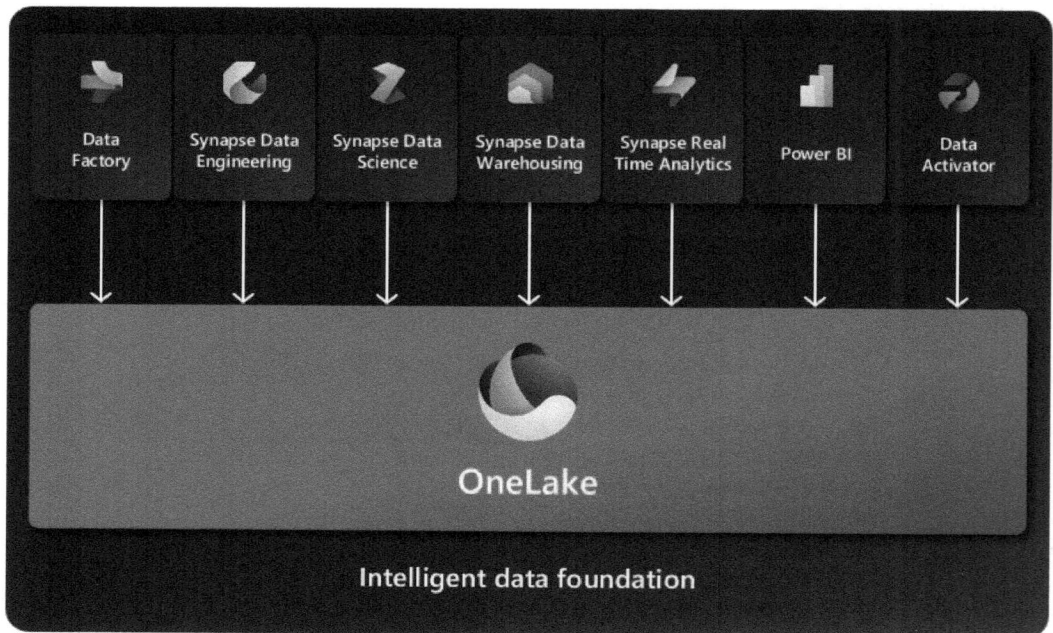

Figure 1.5 – OneLake is shared by all the engines

OneLake and OneCopy

OneLake is based on a SaaS foundation, and underneath, it is built on top of **Azure Data Lake Storage** (**ADLS**) Gen2, supporting any type of file whether structured, semi-structured, or unstructured. OneLake supports the same ADLS Gen2 **Application Programming Interfaces** (**APIs**) and **Software Development Kits** (**SDKs**) that are compatible with existing ADLS Gen2 applications, including Azure Databricks. This means that you can continue to leverage all your existing investments and integrations with other services that you've spent years building. You can think of all your data stored in OneLake as being stored underneath in a big storage account for the Fabric tenant. For every workspace that you create, a container appears in that storage account. Furthermore, any data items you store are stored in a folder hierarchy within those containers.

OneLake gives customers the ability to store one copy of their data for use with multiple analytics engines, which means all the analytics engines can access each other's data. All the architects out there are probably thinking, "Does this mean I don't have to do all that data copying to give my SQL people access to the data in my lake? And does that mean I don't have to copy the data from my warehouse to a dataset in Power BI to be able to report on it?" Yes, that is correct. Along with OneLake comes the concept of **OneCopy**, which means every Fabric computing engine can see and interact with all the data.

OneLake eliminates today's pervasive and chaotic data silos created by different developers by provisioning and configuring their own isolated storage accounts. Instead, OneLake provides a single, unified storage system for all developers, where the discovery and sharing of data is trivial, and compliance with policy and security settings is enforced centrally and uniformly across all the engines.

Additionally, regarding the OneSecurity feature, you can centrally define security policy once in one place, which will be honored by all the workloads across all the engines in Fabric.

Open format

In addition to OneLake, there is one other key change in Microsoft Fabric that enables all the functionalities in Fabric: standardization for the open source Delta Lake format. Every computing engine in Fabric now, by default, reads and writes data in the Delta Lake format. This standardization of the data on a single yet popular open format provides a way to prevent the need to copy data from one computing engine to another, for example, from a lakehouse into a warehouse or vice versa. All tabular data are stored in OneLake in an open source Delta Lake format when stored in the tables section of the lakehouse.

> **Important note**
> In the world of big data, Delta Lake is one of the preferred methods for storing data. With its vibrant and active community, new releases come out frequently and have better read and write performance and newer features for wider adoption and support.

Shortcut

The shortcut feature in OneLake is a reference to the data stored in other file locations; this makes data sharing as simple and easy as sharing files in OneDrive, removing the need for data duplication. As shown in *Figure 1.6*, shortcuts also allow for the instant linking of the data that already exists in Azure and in other clouds without any data copying and movement beforehand, making OneLake the first multi-cloud data lake. These file locations can be found within the same workspace or across different workspaces, for example, any lakehouses within the current OneLake or storage accounts that are external to the current OneLake asset in ADLS or Amazon S3. No matter where the location is, the reference makes it appear as though the files and folders are stored locally. In this way, it creates a data abstraction and data virtualization layer for all the data in your organization.

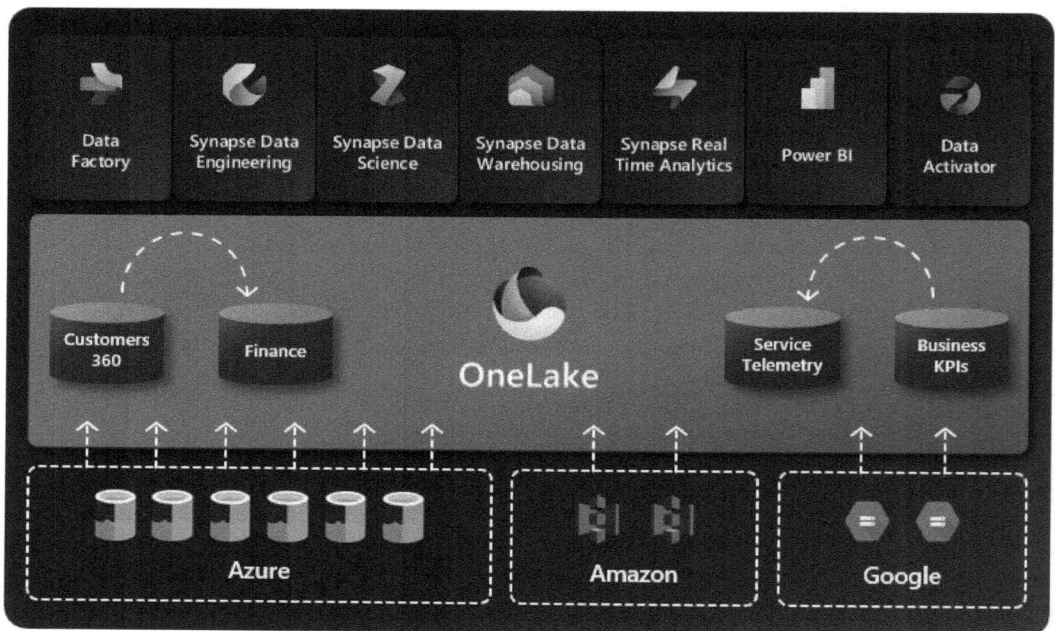

Figure 1.6 – OneLake shortcut

For the teams working independently in different workspaces, shortcuts help to combine the data across different business groups and domains into a virtual data product to fit a user's specific needs. Employing this data virtualization on all of your enterprise data opens the possibility of building data mesh architecture (https://www.datamesh-architecture.com/) quickly.

Additionally, Fabric allows you to create a data domain, one of the core components of Data Mesh; an example is shown in *Figure 1.7*:

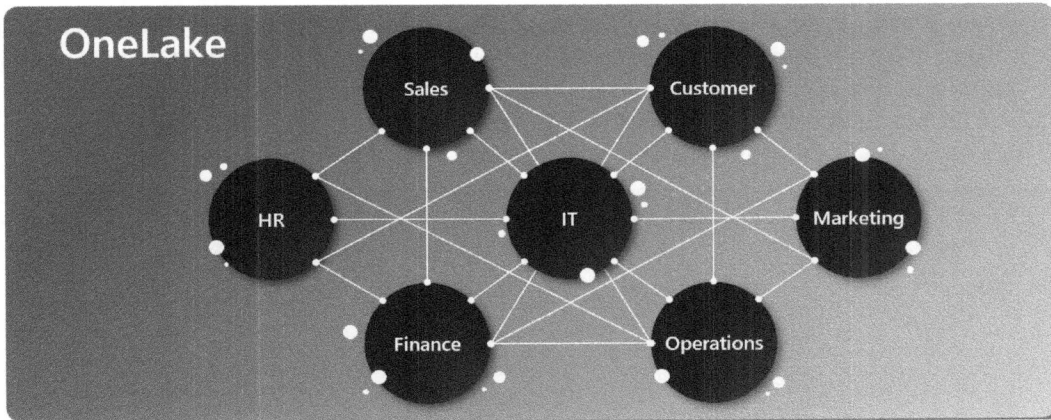

Figure 1.7 – OneLake is a data domain that is used to create hub-and-spoke data mesh architecture

In Fabric, a domain is a way of logically grouping together all the data in an organization and the related code artifacts that are relevant to a particular area or field. One of the most common uses for domains is to group data according to business departments, making it possible for departments to manage their data and related code according to their specific regulations, restrictions, and needs. This ability to create data domains in Fabric offers the following capabilities when building data mesh architecture:

- Workspaces and artifacts for different data domains contribute to building the same data lake

- Without data movement, data from different domains can be analyzed, blended, and transformed together

- Data is secured and governed in one place while remaining easily discoverable and accessible by all who should have access across the organization

- Data can be certified by domain experts to enable trust for data that are discovered

> **Important note**
>
> As of the time of writing (October 2023), support for creating shortcuts is available for other Fabric lakehouses, ADLS Gen 2 storage accounts, and Amazon S3 storage accounts. Support for Google Storage is planned for the future.

OneSecurity

With the OneSecurity feature, Fabric offers a shared universal security model that is enforced across all the engines in Fabric, as shown in *Figure 1.8*. This means that you are able to define security once in the lakehouse and have those permissions honored by every engine in Fabric (Spark, SQL, and Power BI). This security definition can be used for data access permissions for individual tables or files and folders in the lakehouse and can be granted to individual users and Microsoft Entra ID groups. You will learn more about security in *Chapter 9, Security and Governance Overview*.

Figure 1.8 – OneSecurity is a shared universal security model

Empower every business user

Microsoft 365 applications are among the most widely used applications on the planet. They help Microsoft 365 application users become part of the data-driven culture and make better decisions based on their organizational data. Microsoft Fabric deeply integrates with Microsoft 365 applications. For example, Power BI is a core part of Microsoft Fabric and is already infused across Microsoft 365 applications. Power BI has deep and native integration with popular Microsoft 365 applications, such as Microsoft Excel, Microsoft Teams, PowerPoint, and SharePoint, and this integration opens the possibility of easily discovering and accessing data from OneLake by using Microsoft 365 applications; this provides flexibility to organizational business users to gain more value from your OneLake data.

With Fabric, you can turn your Microsoft 365 applications into hubs for uncovering and applying insights. For example, users in Microsoft Excel can directly discover and analyze data in OneLake and generate a Power BI report with a click of a button. In Teams, users can infuse data into their everyday work using embedded channels, chat, and meeting experiences. Business users can bring data into their presentations by embedding live Power BI reports directly in Microsoft PowerPoint. Power BI is also natively integrated with SharePoint, enabling the easy sharing and dissemination of insights.

Additionally, when you consume data in Power BI from a lakehouse, Power BI uses a new groundbreaking technology called Direct Lake to directly load parquet-formatted files (part of the Delta Lake tables created by Fabric engines) from a lakehouse without having to import or duplicate data into a Power BI dataset. This combines the best of existing data-access methods (Import mode and Direct Query mode) and provides a fast path to load the data from the lakehouse straight into the Power BI engine, ready for analysis. You will learn more about this in *Chapter 2, Understanding Different Workloads and Getting Started with Microsoft Fabric*, in the *Power BI* section.

AI powered

For the native integration of Azure OpenAI Service (`https://azure.microsoft.com/en-us/products/cognitive-services/openai-service/`), Microsoft Fabric aims to empower every user at all levels with AI by helping them unlock the full potential of data, enabling you and other developers, as well as the business users in your organization, to leverage the power of generative AI against your own organizational data and assist business users in finding insights quickly. With the availability of **Copilot** across all workloads, this experience will provide an option for you to use natural or conversational language to create data pipelines and dataflows, generate code and entire functions (in SQL, Spark, and so on.), build machine learning models, document your code, and visualize the results with automated report creation. Further, you will be able to create and customize your own conversational language experiences that combine Azure OpenAI Service models with your own organizational data and publish them as contextualized AI plug-ins within your organization so that you can leverage the Copilot experience to get answers.

In Microsoft Fabric, Copilot builds on Microsoft's existing commitments to data security and privacy for enterprises by putting people first. Copilot inherits an organization's security, compliance, and privacy policies. Microsoft does not use your organizational data to train the base foundational language models that power Copilot. You will learn more about Copilot integration in Microsoft Fabric in *Chapter 11, Overview of AI Assistance and Copilot Integration*.

Unified business model with universal compute capacity

As discussed earlier, when you build a data analytics system today, you typically combine multiple products—often from multiple vendors—to build different components in a single analytics system. This means computing capacity is provisioned and charged for the multiple components (for the multiple products used) in the system, such as data integration, data engineering, data warehousing, and business intelligence. This not only burdens you with managing the overall cost but also, when one of the components is idle, its capacity cannot be used by another component. Thus, this can cause significant wastage and overall increased **Total Cost of Ownership (TCO)**.

Microsoft Fabric simplifies this whole experience of purchasing and managing computing resources with its universal compute capacity, which uses **capacity units (CUs)**, as shown in *Figure 1.9*. Universal capacities provide the computing resources for all the engines in Fabric—from Data Factory ingest and transform to Data Engineering, Data Science, Data Warehouse, Real-Time Analytics, and all the way to Power BI for data visualization; in other words, you can purchase a single pool of CUs to power all Fabric engines. With this all-in-one and all-inclusive approach, you can create a system that leverages all engines freely without any friction to your experience or cost. This unified business model significantly reduces costs, as any unused computing capacity in one engine can be utilized by any of the other engines in Fabric, and you get a transparent view of your consumption cost at the artifact or item level by using the Fabric **Capacity Metrics** app.

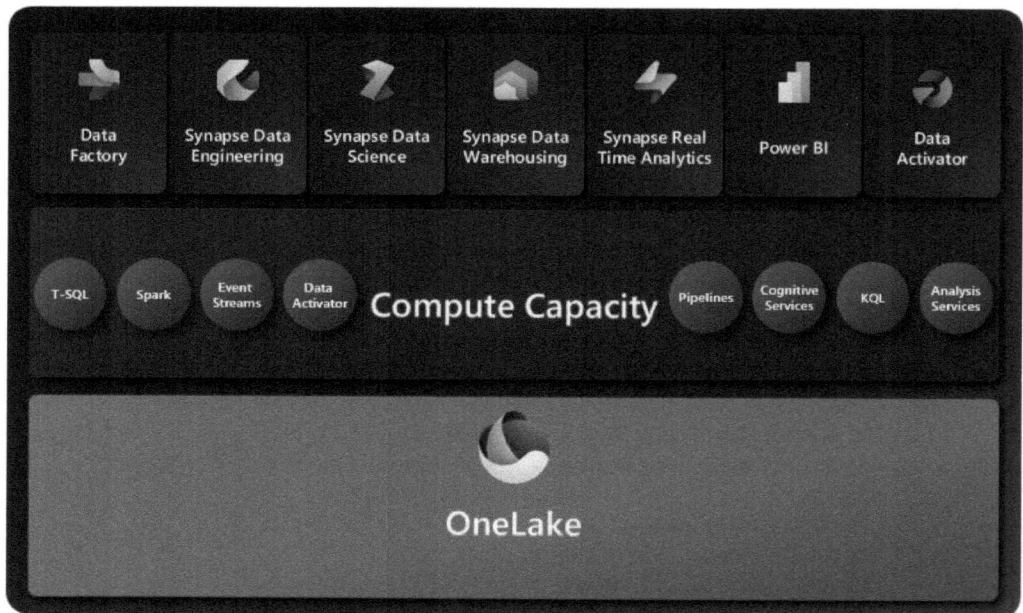

Figure 1.9 – Universal compute capacity

> **Important note**
>
> Rather than provisioning and managing separate computing capacities for each engine, with Fabric, you purchase a universal compute capacity, which provides the computing resources for all the engines in Fabric. These computing capacities are shareable and can be used across engines concurrently. They do not need to be pre-allocated by the engines. Additionally, you will need to pay for the storage space you have consumed. This means that your bill is determined by two variables: the amount of computing resources you provision (to be used across all the engines in Fabric without any restrictions and limitations) and the amount of storage you use for data storage.

A single capacity can power all engines concurrently and does not need to be pre-allocated across the engines. This means that there is no need to size (in advance) the individual engines or to split the capacity across engines. Moreover, a single capacity can be shared among multiple users and projects without any limitations on the number of workspaces or creators that can utilize it (`https://blog.fabric.microsoft.com/en-us/blog/announcing-microsoft-fabric-capacities-are-available-for-purchase`). The consumption of resources by Fabric engines is only bound by the amount of computing required to serve data to your users and can be easily increased with a **Stock Keeping Unit** (**SKU**) upgrade or on-demand using the **Auto-Scale** feature.

Summary

In this chapter, you have learned about Microsoft Fabric as a unified platform. It provides all the natively integrated capabilities with which to design and build end-to-end analytics systems, all the way from Data Factory (for data ingestion) and Data Engineering (for data transformation) to Data Science, Data Warehouse, Real-Time Analytics, and Power BI for data visualization.

You also learned about core capabilities, such as OneLake and OneCopy, and how they break data silos and remove the need for data redundancy across different systems by using data storage format standardization (the open source Delta Lake format), which is used by all Fabric engines, making the platform open at every layer and able to avoid vendor lock-ins. You learned about shortcuts and how they let you create data virtualization layers for all your enterprise data (with multi-cloud support), providing access without the need for data movement and copying.

Finally, you learned about how the platform provides a unified business model that uses universal compute capacity and how this simplifies the purchasing and managing of computing resources to optimize resource utilization and reduce the total cost of ownership.

Now that you have a basic understanding of Microsoft Fabric and the different workloads it supports, it's time to dive a bit deeper into each of the workloads and understand the different use cases it can be used for; this will be covered in the next chapter.

2

Understanding Different Workloads and Getting Started with Microsoft Fabric

Microsoft Fabric brings all the data and analytics tools together to address the need for every aspect of an organization's analytics. With its unification of different capabilities, it offers different types of workloads so that you can design and build your end-to-end analytics systems.

In the previous chapter, you learned about Fabric, its core capabilities, and the different types of workloads it supports at a high level. In this chapter, you will dive deeper into each type of workload and the core capabilities each of these workloads provides. This will help you make timely and better decisions when you're building your end-to-end analytics systems.

Here is what you will learn about as part of this chapter:

- Getting started with Microsoft Fabric
- Data Factory
- Data engineering
- Data warehouses
- Data Science
- Real-Time Analytics
- Power BI

Let's get started!

Getting started with Microsoft Fabric

In this section, you will learn how to enable Microsoft Fabric in an existing Power BI tenant or create a new Fabric tenant if you don't have one already. Then, you will create your first Fabric workspace, which you will use to carry out all subsequent chapters' exercises.

Enabling Microsoft Fabric

Microsoft Fabric shares the same Power BI tenant. If you have a Power BI or Microsoft Fabric tenant already created, you have two options to enable Fabric (more at `https://learn.microsoft.com/en-us/fabric/admin/fabric-switch`) in that tenant. For each of these options, depending on the configuration you select, Microsoft Fabric becomes available for everyone in the tenant or to a selected group of users:

> **Note**
>
> If you are new to Power BI or your organization doesn't have a Power BI/Fabric tenant yet, you can set one up and use a Fabric trial by visiting `https://aka.ms/try-fabric` to sign up for a Power BI free license. After that, you can start the Fabric trial; this will be covered later in this section when we discuss trial capacity. The Fabric trial includes access to the Fabric product experiences and the resources to create and host Fabric items.
>
> At the time of writing, the Fabric trial license allows you to work with Fabric for 60 days for free. At that point, you will need to provision Fabric's capacity to continue using Microsoft Fabric.

- **Enable Fabric at the tenant level**: If you have admin privileges, you can access the **admin center** from the **Settings** menu in the top-right corner of the Power BI service. From here, you can enable Fabric on the **Tenant settings** page. When you enable Microsoft Fabric using this setting, users can create Fabric items in that tenant. To do that, navigate to the **Tenant settings** page in the **Admin portal** page of the tenant, expand the **Users can create Fabric items** field, toggle the switch to enable or disable it, and then hit **Apply**:

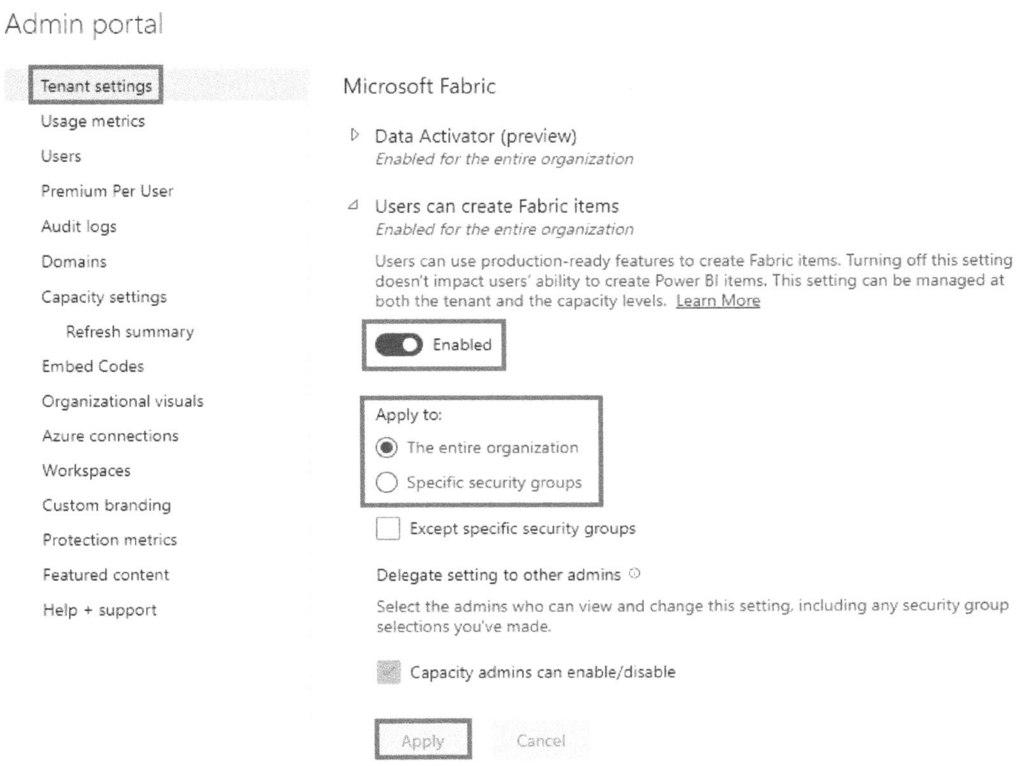

Admin portal

Tenant settings	Microsoft Fabric
Usage metrics	
Users	▷ Data Activator (preview)
Premium Per User	*Enabled for the entire organization*
Audit logs	△ Users can create Fabric items
Domains	*Enabled for the entire organization*
Capacity settings	Users can use production-ready features to create Fabric items. Turning off this setting doesn't impact users' ability to create Power BI items. This setting can be managed at both the tenant and the capacity levels. Learn More
Refresh summary	
Embed Codes	🔘 Enabled
Organizational visuals	
Azure connections	Apply to:
Workspaces	⦿ The entire organization
Custom branding	◯ Specific security groups
Protection metrics	☐ Except specific security groups
Featured content	Delegate setting to other admins ⓘ
Help + support	Select the admins who can view and change this setting, including any security group selections you've made.
	☑ Capacity admins can enable/disable
	Apply Cancel

Figure 2.1 – Microsoft Fabric – Tenant settings

- **Enable Fabric at the capacity level**: While it is recommended to enable Microsoft Fabric for the entire organization at the tenant level, there may be times when you would like it to be enabled for a certain group of people at the capacity level. To do that, from the **Tenant Admin** portal, navigate to the **Capacity settings** page, identify and select the capacity for which you want Microsoft Fabric to be enabled, and click on the **Delegate tenant settings** tab at the top. Then, in the **Microsoft Fabric** section of this page, expand the **Users can create Fabric items** setting, toggle the switch to enable or disable it, and then hit **Apply**:

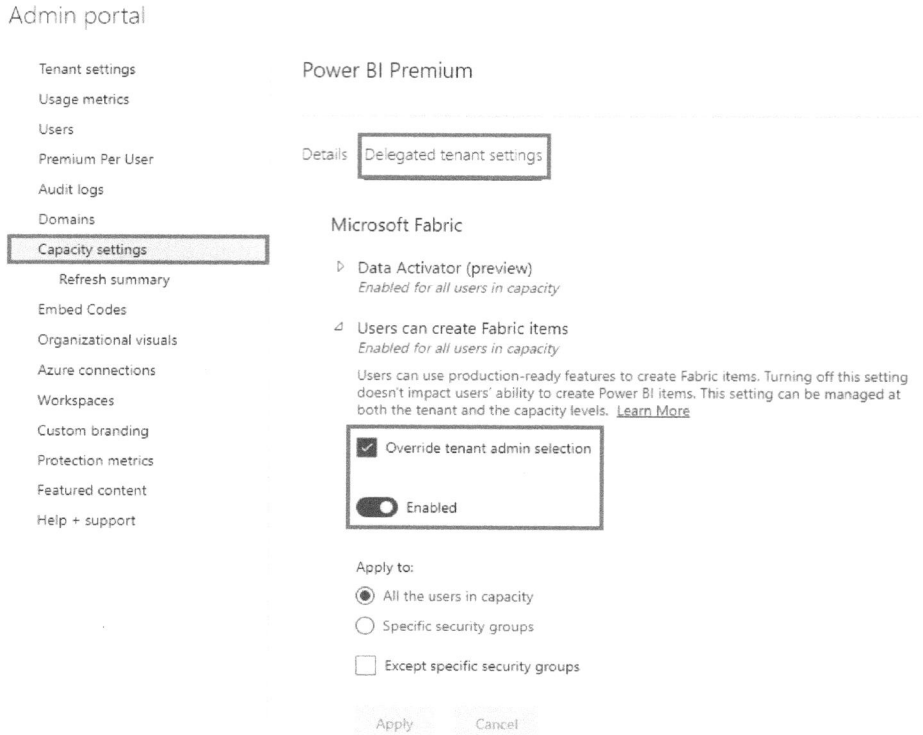

Figure 2.2 – Microsoft Fabric – Capacity settings

In both the previous scenarios, it's assumed you have paid for the capacity that's already available. However, if you don't have this yet, you can use a Fabric trial (more at https://learn.microsoft. com/en-us/fabric/get-started/fabric-trial) to create Fabric items for a certain duration if you want to learn or test the functionalities of Microsoft Fabric. For that, open the Fabric home page (by visiting https://app.fabric.microsoft.com/home) and select **Account manager**. Then, click on **Start Trial** and follow the wizard's instructions to enable a Fabric trial with trial capacity.

> **Note**
>
> To learn more about and try out different capabilities in Fabric, Microsoft provides free **trial capacity**. With this trial capacity, you get full access to all the Fabric workloads/experiences and its features, including the ability to create Fabric items and collaborate with others, as well as OneLake storage of up to 1 TB. However, the usage of this trial capacity is intended for trial and testing only, not for production usage.

Checking your access to Microsoft Fabric

To validate if Fabric is enabled and you have access to it in your organization's tenant, sign into Power BI and look for the Power BI icon at the bottom left of the screen. If you see the Power BI icon, select it to see the experiences that are available within Fabric:

Figure 2.3 – Microsoft Fabric – workloads switcher

If the icon is present, you can click the **Microsoft Fabric** link at the top of the screen (as shown in *Figure 2.3*) to switch to the Fabric experience or click on the experience you want to switch to:

Figure 2.4 – Microsoft Fabric – home page

Note that if the icon isn't present, Fabric isn't available to you. In that case, please follow the steps (or work with your Power BI or Fabric admin) mentioned in the previous section to enable it.

Creating your first Fabric-enabled workspace

Once you have confirmed that Fabric is enabled in your tenant and you have access to it, the next step is to create your Fabric workspace. You can think of a Fabric workspace as a logical container that will contain items such as lakehouses, warehouses, notebooks, and pipelines. Follow these steps to create your first Fabric workspace:

1. Sign into Power BI (`https://app.powerbi.com/`).
2. Select **Workspaces** | **+ New workspace**:

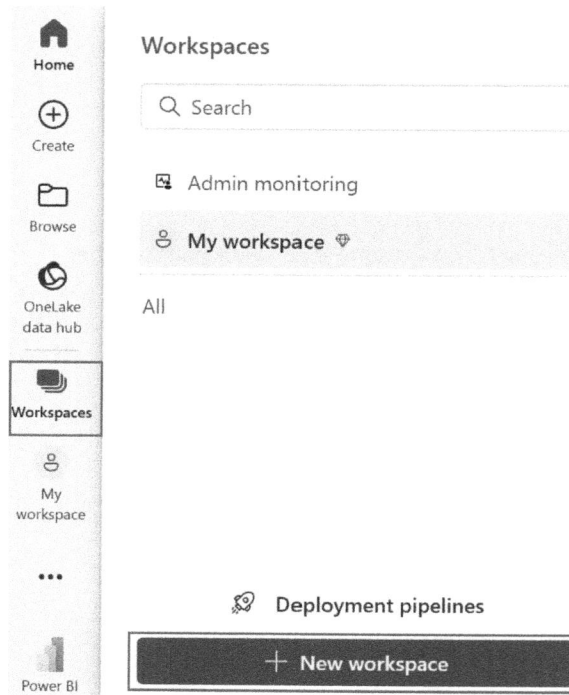

Figure 2.5 – Creating a new workspace

3. Fill out the **Create a workspace** form, as follows:

    • **Name**: Enter `Learn Microsoft Fabric` and some characters for uniqueness.

    • **Description**: Optionally, enter a description for the workspace:

Create a workspace

Name *

Learn Microsoft Fabric

Available

Description

This Fabric workspace contains all the items work through all the exercises of this book.

Domain (preview) ⓘ

Assign to a domain (optional)   ⌄

Learn more about workspace settings ⎘

Workspace image

↑ Upload

↺ Reset

Figure 2.6 – Create a workspace – details

- **Advanced**: Select **Fabric capacity** under **License mode** and then choose a capacity you have access to. If not, you can start a trial license, as described earlier, and use it here.

4. Select **Apply**. The workspace will be created and opened.

5. You can click on **Workspaces** again and then search for your workspace by typing its name in the search box. You can also pin the selected workspace so that it always appears at the top:

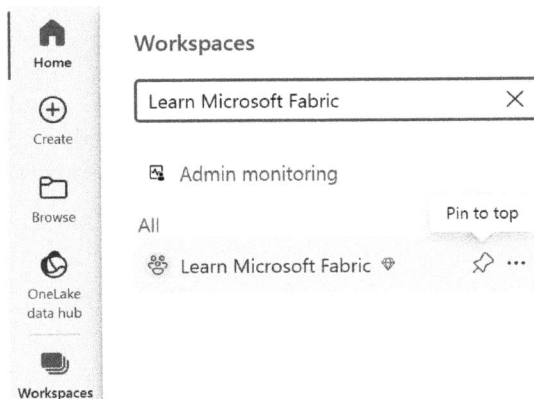

Home

⊕ Create

Browse

OneLake data hub

Workspaces

Workspaces

Learn Microsoft Fabric   ✕

⊞ Admin monitoring

All   Pin to top

⚇ Learn Microsoft Fabric ◈   ✎ ⋯

Figure 2.7 – Searching for a workspace

6.   Clicking on the name of the workspace will open that workspace. A link to it will become available in the left-hand side navigation bar, allowing you to switch from one item to another quickly. Since we haven't created anything yet, there is nothing here. You can click on **+New** to start creating Fabric items:

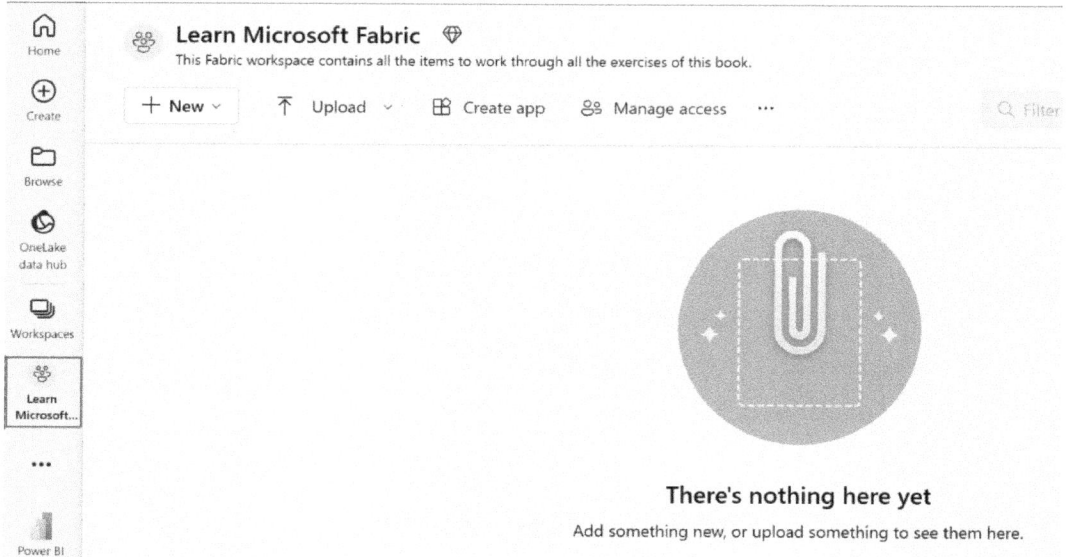

Figure 2.8 – Switching to a workspace

With a Microsoft Fabric workspace set up, let's review the different workloads that are available.

Data Factory

The variety, velocity, and variety of data that organizations need to handle is expanding each day and they need an **extract, transform, and load** (ETL) tool that can keep pace. They also need to orchestrate activities across all the workloads within Fabric and compute engines outside Fabric. Azure Data Factory has a long history of delivering large-scale ETL functionality and was brought into Microsoft Fabric and updated to leverage the new **Software-as-a-Service (SaaS)** foundation.

While many of the concepts from Azure Data Factory can be transferred to Fabric Data Factory, there are some notable changes of which to be aware. Before diving into the major areas of Data Factory, it's important to understand the key terminology that will be used throughout this book:

- **Azure Data Factory**: Microsoft's PaaS ETL-as-a-service that's delivered through Azure.
- **Fabric Data Factory**: Referred to simply as "Data Factory" throughout this book, this is the next generation of Azure Data Factory's functionality delivered through the Microsoft Fabric SaaS service.
- **Pipeline**: A grouping of one or more activities that are executed together to perform a specific task.
- **Activity**: A unit of work inside a pipeline. Activities can move data, transform data, or perform control flow activities that run on Data Factory's compute or an external compute engine.
- **Connections**: These define the settings that are used to connect to a data source or service, including URLs, server names, and credentials.
- **Dataflow**: This is the transformation engine of Microsoft Fabric. It uses Power Query to deliver a low to no-code data transformation experience.

As you will see when you work with all the workloads in Microsoft Fabric, there is a landing page that helps you get started quickly with Data Factory by removing the "noise" of the other experiences that may not be relevant to an ETL developer. When navigating to Fabric, the Data Factory experience can be accessed by clicking on the experience switcher in the bottom-left corner of the user interface and selecting **Data Factory**:

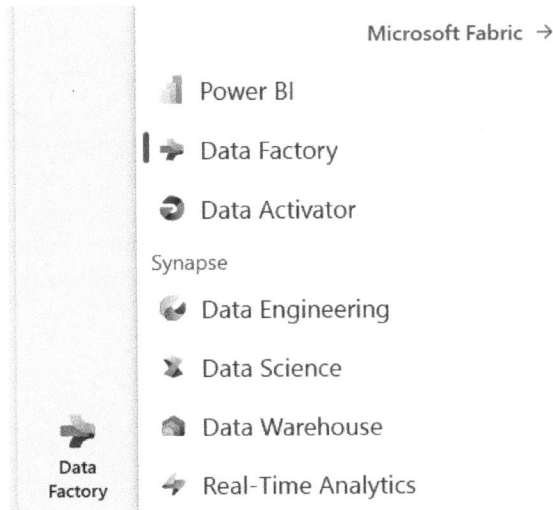

Microsoft Fabric →

Power BI

Data Factory

Data Activator

Synapse

Data Engineering

Data Science

Data Warehouse

Real-Time Analytics

Data Factory

Figure 2.9 – Data Factory – workload switcher

Across the top of the workspace screen, you can choose to create a pipeline or a dataflow to get started quickly:

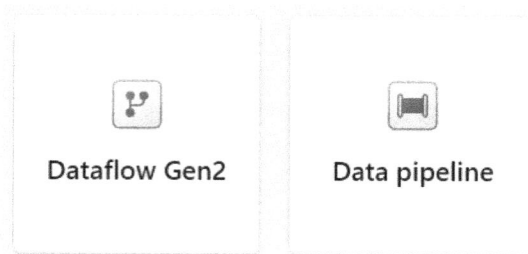

Figure 2.10 – Data Factory – workload options

All the Data Factory items can be found by navigating from the workspace view, clicking **New** | **Show all**, and locating the **Data Factory** section:

Data Factory

Empower your organization to get value from data faster than ever.

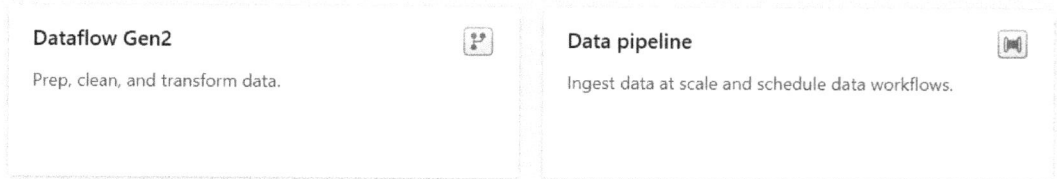

Dataflow Gen2	Data pipeline
Prep, clean, and transform data.	Ingest data at scale and schedule data workflows.

Figure 2.11 – Data Factory work item creation options

Finally, Data Factory can be found woven throughout Fabric through shortcuts so that you can get started with relevant activities from many different places. For instance, when working with a data warehouse, clicking the **Get data** button on the ribbon will give you the option to create a new pipeline and launch into the copy data wizard. Here, the **New Dataflow Gen2** button will create a blank dataflow. The same options are available as quick actions when creating a new lakehouse or data warehouse so that you can load data with as little friction as possible:

Get data in your lakehouse

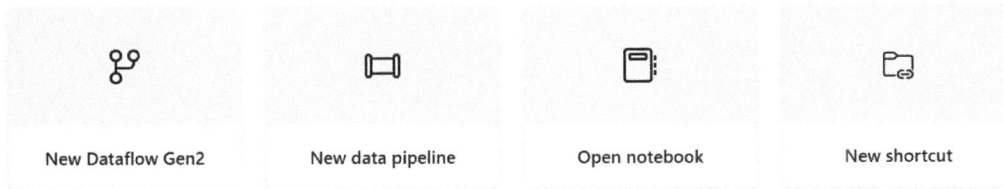

| New Dataflow Gen2 | New data pipeline | Open notebook | New shortcut |

Figure 2.12 – Get data in your lakehouse

Now that you've learned about Data Factory, let's move on to creating different components in Data Factory.

Pipelines

Data pipelines are the foundation of Data Factory. Ensuring the right activity is run in the right order at the right time is vital for any ETL engine. A process that loads a table and then immediately truncates that same table, thus leaving it empty, would be useless. Precedence constraints in a pipeline ensure activities are run in the proper order:

Figure 2.13 – Example of a pipeline flow

Activities can be configured so that you can move forward in the pipeline under one of four conditions:

- **On success**: When an activity is completed successfully, the next activity will execute.

- **On fail**: When an activity fails, the next activity will execute.

- **On completion**: The next activity will execute, irrespective of whether the prior activity succeeded or failed.

- **On skip**: The next activity will execute if the prior activity was not executed. Consider a chain of three activities where the first activity fails, the second activity is configured to run on success, and the third activity is configured to run on skip. In this scenario, the third activity, "on skip," would be executed.

Pipelines can be configured to run based on a wall clock with some configurability for the recurring schedule. Simply define the start and end time for the schedule and how often the pipeline will run (**By the minute**, **Hourly**, **Daily**, or **Weekly**):

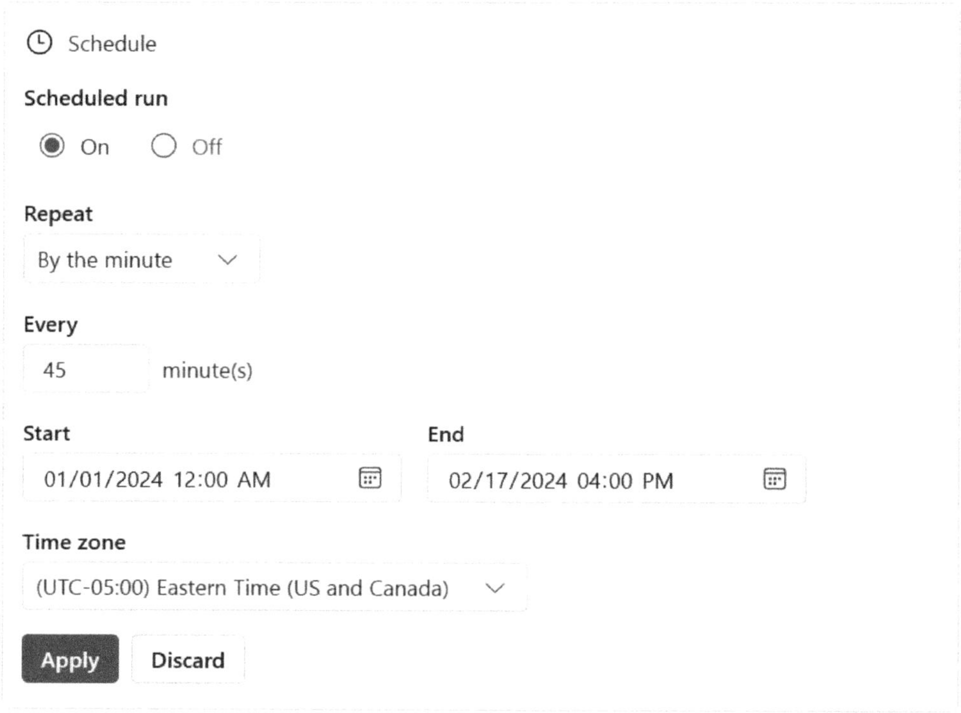

Figure 2.14 – Scheduling options

Users can also run pipelines manually by clicking the **Run** button on the ribbon while editing a pipeline.

Activities

An activity is a defined unit or piece of work to be done within a pipeline; there must be at least one activity in a pipeline. At the time of writing, there are more than 20 activities. The most basic – and likely commonly used – activity is "copy." This allows you to move data between any two supported source/sink combinations. Often, this will be a source system, which generates data, and the bronze layer in a lakehouse or a stage table in a data warehouse.

Activities can be added to the canvas by clicking the respective icon and label on the ribbon. Frequently used activities can be found on the **Home** tab. All the available activities can be found on the **Activities** tab.

Connections

Most activities will require a way to interact with data, whether it's via a lookup that is used to get the last update data from a control table, a copy activity connecting to a source or sink, or a HTTP call to a web service. Connections store all the relevant information for how Fabric will communicate and authenticate with the specified data connector.

This is a key departure from Azure Data Factory, where all connections are managed through linked services and datasets. In Fabric, connections are defined globally and can be shared with specific individuals and used across workspaces. It is worth noting that there is also no integration runtime to specify with the connection as the compute for Fabric pulls from a shared pool of **capacity units** (**CUs**).

There are more than 135 data connectors available. Not all connectors can be used across all activities. A REST connector, for instance, can be used as a source or sink in a copy activity but cannot be used in a lookup activity. A comprehensive list of available connections and what activities can use each connector can be found at `https://learn.microscft.com/en-us/fabric/data-factory/connector-overview`.

Dataflow Gen2

The dataflow activity is set apart from other activities because it is also a separate item inside the Fabric workspace. For any users coming from Power BI, dataflow is a familiar term, but these items should not be confused. Power BI's Dataflow Gen1 continues to exist alongside the new Dataflow Gen2 that was introduced in Microsoft Fabric. At first glance, these two dataflows look similar as both leverage the Power Query experience for authoring. However, this is where the similarities end. The new Dataflow Gen2 autosaves during development, allows you to specify an output destination, integrates directly with Data Factory pipelines for scheduling and orchestration, and leverages a new, higher-scale compute architecture.

> **Note**
> Dataflow Gen2 can be integrated into pipelines by using the dataflow activity.

For the no-code and low-code developers, Dataflow Gen2 is the perfect way to build ETL processes using a familiar interface and perform simple or complex data transformations while still being able to work with large-scale data. Data can be written to a variety of destinations, including Fabric lakehouses, Azure SQL Database, Azure Data Explorer, and Azure Synapse Analytics.

Loading data

Perhaps the most important functionality of Data Factory is the ability to load data at scale. Data Factory in Fabric provides two main ways to accomplish this task. The first is the previously discussed Dataflow Gen2, which provides a no-code experience for users who may not be professional developers or for those who just want to get up and running quickly. The second method is using the copy activity.

There is a bit of overlap in the use case and functionality for the copy activity and Dataflow Gen2 in that both provide a no-code and low-code user experience. However, as stated earlier, Power BI users will feel more comfortable with the dataflow experience because it uses the Power Query interface. Both data loading methods also handle any size of data you throw at them. The biggest difference between the two loading methods is that the copy activity does not support as many data sources while supporting a much wider range of data sinks (destination) and the copy activity allows for almost no transformation while dataflows provide a very rich transformation experience.

Data engineering

The amount of data an organization needs to ingest and process at scale is growing faster than ever before, ranging from tabular data to unstructured documents, images, videos, IoT sensors, and more. Hence, the role of data engineering is increasingly becoming complex yet important in any organization's analytics journey. Data engineering capabilities in Fabric allow you to enrich your data for higher quality and organize it in a way that is easily accessible to the right individuals with the right access and at the right time. These native data engineering capabilities allow data developers and data engineers to quickly and efficiently build data transformation flows that allow them to collect, store, process, and analyze large volumes of data by leveraging the power of open source Apache Spark (`https://spark.apache.org/`) to transform their data at scale and build out a robust lakehouse architecture. When you switch to the data engineering experience, you will find the following options to work with:

| Lakehouse | Notebook | Environment (Preview) | Spark Job Definition | Data pipeline | Import notebook | Use a sample |

Figure 2.15 – Fabric Data Engineering workload options

Now that you've learned about the data engineering capabilities in Fabric at a high level, it's time to dive deep into some of these capabilities in detail.

Lakehouse

In Microsoft Fabric, a lakehouse is a data storage layer that allows organizations to store and manage virtually any type of data (structured, semi-structured, and unstructured data) in a single location, allowing various tools and frameworks to process and analyze that data as per the organization's need and individual's preference. Data engineers can choose from various ways of bringing data into the lakehouse, including dataflows and pipelines, and they can even use shortcuts (refer to the previous chapter for details about shortcuts) to create virtual folders and tables without the data ever leaving their external storage accounts.

A lakehouse combines the best of the data lake and warehouse, removing data duplication and friction of ingesting, transforming, and sharing organizational data, all in the open format of Delta Lake (`https://delta.io/`). Ingested data comes into the lakehouse by default in the Delta Lake format, and tables are automatically discovered and registered in a metastore on behalf of users.

> **Note**
>
> Automatic table discovery and registration is a feature of a lakehouse that provides a fully managed file-to-table experience for data engineers and data scientists. Users can drop a file into the managed area of the lakehouse (that is, tables) and the file will be automatically validated for supported structured formats (currently only for Delta Lake format) and will be registered in the metastore with the necessary metadata, such as column names, formats, compression and more. Users can then reference the file as a table and use SparkSQL syntax to interact with the data. This also means that any Delta Lake format files (Parquet and a transaction log, for example) are automatically registered as a table and will also be available from the SQL endpoint so that they can be queried with T-SQL.

A lakehouse also streamlines the process of collaborating on top of the same and single copy of the data. Since all the data is stored in the Delta Lake format by default, different data professionals can easily work together on the same data. Additionally, each lakehouse comes with a SQL endpoint that provides data warehousing capabilities, including the ability to run T-SQL queries, create views, and define functions on the data stored in the lakehouse. Every lakehouse also comes with a semantic dataset, enabling **business intelligence (BI)** users to build reports directly on top of lakehouse data. Power BI can connect to the lakehouse data using the new Direct Lake mode, which allows Power BI to read the data directly from the lakehouse with no data movement and with great performance.

> **Note**
>
> Direct Lake is a fast path to load data from a lakehouse straight into the Power BI engine, ready for analysis. You'll learn more about Direct Lake in the *Power BI* section of this chapter.

With the OneSecurity feature, you can define security once in the lakehouse and have those permissions enforced by every engine in Fabric (Spark, SQL, and Power BI). This security definition can be for data access permissions for individual tables or files and folders in the lakehouse and can be granted to individual users and **Azure Active Directory** (**AAD**) groups. You will learn more about security in *Chapter 9, Security and Governance Overview*.

Powered by Apache Spark

Both data engineering and data science experiences in Fabric are powered by Apache Spark, an industry-leading open source big data computing framework. To remove friction in getting started, the Spark Runtime – the latest and stable version of Apache Spark, along with Delta Lake – comes pre-wired with every Microsoft Fabric workspace.

> **Note**
>
> Apache Spark can be used to perform a variety of data processing tasks, including batch processing, streaming processing, and **machine learning** (**ML**). It is a popular choice for large-scale big data analytics because it is distributed, fast, scalable, fault-tolerant, and versatile. You can learn more about Apache Spark at `https://spark.apache.org/`.

To leverage the Spark computing framework in Fabric, you can use Notebooks or Spark Jobs. Notebooks are a convenient way to run Spark code interactively and collaboratively, while Spark Jobs is a more efficient way to run Spark code in batch mode.

While Fabric provides data engineering and data science workloads powered by open source Apache Spark so that you don't have to deal with vendor lock-in, it has built several features related to performance, security, scale, and more to make the Spark runtime in Fabric enterprise-ready. For example, there are a variety of optimizations built into the Spark runtime to ensure data engineers always have a performant experience. These include Spark query optimizations such as partition caching, but also Delta optimizations such as V-Order. Additionally, the Autotune feature, with its built-in and behind-the-scenes ML models, automatically analyzes previous Spark job runs and tunes Spark query-level configurations (number of partitions, broadcast join threshold, and partition size) to improve performance.

> **Note**
>
> V-Order is the secret sauce in Fabric from Microsoft that optimizes data writes to Parquet files while still maintaining 100% open source Parquet file format compliance. Internally, V-Order works by applying special sorting algorithms, row group distribution, and dictionary encoding, hence resulting in optimized compression on Parquet files before a data write is made to these files. This optimized compression results in a much smaller storage size footprint for these files for the same dataset and requires less network, disk, and CPU resources in compute engines (such as Power BI, SQL, Spark, and others) for them to read it subsequently, providing cost efficiency and performance. All Microsoft Fabric engines automatically write Delta Lake with V-Order, meaning data is automatically optimized for BI reporting, resulting in great query performance when using Power BI. To learn more, go to `https://learn.microsoft.com/en-us/fabric/data-engineering/delta-optimization-and-v-order`.

In the cloud world, often, compute and storage are separated so that you can scale them independently and still save on consumption costs. This also means that since you don't have a persistent cluster running all the time like you do on-premises, it takes a couple of minutes for your Spark cluster to be created and a new Spark session to be set up for your job to get started. Microsoft Fabric solves this problem with **starter pools**, which are kept "live," meaning Spark sessions now start within 5 to 15 seconds from the moment you run your notebook, at no additional cost to you.

Starter pools come pre-wired to Fabric workspaces, meaning you can get started running Spark with no cluster setup necessary. Additionally, high concurrency mode configuration enables users to share Spark sessions across multiple notebooks. This means attaching a notebook to an already existing high concurrency mode session results in a lightning-fast session startup speed (less than 5 seconds), in addition to cost saving, by having the same set of underlying hardware resources running multiple jobs in parallel.

While the Spark runtime in Fabric provides auto-optimization out of the box so that you can focus more on creating business values for your organization, there are times when you need more control in managing your Spark workloads. For those kinds of scenarios, in addition to starter pools with default configuration, Fabric allows you to create custom pools and configure parameters such as node size, number of nodes, executors, and auto-scale. To do this, you must follow these steps:

1. Open your Fabric workspace and click on the **Workspace settings** link at the top.

2. Click on **Data Engineering/Science** on the **Workspace settings** pane and then click on **Spark settings**:

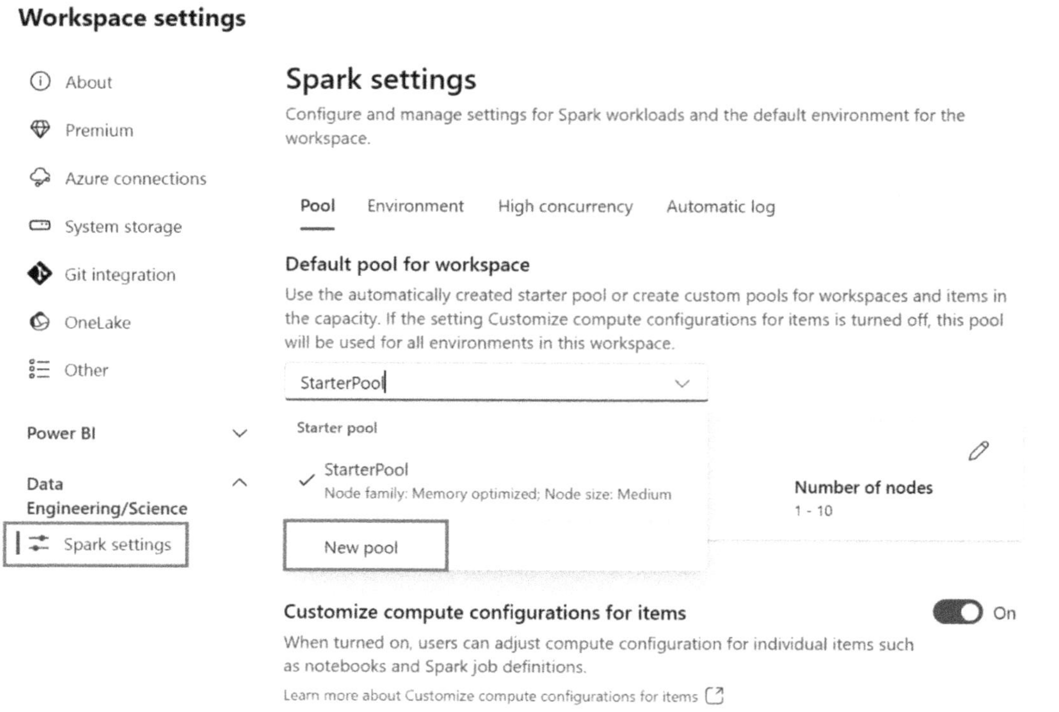

Workspace settings

Figure 2.16 – Spark compute settings

Developer experience

Microsoft Fabric aims to provide a delightful authoring experience for data engineers and data scientists, irrespective of their tooling of choice. In this section, you will learn more about the richer browser-based notebook authoring experience and **Visual Studio (VS)** Code integration for **integrated development environment (IDE)**-based development on your local machine.

Notebooks

For data engineers and data scientists, Microsoft Fabric includes immersive browser-based authoring experiences with notebooks to help you develop Apache Spark jobs and ML experiments that provide rich visualization and markdown text. You can use notebooks that provide native lakehouse integration, real-time collaboration with commenting support for co-authoring abilities, and auto-saving support, just like in Microsoft Office. Notebooks have lightweight scheduling that you can use to schedule a notebook's execution or can be added to pipelines for more complex data integration workflows. While a notebook has a default language to choose from (PySpark, Scala, Spark SQL, or Spark R), which automatically applies to all the cells in the notebook, you can use magic commands to change or switch the language of a specific cell.

Notebooks fully integrate with Spark monitoring experiences inside the notebook cells. Furthermore, you can navigate to the full-blown monitoring hub, where you can monitor all current and past Spark jobs, in addition to other Fabric items. You can drill down into job details, view associated notebooks and pipelines, explore notebook snapshots, and navigate to the Spark **user interface** (**UI**) and history server that comes with open source Apache Spark.

Notebooks also come with **Spark Advisor**, which analyzes code and Spark executions to provide real-time advice, help users avoid common mistakes, and promote best practices. This built-in Spark Advisor auto-scans and analyzes Spark executions, classifying error types and identifying the root cause of 150+ errors. This helps streamline the process of troubleshooting to identify and resolve errors.

While Fabric Spark includes several popular libraries already, there will be times when you'll want to make use of ad hoc libraries during your session. With Fabric Spark, you can install popular Python and R libraries in-line while leveraging commands such as `pip` or `conda install`, while also installing libraries at the workspace level. Additionally, as an advanced notebook capability, it provides development support with the ability to reference notebooks in notebooks for more modularized ways of working. During execution, it captures execution snapshots for each execution instance for troubleshooting.

VS Code integration

Often, there will be people who prefer to work in a local IDE. Fabric provides the Synapse VS Code extension, which enables users to work (author, run, and debug) with their notebooks and Spark Jobs and lakehouses straight from a local development environment. Users can benefit from full local debugging support while still using Spark clusters in their remote Fabric workspace. Furthermore, working in VS Code's IDE provides flexibility in working offline with a local environment and pushing changes online when needed.

> **Note**
> VS Code is one of the most popular lightweight source code editors; it runs on your desktop and is available for Windows, macOS, and Linux.

Spark Job Definition

While notebooks and VS Code allow you to develop your Spark applications interactively, there are times when you will have a job already developed and you would like that job to be executed as a batch or stream job, either on-demand or as per a defined schedule. For that, you can leverage **Spark Job Definition** (**SJD**) in Microsoft Fabric, which allows you to upload existing binary files (JAR, Python, or R files), tweak Spark configurations, add lakehouse references, and submit your jobs. Just like notebooks, SJDs come with monitoring, scheduling, and pipeline integration capabilities.

You will learn more about all these data engineering capabilities in the next chapter.

Data Warehouse

Businesses rely on a single version of truth to operate effectively and the tool of choice for data-driven organizations around the globe has long been the data warehouse. Names such as Ralph Kimball and Bill Inmon are synonymous with design patterns, and Kimball's *The Data Warehouse Toolkit* could be found on the desk of just about any BI developer in the 2010s. While the technology has changed and the lakehouse is becoming more popular, the value of a data warehouse remains and companies are embarking on new warehouse projects every day.

The decision between a data warehouse and a lakehouse in Fabric is largely one of skillset rather than technology. Data Factory ETL tooling, Power BI datasets, SQL, and Spark all work seamlessly over both lakehouses and warehouses, and they both deliver massive scale and high performance. The primary difference comes down to the skillset: Spark for lakehouses versus T-SQL for data warehouses.

If companies have developer teams that have a background in SQL, then the warehouse is often going to be the easiest and quickest path forward. The major benefit that you will see in future chapters is that those skills can also be complementary. It is not uncommon to see a lakehouse and a data warehouse on the same architecture diagram. Thanks to the advances in Fabric, integrating a lakehouse and warehouse is more seamless than ever before.

Fabric Data Warehouse combines the scale of Synapse-dedicated SQL pools, the open Parquet format for data storage, the T-SQL query language that countless data professionals use daily, direct integration with Power BI, and a new compute infrastructure to produce the best-of-breed data warehousing and analytics solutions.

When switching to the Data Warehouse experience, you will be greeted with the option to create a blank warehouse, a sample warehouse pre-populated with tables and data, or start bringing data in using pipelines and dataflows that were previously seen in the Data Factory experience:

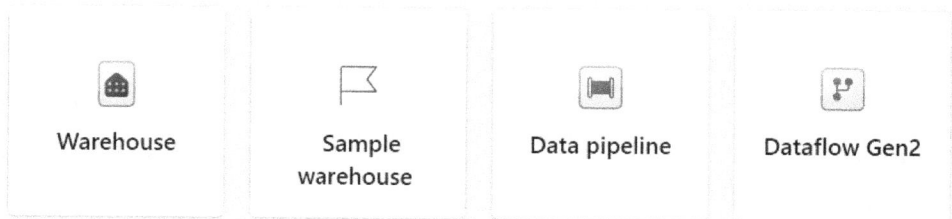

| Warehouse | Sample warehouse | Data pipeline | Dataflow Gen2 |

Figure 2.17 – Fabric Data Warehouse workload options

Now that you've learned about the data warehousing capabilities in Fabric at a high level, it's time to dive deep into some of these capabilities in detail.

Simplifying the Data Warehouse experience

Many complexities come with managing databases, and data warehouses are not immune to those challenges. With Fabric Data Warehouse, the goal is to reduce as many of those points of friction, thereby allowing data professionals to focus on delivering a robust, actionable platform, and allowing business professionals to focus on delivering business value.

For DBAs, this means that statistics will always be up to date, indexes don't need to be rebuilt, and backups are handled automatically, leaving them to focus on architectural and security-related tasks. For developers, there is a reduced emphasis on indexing strategies and data distribution so that they can spend time building a quality data model. Business users also don't need to worry about where or how the data is stored and how that will impact their report performance – they can focus on the value users will get out of the reports they develop.

Another way the warehouse is being simplified is to allow all the different personas to bring their skill sets to the table and work together. No longer does the data warehouse team need to have a deep T-SQL skillset to be successful. The user base can consist of both code-first developers using SQL and low-code developers using Dataflow Gen2 all on top of the same tables. That means integrating these two skill sets happens seamlessly rather than requiring months-long processes and backlogs to manage them.

Finally, a change that will benefit all users of the warehouse is the fact that compute and storage are truly separated in Fabric. No longer will administrators need to look at usage patterns and try to find a window of low activity to scale the warehouse engine up before the nightly batch kicks off, and then another window to lower it back down to daily business levels. Compute is provisioned and deprovisioned on demand as new queries come in. True separation of compute and storage means that storage scales independently as the data footprint grows and queries will provision the appropriate amount of compute based on the amount of data being scanned. This reduces the overall cost of ownership compared to other data warehouse solutions. Altogether, this means customers only pay for what they are using.

Open and lake-centric

A key tenant of the entire Fabric experience is the focus on delivering a lake-centric and open data solution. While data lakes have traditionally allowed users to use the file format of their choice, data warehouses are generally based on proprietary database technologies. This means the data is locked into the vendor platform. Sure, there are ways to get to the data. With database engines, you can generally use an ETL tool to export the data, or there might be a built-in data export utility that will create human-readable files. This process is time-consuming, costly, and error-prone.

The Fabric Data Warehouse has been created to operate natively on top of the open Paquet format, which means that all user data is always accessible to the end user. You can even navigate to the warehouse using the OneLake file explorer on your local computer, as seen in *Figure 2.18*, locate the data files, and copy them to another location for use:

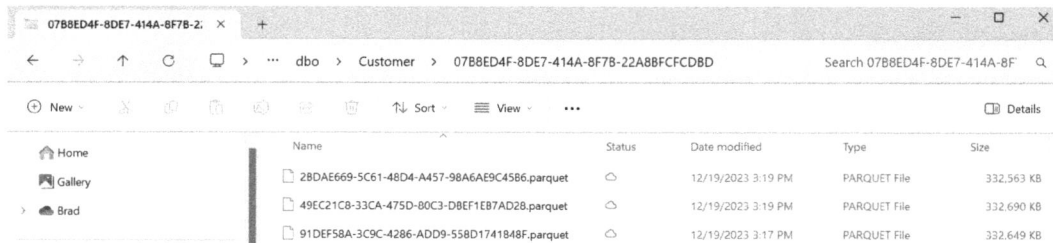

Figure 2.18 – Lakehouse explorer view of the data

Working on Parquet files means there is no vendor lock-in, and you are always in control of your data; there are no proprietary formats. The other major advantage of standardizing on Parquet is that all the data processing engines of Fabric are reading and writing the same format, allowing a single copy of the data to be used by Spark, SQL, and even Power BI.

Combining the lakehouse and data warehouse

A major point of frustration in many analytics projects is having to duplicate data to leverage different compute engines. Often, that means storing a copy of the data in a data lake only to duplicate the gold layer of data inside a staging area of a data warehouse to then merge that data downstream into the final dimensional model.

From a SQL perspective, standardizing on the open Delta format allows any table created in the lakehouse to be read by the SQL engine, which runs over the top of the lakehouse and warehouse by using the newly introduced cross-database querying capabilities. The result is a SQL query that is able to span data stored in the lakehouse and warehouse at the same time.

> **Note**
> Each lakehouse has a SQL endpoint provisioned by default. This SQL endpoint is a logical warehouse that's created automatically allowing T-SQL queries to run against tables in the lakehouse.

From a Spark perspective, standardizing on the open Delta format allows any warehouse tables to be accessed by the Spark engine using shortcuts without the need to copy the data out to the data lake or use inefficient JDBC-type connections to the SQL endpoint.

Many organizations have a mix of data professionals, with the data lake team being more Spark-focused and the warehouse team being more SQL-focused. Cross-database queries and shortcuts bridge the gap by combining the warehouse and lakehouse so that each team can fully prepare their slice of the data and combine the datasets at runtime.

Loading data

Data can be loaded into the warehouse using a variety of methods, including the T-SQL COPY command, Data Factory copy activities, and Dataflow Gen2. Each provides a different level of comfort for developers for their skillset and various levels of on-the-fly data transformation. The one thing that is common across all these methods is the ability to load data quickly and easily.

For SQL developers, the most familiar loading method is likely to be the T-SQL COPY command. Using just a line or two of code, you can perform a high throughput data copy from an Azure storage account or a lakehouse. Simply specify a few pieces of information inline, such as the file type, relevant parsing information such as header rows and delimiters for CSV files, the URL to the location of the data, and the credentials needed to access the data, and then run the command to ingest the data. The COPY command allows wildcards in the storage URL to facilitate loading multiple files from multiple folders with a single command:

```
COPY INTO [dbo].[MyTable]
FROM 'https://mystorageaccount.blob.core.windows.net/mycontainer/
curated/weather/florida_weather.parquet'
WITH (
    CREDENTIAL =
            (
            IDENTITY = 'SHARED ACCESS SIGNATURE',
            SECRET = ''
            ),
    FILE_TYPE = 'PARQUET'
);
```

For those who prefer a UI-based data ingestion experience, Data Factory offers the copy activity. One advantage over the T-SQL-based approach is an expanded list of data sources. Where the T-SQL COPY command needs data to be in Azure storage or a lakehouse, the Data Factory copy activity can pull data from dozens of data sources – relational or non-relational, cloud-based or on-premises. Because Data Factory allows a large amount of dynamic content, it is easy to build a data-driven framework to import data from many tables using a loop and a single copy activity:

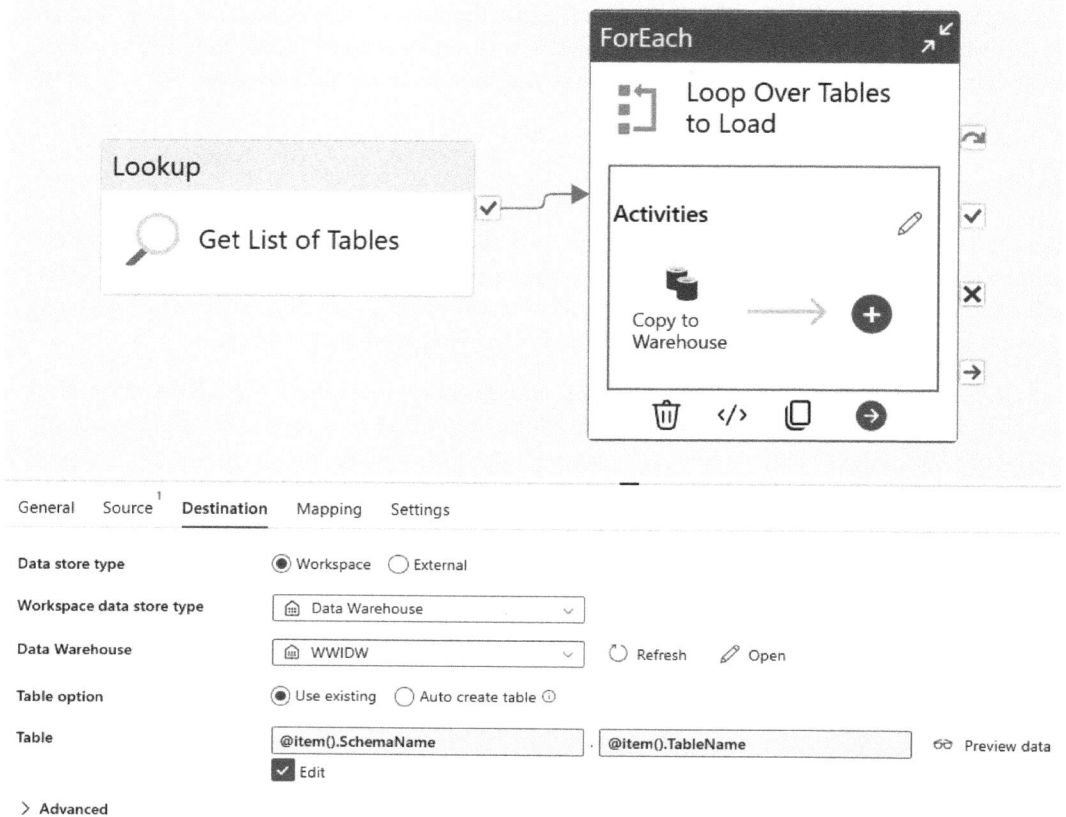

Figure 2.19 – A pipeline to load data for multiple tables in a loop

Finally, for developers coming from Power BI or anyone who needs to perform data transformation on data as it's loaded, Dataflow Gen2 could be the perfect solution. Dataflow Gen2, as discussed in the *Data Factory* section of this chapter, and its interface, as shown in *Figure 2.20*, uses the familiar Power Query interface to select a data source from over 100 different connectors, perform data transformation using a step-based approach, and put the data into the warehouse without the need to write a single line of code. These dataflows can then be added to a pipeline and scheduled as part of a larger ETL process:

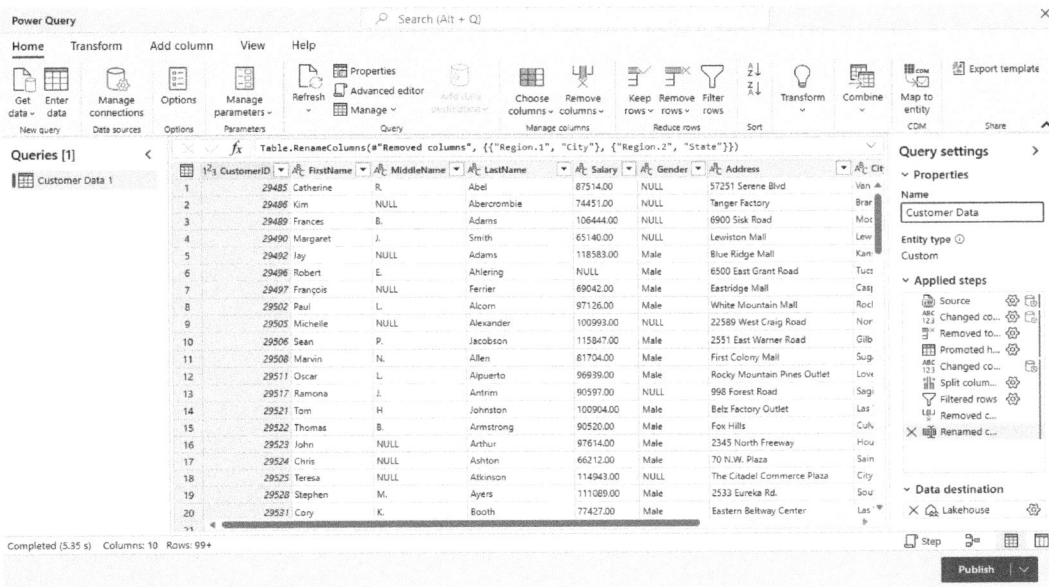

Figure 2.20 – Dataflow Gen 2 interface

Querying the warehouse

The primary method of interacting with any data warehouse is through writing queries. Some queries are written by users from scratch. Other queries are generated for the user by a reporting tool such as Power BI. Regardless of the amount of code you are prepared to write, Fabric aims to provide a world-class experience directly in the browser. For users who prefer to connect using client tools, that option still exists as well.

The web-based query editor, as shown in *Figure 2.21*, delivers everything a user would expect from a modern IDE. The object explorer allows you to explore the database and table structures, while right-click menus offer shortcuts to script tables, generate a SELECT TOP 100, and save queries for later use. Meanwhile, the query window has built-in IntelliSense, a customizable result pane for viewing results, and the ability to easily highlight code and turn it into a view:

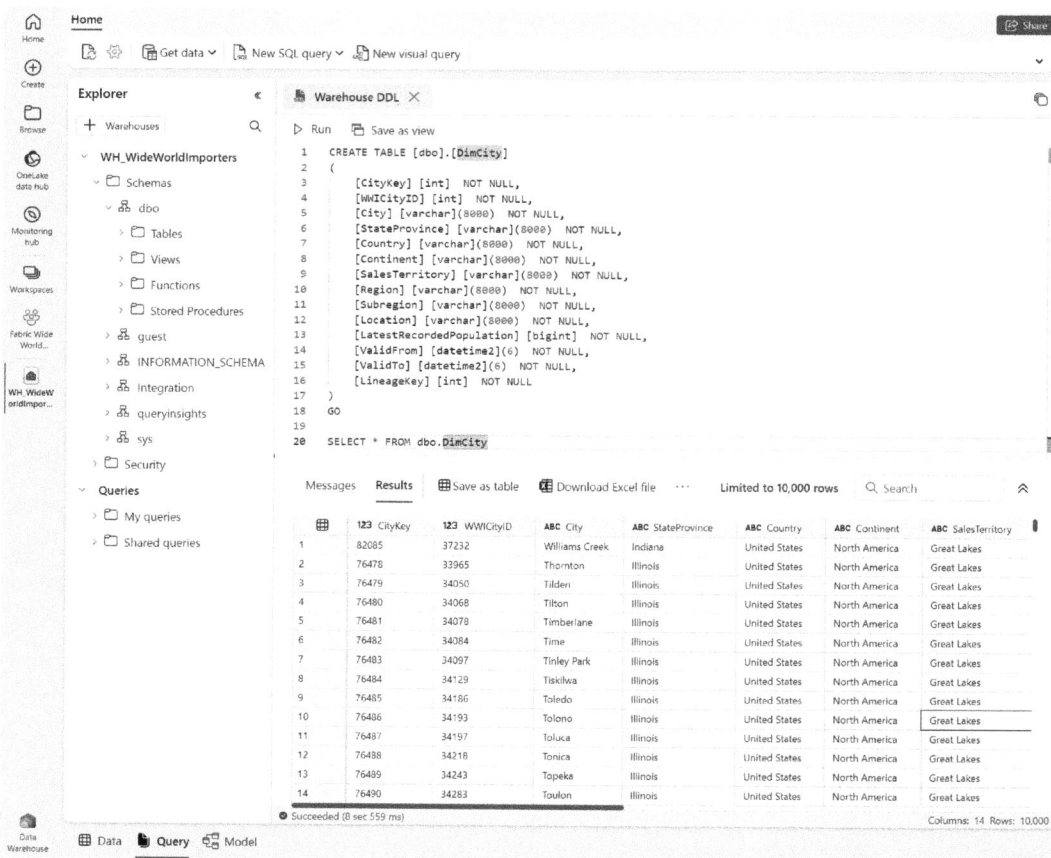

Figure 2.21 – Running SQL queries

Keeping with the theme of enabling as many users as possible to be successful in Fabric, the data warehouse has a robust visual query editor that uses a drag-and-drop experience that, like many other Fabric experiences, will be familiar to users of Power BI. While this is not the full Power Query experience, it does offer many of the same capabilities, such as combining tables, performing group by operations, and doing data cleanup through data type conversions and string manipulation:

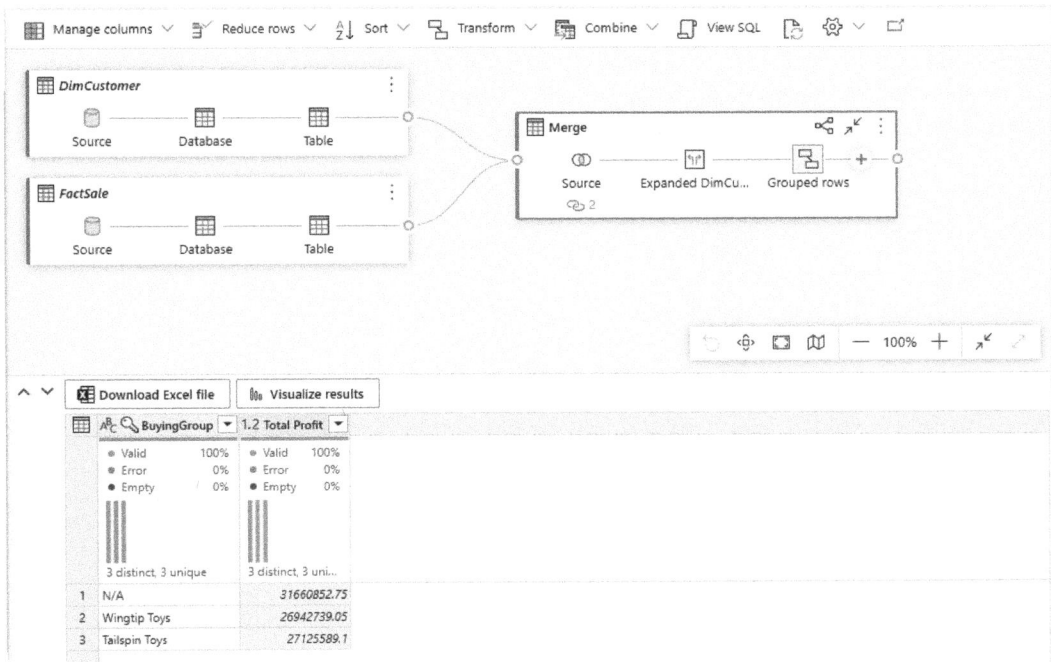

Figure 2.22 – No-code data transformation experience

Not every user or operation is best suited for a browser-based query editor. DBAs often work on many versions of SQL across on-premises and cloud environments and they want to do all their work in a single tool. SQL Server Management Studio has a large user base with many excellent plugins that streamline development processes. Azure Data Studio is built on the foundation of VS Code and therefore has a rich set of extensions available. There will always be a market for client tools running locally on a user's computer.

Fabric makes connecting with client tools easy by providing a single SQL endpoint per workspace, where you can connect to any data warehouse or lakehouse in the workspace. To get the server name to use in client tool connections, go to the workspace view, click the ellipsis next to a warehouse or SQL endpoint, and select **Copy SQL connection string**:

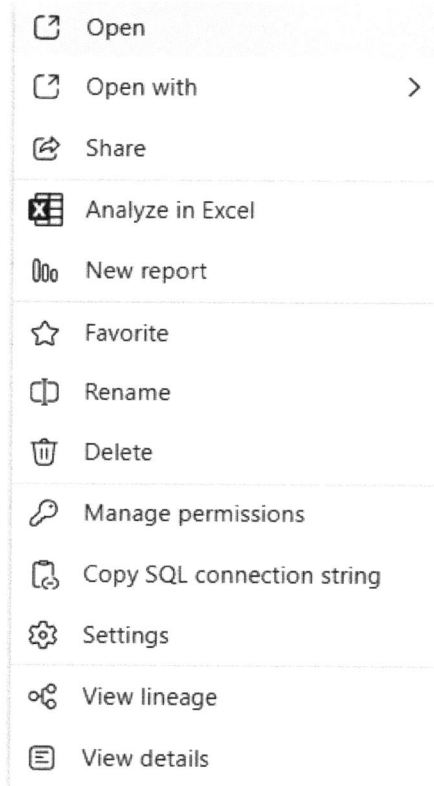

Figure 2.23 – Getting SQL endpoint connection details

The resulting dialog box will allow you to copy the complete server name, which can then be used in the SSMS or ADS connection details:

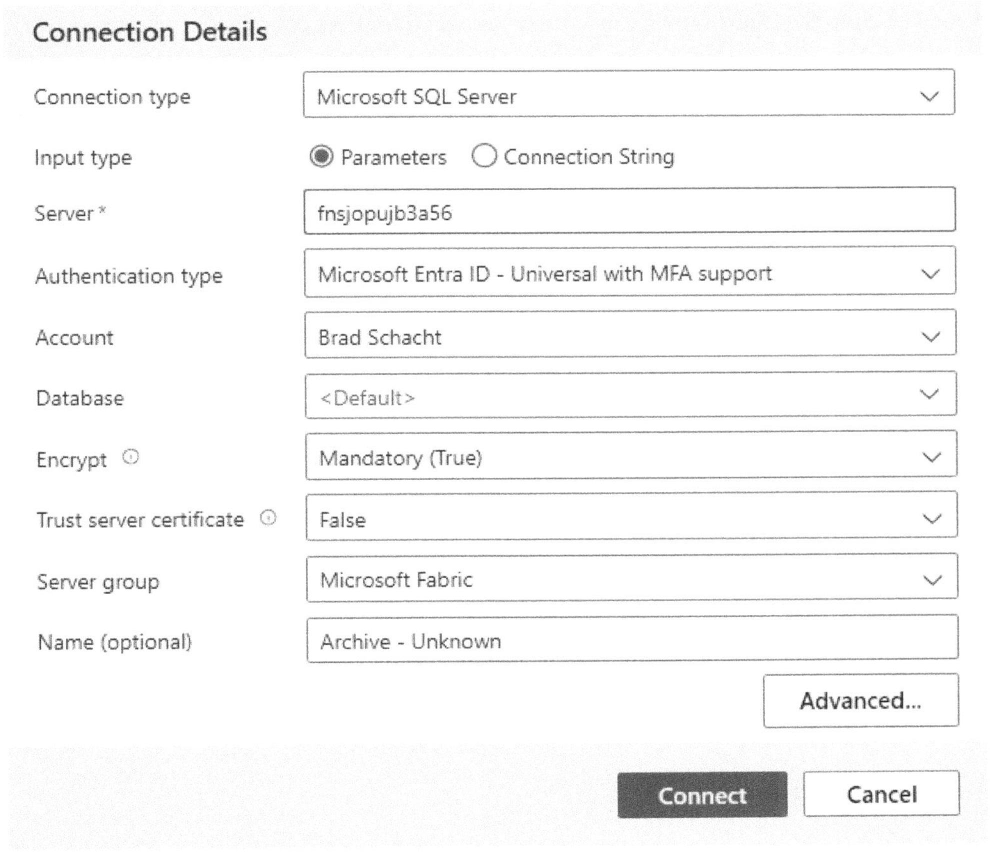

Connection Details

Connection type	Microsoft SQL Server ⌄
Input type	◉ Parameters ○ Connection String
Server *	fnsjopujb3a56
Authentication type	Microsoft Entra ID - Universal with MFA support ⌄
Account	Brad Schacht ⌄
Database	<Default> ⌄
Encrypt ⓘ	Mandatory (True) ⌄
Trust server certificate ⓘ	False ⌄
Server group	Microsoft Fabric ⌄
Name (optional)	Archive - Unknown

Advanced...

Connect   Cancel

Figure 2.24 – Specifying connection details to connect

You will learn more about all these data warehouse capabilities in *Chapter 4, Building an End-to-End Analytics System – Data Warehouse.*

Data Science

The goal of the Data Science experience in Microsoft Fabric is to empower data scientists, developers, and business users to develop a complete end-to-end data science workflow for data enrichment (acquisition, transformation, data exploration, and feature engineering) and predictive business insights with **artificial intelligence (AI)** and ML-based models. It empowers you, as a data scientist and developer, to execute a wide range of tasks across the entire data science process, starting from data exploration, preparation, and cleansing to experimentation, feature engineering, model training, model scoring, and serving predictive insights to end users, BI reports, or other tools.

When you switch to the Data Science experience, you will find these options to work with:

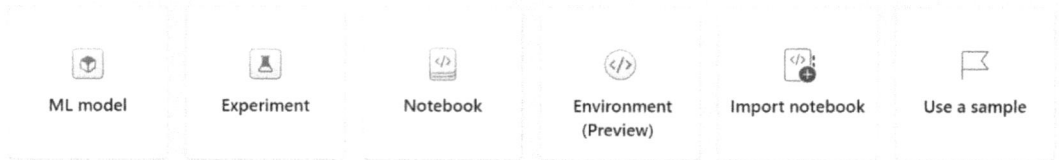

Figure 2.25 – Data Science workload options

Having learned about the data science capabilities in Fabric, it's time to dive deep into some of these capabilities in detail.

SynapseML

The SynapseML Spark library is a simple, distributed, and scalable ML open source library for Spark from Microsoft. This library is pre-installed and pre-configured in Fabric Spark so that you can use it directly without any additional setup needed. The core capability of this library is for you to use it as a scalable ML tool with its easy-to-use APIs for applying ML algorithms and enriching data at scale in a distributed manner by leveraging the power of Spark. SynapseML contains several distributed ML algorithms, such as LightGBM. In addition, its integration with MLflow allows full support for model tracking, versioning, and MLOps. The SynapseML library also allows you to work with pre-trained AI models from Azure Cognitive Services and leverage Azure OpenAI features.

MLflow integration

The built-in MLflow (`https://mlflow.org/docs/latest/index.html`), powered by Azure ML, provides capabilities for ML model and experiment tracking to track and compare their different experiment runs and model versions using standard MLflow APIs. Additionally, the Data Science experience extends MLflow auto-logging to automatically log the key metrics, parameters, and items of a ML model during training.

> **Note**
> MLflow is an open source platform for managing the end-to-end ML life cycle. You can read more about it at `https://mlflow.org/docs/latest/index.html`.

FLAML integration for automated ML (AutoML)

The native integration of FLAML (`https://microsoft.github.io/FLAML/`) in Fabric's Data Science experience offers an automated process of optimizing ML models and hyperparameter tuning. This process can also be easily tuned so that it can be used with SparkML and SynapseML models and is further supported by code-first integration to parallelize AutoML trials with Spark. Additionally, costs can be reduced by parallelizing hyperparameter trials with Spark.

MLflow can be used to automatically capture hyperparameter metrics and parameters, making it easier to build ML models quickly and efficiently.

> **Note**
> FLAML is a fast library for AutoML and parameter tuning. It finds accurate models or configurations with low computational resources for common ML and AI tasks. It frees users from selecting models and hyperparameters for training or inference, with smooth customizability. You can learn more at `https://microsoft.github.io/FLAML/`.

Data Wrangler

For citizen developers, Fabric offers a low-code yet powerful and intuitive tool called Data Wrangler for exploratory data analysis. Data Wrangler makes data cleansing and preparation easier than ever before by providing you with a built-in dynamic data display, built-in statistics, and nice and intuitive chart-rendering capabilities way. You, as a developer, an engineer, or a business user, can use its intuitive interface to apply a variety of data cleansing and data preparation operations in a matter of clicks, update the data displayed in real time, and generate code that can be saved back to the notebook as a reusable fashion for future. This generated code can be further enhanced, when necessary, to suit your changing needs.

Semantic Link

Data scientists can now easily tap into the semantic model developed by business analysts and leverage the hidden knowledge within the semantic model, which contains key measures and business logic, without copying or moving the data. This avoids duplication of effort and improves collaboration among data scientists and business analysts. Furthermore, Semantic Link helps validate data and detect data quality issues.

You will learn more about all these data science capabilities in *Chapter 6, Building an End-to-End Analytics System – Data Science*.

Real-Time Analytics

Everything in the world of data is moving more quickly every day. We track packages, view stats for sporting events, monitor engine health, and watch airplanes move across the globe all in real time. Users are increasingly asking for data to be as close to real time as possible because, in today's competitive landscape, minutes and seconds often matter. The challenge for data professionals is collecting this data and making sense of it all. Fabric's Real-Time Analytics experience is the answer.

Streaming datasets are often fast and large and require parsing. Logs, device data, and telemetry arrive in the form of semi-structured payloads that need to be parsed and indexed before they can be analyzed. Real-Time Analytics provides automatic data ingestion, indexing, and partitioning, all while keeping the data in the open Delta format, which can be read by all the Fabric compute engines.

When you switch to the Real-Time Analytics experience, you will find the following options to work with:

Figure 2.26 – Real-Time Analytics workload options

Next, we will dive deep into some of these capabilities in detail.

Eventstreams

Capturing data with Fabric is made simple with eventstreams. This functionality, which is part of the Real-Time Analytics experience, is a no-code solution that provides a single location to capture, transform, and route events to a variety of destinations. The source for an eventstream can be a built-in sample dataset (NYC Taxi or Stock Market data), an Azure Event Hub, or a custom application such as Kafka:

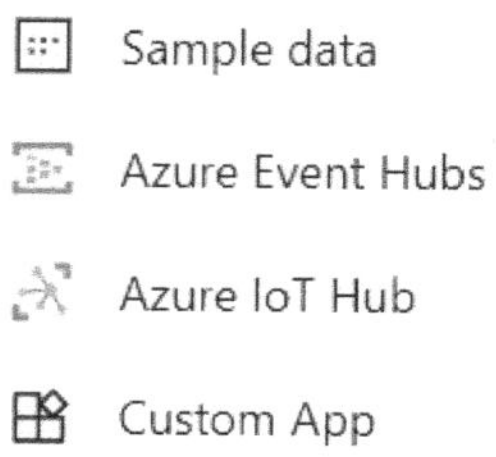

Figure 2.27 – New event sources

Data can be sent to one or more destinations in a single eventstream, including a custom application, a Fabric lakehouse, or a KQL database. The eventstream editor provides options to modify the schema of the incoming data and features the ability to remove columns, rename columns, and change the data type of a column. Simple transformations can also be applied, such as filtering, aggregating, and unioning data. Users can always view a live preview of the raw data being ingested and transformed, as well as data being written to each destination:

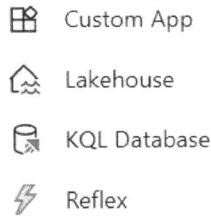

Custom App

Lakehouse

KQL Database

Reflex

Figure 2.28 – New destination for events

The total number of sources and destinations combined cannot exceed 11 in a single eventstream.

KQL databases

Similar to other analytics engines, the Real-Time Analytics experience uses a database for logically grouping data called a **KQL database**. A Fabric workspace can contain zero or more KQL databases. Each database can contain zero or more tables. While most developers will use their web browser as their primary method for interacting with a KQL database, a URI is also provided by which queries can be executed:

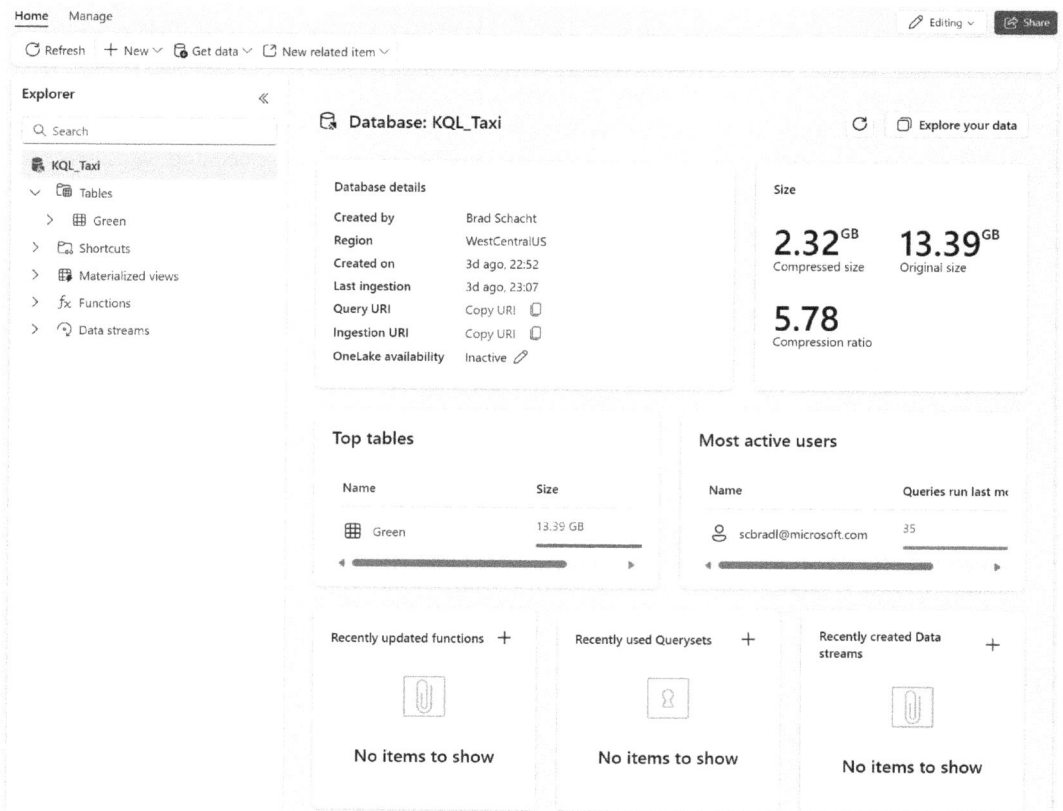

Figure 2.29 – The KQL database user interface

In addition to data being streamed in through an eventstream, data can be imported from files on your computer, Azure storage, Amazon S3, OneLake, using a copy activity in a pipeline with the KQL database as the sink, or using Dataflow Gen2 with the SQL database as the destination.

KQL queryset

A KQL queryset interface, as shown in *Figure 2.30*, uses the **Kusto Query Language** (**KQL**) to run queries against a KQL database. As its name suggests, a queryset can contain multiple queries, organized in tabs, each with a connection to a KQL database. Like SQL scripts in Fabric, KQL querysets can be shared to enable collaboration with multiple users on the same queries:

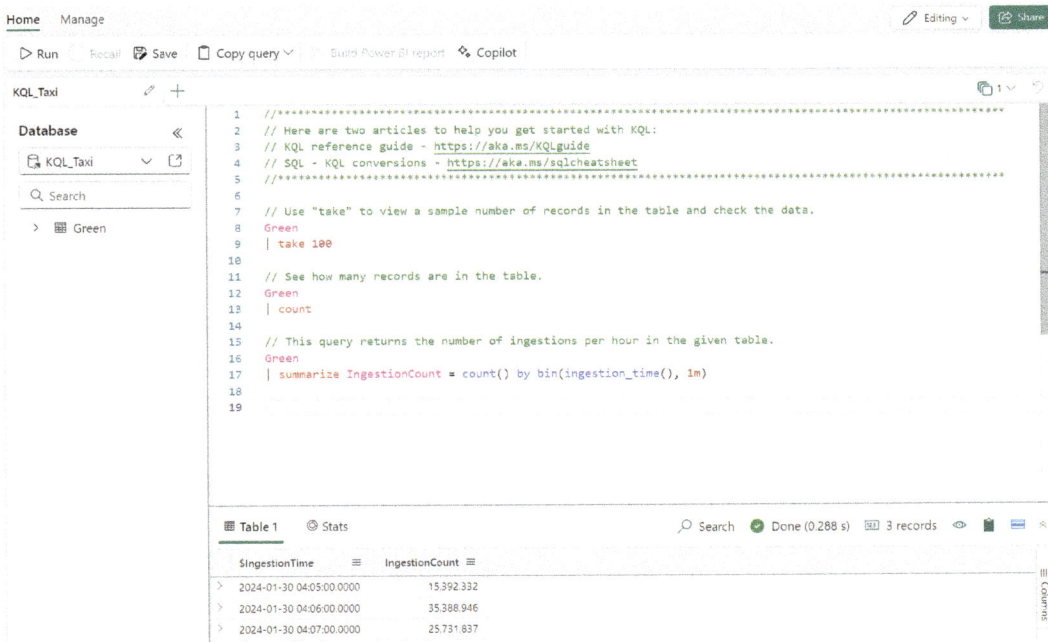

Figure 2.30 – KQL queryset user interface

While KQL is a very logical language and, therefore, relatively easy to learn the basics of, anyone with a SQL background can use those skills since KQL databases will accept T-SQL queries and automatically convert them into KQL. To aid in learning KQL, you can even type `explain` before a T-SQL query and the KQL version of the query will be displayed. It's worth noting that not all T-SQL functionality or queries can be automatically converted into KQL or operate the same. For instance, typing `SELECT *` is supported, but the columns may not be returned in the order the user may expect.

Power BI

Power BI is consistently rated as the leading BI tool in the market as it consists of a desktop application called Power BI Desktop for data model and report development, a service for hosting and distributing content, and a mobile app for consuming reports on the go. The broader Fabric workloads have adopted the foundation created by the Power BI online platform to create a portfolio of experiences all leading up to dataset and report creation. Like all the workloads discussed in this chapter, Power BI can be used independently or as part of an end-to-end solution.

The data that's analyzed and visualized in a Power BI report can come from more than 100 data sources, including Fabric lakehouses and Fabric warehouses. The experiences are more deeply integrated than any other analytics solution available today.

As shown in *Figure 2.31*, building a report from the Power BI experience page is as simple as pasting data into a table or using an existing dataset that someone else in the organization has already published:

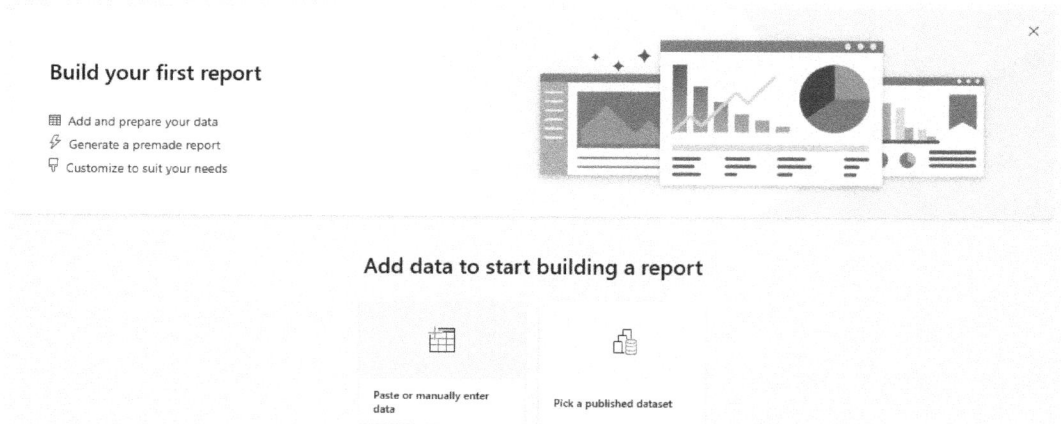

Figure 2.31 – Creating a Power BI report

Power BI is also woven into each Fabric experience. From a lakehouse, you can create a new dataset and report from the ribbon:

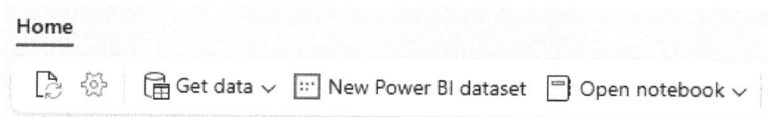

Figure 2.32 – Different options for Power BI

From a SQL endpoint or a data warehouse, you can highlight any query text and select the **Visualize results** button to create a dataset and launch directly into report development:

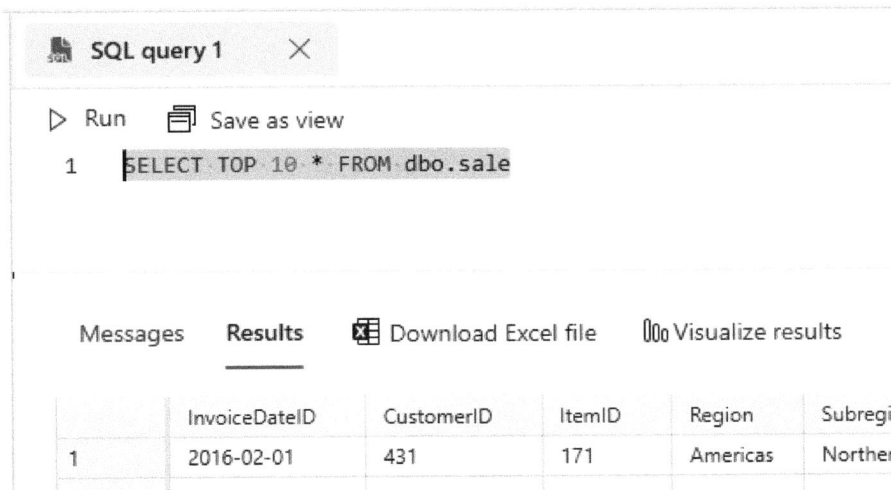

Figure 2.33 – Writing SQL queries

Now, it's time to dive deep into some of these capabilities.

Reports

Power BI reports are the visualization on top of a dataset. Sure, Excel can connect to a dataset, but reports offer so much more than pivot tables and charts. Featuring one or more pages, a report is highly interactive and consists of visualizations that tell a story about the data. By default, visualizations that use related data will filter each other as a user clicks on different elements as they interact with the report. Here is a list of core functionalities you will notice on the Power BI report canvas:

- **Pages or tabs**: A way to organize data inside a report, each containing a set of related visualizations.

- **Filters**: You can limit the data that's displayed on a report page using simple selection-based toggles or more complex, advanced criteria. Filters can be applied as granularly as a single visualization.

- **Visualizations**: A representation of data. While many visualizations are included by default, additional visualizations can be added to the report via Power BI Custom Visuals. *Figure 2.34* shows a report with a donut chart and other visualizations as an example:

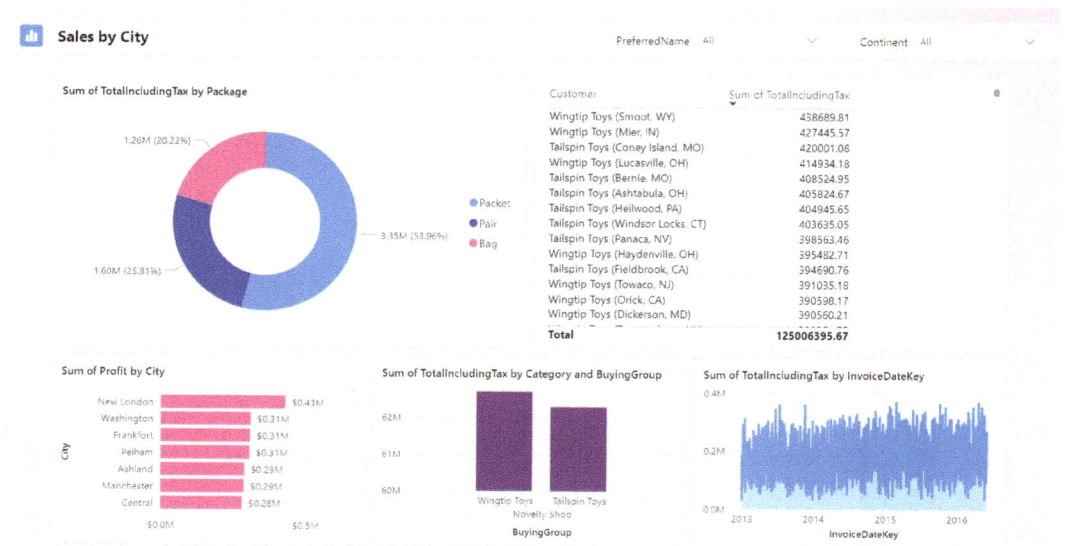

Figure 2.34 – Power BI report example

Datasets

Power BI datasets centralize data from one or more sources in a ready-for-reporting semantic model. Datasets can be created in Power BI Desktop and deployed to the service, created in Power BI, or created for the user by Fabric items. Within datasets, relationships are defined between tables, data quality considerations are considered, columns are renamed to align with business terms, and calculations are created so that everyone in the business is looking at a common set of metrics. The dataset is the single source of truth for all reporting needs.

There are three traditional types of datasets:

- **Import mode**: Data is stored or cached inside the dataset; the source is touched at refresh time and then all subsequent reporting references only the dataset.

- **DirectQuery**: Only metadata is stored in the dataset; when a report is used, a query is generated and executed against the source system. The tradeoff between these two modes is that import mode produces exceptional performance at the cost of refresh time and data latency. DirectQuery gives an up-to-date view of the data at the cost of report performance as the data needs to be retrieved with each report interaction.

- **Composite**: This option combines tables that are in both import mode and DirectQuery mode in the same report.

Each lakehouse and data warehouse comes with a default dataset. An example is shown in *Figure 2.35*:

	WideWorldImportersLH	Lakehouse
	WideWorldImportersLH	Semantic model (default)
	WideWorldImportersLH	SQL analytics endpoint

Figure 2.35 – Lakehouse default items

Relationships are not built into the default dataset by default, but they can be added manually by navigating to the modeling section of the lakehouse or warehouse items and then dragging and dropping columns between tables. This experience will be familiar to users of Power BI Desktop when it comes to creating relationships. All tables in the lakehouse or warehouse are automatically added to the default dataset, which means database developers do not need to continually update the dataset, and report developers will always know what tables and columns are available to them:

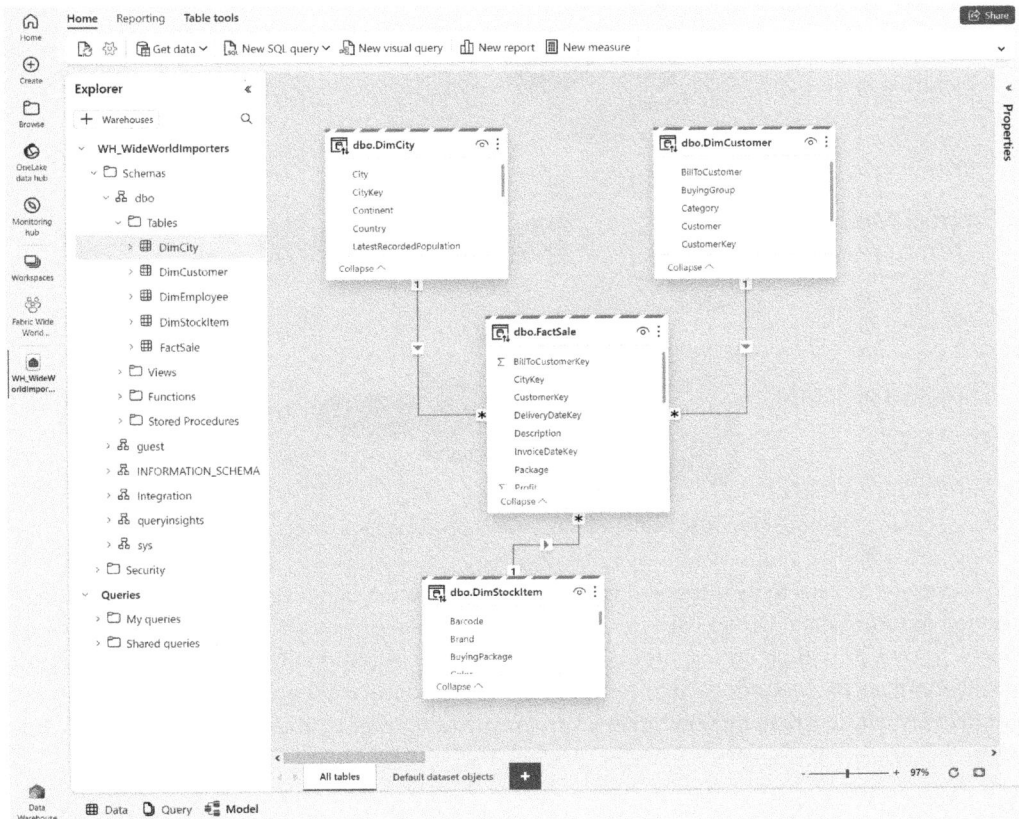

Figure 2.36 – Data model for your data in a lakehouse

There is also a sync process that adds new tables and views to the default dataset, but users can manually update the dataset at any time.

Direct Lake

With Fabric, a new type of dataset has been introduced that joins the three modes that were explained previously: Direct Lake. Using the core Fabric concept of OneCopy for data stored in OneLake that can be accessed by all compute engines, this Power BI dataset mode reads data directly from the Delta files within the lakehouse and data warehouse. There is no ingestion time, no refresh schedule, and no data latency. As shown in *Figure 2.37*, Direct Lake combines the performance benefits of import mode with the real-time nature of DirectQuery mode:

> **Note**
> To use Direct Lake, a workspace requires Power BI Premium P or Fabric F SKU capacities. It is not supported by Power BI Pro, Premium Per User, or Power BI A SKUs.

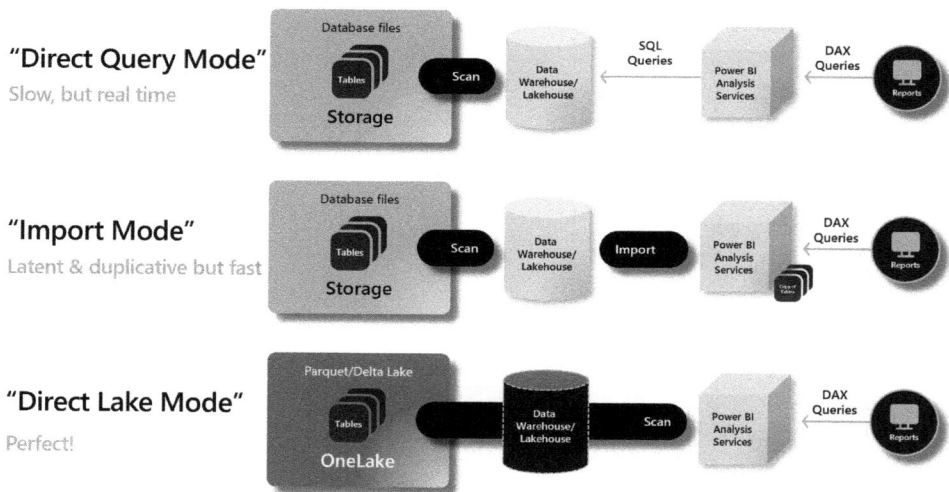

Figure 2.37 – Direct Lake versus import mode versus DirectQuery

While DirectQuery needs to be translated into source system query languages and then have a query be executed to return data, Direct Lake has no query generation or execution as the Parquet files are read natively, thus providing import mode-level performance. Additionally, because no data import occurs, all changes to the underlying files are reflected in each visual update. This makes Direct Lake perfect for datasets that are very large, take a long time to import, and appear in near-real-time reporting scenarios.

Summary

Microsoft Fabric is designed from the ground up for the age of AI and is delivered as a single SaaS platform. In this chapter, you saw how quickly you can set up a Microsoft Fabric tenant and create a Fabric workspace. You also learned about different types of workloads (Data Factory, Data Engineering, Data Warehouse, Data Science, Real-Time Analytics, and Power BI) and how they provide a unified experience in building analytics systems.

With this knowledge, it's time to dive deeper into each of these workloads and build an end-to-end analytics system. In the next chapter, you will build your first analytics system in Fabric based on the lakehouse architecture, followed by another one based on a modern data warehouse.

Part 2:
Building End-to-End
Analytics Systems

This part of the book walks you through building end-to-end analytics systems in Microsoft Fabric for different types of use cases, such as lakehouses, data warehouses, real-time analytics, and data science.

This part contains the following chapters:

- *Chapter 3, Building an End-to-End Analytics System – Lakehouse*
- *Chapter 4, Building an End-to-End Analytics System – Data Warehouse*
- *Chapter 5, Building an End-to-End Analytics System – Real-Time Analytics*
- *Chapter 6, Building an End-to-End Analytics System – Data Science*

3
Building an End-to-End Analytics System – Lakehouse

Traditionally, for their analytics needs, companies have struggled to manage two different analytics systems: a relational data warehouse to manage and process primarily structured data and a data lake for big data processing (primarily unstructured data). This has not only created data silos and redundancy across multiple systems but has also increased the overall effort to develop and manage the increased total cost of ownership. **Microsoft Fabric** bridges this gap by unifying different data stores (data warehouses and data lakes) by standardizing data storage using the **Delta Lake** format in **OneLake** for lakehouses.

In this chapter, we are going to take an example of a retail organization and build its end-to-end analytics system based on a lakehouse from start to finish—all the way from data ingestion and transformation to reporting and visualization. The key stages are as follows:

- Creating a lakehouse using **Medallion architecture** (Bronze, Silver, and Gold)

- Ingesting data from the source to the Bronze zone in an "as-is" format (or in a row format)

- Transforming and loading data into the Silver and Gold zones as Delta Lake tables

- Understanding the concept of one data copy in OneLake and accessing it from a lakehouse using **Spark** or from an SQL endpoint using SQL query

- Creating Power BI reports based on data from a lakehouse using **Direct Lake** and, without copying the data over, analyzing sales data across different dimensions

- Orchestrating data ingestion and transformation flow using a data pipeline and notebooks and schedules to run either on demand or according to a defined schedule

- Building a data domain within the journey of implementing a **data mesh** architecture

This approach can be taken by any organization from any industry. To learn these stages, we will cover the following specific topics in this chapter:

- Understanding end-to-end scenarios
- Storage
- Ingestion
- Transformation
- Analyze
- Orchestrate data ingestion and transformation flow and schedule notebooks and pipelines
- Data meshes in Fabric: a primer

Technical requirements

This chapter assumes that you have followed the instructions mentioned in the *Getting started with Microsoft Fabric* section in the previous chapter to create/enable Fabric in your tenant and have created a Fabric workspace to work in.

The code files for this chapter are available on GitHub: `https://github.com/PacktPublishing/Learn-Microsoft-Fabric/tree/main/ch3`.

Once you arrive at this link, you can open an individual notebook and then click on the **Download raw file** icon at the top right of the preview pane to download this individual notebook file.

You can also click on `https://github.com/PacktPublishing/Learn-Microsoft-Fabric/` and then click on **Download ZIP** under the **Code** button at the top of the middle of the screen to download all notebook files in one go.

Understanding end-to-end scenarios

A lakehouse in Microsoft Fabric is a data storage layer that allows organizations to store and manage virtually any type of data (structured, semi-structured, and unstructured data) in a single location, allowing various tools and frameworks to process and analyze such data as per organizational needs and/or an individual's preference.

A lakehouse combines the best aspects of a data lake and a data warehouse, removing the data duplicity and friction of ingesting, transforming, and sharing organizational data, all in the open format of Delta Lake. Ingested data flow into the lakehouse by default in the Delta Lake format (`https://delta.io/`), and tables are automatically discovered and registered in the metastore on behalf of users so that they're available to seamlessly work with all the engines within Fabric.

A data analytics system based on a lakehouse typically follows Medallion architecture (`https://learn.microsoft.com/en-us/azure/databricks/lakehouse/medallion`), which recommends taking a multi-layered approach to building a single source of truth for enterprise data products by describing a series of data zones (Bronze, Silver, and Gold) that denote the quality of the data stored in the lakehouse at each stage. For example, the terms Bronze, Silver, and Gold (sometimes referred to as raw, validated, and enriched, respectively) describe the quality of the data in each of these layers.

End-to-end scenario implementation involves an understanding of the architecture, sample data, data model, and the data and transformation flow. We will look at each in the following subsections.

Understanding the end-to-end architecture

A typical data analytics system has different components and layers overall, as shown in *Figure 3.1*. In this chapter, we will design and build each of these components in developing an end-to-end lakehouse-based data analytics system:

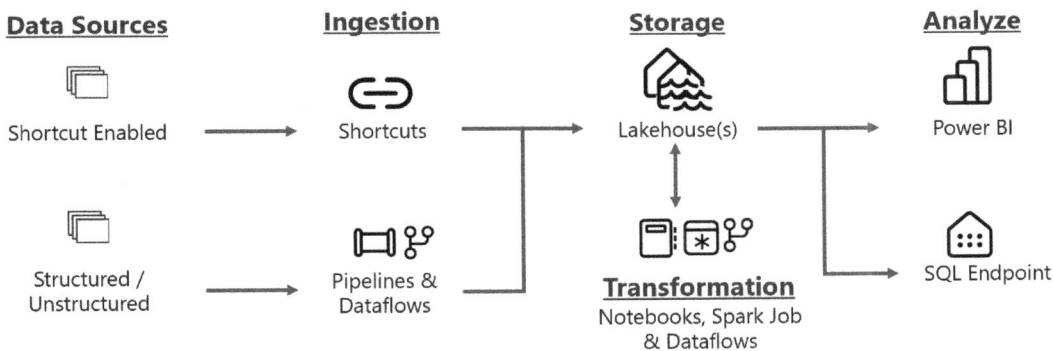

Figure 3.1 – Reference architecture for a lakehouse in Fabric

Let's review these components:

- **Data Sources**: You can easily and quickly connect a variety of different data sources to ingest data from on-premises data sources to **Azure Data Services** and other cloud platforms (Amazon or Google) with Fabric. Data Engineers can choose various ways of bringing data into the lakehouse, including dataflow and pipelines, or they can even use shortcuts (refer to *Chapter 1, Overview of Microsoft Fabric and Understanding Its Different Concepts*, for details about shortcuts) to create virtual folders and tables without the data ever leaving their external storage accounts.

- **Ingestion**: With 150+ native connectors as part of the pipeline and drag-and-drop data transformation with dataflow, you can quickly build insights for your organization. **Shortcut** is a new feature in Fabric that provides a way to connect to existing data without having to copy or move it.

- **Transformation and Storage**: For data transformation, Fabric offers intuitive no-code/low-code user experiences with pipeline and dataflow as well as pro-developer experiences in case the user prefers writing code in Spark with notebook or prefers writing in T-SQL. Based on your background and experience, you can use either of these methods or both in single-data transformation flow. For data storage in OneLake, Fabric unifies storage using the Delta Lake format and maintains one copy of the data in the lakehouse, meaning there is no data duplicity and all the engines of Fabric work on the same copy of the data. This makes it simpler and easier for you to implement a Medallion architecture or data mesh data architecture for your organization based on your requirements.

- **Analyze**: Once you have transformed and prepared your data, you or your end users, with appropriate permission, can consume it with Power BI for reporting, visualization, and dashboards. With the new **Direct Lake** mode in Power BI, you can consume this data directly from the lakehouse without any necessary data movement and get the same performance while scaling the existing import mode. Further, each lakehouse comes with a built-in SQL endpoint, which can be used by users to connect to the lakehouse from other reporting tools and query the data using SQL.

Understanding sample data and data models

For the purpose of building end-to-end data analytics systems based on lakehouses, you are going to use the **Wide World Importers** (**WWI**) sample database provided by Microsoft. WWI is an importer, distributor, and reseller of novelty goods and falls into the retail industry domain. You can learn more about their company profile and operation at `https://learn.microsoft.com/en-us/sql/samples/wide-world-importers-what-is`.

Please note the data model in this database contains several facts tables and associated dimension tables; however, for the simplicity of this chapter, you will consider one fact table and its associated dimensions in the **Star** schema, as outlined in the following:

- Fact: Sale
- Dimension: Customer
- Dimension: Employee
- Dimension: City
- Dimension: Date
- Dimension: Stock Item

Understanding data and transformation flow

The source data are in the **comma-separated values** (**CSV**) file format in an un-partitioned structure, stored in a folder for each table in a remote **Azure Data Lake** storage account. To demonstrate the full or historical load as well as the incremental data load, for one of the fact tables (**Sale**) you have one folder with all the historical data for several months and another folder for only the incremental data for 3 months. You will learn both approaches to data loading in the *Transformation* section of this chapter.

Since a lakehouse item in Fabric is equivalent to a schema, you will create three lakehouses to represent the three data zones (Bronze, Silver, and Gold) of the Medallion architecture, as shown in *Figure 3.2*:

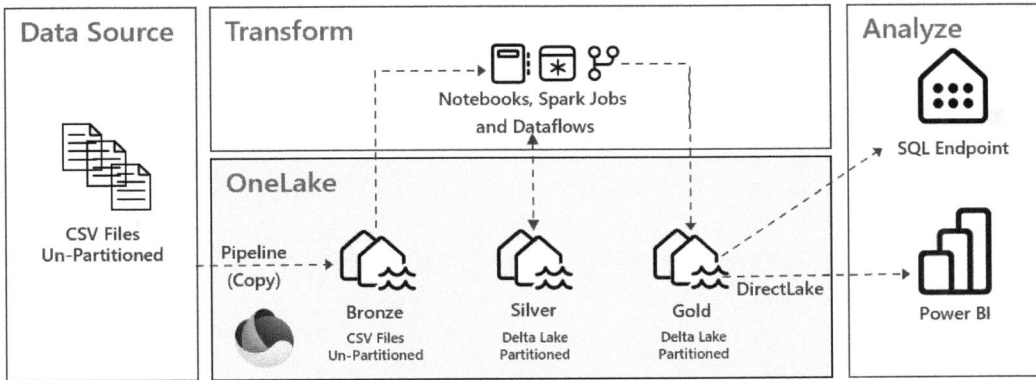

Figure 3.2 – Implementing Medallion architecture in Fabric

For data ingestion, you will be using **Data Factory Pipeline** to copy data from the source to the Bronze (or raw) lakehouse in the as-is format. Then, you will use **Spark notebooks** to transform and write (both historical and incremental) data to the Delta Lake tables in the Silver lakehouse. Finally, you will create business aggregates by creating Delta Lake tables in the Gold lakehouse using Spark notebooks.

Furthermore, you will learn to use Power BI and Direct Lake to create reports/dashboards that query data directly from the lakehouse and how to make use of an SQL endpoint to connect to the lakehouse and run SQL-based queries for analytics if you intend to use third-party tools for reporting.

With an understanding of the end-to-end scenario, let's switch to its implementation.

Storage

In this section, you will create three lakehouses (each representing each zone of the Medallion architecture) by following these steps:

1. When logged into Fabric tenant, select the **Workspaces** flyout on the left-hand side.

2. Search for the workspace that you created in *Chapter 2, Understanding Different Workloads and Getting Started with Microsoft Fabric*, by typing its name in the search textbox at the top and clicking on your workspace to open it. You can also pin it so that it always appears at the top of the list.

3. From the workload switcher located at the bottom left of the screen, select **Data Engineering**.

4. In the **Data Engineering** experience, select the **Lakehouse** type of item to create a lakehouse under + **New**.

5. Enter wwi_bronze in the **Name** box and click on **Create**. The new lakehouse will be created and automatically opened.

Repeat *steps 4–5* to create two more lakehouses named wwi_silver and wwi_gold. When you switch to the workspace again, you should see all your lakehouses, along with their default datasets and corresponding SQL endpoints, as shown in the following:

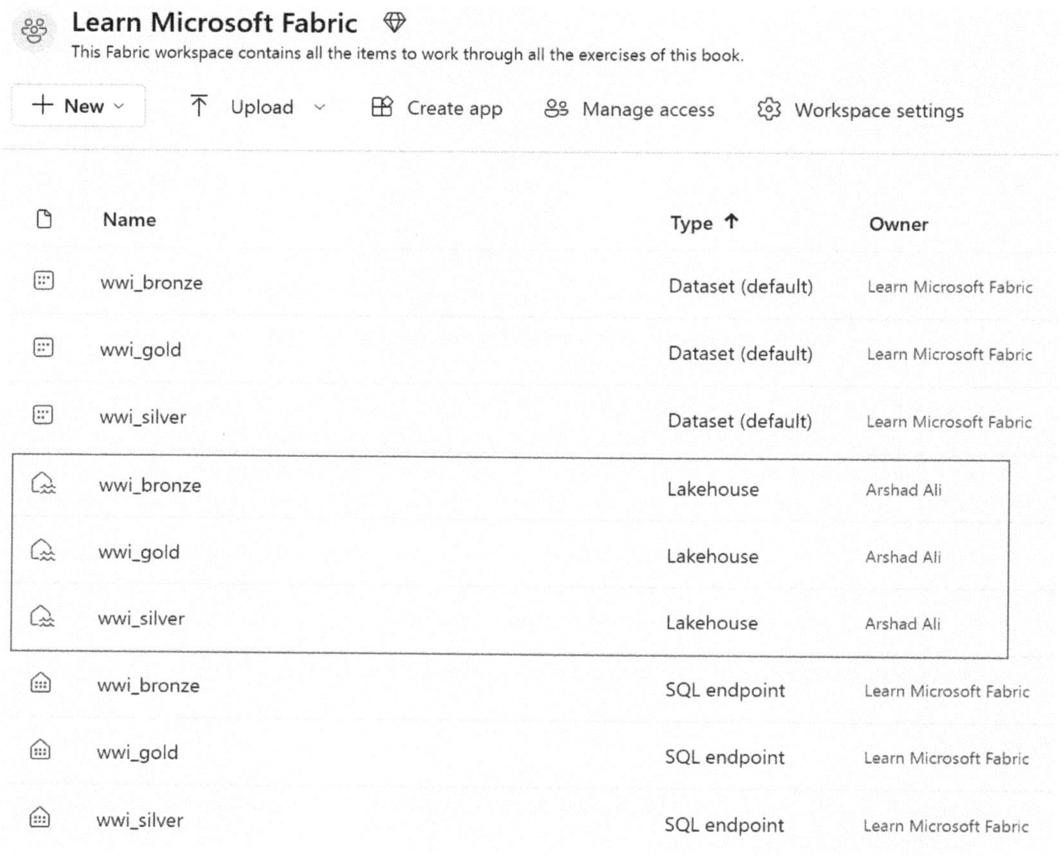

Learn Microsoft Fabric

This Fabric workspace contains all the items to work through all the exercises of this book.

| + New ˅ | ↑ Upload ˅ | ⊞ Create app | ⚇ Manage access | ⚙ Workspace settings |

	Name	Type ↑	Owner
⊞	wwi_bronze	Dataset (default)	Learn Microsoft Fabric
⊞	wwi_gold	Dataset (default)	Learn Microsoft Fabric
⊞	wwi_silver	Dataset (default)	Learn Microsoft Fabric
⌂	wwi_bronze	Lakehouse	Arshad Ali
⌂	wwi_gold	Lakehouse	Arshad Ali
⌂	wwi_silver	Lakehouse	Arshad Ali
⌂	wwi_bronze	SQL endpoint	Learn Microsoft Fabric
⌂	wwi_gold	SQL endpoint	Learn Microsoft Fabric
⌂	wwi_silver	SQL endpoint	Learn Microsoft Fabric

Figure 3.3 – Different zones of Medallion architecture

Physical locations

When a lakehouse is created, it is created with two physical locations for the storage of your data:

- **Tables**: This is the main container or managed area to host tables of all types (CSV, Parquet, Delta, managed tables, and unmanaged or external tables (`https://www. oreilly.com/library/view/learning-spark-2nd/9781492050032/ ch04.html#:~:text=Managed%20Versus%20UnmanagedTables`). All tables, whether automatically or explicitly created, will show up as a table under this managed area of the lakehouse. Any Delta Lake format files (Parquet + transaction log) stored in this area are automatically recognized as tables.

- **Files**: This is an unmanaged area for your lakehouse to store data under virtually any file format. Any Delta Lake format files (Parquet + transaction log) stored in this area are not automatically recognized as tables. If a user wants to create a table over a Delta folder in the unmanaged area, they will have to explicitly create an external table with the location pointer linking to the unmanaged folder containing the Delta Lake files.

The main distinction between the managed area (tables) and the unmanaged area (files) is the automatic table discovery and registration process that only runs over any of the folders created in the managed area and not in the unmanaged area.

After creating lakehouses to represent each stage of the Medallion architecture, it's time to ingest data into the Bronze zone.

Ingestion

In this section, you will use a **Pipeline** (Data Factory) to ingest sample data from a source (Azure storage account) to the **Files** section of the Bronze zone (**wwi_bronze**) of the Medallion architecture:

1. Choose the workspace that you created in *Chapter 2, Understanding Different Workloads and Getting Started with Microsoft Fabric*, from the **Workspaces** fly out on the left-hand side and open it. Create a **Data pipeline** from the +**New** button on the workspace page. If you don't see an option for **Data pipeline**, click on the **Show All** menu item at the bottom and then select **Data pipeline** under **Data Factory**.

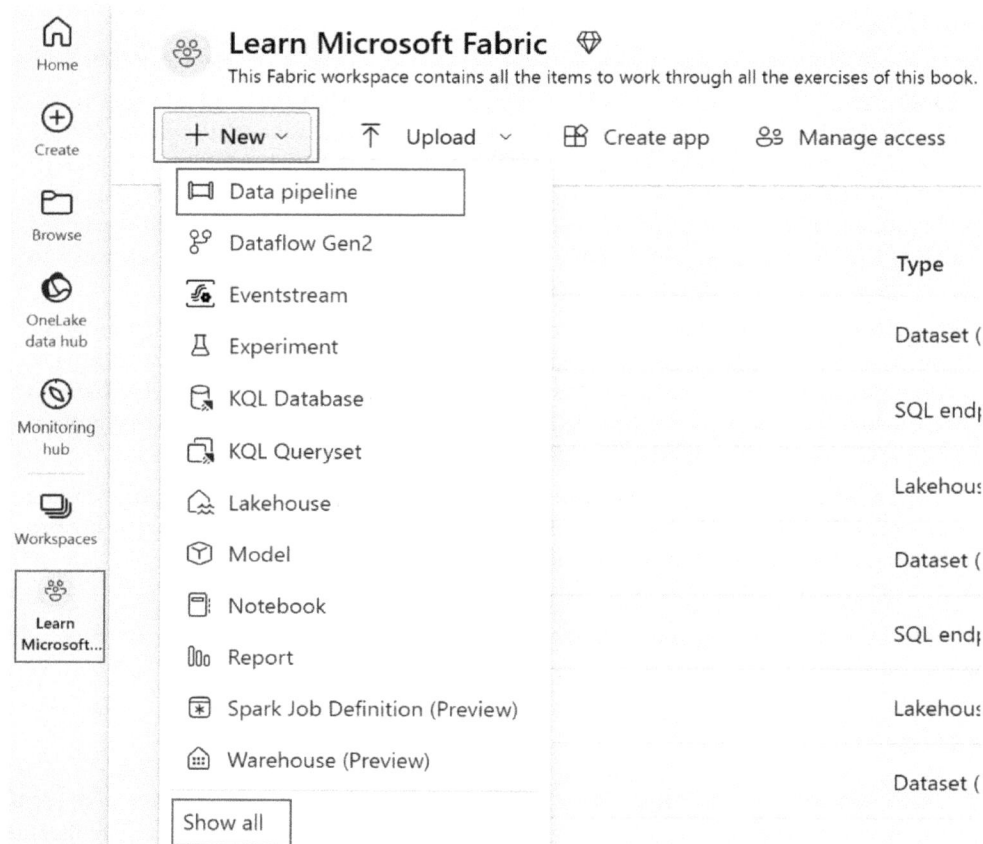

Figure 3.4 – Creating a new data pipeline

2. For the **New pipeline**, specify the name as `IngestDataFromSourceToBronze` and click on **Create**. This will create a new data factory pipeline and open its canvas on the screen to work on.

3. On the newly created data factory pipeline, click on **Add pipeline activity** to add an activity to the pipeline, and click on **Copy data**. This will add the copy data activity to the pipeline canvas.

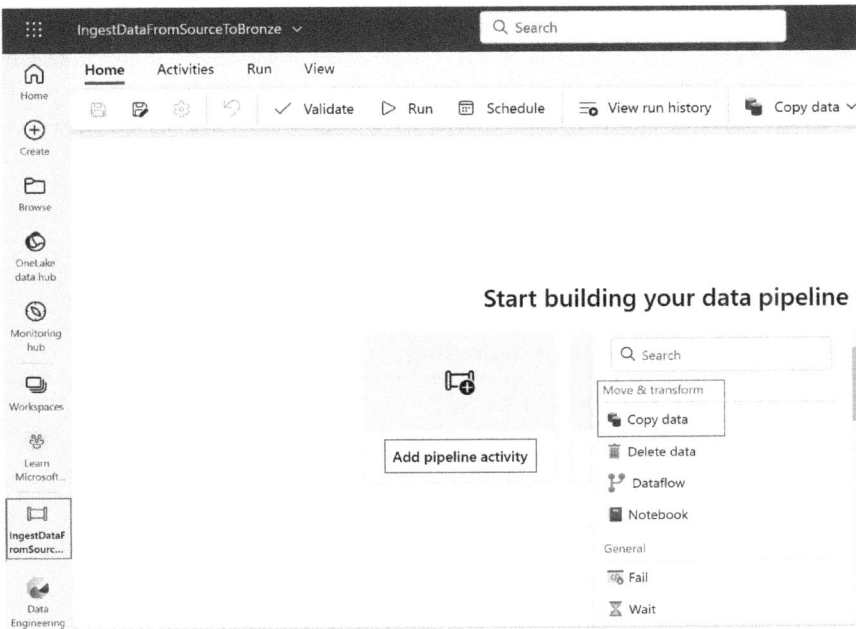

Figure 3.5 – Creating a Copy data activity

4. Select the newly added **Copy data** activity to the canvas, which will show activity properties at the bottom. Under the **General** tab, specify the name for the copy data activity as Data Copy to Bronze. Under the **Source** tab of the selected copy data activity, select **External** as the **Data store type** and then click on + **New** to create a new connection to an external data source from which you need to ingest data.

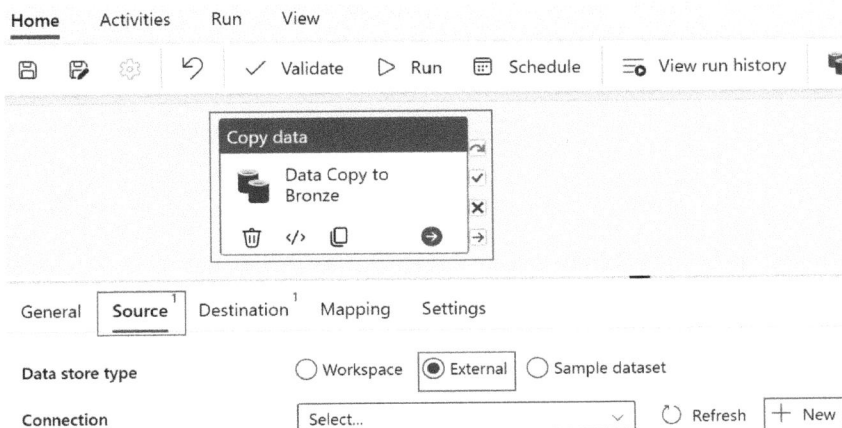

Figure 3.6 – Creating a copy data activity: define source

5.   For this scenario, you will be using sample data that are available in a public container from Azure blob storage; you will connect to this container to copy its data. On the **New** connection wizard, select **Azure Blob Storage** as the source and then click on **Continue**. On the next screen of the **New** connection wizard, please specify these details and click on the **Create** button to create the connection to the identified data source.

Configuration	Value
Account name or URI	`https://azuresynapsestorage.blob.core.windows.net/sampledata`
Connection	**Create new connection**
Connection name	`wwisampledata`
Authentication kind	**Anonymous**

Table 3.1 – New connection configuration

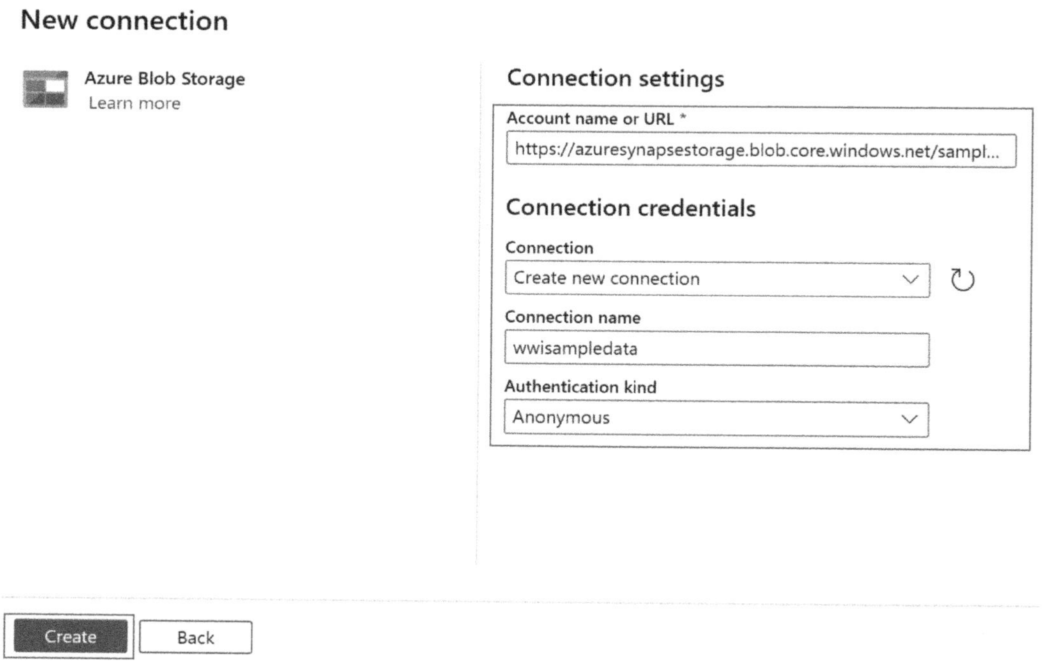

New connection

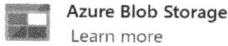

Figure 3.7 – Creating a new connection to the data source

6. Once the new connection is created, you will return to the **Source** tab of the **Copy data** activity, and the newly created connection will be selected by default. Please specify these properties before moving to the **Destination** tab:

Configuration	Value
Data store type	`External`
Connection	`wwisampledata`
File path type	`File path`
File path	Container name (first text box) – `sampledata` Directory name (second text box) – `WideWorldImportersDW/csv`
Recursively	`Checked`
File Format	`Binary`

Table 3.2 – Source configuration

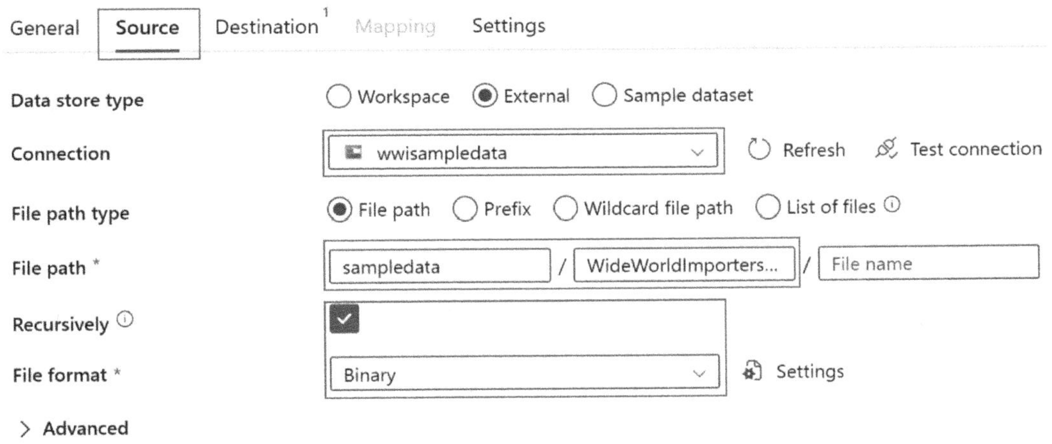

| General | **Source** | Destination [1] | Mapping | Settings |

Data store type   ○ Workspace   ● External   ○ Sample dataset

Connection   [🖬 wwisampledata   ∨]   ○ Refresh   ✎ Test connection

File path type   ● File path   ○ Prefix   ○ Wildcard file path   ○ List of files ⓘ

File path *   [sampledata   ] / [WideWorldImporters...] / [File name   ]

Recursively ⓘ   [✔]

File format *   [Binary   ∨]   🗒 Settings

> Advanced

Figure 3.8 – Creating a copy data activity: source configuration

7.   Under the **Destination** tab of the selected **Copy data** activity, please specify these properties:

Configuration	Value
Data store type	`Workspace`
Workspace data store type	`Lakehouse`
Lakehouse	`wwi_bronze`
Root Folder	`Files`
File path	Directory name (first text box) – `wwi`
File Format	`Binary`

Table 3.3 – Destination configuration

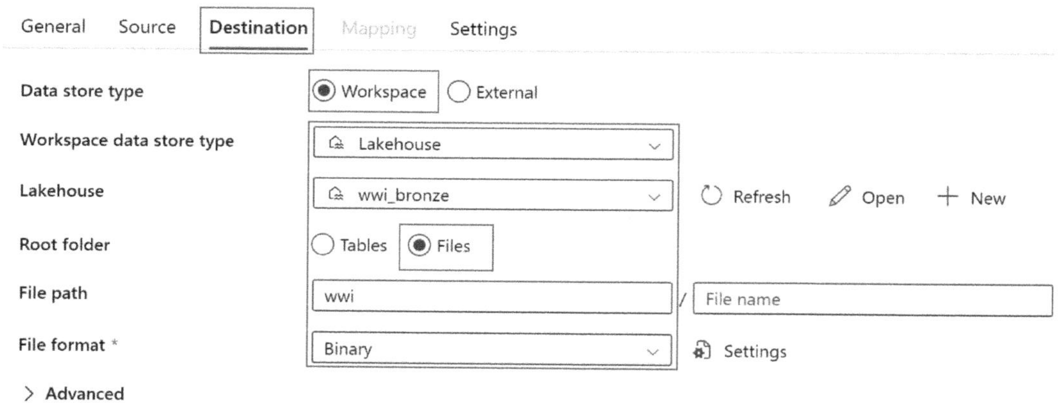

Figure 3.9 – Creating a copy data activity: destination configuration

8.   At this time, you have completed configuring the **Copy data** activity. Click on the **Save** button under the **Home** menu bar on the top left, as shown in *Figure 3.10*, to save all these details and click on **Run** to kick off the execution of this pipeline and its activity. You can also schedule pipelines to refresh data at defined intervals to meet your business requirements; however, for now, you will run the pipeline on demand once by clicking on the **Run** button. This will trigger data copying from the underlying data source to the specified lakehouse and might take couple of minutes to complete. You can monitor the execution of the pipeline and its activity under the **Output** tab, which appears when you click anywhere on the canvas. Optionally, you can click on the **glass** icon to look at the details (number of files, amount of data transfer, transfer rate, and so on) of the data transfer.

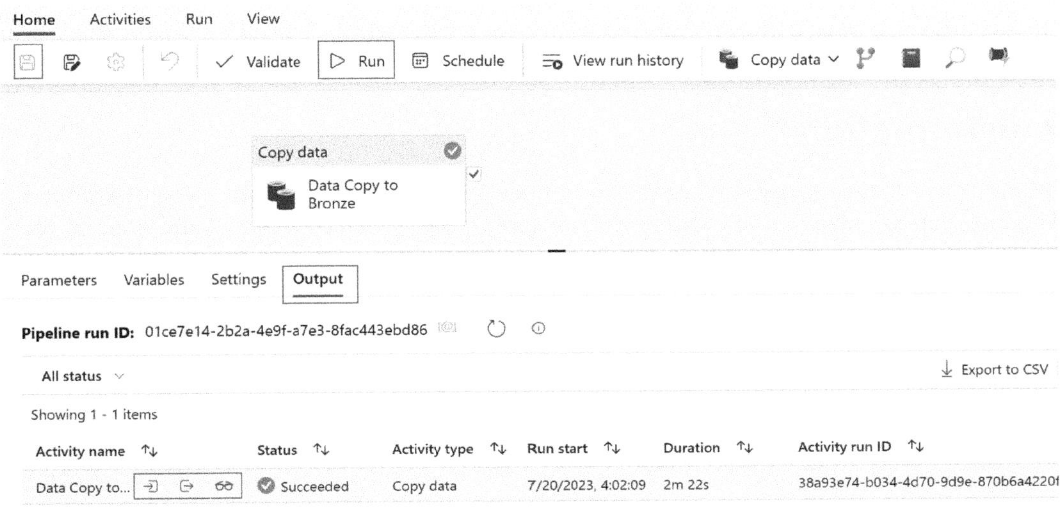

Figure 3.10 – Execution of the copy data activity

9.   Once the data copy is completed, you can go to the items view of the workspace and click on the **wwi_bronze** lakehouse to launch the lakehouse explorer to view this selected lakehouse. In the lakehouse explorer view, you will notice a new folder **wwi** under **Files** has been created and the raw data in the CSV format for all the tables have been copied here.

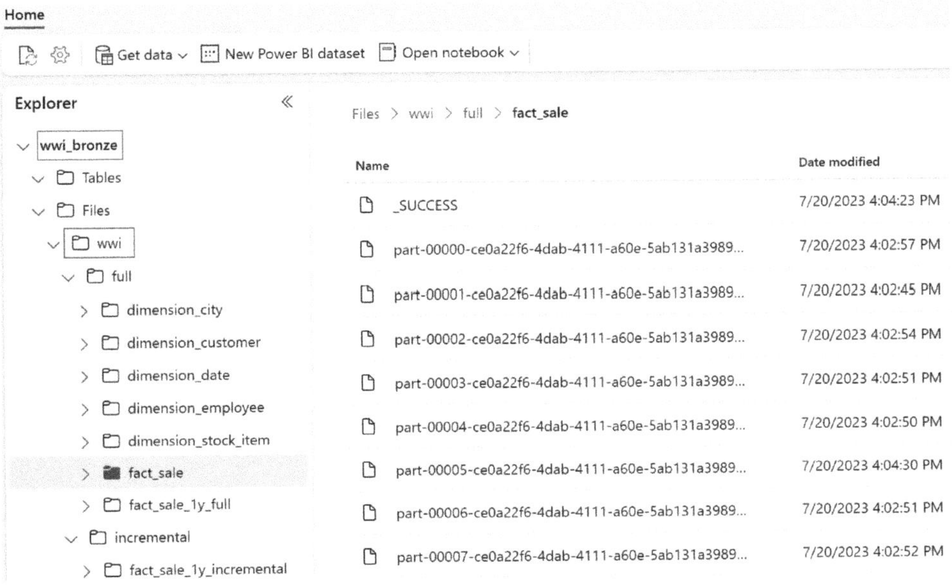

Figure 3.11 – Verifying the data that have landed into the lakehouse (Bronze zone)

Now that you have ingested raw data from the source to the Bronze zone of the Medallion architecture, we will transform and move these to the Silver zone next.

Transformation

Now that you have already ingested the raw data from the source to the **Files** section of the **wwi_bronze** lakehouse, you can take this data and transform and prepare it to create Delta Lake tables in the **wwi_silver** lakehouse as a next step.

Importing notebooks

The first step is to import notebooks using the following steps:

1. Download the notebooks found in the `ch3` folder of this chapter's GitHub repo (`https://github.com/PacktPublishing/Learn-Microsoft-Fabric/tree/main/ch3`) to your local machine. If required, unzip or uncompress them.

2. From the workload switcher located at the bottom left of the screen, select **Data engineering**. Select **Import notebook** from the **New** section at the top of the landing page of the **Data Engineering** experience.

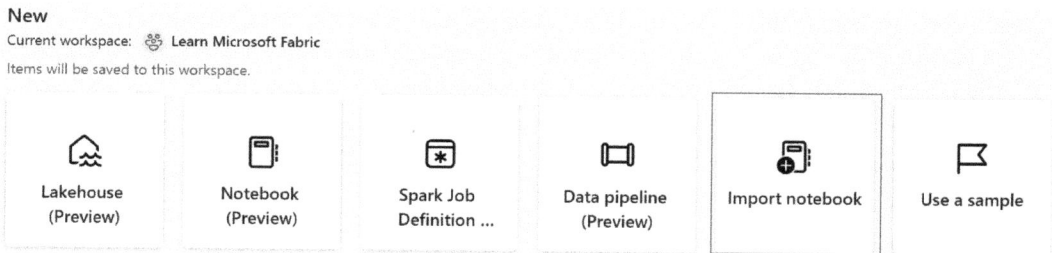

New

Current workspace: Learn Microsoft Fabric

Items will be saved to this workspace.

| Lakehouse (Preview) | Notebook (Preview) | Spark Job Definition ... | Data pipeline (Preview) | Import notebook | Use a sample |

Figure 3.12 – The option to import notebooks

3. Select **Upload** from the **Import status** pane that opens on the right-hand side of the screen. Select all three notebooks that were downloaded and/or unzipped in *step 1* and hit **Open**. A notification indicating the status of the imports will appear in the top-right corner of the browser window after the import process is completed.

4. After the import of the notebooks is successful, you can go to the items view of the workspace and see these newly imported notebooks.

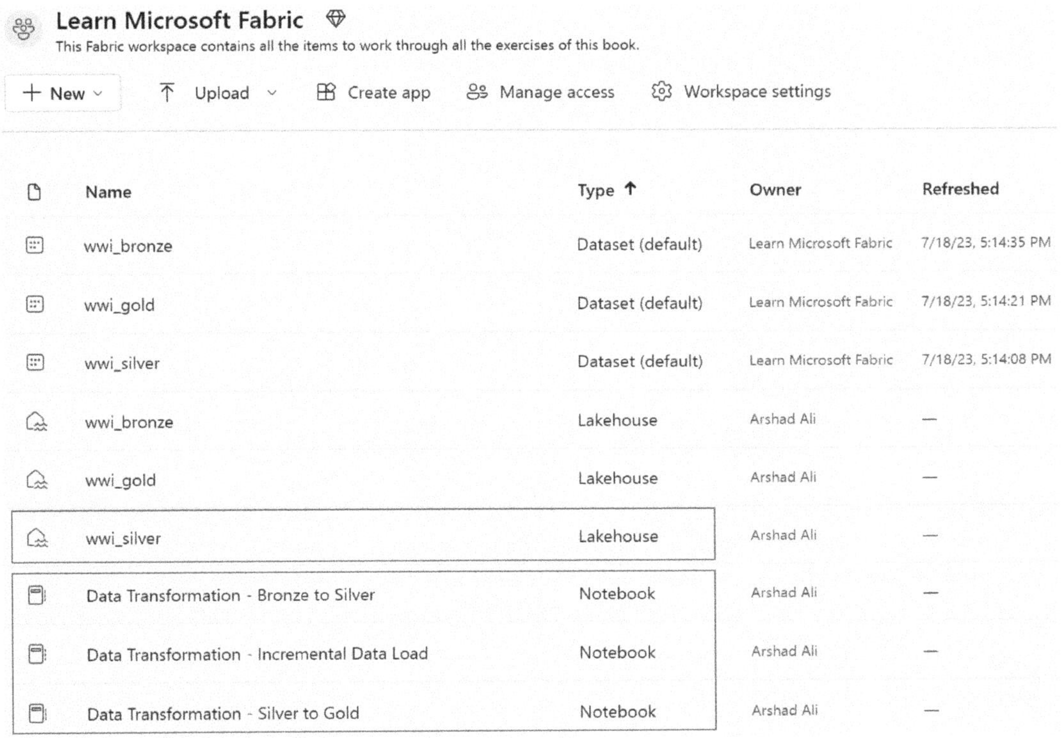

Learn Microsoft Fabric ◈

This Fabric workspace contains all the items to work through all the exercises of this book.

+ New ∨   ↑ Upload ∨   ⊞ Create app   ⚇ Manage access   ⚙ Workspace settings

	Name	Type ↑	Owner	Refreshed
⊞	wwi_bronze	Dataset (default)	Learn Microsoft Fabric	7/18/23, 5:14:35 PM
⊞	wwi_gold	Dataset (default)	Learn Microsoft Fabric	7/18/23, 5:14:21 PM
⊞	wwi_silver	Dataset (default)	Learn Microsoft Fabric	7/18/23, 5:14:08 PM
⌂	wwi_bronze	Lakehouse	Arshad Ali	—
⌂	wwi_gold	Lakehouse	Arshad Ali	—
⌂	wwi_silver	Lakehouse	Arshad Ali	—
▤	Data Transformation - Bronze to Silver	Notebook	Arshad Ali	—
▤	Data Transformation - Incremental Data Load	Notebook	Arshad Ali	—
▤	Data Transformation - Silver to Gold	Notebook	Arshad Ali	—

Figure 3.13 – Verifying imported notebooks

Creating a shortcut (for Files): Silver zone

In this section, you will create a shortcut to the Bronze zone from the Silver zone so that you can easily access the Bronze zone content from the Silver zone. Please note you can access it directly if all lakehouses are in the same workspace and by specifying the full path; however, a shortcut simplifies the experience, especially when you are accessing lakehouses across workspaces. Let's go through the steps:

1. Click on the **wwi_silver** lakehouse to open it from the items view of the workspace. Once the **wwi_silver** lakehouse is opened, right-click on **Files** in the tree view, and then click on **New shortcut** to create a shortcut to reference the **wwi_bronze** lakehouse from the **wwi_silver** lakehouse.

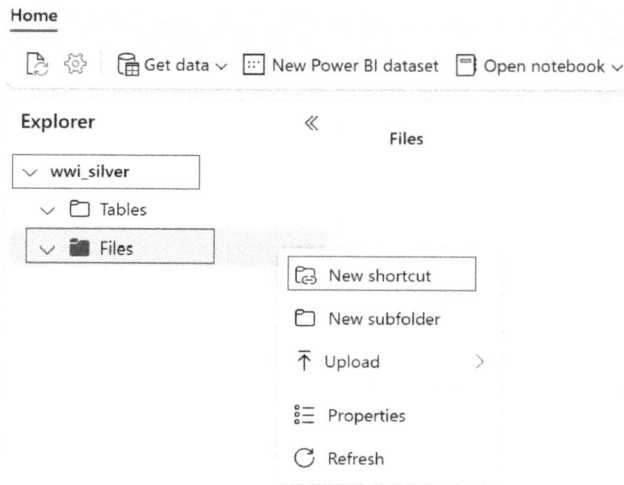

Figure 3.14 – Creating a shortcut under Files

2.   On the **New shortcut** wizard, select **Microsoft OneLake** under **Internal sources** and then select the **wwi_bronze** lakehouse. Finally, on the last screen of the wizard, select the **wwi** folder from the Bronze zone as a source for this shortcut and click on the **Create** button. After the shortcut is created, you should be able to browse all the contents of the Bronze zone while still being in the Silver zone.

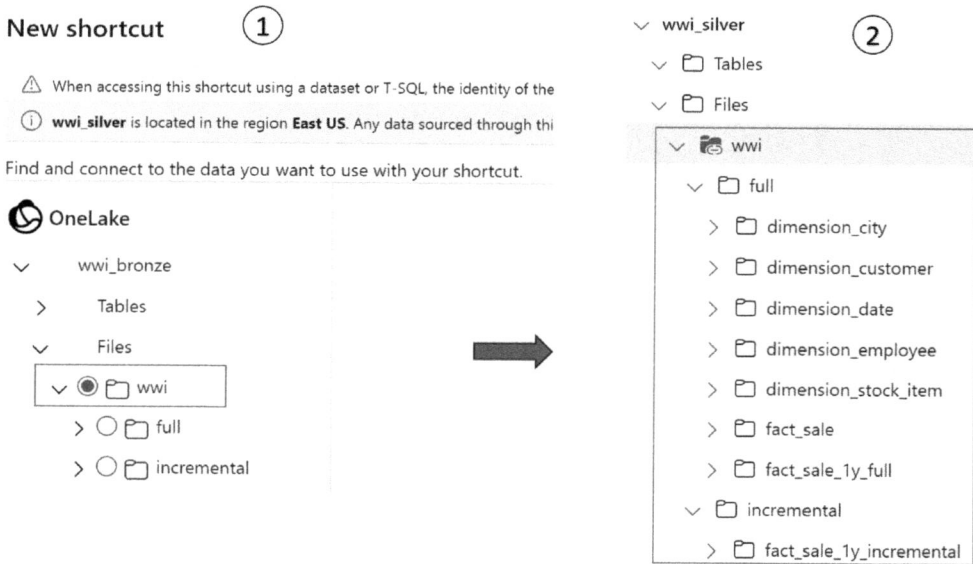

Figure 3.15 – Creating a shortcut under Files: specifying configuration

Opening notebook and executing commands (loading to the Silver zone)

1. Open the **wwi_silver** lakehouse if it is not already opened. Next, click on **Open notebook |
    Existing notebook** from the ribbon at the top. From the list of existing notebooks, select the
    Data Transformation – Bronze to Silver notebook and click on the **Open** button.

Home

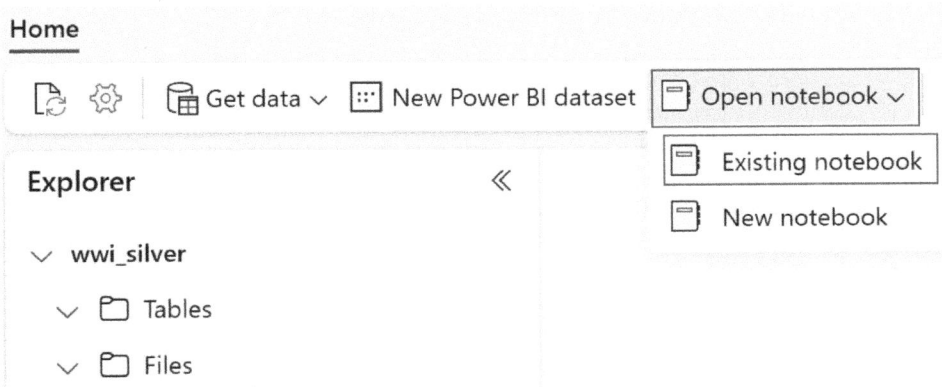

Figure 3.16 – Open an existing notebook

2. Once the notebook is opened, in the **Lakehouse explorer** view, you will notice the notebook
    is already linked to your opened lakehouse. If it doesn't link by itself, you can click on **Add
    lakehouse**, click on **Existing lakehouse**, and then select the **wwi_silver** lakehouse to make it
    a default lakehouse for the notebook. You can learn more about notebooks and their different
    capabilities here:

    *   https://learn.microsoft.com/en-us/fabric/data-engineering/
        how-to-use-notebook

    *   https://learn.microsoft.com/en-us/fabric/data-engineering/
        author-execute-notebook

3. Click on **Run All** under **Home** at the top to start the execution of the notebook and all its cells
    in sequence, or click the **Run** icon on the left of the cell or hit *Shift + Enter* while control is
    located in the cell to execute code from that specific cell. As is shown in the following, the first
    cell of the notebook loads data for the **City** dimension from the Bronze zone (which exists in
    the CSV format) using the shortcut you created to the Silver zone (in the Delta Lake format).
    This cell first defines a variable and assigns the name of the table for which the data is being
    loaded for. Next, it defines the schema of the data coming from the set of CSV files for this
    specific table. This explicit definition of the schema optimizes data load performance. Finally,
    it reads raw data from the CSV files from the Bronze zone and writes it as a Delta Lake table

(**dimension_city**). This is an example of applying simple transformation; however, based on your needs, you can make the transformation as complex as it needs to be:

```python
from pyspark.sql.types import *
table_name = 'dimension_city'
dimension_city_schema = StructType([
    StructField('CityKey', IntegerType(), True),
    StructField('WWICityID', IntegerType(), True),
    StructField('City', StringType(), True),
    StructField('StateProvince', StringType(), True),
    StructField('Country', StringType(), True),
    StructField('Continent', StringType(), True),
    StructField('SalesTerritory', StringType(), True),
    StructField('Region', StringType(), True),
    StructField('Subregion', StringType(), True),
    StructField('Location', StringType(), True),
    StructField('LatestRecordedPopulation', LongType(), True),
    StructField('ValidFrom', TimestampType(), True),
    StructField('ValidTo', TimestampType(), True),
    StructField('LineageKey', IntegerType(), True)])

df = spark.read.format("csv").schema(dimension_city_schema).
option("header","true").load('Files/wwi/full/' + table_name)
df.write.mode("overwrite").format("delta").save("Tables/" +
table_name)
```

> **Important note**
>
> The first thing you would have noticed when executing this cell is that you didn't have to specify the underlying Spark pool or Spark cluster details because Fabric provides these through the concepts of **Live Pool**; that is, every Fabric workspace comes pre-wired with a default Spark pool, called **Starter Pool**. This means that when you create notebooks, you don't have to worry about specifying any Spark configurations or cluster details (or something like that), and when you execute your first command in the notebooks, the Live Pool kicks in and is up in a few seconds after establishing your Spark session and starts executing the code in the cell. Subsequent code execution is almost instantaneous in this notebook as long as the Spark session is active. You can read more about it at https://learn.microsoft.com/en-us/fabric/data-engineering/spark-compute.

4. This notebook (**Data Transformation – Bronze to Silver**) contains further code for transforming and loading data for the rest of the dimensions (Customer, Date, Employee, and Stock Item). Since the process to load other dimensions remains the same as loading data for the **City** dimension, in *step 3*, and for the sake of simplicity, we have not included this code here. However, we suggest you run them to have all these dimensions ready in the Silver zone.

> **Important note**
>
> **V-Order optimization:** All the compute engines in Fabric transparently leverage Microsoft's unique VertiParquet technology when writing data into a Delta Lake table. VertiParquet transparently optimizes the Delta Lake files in a way that is highly optimized by Fabric compute engines, often resulting in a 3–4-fold improvement in compression and up to a 10-fold improvement in performance acceleration (in comparison to Delta Lake files not optimized using VertiParquet) while still maintaining full open source Delta Lake format compliance. You can refer to `https://learn.microsoft.com/en-us/fabric/data-engineering/delta-optimization-and-v-order` to learn more.

5. For the fact table (**Sale**), you will apply the same transformation of definition for the appropriate data types for each of the columns:

```
From pyspark.sql.types import *
from pyspark.sql.functions import col, year, month, quarter
table_name = 'fact_sale'
fact_sale_schema = StructType([
    StructField('SaleKey', LongType(), True),
    StructField('CityKey', IntegerType(), True),
    StructField('CustomerKey', IntegerType(), True),
    StructField('BillToCustomerKey', IntegerType(), True),
    StructField('StockItemKey', IntegerType(), True),
    StructField('InvoiceDateKey', TimestampType(), True),
    StructField('DeliveryDateKey', TimestampType(), True),
    StructField('SalespersonKey', IntegerType(), True),
    StructField('WWIInvoiceID', IntegerType(), True),
    StructField('Description', StringType(), True),
    StructField('Package', StringType(), True),
    StructField('Quantity', IntegerType(), True),
    StructField('UnitPrice', DecimalType(18,2), True),
    StructField('TaxRate', DecimalType(18,3), True),
    StructField('TotalExcludingTax', DecimalType(29,2), True),
    StructField('TaxAmount', DecimalType(38,6), True),
    StructField('Profit', DecimalType(18,2), True),
    StructField('TotalIncludingTax', DecimalType(38,6), True),
    StructField('TotalDryItems', IntegerType(), True),
    StructField('TotalChillerItems', IntegerType(), True),
    StructField('LineageKey', IntegerType(), True)])
```

In addition to defining the structure, you will also add computed columns (`Year`, `Quarter`, and `Month`) for the different date sections. Finally, you will use `partitionBy` Spark API to partition the data before writing them as a Delta table based on the newly created data part columns (Year and Quarter). Since the fact table contains data for over 50 million rows, this process might take a couple of minutes to complete:

```
df = spark.read.format("csv").schema(fact_sale_schema).
option("header","true").load('Files/wwi/full/' + table_name)
df = df.withColumn('Year', year(col("InvoiceDateKey")))
df = df.withColumn('Quarter', quarter(col("InvoiceDateKey")))
df = df.withColumn('Month', month(col("InvoiceDateKey")))
df.write.mode("overwrite").format("delta").
partitionBy("Year","Quarter").save("Tables/" + table_name)
```

6. Once you have executed all the cells or commands in the notebook, you can verify all the created tables under the **Tables** section of the lakehouse; if these are not visible, right-click on the section and hit **Refresh**. Now, you can reference and use these tables based on your needs; here is an example of using SparkSQL commands to aggregate data from the fact table:

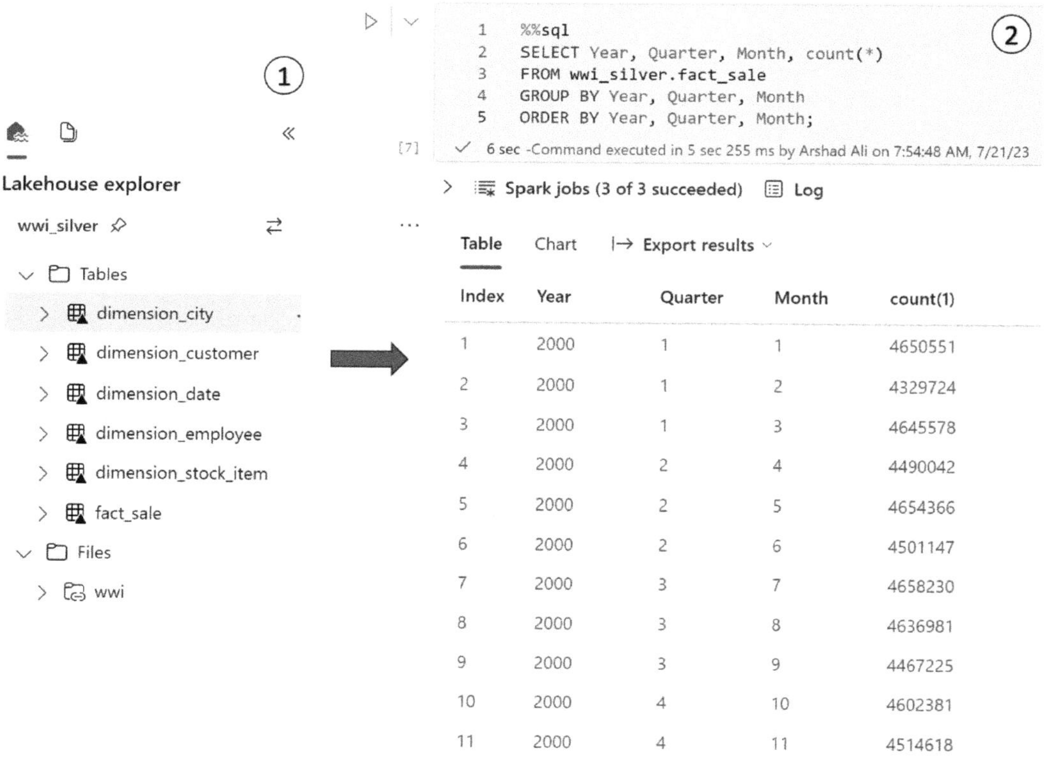

Figure 3.17 – Validating created tables and their data

Incremental data load

While one-time historical data migration is the first step, you need to build a process to incrementally integrate data from various sources on a regular basis based on business needs and a defined frequency. Please note that in *Figure 3.17* in the previous section, the **Sale** fact table has historical data for 11 months already loaded in the table. Now, let's look at how you can incrementally load data into this table as the new data arrives:

1. To demonstrate the process and capabilities for subsequent incremental data loading, you will use the fact table (**Sale**), which, at the source in the Bronze zone, has one parent folder with all the historical data for 11 months and another folder for just incremental data for 3 months. As part of the last step in the previous section, you have already ingested data for 11 months. Now, you need to load incremental data into this table. The incremental data in the source folder (which you are going to use here) have updated data for Oct and Nov and new data for Dec, so the Oct and Nov data should be updated, and the new data for Dec should be written afresh into the lakehouse sale fact table, as depicted here:

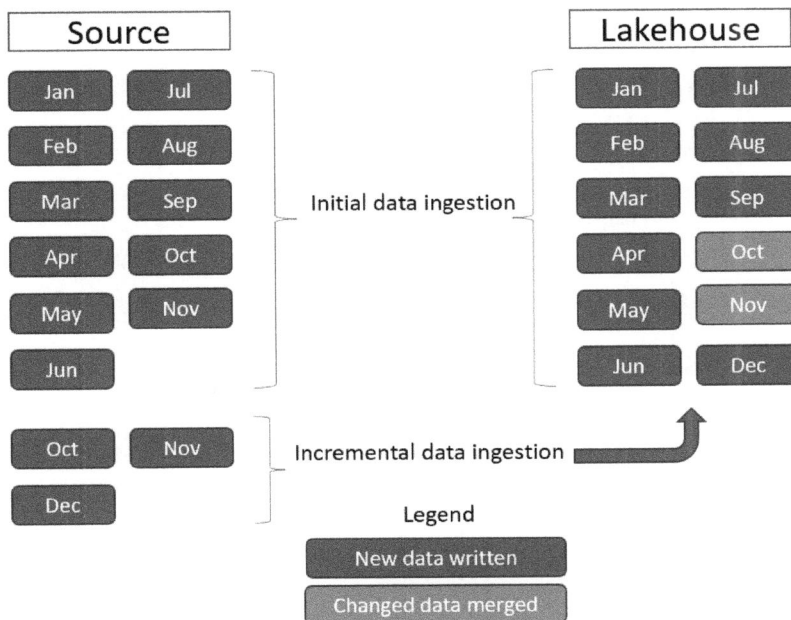

Figure 3.18 – Data load patterns (historical versus incremental)

2. Open the **wwi_silver** lakehouse if it is not already opened. Next, click on **Open notebook | Existing notebook** on the ribbon at the top. From the list of existing notebooks, select the **Data Transformation – Incremental Data Load** notebook and click on the **Open** button. Once the notebook is open, in the **Lakehouse explorer** you will notice the notebook is already linked

to your opened lakehouse. If it doesn't link by itself, you can click on **Add lakehouse**, click on **Existing lakehouse**, and then select the **wwi_silver** lakehouse to make it a default lakehouse for the notebook.

3. Now, you need to read the incremental data from the source—in this case, from the Bronze zone, as we have already ingested this data here. The following code block reads this incremental raw data from the CSV files coming from the Bronze zone, adds additional computed columns to it, and creates a temporary Spark view to reference it later during merging.

```
From pyspark.sql.functions import col, year, month, quarter
df = spark.read.format("csv").option("header","true").
load('Files/wwi/incremental/fact_sale_1y_incremental')
df = df.withColumn('Year', year(col("InvoiceDateKey")))
df = df.withColumn('Quarter', quarter(col("InvoiceDateKey")))
df = df.withColumn('Month', month(col("InvoiceDateKey")))
df = df.createOrReplaceTempView("fact_sale_incremental")
```

4. Here is a look at the incremental data, and, as mentioned earlier, it has changed or modified data for Oct and Nov (which need to be updated into the target) and new data for Dec (which need to be inserted into the target).

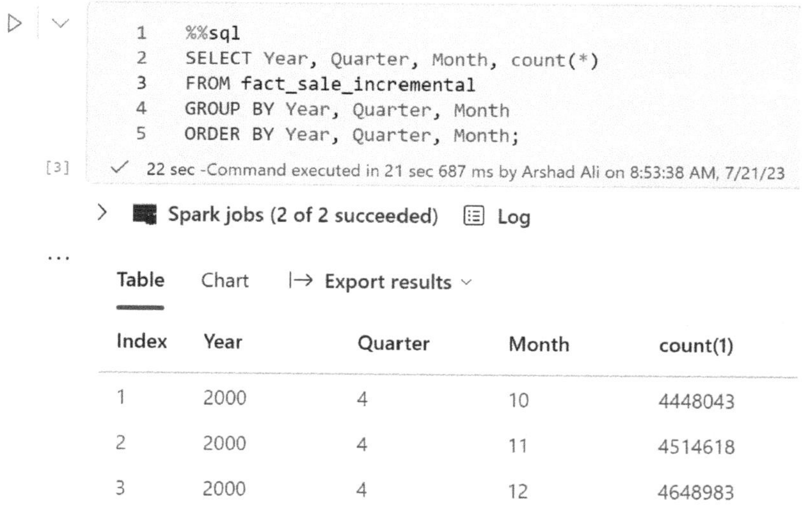

```
1  %%sql
2  SELECT Year, Quarter, Month, count(*)
3  FROM fact_sale_incremental
4  GROUP BY Year, Quarter, Month
5  ORDER BY Year, Quarter, Month;
```

[3]   ✓ 22 sec -Command executed in 21 sec 687 ms by Arshad Ali on 8:53:38 AM, 7/21/23

> 🟦 Spark jobs (2 of 2 succeeded)   ▤ Log

...

Table   Chart |→ Export results ∨

Index	Year	Quarter	Month	count(1)
1	2000	4	10	4448043
2	2000	4	11	4514618
3	2000	4	12	4648983

Figure 3.19 – Validating incremental data

5. Delta Lake in Spark allows merge statements (https://docs.delta.io/latest/delta-update.html#-delta-merge) to merge incremental data into a Delta table as and when it arrives from the source. As part of the process, existing rows are updated with new information if they match the joining conditions; if not, these new incoming rows are

inserted as new rows in the target table. This makes incremental data merging in the big data world so much easier. The following cell updates data into a target Delta Lake table. With the ON clause, you specify the key columns to match records from both sides and include columns from the target table to filter out only the partitions necessary for this merge. This improves the performance of your merge statements by pruning all the other partitions that are not necessary for this merge statement. Depending on the data volume and compute capacity available, the execution time varies and might take a couple of minutes; at the end of the execution, it will show stats about the operation, such as the number of rows affected, the rows updated, the rows deleted, and the rows inserted. At this time, if you execute the command from *step 6* of the previous section again, you should now see data that cover 12 months:

```sql
%%sql
MERGE INTO wwi_silver.fact_sale target
USING fact_sale_incremental source
ON
   source.SaleKey = target.SaleKey AND source.InvoiceDateKey =
target.InvoiceDateKey - Unique key for update identification
   AND target.Year IN (2000) AND target.Quarter IN (4) -
Partition Pruning for optimized performance
WHEN MATCHED THEN
  UPDATE SET
    target.CityKey = source.CityKey
      , target.CustomerKey = source.CustomerKey
      , target.BillToCustomerKey = source.BillToCustomerKey
      , target.StockItemKey = source.StockItemKey
      , target.DeliveryDateKey = source.DeliveryDateKey
      , target.SalespersonKey = source.SalespersonKey
      , target.WWIInvoiceID = source.WWIInvoiceID
      , target.Description = source.Description
      , target.Package = source.Package
      , target.Quantity = source.Quantity
      , target.UnitPrice = source.UnitPrice
      , target.TaxRate = source.TaxRate
      , target.TotalExcludingTax = source.TotalExcludingTax
      , target.TaxAmount = source.TaxAmount
      , target.Profit = source.Profit
      , target.TotalIncludingTax = source.TotalIncludingTax
      , target.TotalDryItems = source.TotalDryItems
      , target.TotalChillerItems = source.TotalChillerItems
      , target.LineageKey = source.LineageKey
  WHEN NOT MATCHED
    THEN INSERT (
      target.SaleKey, target.CityKey, target.CustomerKey, target.
BillToCustomerKey, target.StockItemKey, target.InvoiceDateKey,
```

```
        target.DeliveryDateKey, target.SalespersonKey, target.
WWIInvoiceID, target.Description, target.Package,
        target.Quantity, target.UnitPrice, target.TaxRate, target.
TotalExcludingTax, target.TaxAmount, target.Profit,
        target.TotalIncludingTax, target.TotalDryItems, target.
TotalChillerItems, target.LineageKey,
        target.Year, target.Quarter, target.Month)
 VALUES (
    source.SaleKey, source.CityKey, source.CustomerKey, source.
BillToCustomerKey, source.StockItemKey, source.InvoiceDateKey,
    source.DeliveryDateKey, source.SalespersonKey, source.
WWIInvoiceID, source.Description, source.Package,
    source.Quantity, source.UnitPrice, source.TaxRate, source.
TotalExcludingTax, source.TaxAmount, source.Profit,
    source.TotalIncludingTax, source.TotalDryItems, source.
TotalChillerItems, source.LineageKey,
    source.Year, source.Quarter, source.Month)
```

6. Delta Lake maintains the history of the changes; as you can see in the following screen, it shows that it wrote data for the first time into this Delta Lake table (version=0) and then merged incremental data into it (version=1). With this history of changes, you can time travel back and forth as per your needs and requirements.

```
1  %%sql
2  DESCRIBE HISTORY wwi_silver.fact_sale
```
✓ 6 sec -Command executed in 5 sec 260 ms by Arshad Ali on 9:10:26 AM, 7/21/23

> 🟥 Spark jobs (1 of 1 succeeded)   ▤ Log

Table   Chart   ⟼ Export results ⌄

Index	version	timestamp	userId	userNa...	operati...	operationParameters
1	1	2023-07-21T16:04:2...	NULL	NULL	MERGE	▶ "{"predicate":"(((CAST(sourc
2	0	2023-07-21T14:44:3...	NULL	NULL	WRITE	▶ "{"mode":"Overwrite","partit

Figure 3.20 – Analyzing the change history of a Delta table

Creating a shortcut (for Tables): Gold zone

The steps to create a shortcut are as follows:

1. Click on the **wwi_gold** lakehouse to open it from the items view of the workspace. Once the **wwi_gold** lakehouse is opened, right-click on **Tables** in the tree view and then click on **New shortcut** to create a shortcut to the reference tables that we created in the previous section within **wwi_silver** from the **wwi_gold** lakehouse.

2. On the **New shortcut** wizard, select **Microsoft OneLake** under **Internal sources** and then select the **wwi_silver** lakehouse. Finally, on the last screen of the wizard, select the **dimension_city** table from the Silver zone as the source for this shortcut and click on the **Create** button.

3. Repeat *steps 1 and 2* for the rest of the dimensions (Customer, Date, Employee, and Stock Item) and fact table (Sale).

4. After the shortcut is created, you should be able to reference all the tables from the Silver zone while still being in the Gold zone, as shown in the following figure. Please note that there is a tiny **link** icon along with the **Delta** icon within the table icon, which indicates that it's a referenced table, created with the shortcut feature.

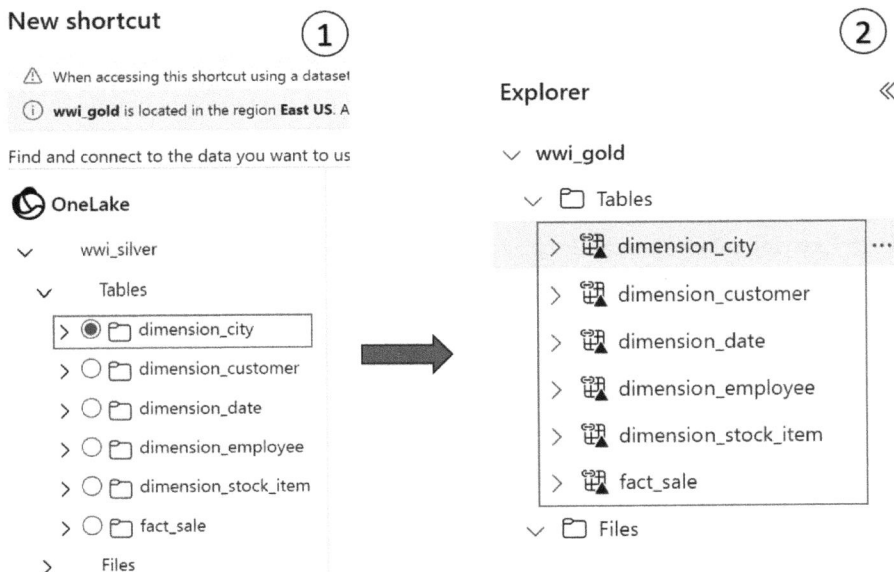

Figure 3.21 – Creating a shortcut under Tables

Now that you have transformed the tables created in the Silver zone, it's time to create business aggregates in the Gold zone.

Creating business aggregates for the Gold zone

An organization might have a group of data engineers working with Scala/Python, whereas there might be other groups of data engineers who prefer to work with SQL (Spark SQL or T-SQL), but all of them intend to work with the same copy of the data. Fabric makes it possible for these different groups, with varied experience levels and preferences, to work and collaborate.

In this section, you are going to create business aggregates for the Gold zone based on the transformed tables from the Silver zone. You are going to learn two different approaches to transform and generate business aggregates, and, as a developer, you can pick the one suitable for you or mix and match these approaches based on your preference without compromising performance:

- **Approach #1**: Use **PySpark** to join and aggregate data for generating business aggregates. This approach would be preferable for someone with a programming (Python or PySpark) background.

- **Approach #2**: Use Spark SQL to join and aggregate data for generating business aggregates. This approach would be preferable for someone with an SQL background who is transitioning to Spark.

Let's get started and try both of these approaches. Before we start, we need to perform the following initial steps:

1. Open the **wwi_gold** lakehouse if it is not already opened. Next, click on **Open notebook | Existing notebook** on the ribbon at the top. From the list of existing notebooks, select the **Data Transformation – Silver to Gold** notebook and click on the **Open** button.

2. Once the notebook is opened, in the **Lakehouse explorer** you will notice the notebook is already linked to your opened lakehouse. If it doesn't link by itself, you can click on **Add lakehouse**, click on **Existing lakehouse**, and then select the **wwi_gold** lakehouse to make it a default lakehouse for the notebook.

3. Click on **Run All** under **Home** at the top to start the execution of the notebook and all its cells in sequence, or click on the **run** icon on the left of the cell or hit *Shift + Enter* while control is located in the cell to execute code from that specific cell.

Approach #1 – using PySpark

In this approach, we will learn how you can use PySpark to join and aggregate data for generating business aggregates. In the following code, we create three different Spark dataframes, each referencing an existing Delta table. Then, we will join these tables using the dataframes, perform group by to generate aggregation, rename a few of the columns, and finally write the dataframe as a Delta table in the **Tables** section of the lakehouse to persist with the aggregated data:

```
Df_fact_sale = spark.read.table("wwi_gold.fact_sale")
df_dimension_date = spark.read.table("wwi_gold.dimension_date")
df_dimension_city = spark.read.table("wwi_gold.dimension_city")
```

```
sale_by_date_city = df_fact_sale.alias("sale") \
.join(df_dimension_date.alias("date"), df_fact_sale.InvoiceDateKey ==
df_dimension_date.Date, "inner") \
.join(df_dimension_city.alias("city"), df_fact_sale.CityKey == df_
dimension_city.CityKey, "inner") \
.select("date.Date", "date.CalendarMonthLabel", "date.Day", "date.
ShortMonth", "date.CalendarYear", "city.City", "city.StateProvince",
"city.SalesTerritory", "sale.TotalExcludingTax", "sale.TaxAmount",
"sale.TotalIncludingTax", "sale.Profit")\
.groupBy("date.Date", "date.CalendarMonthLabel", "date.Day", "date.
ShortMonth", "date.CalendarYear", "city.City", "city.StateProvince",
"city.SalesTerritory")\
.sum("sale.TotalExcludingTax", "sale.TaxAmount", "sale.
TotalIncludingTax", "sale.Profit")\
.withColumnRenamed("sum(TotalExcludingTax)",
"SumOfTotalExcludingTax")\
.withColumnRenamed("sum(TaxAmount)", "SumOfTaxAmount")\
.withColumnRenamed("sum(TotalIncludingTax)",
"SumOfTotalIncludingTax")\
.withColumnRenamed("sum(Profit)", "SumOfProfit")\
.orderBy("date.Date", "city.StateProvince", "city.City")
sale_by_date_city.write.mode("overwrite").format("delta").
option("overwriteSchema", "true").save("Tables/aggregate_sale_by_date_
city")
```

Approach #2 – using Spark SQL

In this approach, we will learn how we can use Spark SQL to join and aggregate data for generating business aggregates. In the following code, we will create a temporary Spark view by joining three tables, perform group by to generate aggregates, and rename a few of the columns:

```
%%sql
CREATE OR REPLACE TEMPORARY VIEW sale_by_date_employee
AS
SELECT
  DD.Date, DD.CalendarMonthLabel
      ,DD.Day, DD.ShortMonth Month, CalendarYear Year
  ,DE.PreferredName, DE.Employee
  ,SUM(FS.TotalExcludingTax) SumOfTotalExcludingTax
  ,SUM(FS.TaxAmount) SumOfTaxAmount
  ,SUM(FS.TotalIncludingTax) SumOfTotalIncludingTax
  ,SUM(Profit) SumOfProfit
FROM wwi_gold.fact_sale FS
INNER JOIN wwi_gold.dimension_date DD ON FS.InvoiceDateKey = DD.Date
INNER JOIN wwi_gold.dimension_Employee DE ON FS.SalespersonKey =
DE.EmployeeKey
GROUP BY DD.Date, DD.CalendarMonthLabel, DD.Day, DD.ShortMonth,
```

```
DD.CalendarYear, DE.PreferredName, DE.Employee
ORDER BY DD.Date ASC, DE.PreferredName ASC, DE.Employee ASC
```

Finally, we will read from the temporary Spark view and write it as a Delta table in the **Tables** section of the lakehouse to persist with the data:

```
Sale_by_date_employee = spark.sql("SELECT * FROM sale_by_date_
employee")
sale_by_date_employee.write.mode("overwrite").format("delta").
option("overwriteSchema", "true").save("Tables/aggregate_sale_by_date_
employee")
```

You can validate the created tables by right-clicking on **Tables** and selecting **refresh** on the **wwi_gold** lakehouse; you will notice that these aggregate tables then appear.

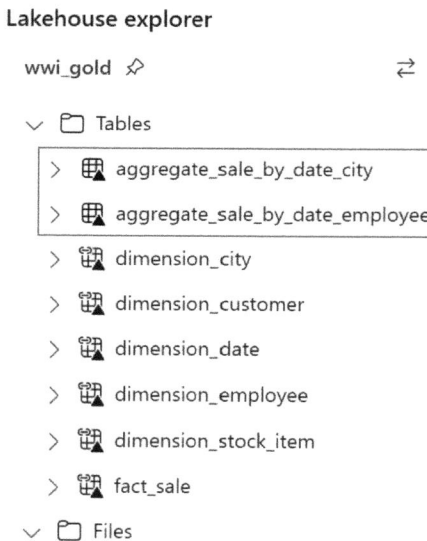

Lakehouse explorer

wwi_gold

> ∨ 🗂 Tables
>   > ⊞ aggregate_sale_by_date_city
>   > ⊞ aggregate_sale_by_date_employee
>   > 🗄 dimension_city
>   > 🗄 dimension_customer
>   > 🗄 dimension_date
>   > 🗄 dimension_employee
>   > 🗄 dimension_stock_item
>   > 🗄 fact_sale
> ∨ 🗂 Files

Figure 3.22 – Validate tables using business aggregates

Please note that both approaches produce a similar outcome. However, based on the developer's background and preference, one approach can be picked up over the other without any need for the developer to learn a new technology; thus, this does not compromise performance.

Furthermore, you might have noticed that you are writing data as Delta Lake files, and then the automatic table discovery and registration feature of Fabric picks this up and registers it in the metastore; this means that you don't need to explicitly call the CREATE TABLE statement to create tables to use this with SparkSQL.

After transforming and preparing our data, it's time to query and analyze them.

Analyze

Now that we have data integrated into the lakehouse and have prepared them for reporting, we'll analyze these data to get insights. We will look at two methods: first, we will use Power BI to create visualizations (reports and dashboards), and then we will use SQL endpoint to connect the lakehouse for running analytical queries.

Power BI

Power BI is natively integrated within the whole Fabric experience; this native integration brings a unique mode of accessing the data (called **Direct Lake**, which we discussed in earlier chapters) from the lakehouse to provide the most performant query and reporting experience. Let's create a report based on the data from the Gold zone:

1. Open the **wwi_gold** lakehouse and click on **SQL endpoint** under mode selection on the top right of the screen to switch to SQL endpoint mode for the selected lakehouse.

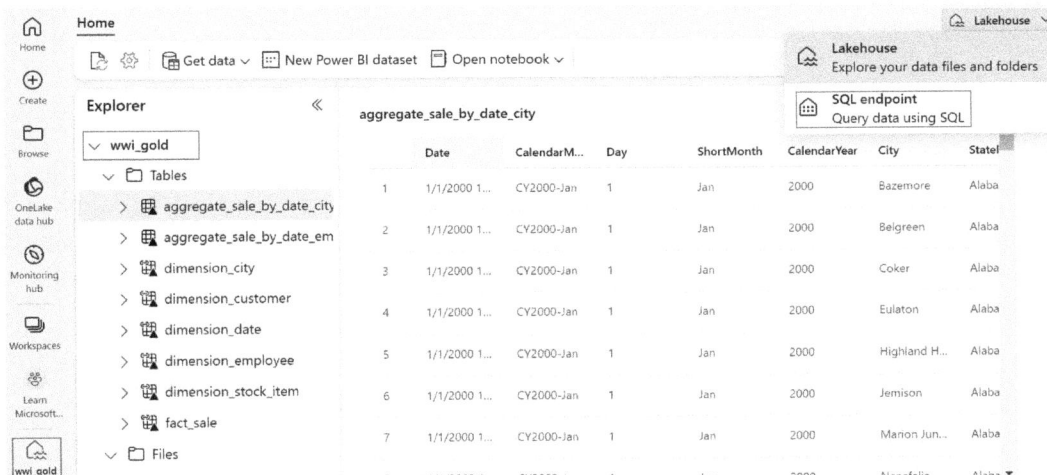

Figure 3.23 – Switching to SQL endpoint mode

2. Once you are in SQL endpoint mode, you should be able to see all the tables you created. If you don't see them yet, please click on the **Refresh** icon at the top under the **Home** menu or click on the ellipsis (…) next to the folder and then on **Refresh**. Next, click on the **Model** tab at the bottom to open the default Power BI dataset.

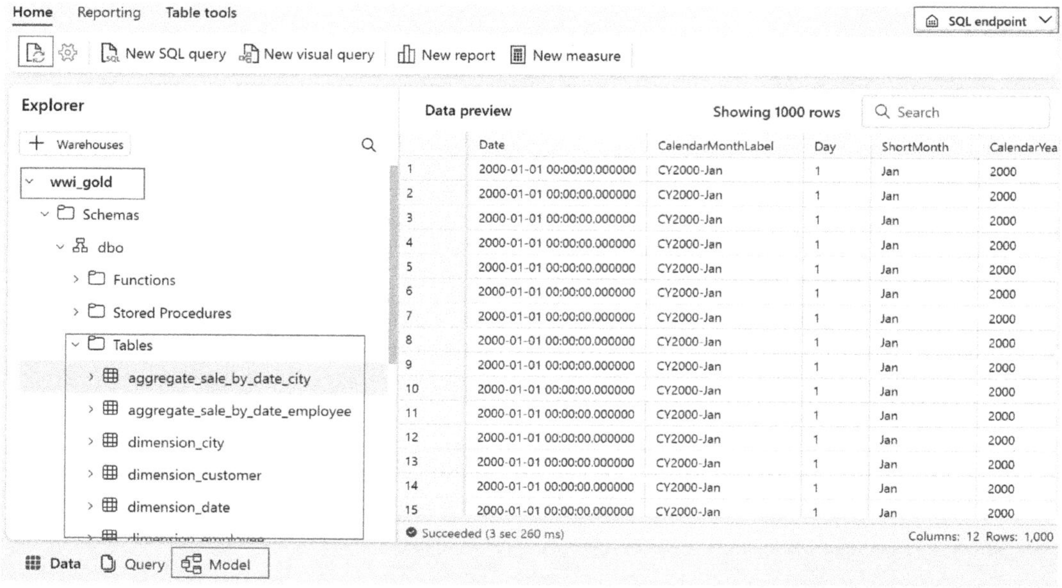

Figure 3.24 – SQL view of the lakehouse tables

3.   For this data model, you need to define the relationship between the different tables so that you can create reports and visualizations based on data coming from different tables. From the **fact_sale** table, drag the **CityKey** field and drop it on the **CityKey** field in the **dimension_city** table to create a relationship. On the **Create Relationship** settings, you will notice the following configurations:

   I.   Table 1 is populated with **fact_sale** and the **CityKey** column.

   II.   Table 2 is populated with **dimension_city** and the **CityKey** column

   III. Cardinality: **Many to one (*:1).**

   IV.   Cross-filter direction: **Single.**

   V.   Leave the box next to **Make this relationship active** checked.

   VI.   Check the box next to **Assume referential integrity**

   VII. Select **Confirm.**

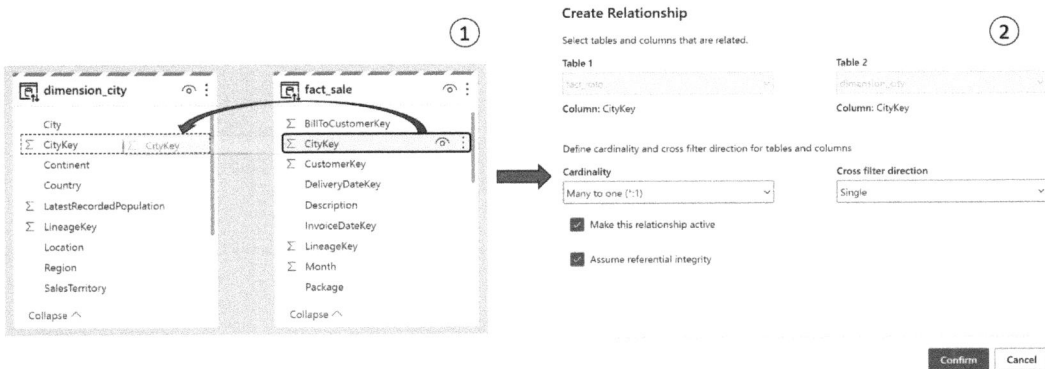

Figure 3.25 – Building a relationship between tables in the data model

> **Important note**
>
> When defining relationships, please make sure you have a many-to-one relationship regarding the fact-to-dimension relationship and not vice versa.

4. Similarly, you need to add these relationships as well:

    - `StockItemKey(fact_sale):StockItemKey(dimension_stock_item)`
    - `Salespersonkey(fact_sale):EmployeeKey(dimension_employee)`
    - `CustomerKey(fact_sale):CustomerKey(dimension_customer)`
    - `InvoiceDateKey(fact_sale):Date(dimension_date)`

5. After adding these relationships, your data model is ready for reporting, as shown in *Figure 3.26*. Click on **New report** to start creating reports/dashboards in Power BI.

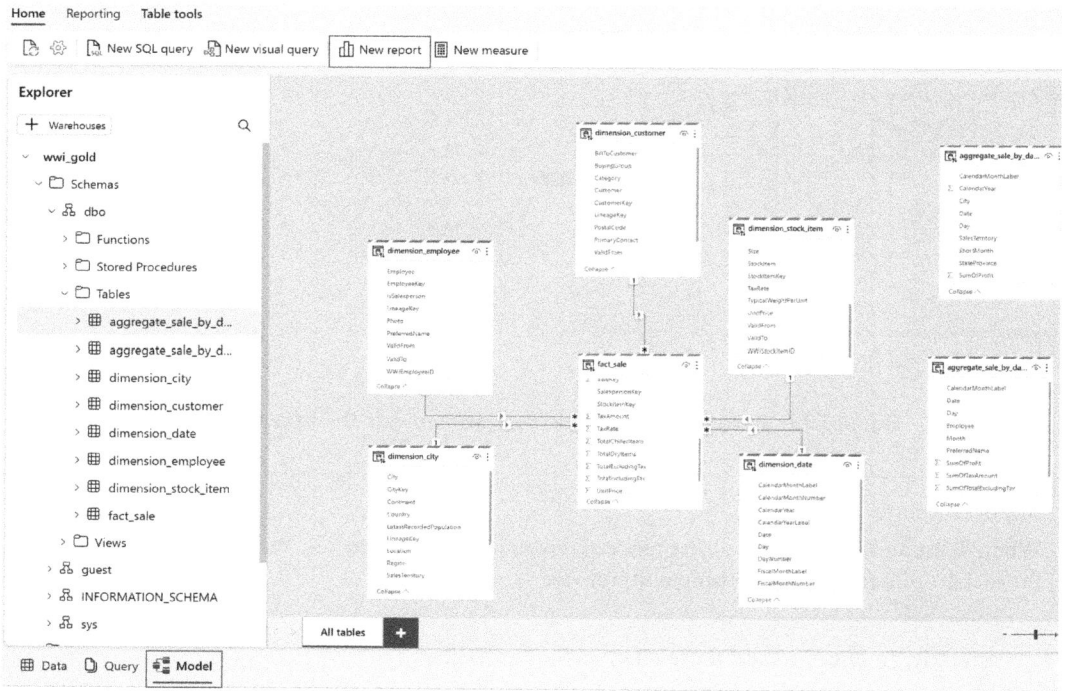

Figure 3.26 – Data model with established relationship (Star schema)

6. Once you land on the Power BI report canvas, you can create reports and dashboards to meet your business requirements by dragging the required columns from the **Data** pane to the canvas and using one or more of the available visualizations.

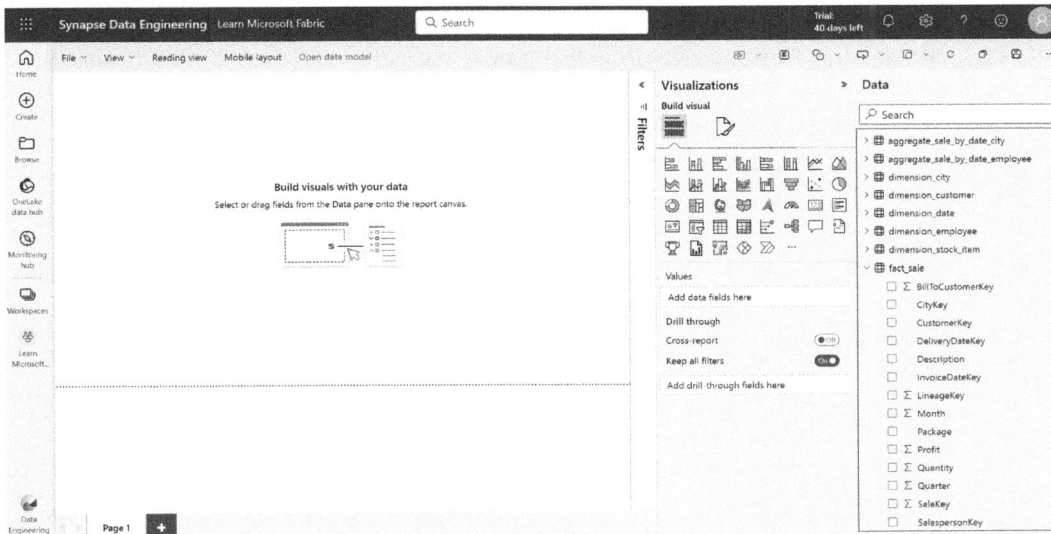

Figure 3.27 – Power BI report canvas

7. You can also add a title for your report. On the right side of the menu bar, as shown in *Figure 3.28*, click on the text box icon (available on the top right of the screen) and drag it to the top left; type in `Wide World Importers - Profit Analysis` as text and then select the typed text and increase the font size to **24**.

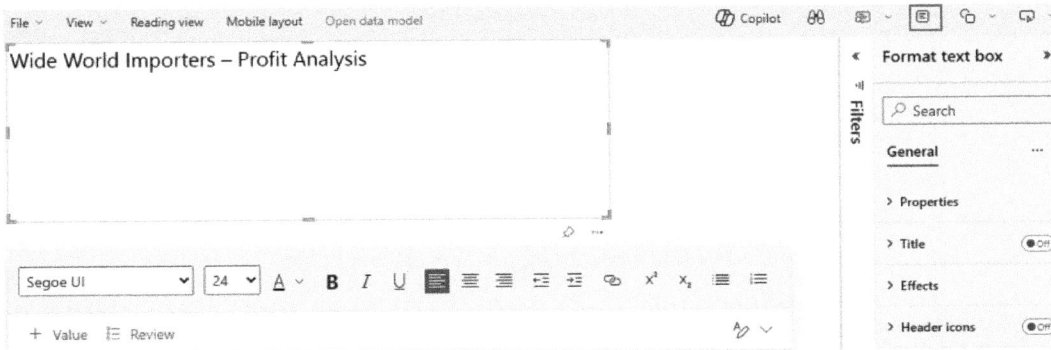

Figure 3.28 – Add a title for your report

8. Next, we will add a row count for the fact table in the report. From the **Data** pane, expand **fact_sale** and drag **CustomerKey** from **fact_sale** to the canvas and drop it. Next, change the visualization type to **Card**. Under **Fields**, you can rename this measure for this report and make sure the aggregation method is selected as **Count**.

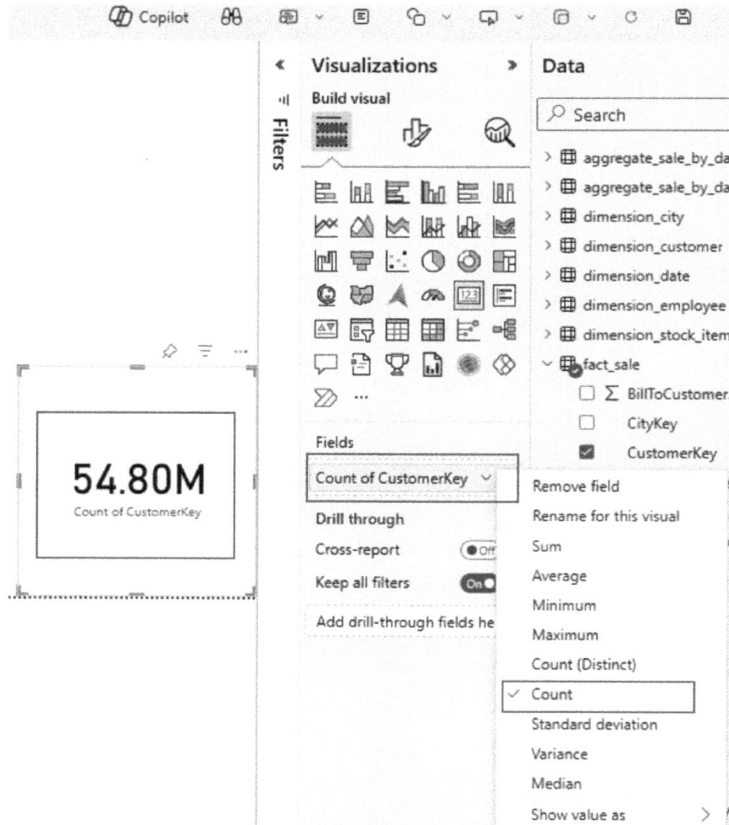

Figure 3.29 – Add a visualization to show record Count

9. To add a bar chart, click anywhere on the blank canvas (or press the *Esc* key) so none of the visuals are selected. From the **Data** pane, expand **fact_sale**, and drag and drop **Profit** measure to the canvas from **fact_sale** to create a column chart. Next, expand **dimension_city**, drag the **SalesTerritory** column from **dimension_city**, and drop it into the same selected visualization. You can also take advantage of the **Search** bar at the top of the **Data** pane, as shown in *Figure 3.29*, to search for a specific field or column that you want to include in your report. With the chart selected, you can click on any of the available visualizations for this chart to change it. In my case, I changed it to a **Pie** chart. However, you can use any other out-of-the-box visualizations that give you better insights.

Wide World Importers – Profit Analysis

Sum of Profit by SalesTerritory

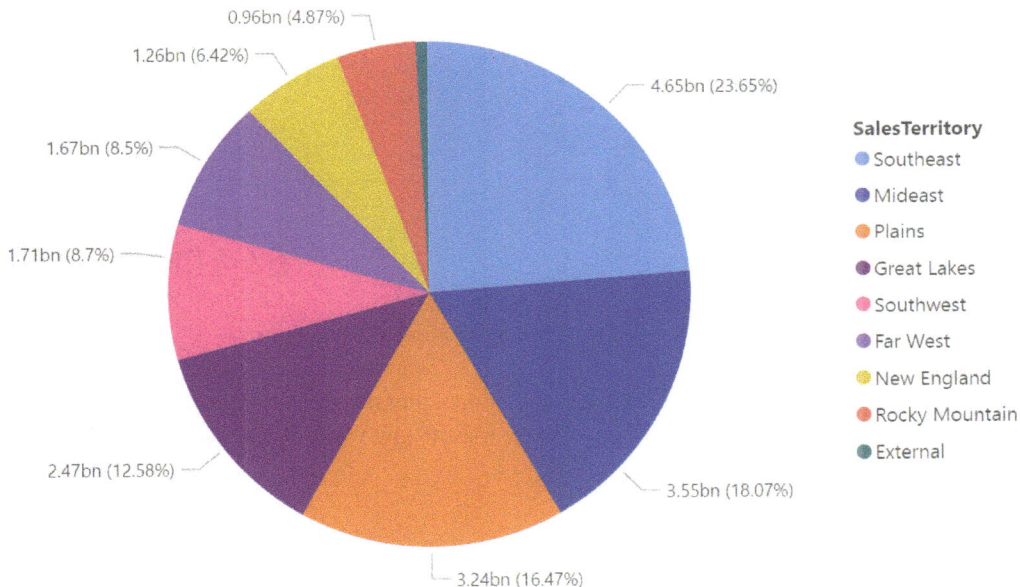

SalesTerritory
- ● Southeast
- ● Mideast
- ● Plains
- ● Great Lakes
- ● Southwest
- ● Far West
- ● New England
- ● Rocky Mountain
- ● External

0.96bn (4.87%)
1.26bn (6.42%)
1.67bn (8.5%)
1.71bn (8.7%)
2.47bn (12.58%)
3.24bn (16.47%)
3.55bn (18.07%)
4.65bn (23.65%)

54.80M

Row Count - Fact Sale

Figure 3.30 – A sample report created with pie chart visualization

10. Now, we will add a stacked area chart to your report. Click anywhere on the blank canvas (or press the *Esc* key) so none of the visuals are selected. From the **Data** pane, expand **fact_sale** and check the box next to **Profit**. Expand **dimension_date** and check the box next to **FiscalMonthNumber**. This will create a line chart showing profit by fiscal month. Now, expand **dimension_stock_item** and check **BuyingPackage** to add it to the chart. This will add this field to the **Legend** field and will add a line for each of the buying packages. Now, while you have selected the chart, click on **Stacked area chart** from the visualization to change it, as shown in the following screenshot:

Wide World Importers – Profit Analysis

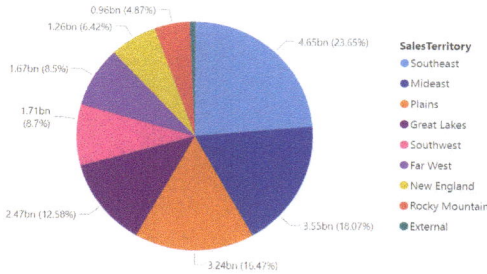

Figure 3.31 – A sample report with multiple visualizations

11. To save this report, select **File | Save** from the ribbon. Enter the name of your report as Profit Analysis Report (or whatever name you want to give) and click on **Save**.

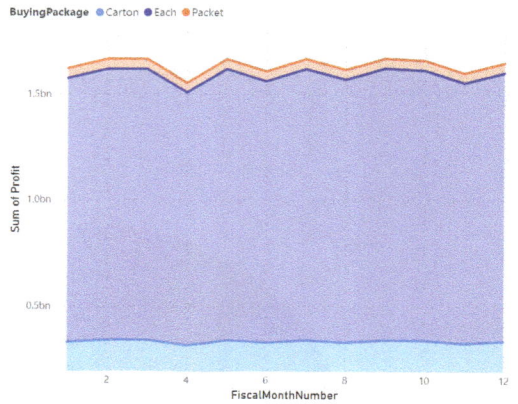

Figure 3.32 – Saving your report

> **Important note**
>
> This is the simplest example of quickly creating a report with different visualizations based on data from the lakehouse and leveraging the new Direct Lake feature. So far, you have barely scratched the surface in terms of creating powerful reports and dashboards in Power BI. As an industry-leading business intelligence tool for reporting and visualization, Power BI provides tons of different capabilities to build powerful reports and dashboards. You can learn more about it in the book *Learn Power BI - Second Edition* (`https://www.packtpub.com/product/learn-power-bi-second-edition/9781801811958`).

SQL endpoint

Each lakehouse comes with a built-in SQL endpoint for easily connecting and querying data in the lakehouse tables. When a lakehouse is created, a secondary item called a SQL endpoint will be automatically generated at the same time with the same name of the lakehouse. This lets consumers of the data use their own client tools, such as **SQL Server Management Studio (SSMS)**, Azure Data Studio, or other third-party reporting tools, to work with the data. Please note that for the lakehouse tables, the data accessed through this SQL endpoint are read-only for reporting and analysis purposes. The steps to connect to this SQL endpoint from Azure Data Studio are as follows:

1. Select and open the workspace you created earlier from the **Workspaces** flyout on the left-hand side.

2. From the workspace items view, locate the item called **wwi_gold** with the **SQL endpoint** type. Click on the ellipses (**…**) next to the item name, select **Copy SQL connection string**, and then click on the **Copy** button to copy it to the clipboard.

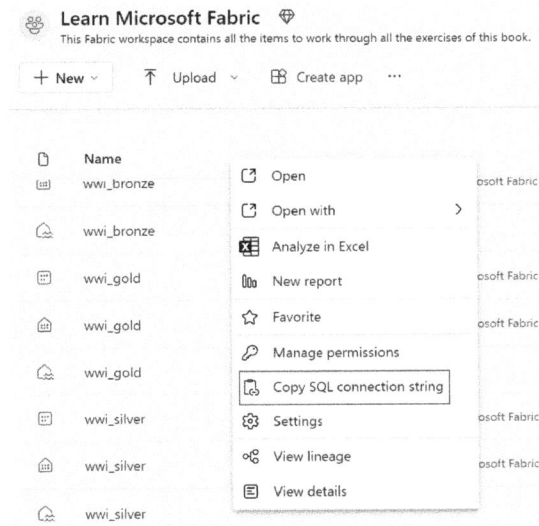

Figure 3.33 – Getting an SQL connection string for your lakehouse

3.   Launch **Azure Data Studio**. If you don't have it installed already, you can install it from here: `https://learn.microsoft.com/en-us/sql/azure-data-studio/download-azure-data-studio`.

4.   Under the **Connection** tab on the left of Azure Data Studio, click on the **New Connection** button or icon and, then, on the **Connection Details** page; paste the **SQL endpoint** connection string from *step 2* into the **Server** textbox. Then, select Azure **Active Directory – Universal with MFA support** as the **Authentication** type, and select your Azure Active Directory username in the **Account** selection box (if your account information is not available yet, you will need to click on **Add an account** to add it), and click on **Connect**.

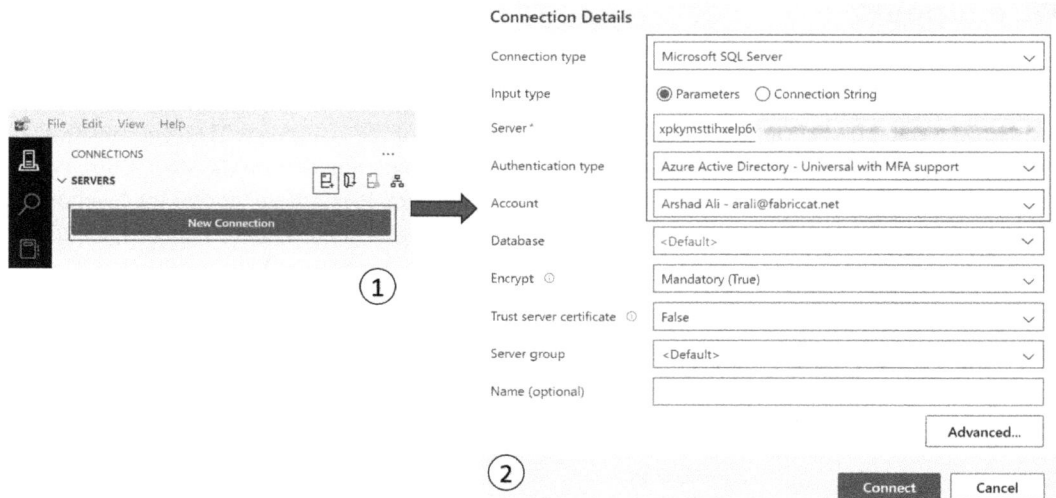

Figure 3.34 – Specify connection details to connect from Azure Data Studio

5.   Once the connection is established, you will notice all the databases (or the endpoints of the lakehouses) from the workspace are listed, as shown in *Figure 3.35*.

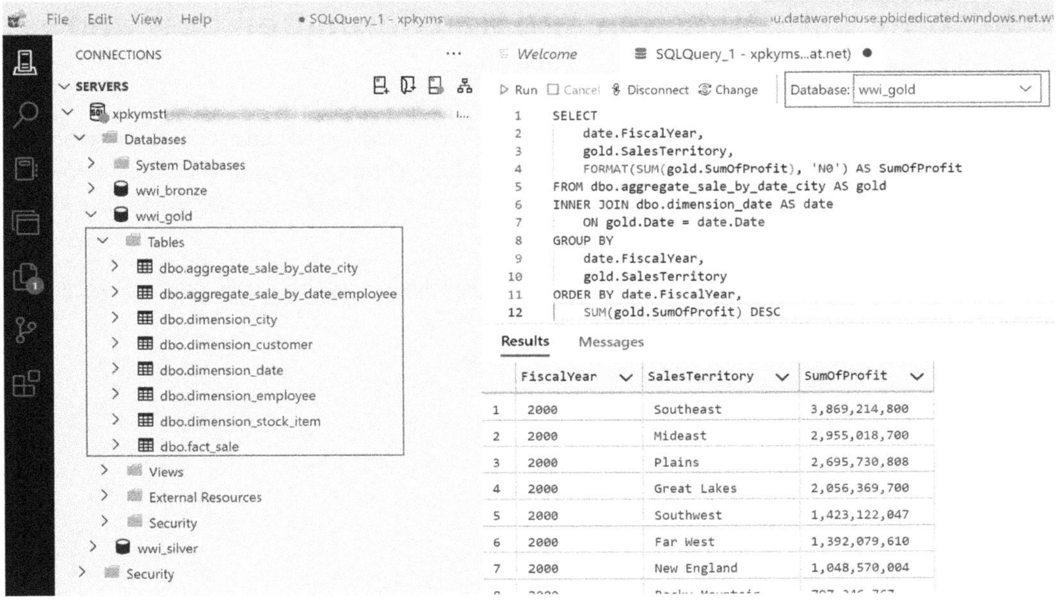

Figure 3.35 – Working with lakehouse tables in Azure Data Studio

From the tree view on the left, navigate to the **wwi-gold** database and expand the tables list. Right-click on any table and choose **Select Top 1000** to view its data. Next, click on the **New Query** from the **File** menu to open a blank query and type the query that follows. Select the **wwi-gold** database under the **Databases** drop-down and then click on the **Run** button to execute the query and explore the results. This is just an example; you can write and execute any SQL queries referencing these tables.

```
SELECT
    date.FiscalYear,
    gold.SalesTerritory,
    FORMAT(SUM(gold.SumOfProfit), 'N0') AS SumOfProfit
FROM dbo.aggregate_sale_by_date_city AS gold
INNER JOIN dbo.dimension_date AS date ON gold.Date = date.Date
GROUP BY date.FiscalYear, gold.SalesTerritory
ORDER BY date.FiscalYear, SUM(gold.SumOfProfit) DESC
```

In this section, you learned about using SQL endpoint to connect to Azure Data Studio; however, the process remains the same even if you are connecting from SQL Server Management Studio or other third-party data query or reporting tools.

Next, we would like to orchestrate and schedule data ingestion and transformation flow to refresh the new data as they arrive.

Orchestrate data ingestion and transformation flow and schedule notebooks and pipelines

Fabric provides flexibility in how you schedule your jobs. For example, you can schedule a notebook by clicking on the settings (cogwheel) icon at the top under the **Home** menu tab when the notebook is open or by clicking on the ellipsis (**…**) next to the name of the notebook in the workspace item view and then clicking on the **Setting** menu.

On the **Setting** page, click on the **Schedule** tab and define the schedule for this notebook to be executed.

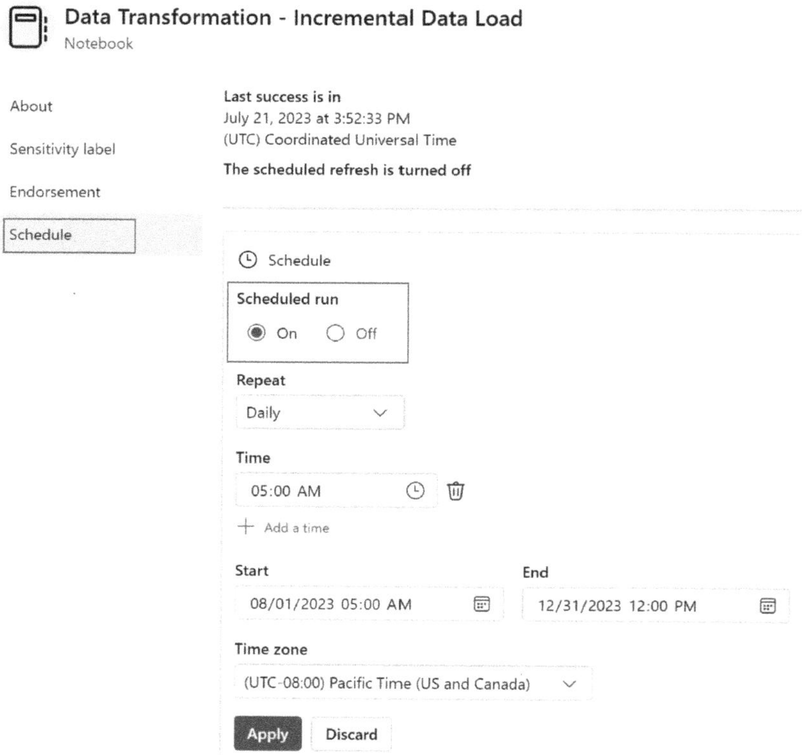

Figure 3.36 – Schedule a notebook

Furthermore, if you have multiple notebooks/jobs, some of which you would like to be executed in parallel while others in sequence, then you can create a data pipeline and define a schedule for when and how frequently this pipeline should be executed. *Figure 3.37* shows an example pipeline that has three activities being executed in sequence (this is just one example; you might have jobs running in parallel or a mix of both parallel and sequential jobs) after the successful completion of the previous one.

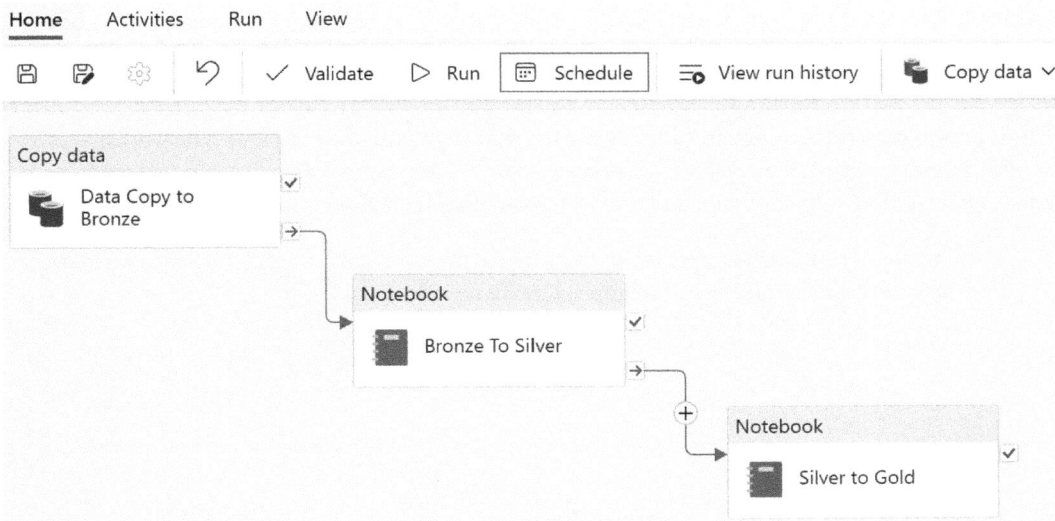

Figure 3.37 – Create a pipeline to orchestrate and schedule activities (including notebooks)

Under the **Home** menu of the opened pipeline, you can click on the **Schedule** button to define the schedule (such as when, how frequently, and the start and end date) for this pipeline to be executed.

Data meshes in Fabric – a primer

A **data mesh** is a federated data architecture that emphasizes decentralizing data across business functions or domains such as marketing, sales, human resources, and more. It facilitates organizing and managing data in a logical way to facilitate the more targeted and efficient use and governance of the data across organizations. This provides more ownership to the producers of a given dataset by encouraging a shift away from the giant, monolithic enterprise-wide data architecture.

> **Important note**
>
> The term data mesh was coined by Zhamak Dehghani (`https://martinfowler.com/articles/data-mesh-principles.html`) and is founded on four principles: "domain-driven ownership of data", "data as a product", "self-serve data infrastructure platform", and "federated governance". A detailed discussion about data meshes is out of the scope of this chapter; however, you can learn more about it at `https://www.datamesh-architecture.com/`.

Microsoft Fabric provides native capabilities to build a data mesh architecture for your organization. It supports organizing data into domains, logically grouping together all the data in an organization that are relevant to a particular function or domain to meet the organization's specific regulations, restrictions, needs, and so on; this enables data consumers to be able to filter and find content by domain. Additionally, it also provides federated governance by delegating governance ability at the domain level, enabling each business function/department to define its own rules and restrictions according to its own specific business needs.

A Fabric admin can create a domain by following the next steps, and they can associate workspaces as part of that domain. When a workspace is associated with a domain, all the items from that workspace are also associated with the domain, and they receive a domain attribute as part of their metadata:

1. Click on the **Admin portal** under the settings icon at the top-right corner of the Fabric homepage, then select **Domains**, and then click on + **Create new domain**.

Figure 3.38 – Creating a data domain

2. For the new domain, specify the name (for example, Retail Sale) and description and hit **Apply**.

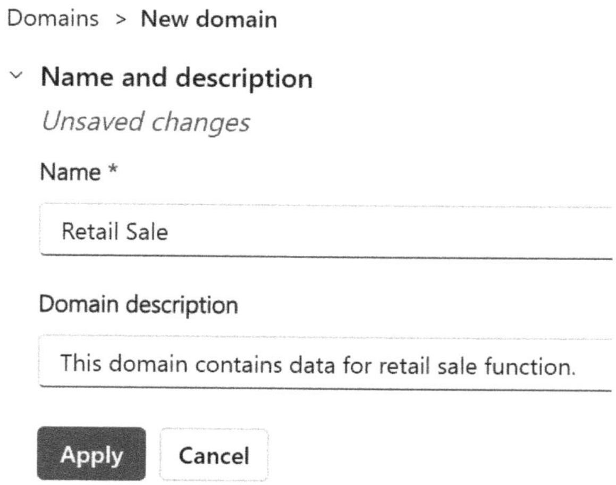

Figure 3.39 – Specifying a name and a description for the data domain

3.   Once the domain is created, you can further modify it to add a domain image to represent your domain, and you can add additional domain admins and contributors. Finally, you are able to associate workspaces with this domain via their name, admins, or capacity.

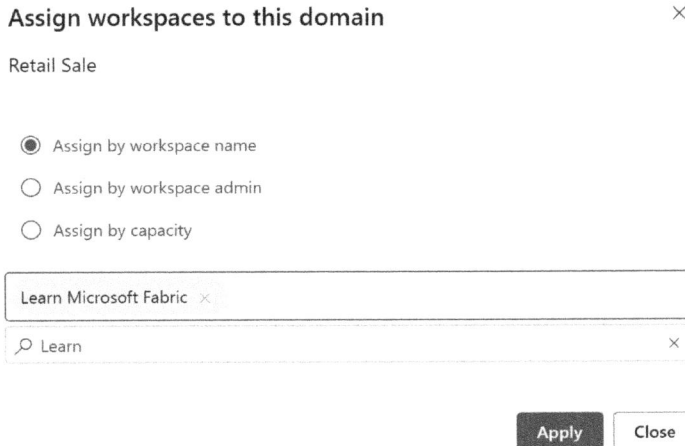

Assign workspaces to this domain   ×

Retail Sale

◉ Assign by workspace name

○ Assign by workspace admin

○ Assign by capacity

Learn Microsoft Fabric ×

🔍 Learn   ×

Apply   Close

Figure 3.40 – Assign workspaces to the data domain

4.   For federated governance, Fabric allows some of the tenant-level settings at the domain level to be overridden. Select the **Delegated** settings tab on the selected domain's configuration page and override these settings appropriately; if this option is grayed out, it means the Fabric admin has not allowed these settings to be overridden at the domain level.

Admin portal

Tenant settings
Usage metrics
Users
Premium Per User
Audit logs
Domains (preview) New
Capacity settings
   Refresh summary
Embed Codes

Domains > **Retail Sale**

Details **Delegated Settings**

Export and sharing settings

◿ Certification
Enabled for a subset of users in domain

Choose whether people in your org or specific security groups can certify items (like apps, reports, or datamarts) as trusted sources for the wider organization.

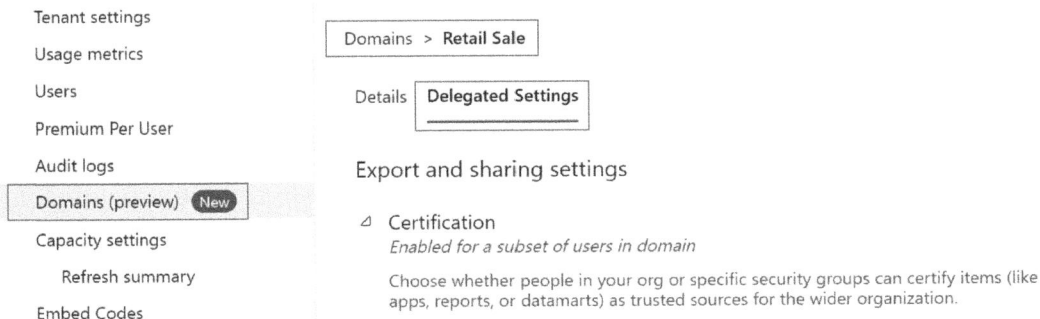

Figure 3.41 – Changing data domain level settings

Summary

Since a lakehouse based on Medallion architecture combines the best of data lakes and data warehouses by breaking silos and removing data duplicity, it's becoming more popular as the de facto standard for building data platform architecture. Microsoft Fabric, with its native capabilities, makes it easy to build data analytics systems based on lakehouses.

In this chapter, you learned about creating an end-to-end lakehouse-based data analytics system. You learned about the different components in this architecture pattern and how to implement them quickly to derive business values. Further, you learned about ingesting data from a data source to your lakehouse using pipelines, transforming this data with notebooks/Spark, and then using Power BI—with its new Direct Lake mode—to create reports and dashboards. You also learned about the capabilities that Fabric provides to build a decentralized data architecture with data meshes.

In the next chapter, you will learn about building an end-to-end analytics system based on data warehouses, where you will learn to use T-SQL for data transformation instead.

4

Building an End-to-End Analytics System – Data Warehouse

While the world of data and analytics makes a shift to the lake-centric approach introduced in the previous chapter, there are still many scenarios that are well served by a traditional data warehouse. Teams of developers often have deep, longstanding SQL skills that can be easily applied to the development of a data warehouse. Other times, an enterprise data lake or lakehouse could feed data into downstream data warehouses that are purpose-built by various **business units** (**BUs**) or departments that serve as the gold layer in a medallion architecture. In some smaller organizations, there just isn't the need for the added complexity of a lakehouse when data is being centralized from all or mostly relational data sources.

In this chapter, you will explore the core functionality of the Fabric data warehouse by building an end-to-end solution that includes ingestion, transformation, and reporting. Many of the concepts in this chapter can be combined with those learned in the prior chapter to create an architecture that combines a lakehouse and a warehouse. We will cover the following topics in this chapter:

- Understanding the end-to-end scenario
- Creating a data warehouse
- Loading data
- Data transformation using **Transact-SQL** (**T-SQL**)
- Orchestrating ETL operations with Data Factory pipelines
- Analyzing data with Power BI

Before you build anything in Fabric, let's get a better understanding of the scenario that will be built.

Understanding the end-to-end scenario

A warehouse in Microsoft Fabric is a relational data store that organizes data into schemas and tables. There are a few different ways for developers to interact with the data warehouse, which are outlined in *Table 4.1*. It is important to note that Spark-based operations against the data warehouse, even those leveraging Spark SQL, are read-only, while T-SQL commands issued from the SQL endpoint are read/write:

	Read-capable on warehouse	**Write-capable on warehouse**
T-SQL	Yes	Yes
Table access via lakehouse shortcut	Yes	No
Power BI	Yes	No
Data Factory pipelines	Yes	Yes
Dataflows Gen2	Yes	Yes

Table 4.1 – A matrix of methods for interacting with the Fabric data warehouse and each method's ability to read or write data

Most of these methods will be illustrated throughout this chapter. This scenario will walk you through three main operations – data ingestion, transformation, and analysis:

- **Ingest**: The data ingestion process presents the largest number of options to weigh. For code-first developers, T-SQL offers high-speed ingestion with the trade-off of a limited set of data sources. Data can be loaded using cross-database queries to the lakehouse or other warehouses, as well as the popular COPY command to access file storage locations such as **Azure Data Lake Storage Gen2 (ADLS Gen2)**. The Data Factory pipeline copy activity can load data from a wider variety of sources than T-SQL and has a GUI for development, but it lacks any meaningful data transformation capabilities. Finally, Dataflows Gen2 offers maximum flexibility, combining a GUI, a vast number of data sources, and the ability to perform data transformation in flight.

- **Transform**: There are two ways to transform data in the warehouse – on ingestion or post-ingestion. For scenarios where the data has been cleaned up by other processes, such as a data lake using the medallion architecture that stored bronze and silver data, you will likely be looking to ingest the data using a T-SQL COPY command, and then perform any additional transformations using T-SQL, often leveraging stored procedures. In other cases, a Dataflow Gen2 would be more applicable if there is no data lake; data is landed directly into the warehouse, and the source necessitates some transformation to the data before it hits the warehouse.

- **Analyze**: There is a wide range of reporting tools, but the focus will be Power BI, using the newly introduced Direct Lake mode. This allows you to build Power BI models directly over the warehouse without the need to perform a data model refresh, which can be a long-running operation on large datasets that are not enabled for incremental refresh. In addition to Power BI, it is very common to see ad hoc queries or other reporting tools use the SQL endpoint to issue T-SQL queries. Queries against the SQL endpoint can leverage cross-database querying to combine data from other warehouses and lakehouses in the same Fabric workspace.

Data and transformation flow

For the purpose of building an end-to-end data analytics system in the data warehouse, you are going to use the **Wide World Importers (WWI)** sample database. A detailed explanation of the data model was given in the previous chapter.

One source table will come from Data Factory's built-in sample datasets and two tables from Parquet files in an unpartitioned structure, stored in a folder for each table in a remote ADLS account. These two sources will be used to illustrate different methods for loading the data: a Data Factory copy activity and T-SQL. In a real-world situation, the data would likely come from various sources into a common data lake, which would then be loaded into the warehouse using T-SQL. However, some smaller solutions or departmental warehouse solutions will load directly into the warehouse using the Data Factory copy activity.

The data warehouse will be split into two sections using schemas. The first uses the `stage` schema, where the raw source data lands, and will include a combination of new and updated records from the source systems. The second uses the `dbo` schema, which will be the final start-schema dimensional model.

The overall flow of the data from source through end-user reporting can be seen in *Figure 4.1*:

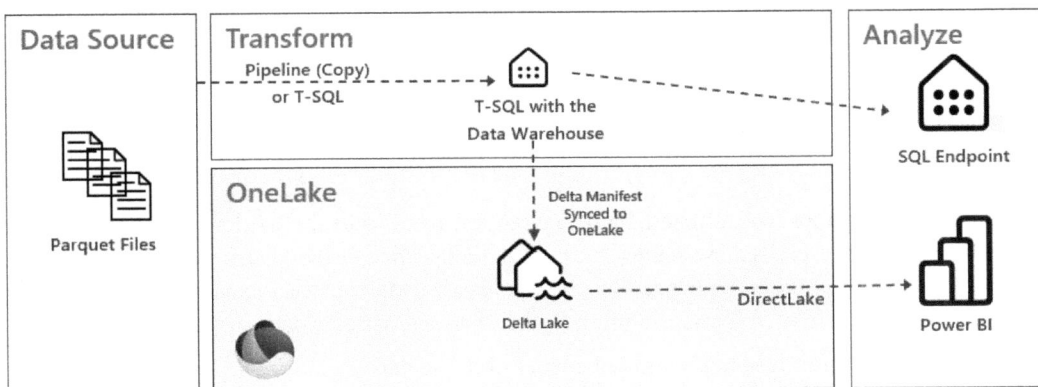

Figure 4.1 – Implementing the medallion architecture in Fabric

For data ingestion, you will be using a Data Factory pipeline and T-SQL to copy data from the sources to the `stage` schema. Then, you will use T-SQL to build an incremental data load from the `stage` to `dbo` schema tables. Finally, you will use Power BI and Direct Lake to create reports/dashboards that query data directly from the data warehouse. Along the way, you will run several T-SQL scripts using the built-in query editor to validate record counts produced by the ETL process.

Creating a data warehouse

In this section, you will create a data warehouse that will store the data used throughout this chapter. To get started, follow these steps:

1. Open your web browser, navigate to Microsoft Fabric (`https://app.fabric.microsoft.com`), and sign in.

2. From the list of experiences, select **Synapse Data Warehouse**:

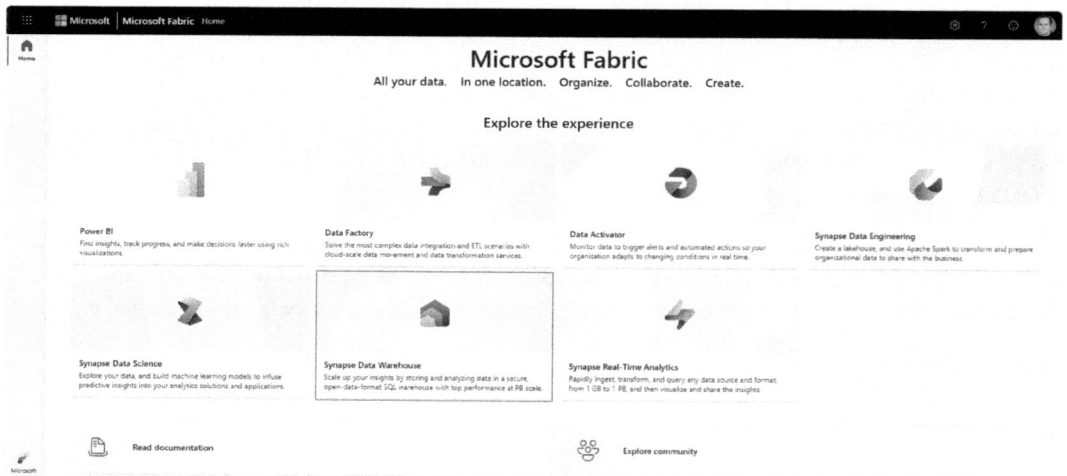

Figure 4.2 – Microsoft Fabric landing page and experience list

3. Select **Workspaces** from the left-hand navigation bar. Go to the workspace called **Learn Microsoft Fabric**, created in *Chapter 2, Understanding Different Workloads and Getting Started with Microsoft Fabric*, by typing its name in the search textbox at the top and clicking on your workspace to open it. You can also pin it so that it always appears on top of the list.

4. Select **New** | **Warehouse** in the top-left corner of the screen:

Data pipeline

Dataflow Gen2

Environment (Preview)

Eventstream

Experiment

KQL Database

KQL Queryset

Lakehouse

ML model

Notebook

Reflex (Preview)

Report

Spark Job Definition

Warehouse

More options

Import item

Import notebook

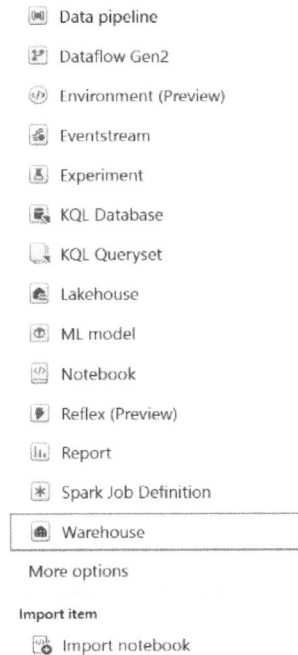

Figure 4.3 – Menu of new items found on the Fabric workspace view

5. On the **New warehouse** dialog box, enter WideWorldImportersDW in the **Name** field, and click on **Create**.

After a few seconds, a **Build a warehouse** landing page will be displayed, and the warehouse will be ready to use. Now, let's look at how to create tables.

Creating tables in a data warehouse

In a warehouse, data is organized in schemas and tables. There can be one or more schemas, the default being dbo, and zero or more tables in a schema. All objects, including views, stored procedures, and functions, are organized inside schemas as well.

Let's look at creating schemas and tables that will be used for the remainder of this chapter:

1. From the ribbon of the **WideWorldImportersDW** data warehouse, select the **New SQL query** dropdown and then select **New SQL query**:

Get data ⌄ | New SQL query ⌄ | New visual query | New report | New measure

Figure 4.4 – The New SQL query option on the Fabric data warehouse ribbon

2. Enter the code found at https://github.com/PacktPublishing/Learn-Microsoft-Fabric/tree/main/ch4/DropAndCreateTables.sql into the query editor. This block of code creates a stored procedure called dbo.DropAndCreateTables, which accepts a parameter for Schema. The code creates the specified schema if it does not exist and then drops and recreates three tables that will be used for the dimensional mode: DimCity, DimDate, and FactSale. Finally, the stored procedure is executed to create tables in two schemas – stage and dbo:

```
DROP PROCEDURE IF EXISTS dbo.DropAndCreateTables
GO

CREATE PROCEDURE dbo.DropAndCreateTables
    @Schema varchar(5)
AS
    BEGIN
    DECLARE @SQL varchar(4000)
    IF NOT EXISTS (SELECT * FROM sys.schemas WHERE name = 'stage')
    EXEC ('CREATE SCHEMA [stage]')

    SET @SQL = 'DROP TABLE IF EXISTS [' + @Schema + '].[DimCity];
    CREATE TABLE [' + @Schema + '].[DimCity](
    [CityKey] [int] NOT NULL,
    [WWICityID] [int] NOT NULL,
    [City] [varchar](50) NOT NULL,
    [StateProvince] [varchar](50) NOT NULL,
    [Country] [varchar](60) NOT NULL,
    [Continent] [varchar](30) NOT NULL,
    [SalesTerritory] [varchar](50) NOT NULL,
    [Region] [varchar](30) NOT NULL,
    [Subregion] [varchar](30) NOT NULL,
    [Location] [varchar](50) NULL,
    [LatestRecordedPopulation] [bigint] NOT NULL,
    [ValidFrom] [datetime2](6) NOT NULL,
    [ValidTo] [datetime2](6) NOT NULL,
    [LineageKey] [int] NOT NULL);

    DROP TABLE IF EXISTS [' + @Schema + '].[FactSale];

    CREATE TABLE [' + @Schema + '].[FactSale](
        [SaleKey] [bigint] NOT NULL,
        [CityKey] [int] NOT NULL,
```

Figure 4.5 – A snippet of the stored procedure to drop and create warehouse tables

3. At the top of the query editor window, click on **Run**. This will create three tables in the stage schema and three tables in the dbo schema:

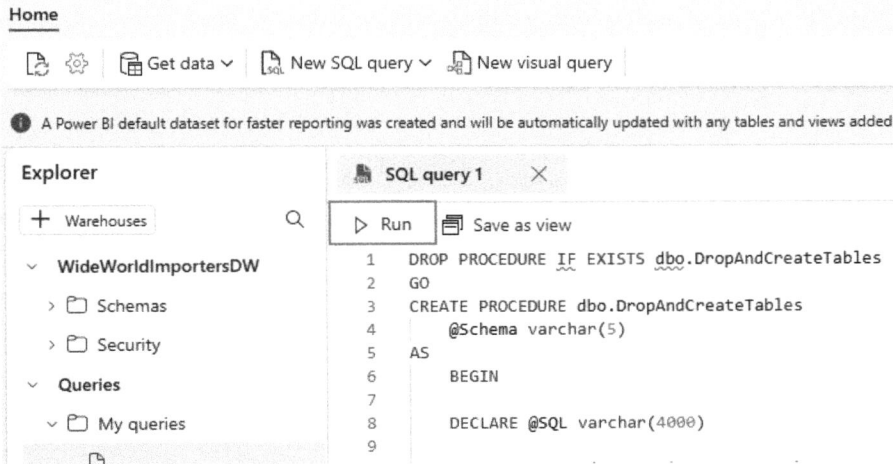

Figure 4.6 – The Fabric data warehouse query view

4.   To ensure all tables were created successfully, right-click on **WideWorldImportersDW** in the **Explorer** window and click on **Refresh**. Then, expand the dbo and stage table nodes:

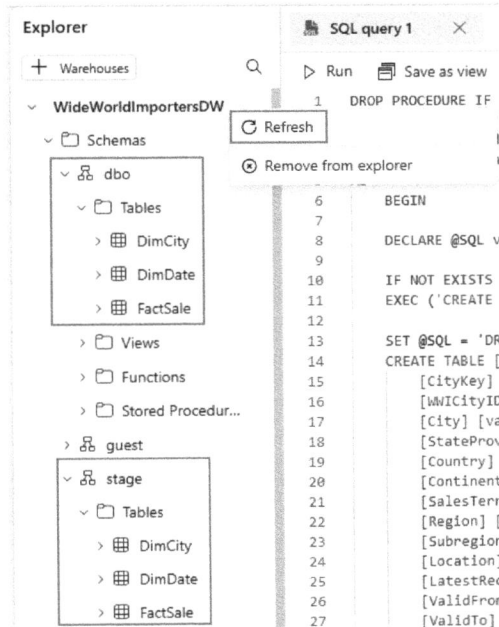

Figure 4.7 – The data warehouse explorer showing three tables have been successfully created in each of the two schemas

5. Scroll to the bottom of the **Explorer** window, right-click on **SQL query 1** in the **Queries | My queries** section, and click on **Rename**:

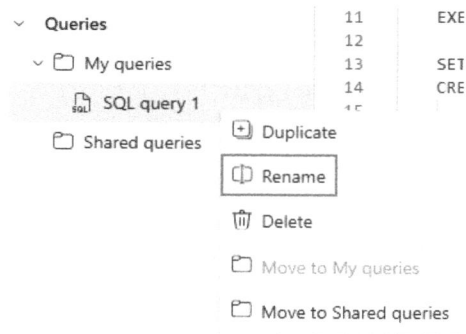

Figure 4.8 – Right-click menu on a script stored in the data warehouse

6. Name the query `Create Tables Stored Procedure` and again click on **Rename**.

With all the tables created, it is time to get data into the warehouse.

Loading data

As previously discussed, there are several ways to load data into a warehouse. In this section, we will explore two methods: the Data Factory copy activity and T-SQL. The loading method you choose will largely depend on two factors: developer skillset and data source connectivity.

Data warehouse professionals are very likely to be proficient in writing T-SQL and may, therefore, gravitate toward a code-based approach that uses the `COPY` command. While analysts may not have as deep of a T-SQL skillset, they may opt for a GUI-based approach with Data Factory. While an individual may want to use a code-based approach, the fact that T-SQL requires the data to come from a narrow set of locations could mean the copy activity is a better fit. There are other factors to consider, such as enterprise standards and ETL frameworks, that may inform a decision on the tool used.

> **Note**
> In a real-world scenario, it is unlikely that you would load data from the same source using different tools. This scenario in this chapter uses different methods for illustrative purposes only to demonstrate multiple tools that are available and should not be considered architectural guidance.

Let's begin by exploring the Data Factory copy activity.

Loading data using the copy activity in Data Factory

For data professionals coming from a data warehouse background, the Data Factory copy activity is likely to be very familiar. It offers the ability to load data from dozens of sources directly into the data warehouse without writing any code. There is very limited data transformation functionality built into the copy activity, but it does offer automatic table creation, column mappings, and pre- and post-load script execution. Pre-load scripts can be especially useful when loading staging tables that need to have the prior run's data removed before the next batch of data is added.

> **Note**
>
> Initially, the pipeline created in this section will be used to load only a single stage table, `stage.DimCity`. You will return to the pipeline later in the chapter to extend it by creating a single pipeline that orchestrates the entire process, from the loading stage to building the dimensional model.

To get started with loading a table using the copy activity inside a Data Factory pipeline, follow these steps:

1. From the ribbon of the **WideWorldImportersDW** data warehouse, select **Get data | New data pipeline**:

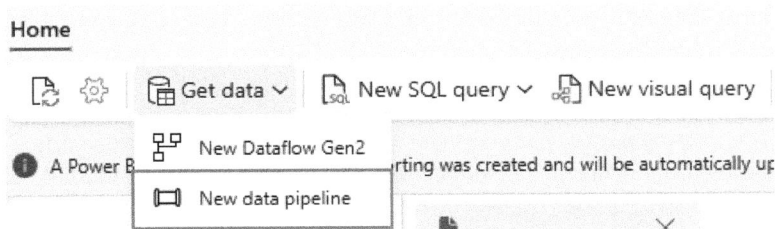

Figure 4.9 – The data warehouse Get data menu

2. In the **New pipeline** dialog, enter `Data Warehouse End to End` as the **Name** value.

3. Click on **Create**. The **Copy data** assistant will open to **Choose data source** page.

4. From the **Sample data** section, select **Retail Data Model from Wide World Importers**:

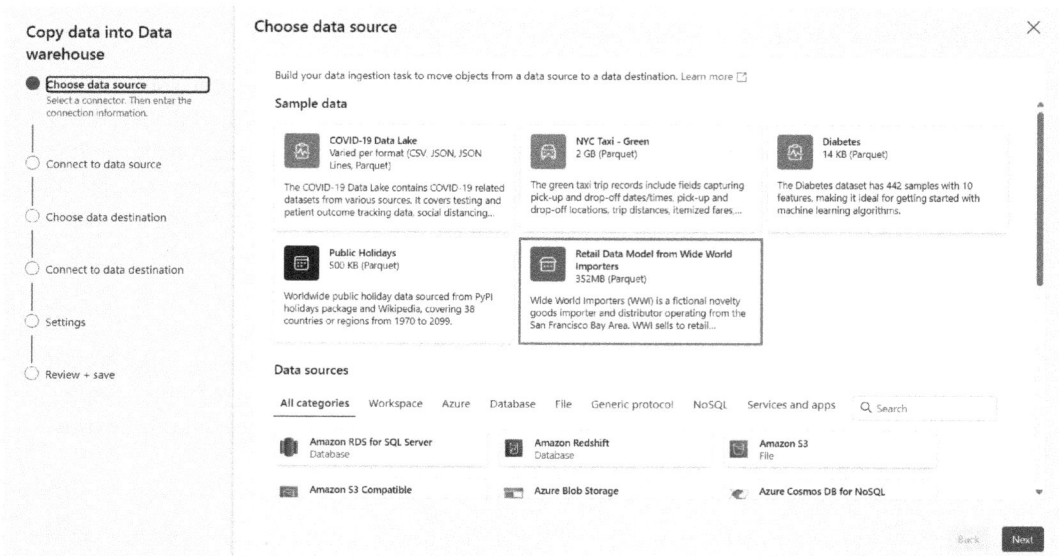

Figure 4.10 – The Choose data source screen of the Copy data assistant

5. Click on **Next**.

6. In the **Select a dataset** section of the screen, select `dimension_city`. After a few seconds, a preview of the data will appear.

7. Click on **Next**.

8. Because the **Copy data** assistant was started from the data warehouse, the **Choose data destination** field should already be populated with **WideWorldImportersDW**, as seen here:

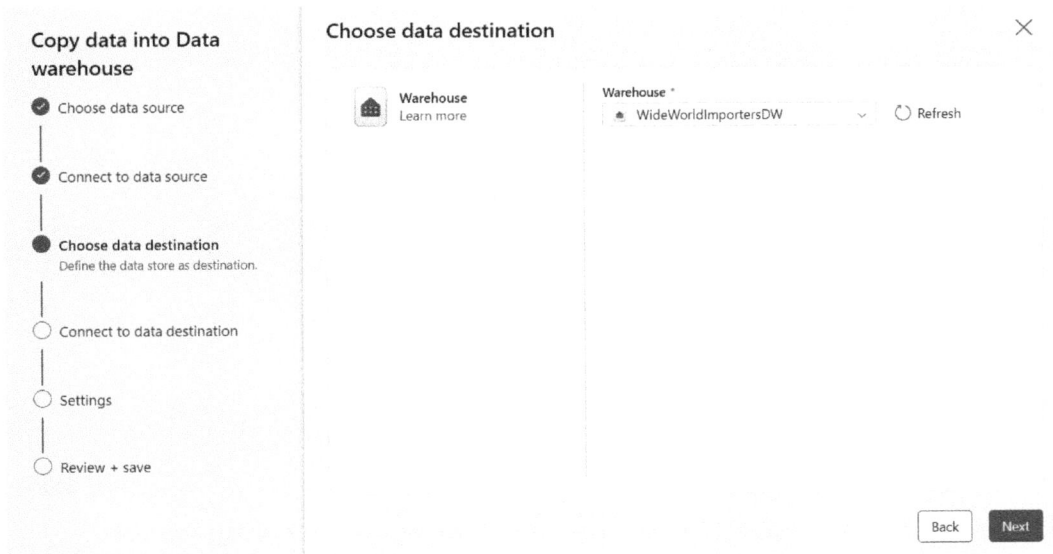

Figure 4.11 – The Choose data destination screen of the Copy data assistant

Click on **Next**.

9.   On the **Connect to data destination** page, configure the following settings:

   - **Load settings**: Load to an existing table
   - **Destination table name**: `stage.DimCity`
   - **Column mappings**: Accept the defaults

   Then, click on **Next**:

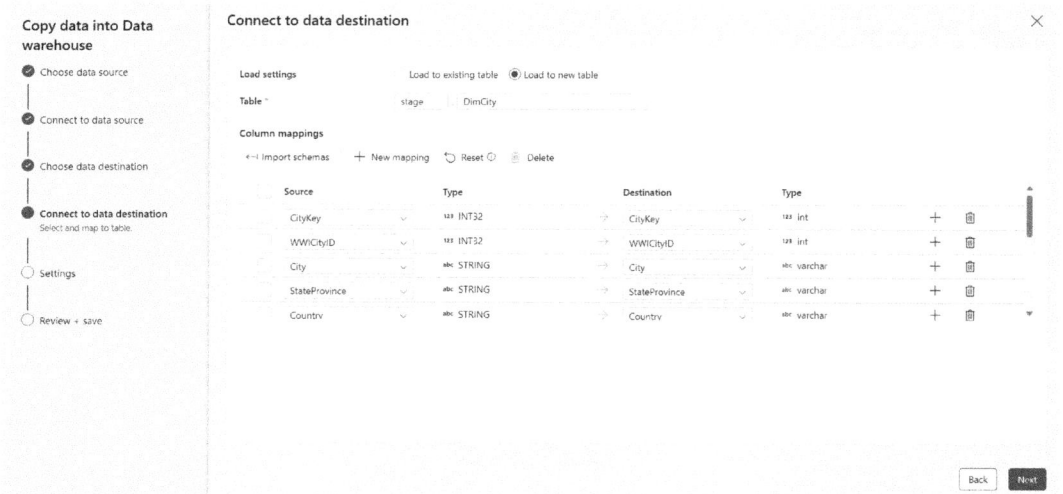

Figure 4.12 – The completed Connect to data destination page of the Copy data assistant

10. On the **Settings** page, ensure the box next to **Enable staging** is checked. Click on **Next**.

11. On the **Review + Save** page, uncheck the box next to **Start data transfer immediately**.

12. Click on **OK**. The **Copy data** assistant will close and land into the pipeline view.

13. Select the **Copy data** activity that was generated. It will have a name in the format of `Copy_xxx`.

14. On the **General** page, change the **Name** value to `CD Load Stage_DimCity`:

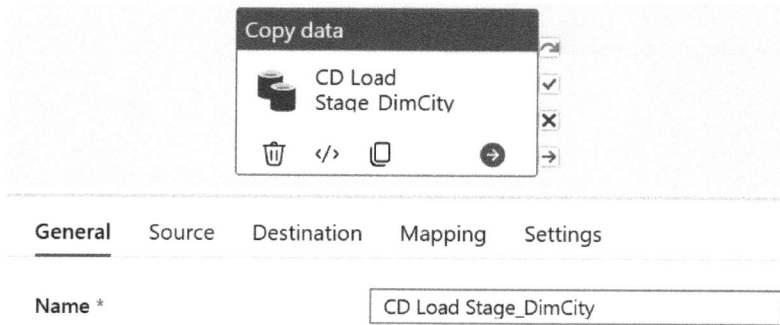

Figure 4.13 – The General settings tab of the Copy data activity

15. From the ribbon, select **Save** to save the changes to the pipeline.

16. From the ribbon, select **Run** to load the `Stage.DimCity` table.

The **Output** tab will display the status of the copy activity change as it moves from queuing to in progress to completed. The whole execution should take less than 1 minute. A sample output can be seen in *Figure 4.14*:

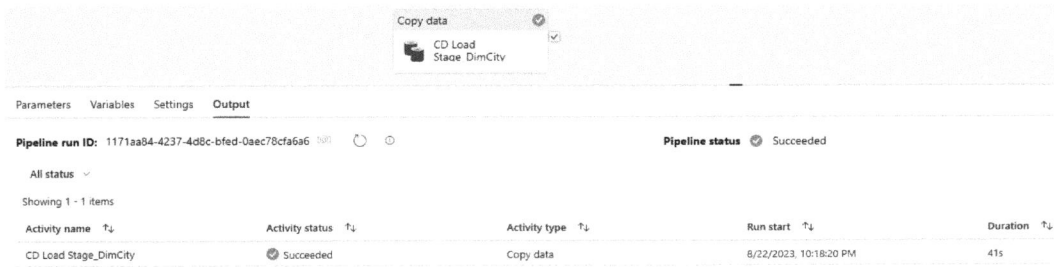

Figure 4.14 – The Output section after running a pipeline with a single Copy data activity

There are a few more steps in the data loading and transformation process that need to be built in the sections that follow, after which you will return to this pipeline and extend it to orchestrate the entire data loading and transformation process. In the meantime, now that you know how to use Data Factory's copy activity, let's look at how to load data using the T-SQL COPY command.

Loading data using T-SQL

T-SQL has a wide user base that spans across all Microsoft first-party database engines and is often the first choice for data warehouse developers because it is familiar, flexible, and fits into their workflow without having to switch contexts or tools.

There are two ways to use T-SQL to load data in bulk. The first is using a cross-database query. This functionality has long existed in SQL Server but is new to Synapse in Fabric. By using a three-part name in the `database.schema.table` format, you can select and subsequently insert data from another warehouse or lakehouse within the same workspace. The COPY command lets you bring in data from file stores by specifying an individual file or a folder. Follow the steps outlined next:

1. Return to the WWI data warehouse by navigating to your workspace and then selecting **WideWorldImportersDW** from the list of workspace items:

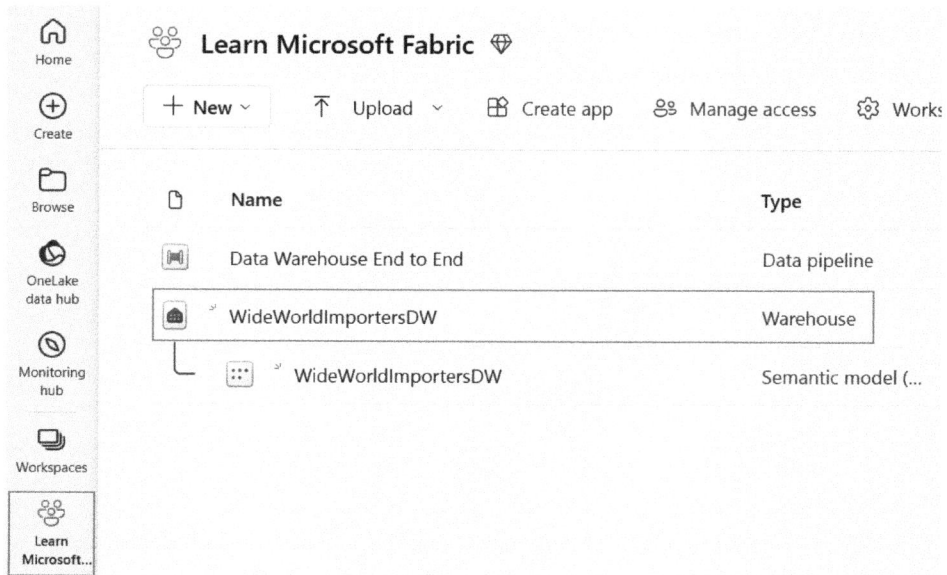

Figure 4.15 – The item view of a Fabric workspace

2. In the bottom-left corner of the screen, navigate to the **Query** view:

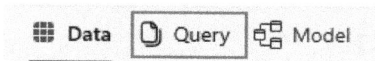

Figure 4.16 – Options for different views available in the data warehouse

3. From the ribbon, select **New SQL query**.

4. In the editor, type the following code:

```
DROP PROCEDURE IF EXISTS dbo.LoadStageTables
GO
CREATE PROCEDURE dbo.LoadStageTables
AS
BEGIN
    COPY INTO [stage].[DimDate]
    FROM 'https://azuresynapsestorage.blob.core.windows.net/
sampledata/WideWorldImportersDW/tables/dimension_date.parquet'
    WITH (FILE_TYPE = 'PARQUET');
    COPY INTO [stage].[FactSale]
    FROM 'https://azuresynapsestorage.blob.core.windows.net/
```

```
sampledata/WideWorldImportersDW/tables/fact_sale.parquet'
    WITH (FILE_TYPE = 'PARQUET');
END
GO
EXEC dbo.LoadStageTables
GO
```

5. Click on **Run** at the top of the query editor window:

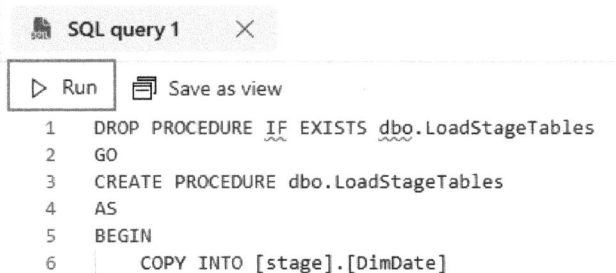

Figure 4.17 – The data warehouse query editor

6. On the tab above the query editor, right-click on **SQL query 1** and then click on **Rename**:

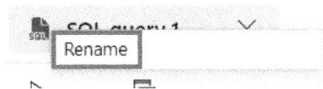

Figure 4.18 – Option menu as it appears on tabs at the top of the data warehouse query editor

7. Name the query Load Remaining Stage Tables and click on **Rename**.

8. To verify all stage tables have loaded successfully, click on **New SQL query** from the ribbon and run the following code:

```
SELECT COUNT(*) AS 'RecordCount', 'stage.DimCity' AS Table_Name
FROM stage.DimCity UNION ALL
SELECT COUNT(*) AS 'RecordCount', 'stage.DimDate' AS Table_Name
FROM stage.DimDate UNION ALL
SELECT COUNT(*) AS 'RecordCount', 'stage.FactSale' AS Table_Name
FROM stage.FactSale
```

9. Verify the record counts as shown in *Figure 4.19*:

```
1   SELECT COUNT(*) AS 'RecordCount', 'stage.DimCity' AS Table_Name FROM stage.DimCity UNION ALL
2   SELECT COUNT(*) AS 'RecordCount', 'stage.DimDate' AS Table_Name FROM stage.DimDate UNION ALL
3   SELECT COUNT(*) AS 'RecordCount', 'stage.FactSale' AS Table_Name FROM stage.FactSale
```

123 RecordCount	ABC Table_Name
1	116295	stage.DimCity
2	6210	stage.DimDate
3	50150843	stage.FactSale

Figure 4.19 – Record counts for the three stage tables that have been created and loaded

10. Using one of the methods discussed earlier in this chapter, rename the script `Stage Table Counts`.

With all the tables for the dimensional model created and loaded, it is time to perform the data transformation steps to prepare the data for reporting.

Data transformation using T-SQL

With the data now loaded, it is time to transform the data into an aggregate reporting table. In this section, you will create and execute a stored procedure that will create an aggregate table that will be used later in this chapter as the base for a Power BI report.

Let's look at transforming data using T-SQL:

1. While still in the query editor of the **WideWorldImportersDW** data warehouse, click on **New SQL query** from the ribbon.

2. In the query window, enter the following code:

> **Note**
>
> The following code should not be used as an example of best practices. In a real-world scenario, loading a data warehouse will involve generating a surrogate key (warehouse key), updating dimension data based on type 1 and type 2 attributes, handling NULL dimension attributes, looking up surrogate key values when loading a fact table, and more. The following code represents a simplified approach to loading dimension and fact tables to show the general loading pattern.

```
DROP PROCEDURE IF EXISTS dbo.LoadDimensionalModel
GO
```

```
CREATE PROCEDURE dbo.LoadDimensionalModel
AS
BEGIN
    UPDATE dbo.DimCity
    SET
        [City] = sdc.[City],
        [StateProvince] = sdc.[StateProvince],
        [Country] = sdc.[Country],
        [Continent] = sdc.[Continent],
        [SalesTerritory] = sdc.[SalesTerritory],
        [Region] = sdc.[Region],
        [Subregion] = sdc.[Subregion],
        [Location] = sdc.[Location],
        [LatestRecordedPopulation] = sdc.
[LatestRecordedPopulation],
        [ValidFrom] = sdc.[ValidFrom],
        [ValidTo] = sdc.[ValidTo],
        [LineageKey] = sdc.[LineageKey]
    FROM stage.DimCity AS sdc
    WHERE dbo.DimCity.CityKey = sdc.CityKey
    INSERT INTO dbo.DimCity
    SELECT * FROM stage.DimCity
    WHERE CityKey NOT IN (SELECT CityKey FROM dbo.DimCity)

    DELETE FROM dbo.DimDate
    INSERT INTO dbo.DimDate
    SELECT * FROM stage.DimDate

    INSERT INTO dbo.FactSale
    SELECT * FROM stage.FactSale WHERE SaleKey NOT IN (SELECT
SaleKey FROM dbo.FactSale)
END
GO
EXEC dbo.LoadDimensionalModel
GO
```

3. Click on **Run** at the top of the query editor window.

4. Using one of the methods discussed earlier in this chapter, rename the script Load Dimensional Model Stored Procedure.

5. To verify all dimensional model tables have loaded successfully, click on **New SQL query** from the ribbon and run the following query:

```
SELECT COUNT(*) AS 'RecordCount', 'dbo.DimCity' AS Table_Name
FROM dbo.DimCity UNION ALL
```

```
SELECT COUNT(*) AS 'RecordCount', 'dbo.DimDate' AS Table_Name
FROM dbo.DimDate UNION ALL
SELECT COUNT(*) AS 'RecordCount', 'dbo.FactSale' AS Table_Name
FROM dbo.FactSale
```

6. Verify the record counts as shown in *Figure 4.20*:

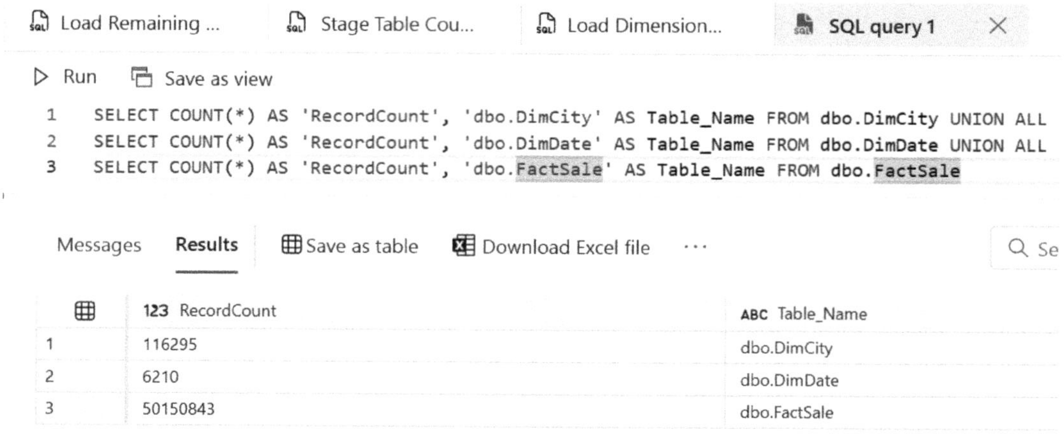

Figure 4.20 – Record counts for the three dimensional model tables that have been created and loaded

7. Using one of the methods discussed earlier in this chapter, rename the script `Dimensional Model Table Counts`.

T-SQL is the most versatile tool for interacting with a data warehouse in Fabric. Not only is it used to create tables and query the database – it is the main tool at your disposal for transforming data within the warehouse. Now that the data is cleaned and transformed, let's look at driving business value through reporting.

Orchestrating ETL operations with Data Factory pipelines

Data Factory pipelines are an extremely useful tool in analytics projects. Earlier in this chapter, you created a data pipeline that runs a **Copy data** activity to load the `stage.DimCity` table. This data was later used in a stored procedure to load a dimensional model table called `dbo.DimCity`. It is now time to extend the pipeline to orchestrate the entire ETL process, which will include the following:

1. Dropping and recreating all `stage` schema tables so that data is not duplicated from prior runs

2. Loading the `stage.DimCity` table using the **Copy data** activity

3. Loading the `stage.DimDate` and `stage.FactSale` tables using the T-SQL `COPY` command by executing a stored procedure

4. Incrementally loading the dimensional model using a stored procedure

Let's extend the pipeline created earlier in the chapter:

1. Return to the pipeline created in the *Loading data* section earlier in the chapter by navigating to your workspace and then selecting **Data Warehouse End to End** from the list of workspace items:

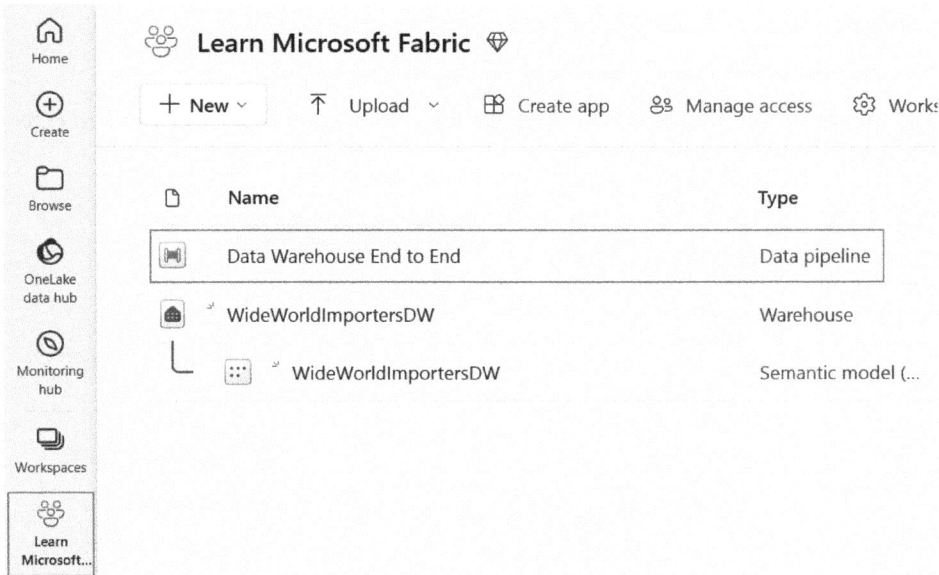

Figure 4.21 – The item view of a Fabric workspace

2. From the **Activities** tab of the ribbon, click on **Stored procedure** to add an activity to the canvas:

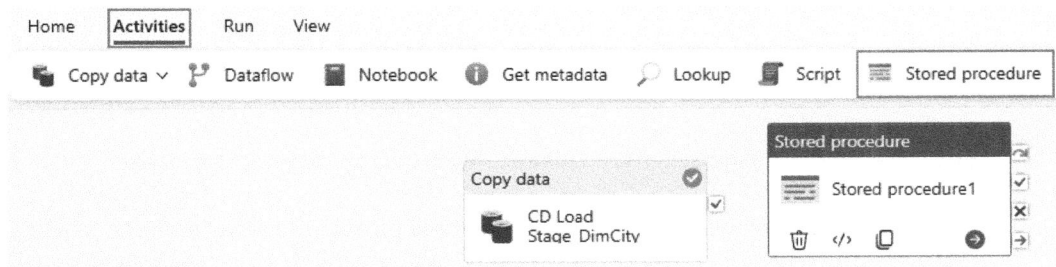

Figure 4.22 – The Activities tab of the Data Factory pipeline editor

3. Select the newly created stored procedure activity on the canvas.

4. On the **General** page of the activity settings, change the **Name** value to `SP Drop and Create Stage Tables`.

5. On the **Settings** page of the activity settings, as shown in *Figure 4.23*, configure the following settings:

   - **Data store type: Workspace**
   - **Warehouse**: **WideWorldImportersDW**
   - **Stored procedure name**: `[dbo].[DropAndCreateTables]`
   - In the **Stored procedure parameters** section, click on **Import**.
   - In the resulting **Value** box of the **Schema** parameter, enter `stage`. Be sure to enter this text in all lowercase:

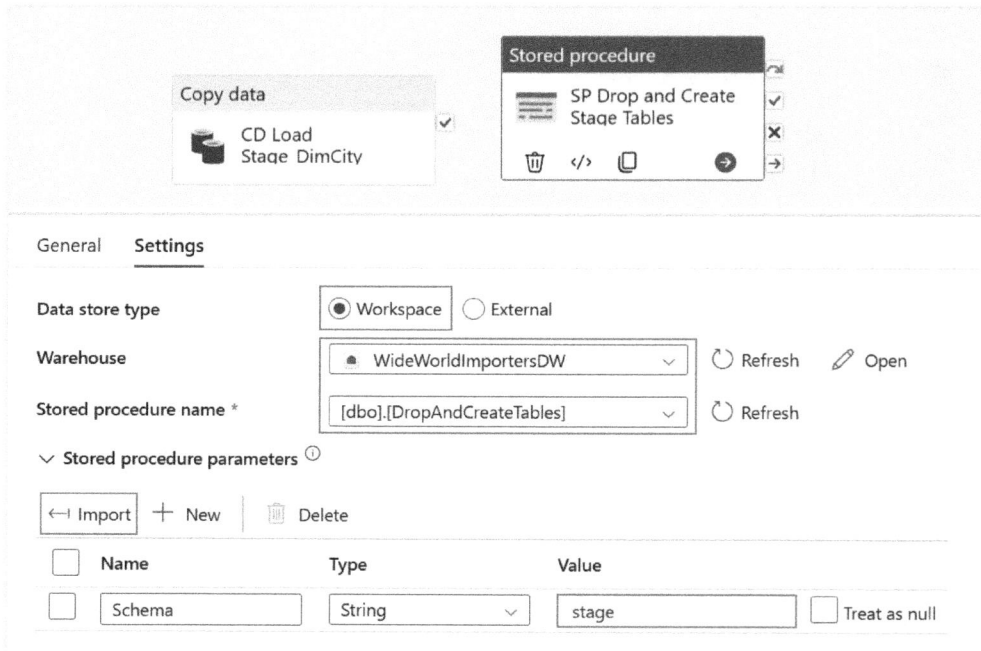

Figure 4.23 – Fully configured stored procedure activity to drop and recreate stage tables

6. Reposition the **SP Drop and Create Stage Tables** stored procedure activity to the left of the `CD Load Stage_DimCity` activity by clicking, holding, and dragging the activity onto the canvas.

7. Connect the **On success** constraint from the stored procedure to the **Copy data** activity:

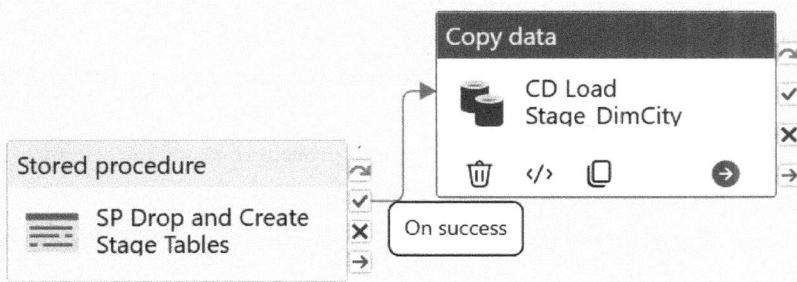

Figure 4.24 – The repositioned pipeline canvas and On success constraint connecting the activities

8. From the **Activities** tab of the ribbon, select **Stored procedure** to add the activity to the canvas.

9. Select the newly created stored procedure activity on the canvas.

10. On the **General** page of the activity settings, change the **Name** value to SP Load Remaining Stage Tables.

11. On the **Settings** page of the activity settings, as shown in *Figure 4.25*, configure the following settings:

   - **Data store type: Workspace**

   - **Warehouse: WideWorldImportersDW**

   - **Stored procedure name**: [dbo] . [LoadStageTables]:

General	**Settings**	
Data store type	● Workspace ○ External	
Warehouse	▲ WideWorldImportersDW ∨	○ Refresh ✎ Open
Stored procedure name *	[dbo].[LoadStageTables] ∨	○ Refresh

Figure 4.25 – Fully configured stored procedure activity to load the remaining stage tables

12. Reposition the **SP Load Remaining Stage Tables** stored procedure activity to the right of the `CD Load Stage_DimCity` activity by clicking, holding, and dragging the activity onto the canvas.

13. Connect the **On success** constraint from the **Copy data** activity to the **SP Load Remaining Stage Tables** stored procedure activity.

14. From the **Activities** tab of the ribbon, select **Stored procedure** to add the activity to the canvas.

15. Select the newly created stored procedure activity on the canvas.

16. On the **General** page of the activity settings, change the **Name** value to `SP Refresh Dimensional Model`.

17. On the **Settings** page of the activity settings, as shown in *Figure 4.25*, configure the following settings:

    - **Data store type: Workspace**

    - **Warehouse: WideWorldImportersDW**

    - **Stored procedure name**: `[dbo].[LoadDimensionalMode]`

18. Reposition the **SP Refresh Dimensional Model** stored procedure activity to the right of the **SP Load Remaining Stage Tables** activity by clicking, holding, and dragging the activity onto the canvas.

19. Connect the **On success** constraint from the **SP Load Remaining Stage Tables** stored procedure activity to the **SP Refresh Dimensional Model** stored procedure activity:

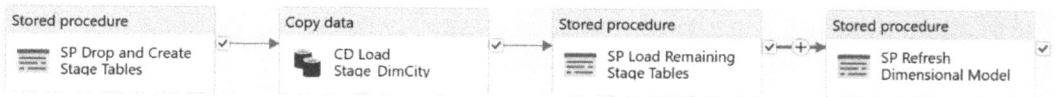

Figure 4.26 – Completed pipeline connecting all data loading and refresh activities

20. From the **Home** tab of the ribbon, click on **Save** to save the changes to the pipeline.

21. From the ribbon, click on **Run** to run the end-to-end data pipeline.

The **Output** tab will display the status of each activity as it begins to run and will change as it moves from a queue to in progress to completed. The whole execution should take about 3 minutes. A sample output can be seen in *Figure 4.27*:

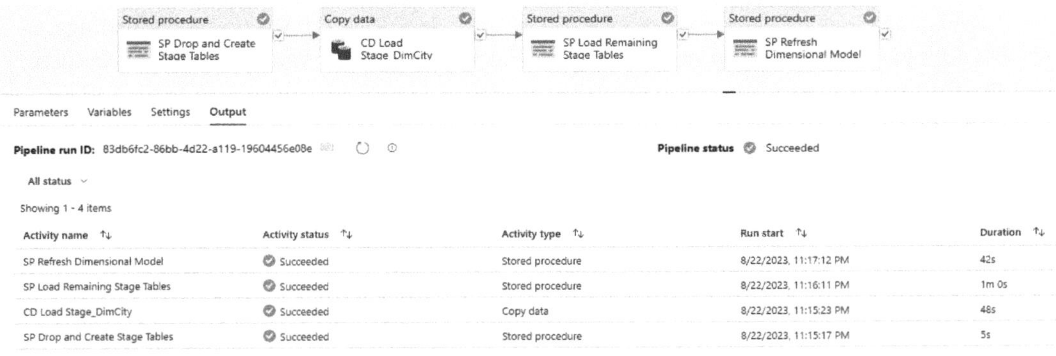

Figure 4.27 – The Output section after running the end-to-end pipeline
to build the WWI data warehouse dimensional model

To this point, you have built a repeatable end-to-end process for incrementally loading the dimensional model. Each time this pipeline is executed, the stage tables will be cleared and reloaded, and the dimensional model tables will update existing records and add new records. With the data loaded, it is time to gain some business value from the warehouse by building a report using Power BI.

Analyzing data with Power BI

The value derived from data is only truly realized when it can be used to make business decisions. To this point, we have explored creating a warehouse, loading tables, and transforming data within a Fabric data warehouse. Now, it is time to refine the data model for reporting. To begin, we will define relationships between the tables in the data model, followed by creating visuals in a Power BI report.

Let's look at setting up a Power BI report:

1. Return to the WWI data warehouse by navigating to your workspace and then selecting **WideWorldImportersDW** with a type of **Warehouse** from the list of workspace items.

2. In the bottom-left corner of the screen, navigate to the **Model** view:

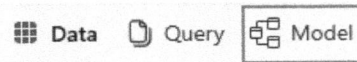

Figure 4.28 – Options for different views available in the data warehouse

3. Create a relationship between the dbo.FactSale and dbo.DimDate tables by dragging the **InvoiceDateKey** field from dbo.FactSale and dropping it onto the **Date** field in dbo.DimDate:

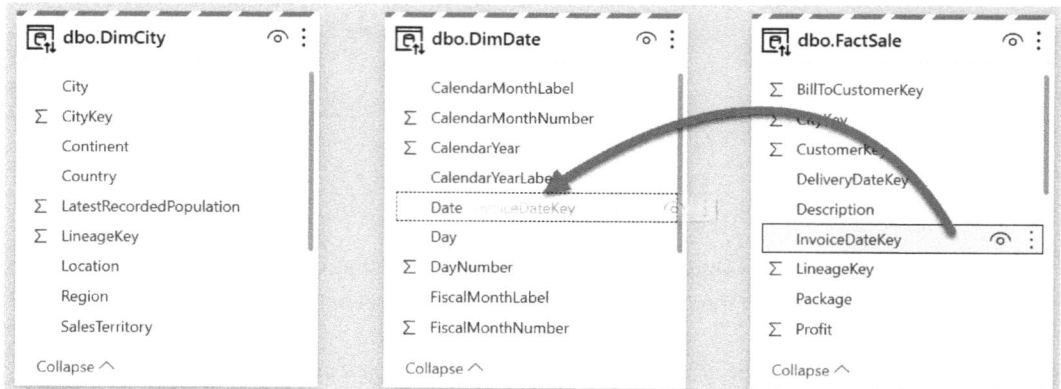

Figure 4.29 – Dragging and dropping fields between tables in the
Model view of the warehouse to create relationships

4. On the **Create Relationship** page, configure the following settings:

    - **Table 1**: dbo.FactSale

    - **Table 2**: dbo.DimDate

    - **Cardinality: Many to one (*:1)**

    - **Cross-filter direction: Single**

    - **Make this relationship active**: Check this box

    - **Assume referential integrity**: Check this box

5. Click on **Ok**:

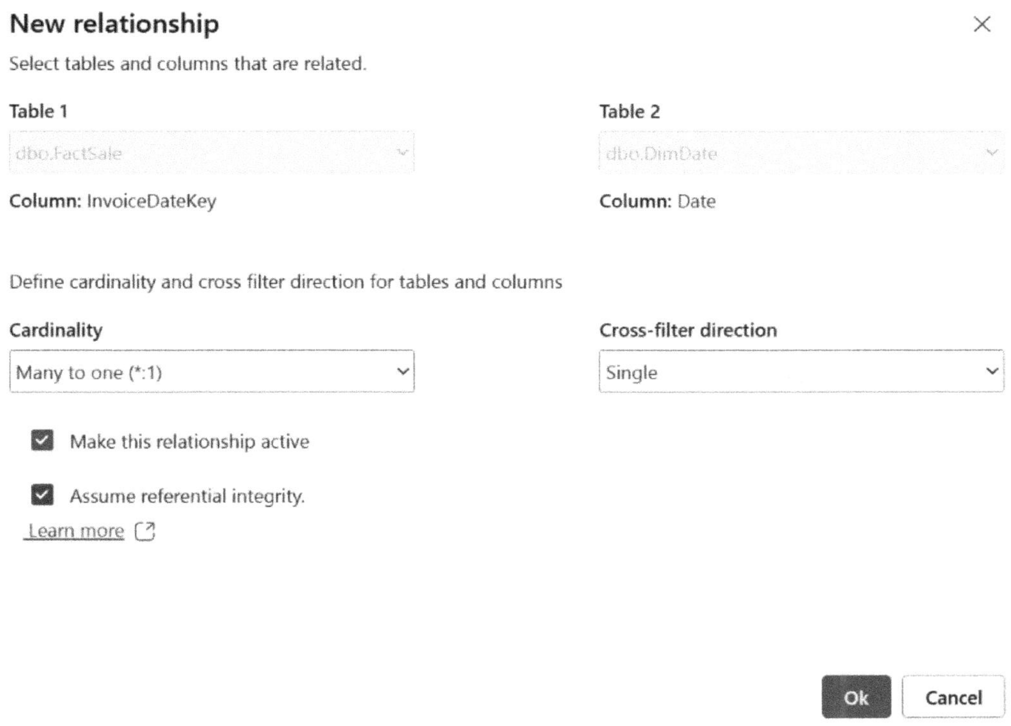

New relationship

Select tables and columns that are related.

Table 1

dbo.FactSale

Column: InvoiceDateKey

Table 2

dbo.DimDate

Column: Date

Define cardinality and cross filter direction for tables and columns

Cardinality

Many to one (*:1)

Cross-filter direction

Single

☑ Make this relationship active

☑ Assume referential integrity.

Learn more

Ok   Cancel

Figure 4.30 – Relationship configuration between the dbo.FactSale and dbo.DimDate tables

6. Repeat this process by dragging the **CityKey** field from dbo.FactSale to the **CityKey** field on dbo.DimCity and configuring and verifying the configuration as follows:

  - **Table 1**: dbo.FactSale

  - **Table 2**: dbo.DimCity

  - **Cardinality: Many to one (*:1)**

  - **Cross-filter direction: Single**

  - **Make this relationship active**: Check this box

  - **Assume referential integrity**: Check this box

7. Click on **Ok**.

8. Hide the stage.DimCity, stage.DimDate, and stage.FactSale tables by clicking the eye icon in the top-right corner of each table, as indicated in *Figure 4.31*. When complete, the data model should look like the following model:

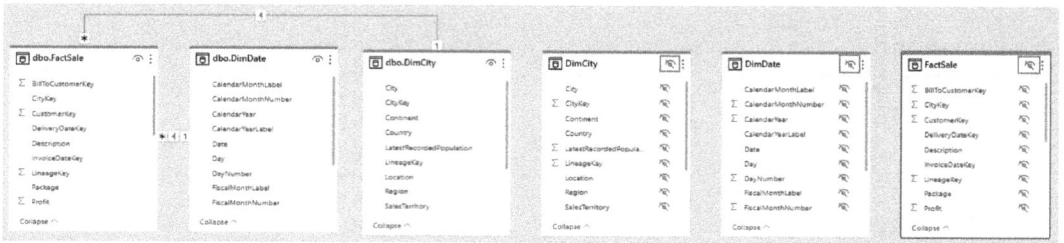

Figure 4.31 – The completed WWI data warehouse data model

9. On the data model canvas, select the `dbo.FactSale` table.

10. On the **Home** tab of the ribbon, click on **New measure**.

11. In the box at the top of the screen, enter the following **Data Analysis Expressions (DAX)** expression:

```
Profit Margin = SUM(FactSale[Profit])/
SUM(FactSale[TotalExcludingTax])
```

12. Press *Enter*. The measure will be created and can be found by scrolling to the bottom of the `dbo.FactSale` table:

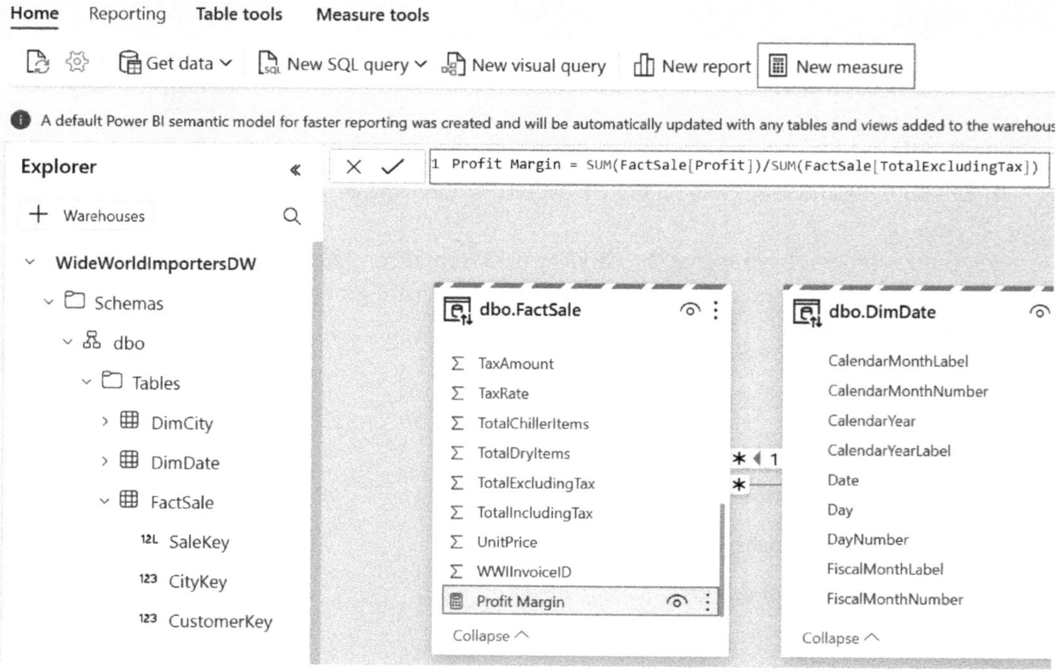

Figure 4.32 – The newly created Profit Margin calculation in the dbo.FactSale table

13. Select the **Profit Margin** calculation in the `dbo.FactSale` table.

14. On the **Properties** pane, change **Format** to **Percentage**:

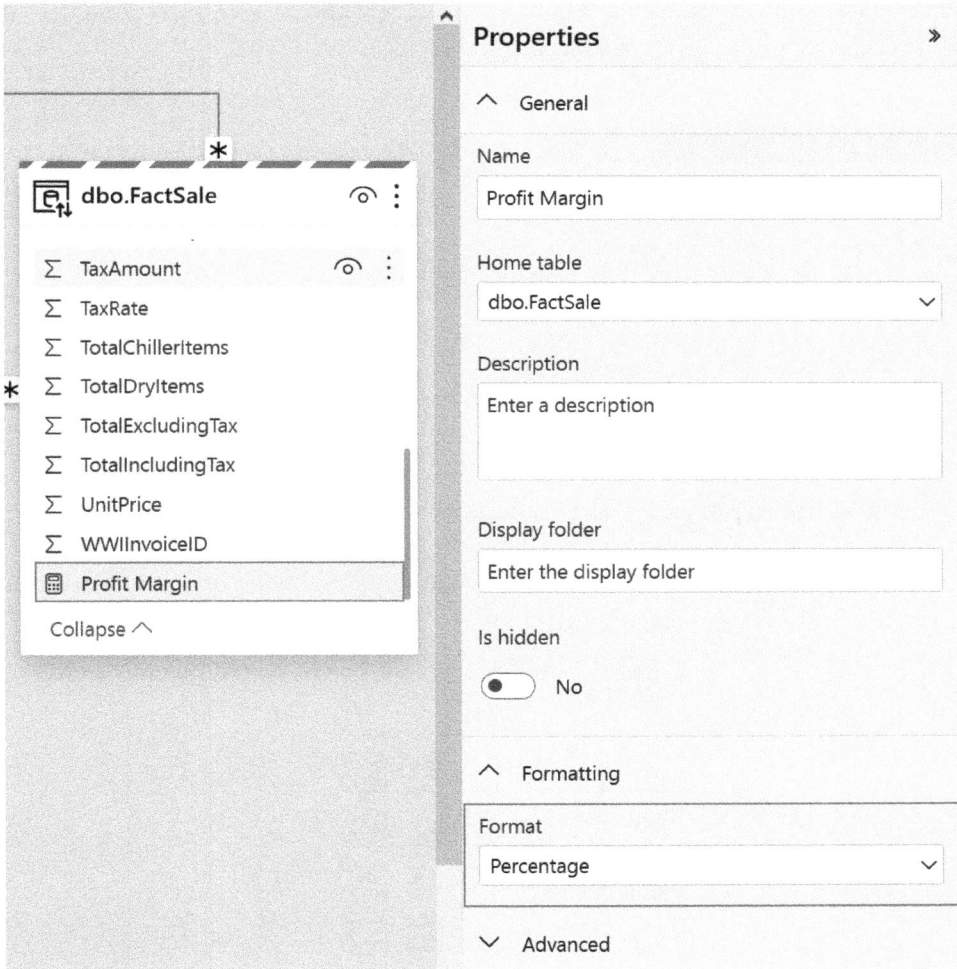

Figure 4.33 – The Properties pane for the Profit Margin calculation

15. Select the **Profit** field in the `dbo.FactSale` table.

16. On the **Properties** pane, change the **Format** value to **Currency**.

17. Select the **TotalExcludingTax** field in the `dbo.FactSale` table.

18. On the **Properties** pane, change the **Format** value to **Currency**.

19. From the **Home** tab of the ribbon, select **New Report**.

20. From the ribbon, select **Text box** to add a textbox to the report canvas.

21. Reposition the textbox to take up a small portion of the top of the report.

22. Enter a title for the report, such as `Wide World Importers - Sales Analysis`.

23. Change the font to a larger size for better visibility:

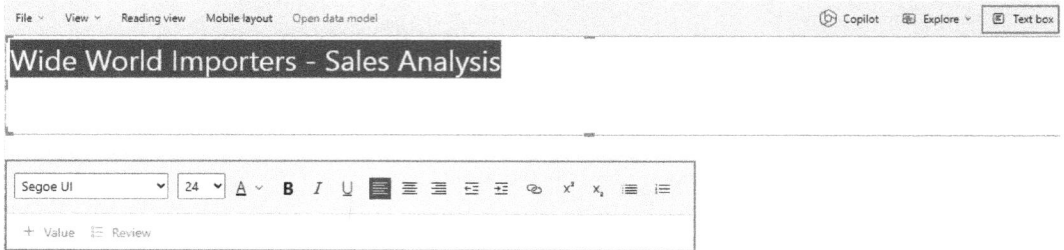

Figure 4.34 – The title of the WWI sales analysis report

24. Click on any blank space on the canvas to unselect the textbox.

25. From the **Visualizations** pane, select the stacked column chart:

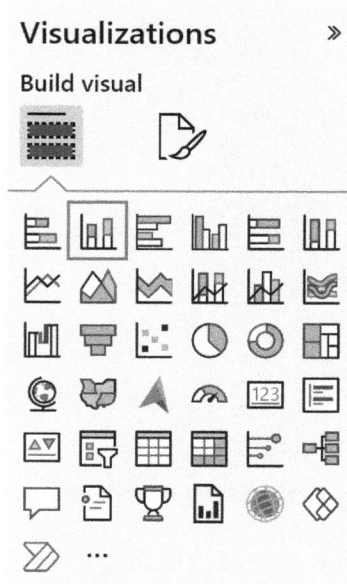

Figure 4.35 – The Visualizations pane in the Power BI report editor

26. Resize the visual to take up the left half of the page.

27. From the **Data** pane, drag and drop the field to the following locations in the **Visualizations** pane:

- **X-axis**: **SalesTerritory** from the `DimCity` table

- **Y-axis**: **TotalExcludingTax** and **Profit** from the `FactSale` table:

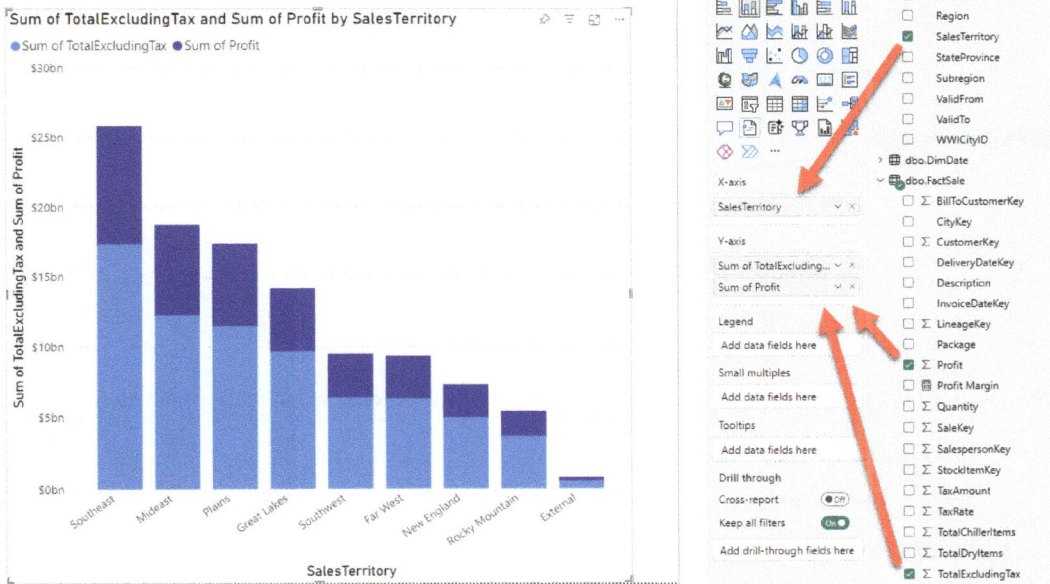

Figure 4.36 – The configured stacked column chart in the sales analysis report

28. Click on any blank space on the canvas to unselect the textbox.

29. From the **Visualizations** pane, select the multi-row card:

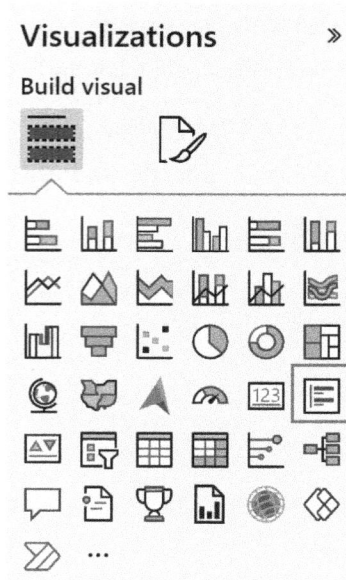

Figure 4.37 – The Visualizations pane in the Power BI report editor

30. From the **Data** pane, drag and drop the following fields to the **Fields** well in the **Visualizations** pane:

- **SalesTerritory** from `DimCity`
- **Profit** from `FactSale`
- **TotalExcludingTax** from `FactSale`
- **Profit Margin** from `FactSale`:

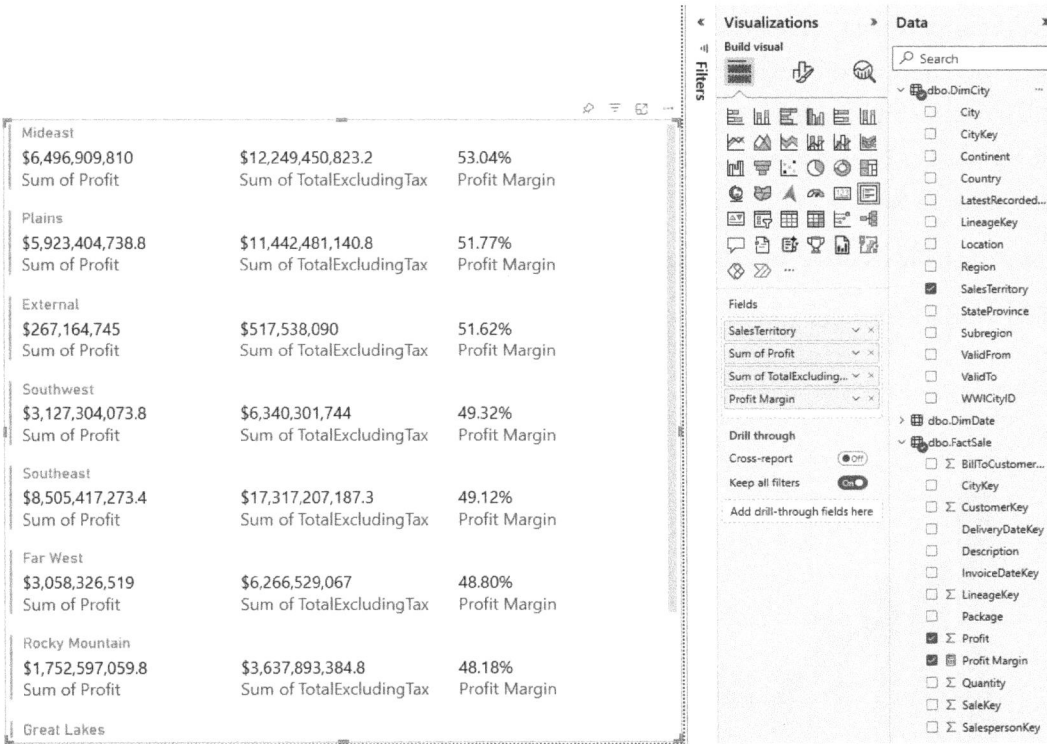

Figure 4.38 – The configured multi-row card visual

31. In the top-right corner of the multi-row card visual, click the ellipsis (…).

32. Select **Sort by** | **Profit Margin**:

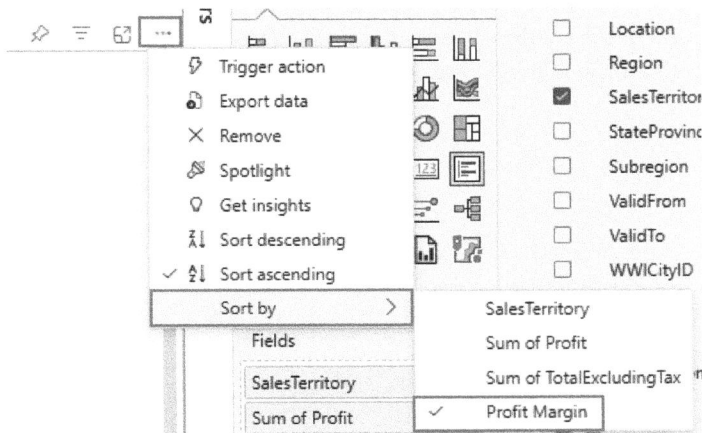

Figure 4.39 – The Sort by setting on the multi-card visual

33. In the top-right corner of the multi-row card visual, click on the ellipsis (**…**).

34. Select **Sort descending**.

35. From the ribbon select **File | Save**.

36. In the box labeled **Enter a name for your report**, type `Sales Analysis`.

37. Click on **Save**.

Upon saving, the report editor will close, and you are free to interact with your finished report:

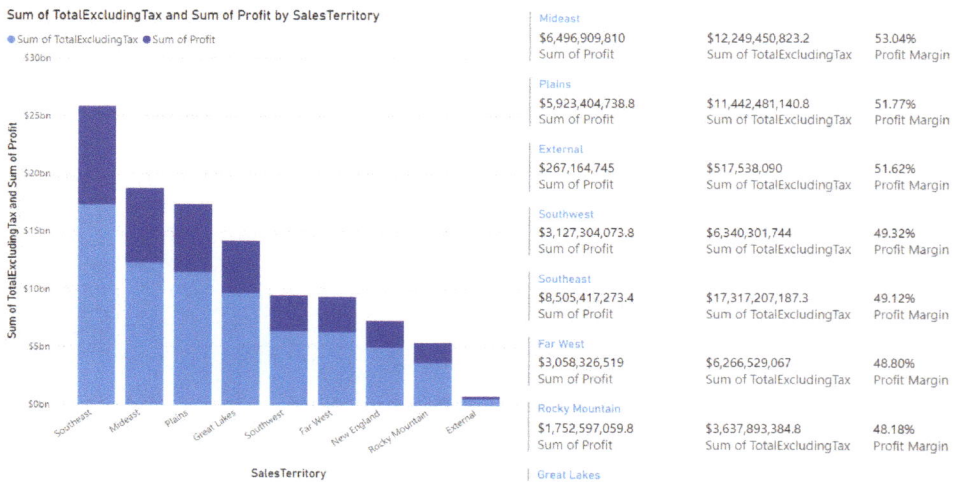

Figure 4.40 – The finalized sales analysis report

Clicking on any section of the column chart will filter the multi-row card visual. Likewise, clicking on a row in the card visual will highlight the corresponding data in the column chart.

Summary

As lakehouse implementations grow in popularity, data warehouses still play a key role in data-driven organizations. Many of the patterns that were explored in the prior lakehouse chapter can also be applied to a data warehouse. The major difference comes in the developer skillset. Lakehouses are Spark-centric, while data warehouses are T-SQL-centric. For the foreseeable future, these two items will live and work in tandem. Fabric provides a seamless experience to combine lakehouses and warehouses through OneCopy, cross-database querying, and standardizing on the Delta format.

In this chapter, you learned how to build out an end-to-end data warehouse analytics system. You learned how to create a data warehouse and a code-first and no-code approach for loading warehouse tables, how to transform data using T-SQL, and how to curate a data model that can then be used in a Power BI report. These are by no means the full extent of the data warehouse functionality but instead represent the foundational elements required for any data warehouse project on Fabric.

In the next chapter, you will learn how to build an end-to-end solution using Fabric Real-Time Analytics; you will use **Kusto Query Language** (**KQL**) to analyze the dataset.

5

Building an End-to-End Analytics System – Real-Time Analytics

Ask a business user how quickly they need their data available for analysis and the response will likely be "in real time." Discuss data latency with an architect and the conversation will involve functionality of the technology stack and cost. The reality for most use cases is that batch data processing is good enough. There are, however, times when real-time data is necessary.

Even in the case of real-time data processing, there will always be some amount of latency. When launching rockets into space carrying astronauts to the International Space Station, every microsecond counts. When transmitting GPS coordinates for directions, a second or two of latency is likely acceptable. When tracking sales at the local electronics retailer, real time starts to look more like microbatches.

There are several aspects of real-time data that need to be dealt with. First, how quickly can the data be transmitted after a datapoint is generated? For device telemetry, that could be instantaneously as a temperature reading is emitted by a sensor and immediately pushed off the measuring device. Meanwhile, **point of sale** (**POS**) transactions may be batched and sent off every 15 minutes. Next, upon being received, the data then needs to be processed. This often involves sending the data to multiple destinations. For instance, this could include one where the raw data will be persisted in long-term storage such as a data lake for later use in purpose-built downstream systems, and another output where a set of calculations based on a tumbling window are generated and displayed on a real-time report.

After data is received and stored, the challenge of how to analyze massive amounts of data remains. And even though Fabric's Real-Time Analytics workload can capture events and route them to multiple locations, it also shines in performing large-scale analysis scanning trillions of records in seconds.

In this chapter, you will explore how Fabric's Real-Time Analytics serves as the receiver, processor, storage, and analytics engine for large time-series datasets with partitioning, indexing, and scaling handled automatically. These same concepts apply to large batch data and streaming data alike. You will learn how to do the following:

- Creating a **Kusto Query Language** (**KQL**) database
- Capturing and delivering data using eventstreams
- Analyzing data with KQL
- Reporting with Power BI

Before you get started in Fabric, let's get a better understanding of the scenario that you will be building out in the remainder of this chapter.

Understanding the end-to-end scenario

Real-time analytics allows for a variety of valid use cases including streaming data processing, low-latency queries on large datasets, and querying complex formats such as nested JSON. There are three important concepts to understand:

- **Eventstreams:** This no-code experience captures, transforms, and routes events to destinations such as KQL databases or Fabric lakehouses.
- **KQL databases:** Data is stored and organized in tables that are organized in databases. A workspace can have multiple databases.
- **KQL queryset:** A KQL query is a request to process and display data in a specific manner. A queryset is a collection of queries from a particular workspace. Each query in a queryset can execute against different workspaces.

This chapter will focus on building a simplified real-time analytics architecture, as shown in *Figure 5.1*, but real-world scenarios often contain a wide array of data sources and downstream consumers. Not all data ingested into a KQL database must be generated in real time or even be real time in nature. Very often, reference datasets, such as a product list, a truck fleet manifest, or a sensor list, will be loaded in batches using a tool such as Data Factory.

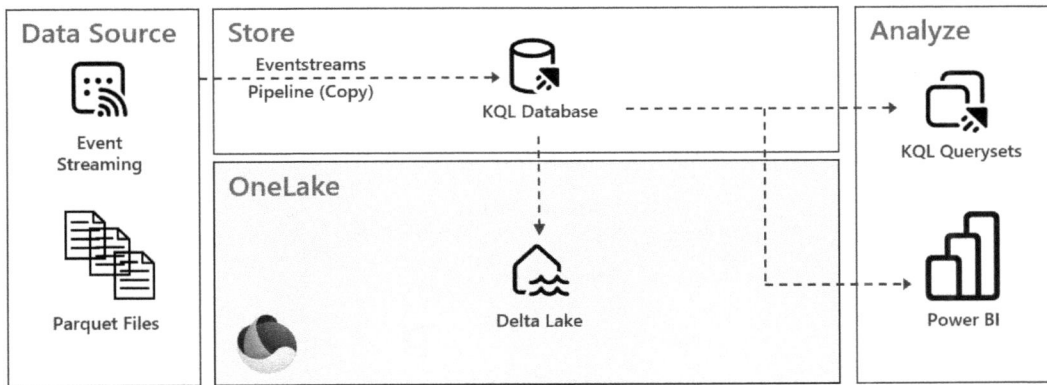

Figure 5.1 – The architecture to be built in Fabric Real-Time Analytics

For this exercise, you will ingest fictional stock exchange trades using an eventstream, store the data in a KQL database, perform ad hoc query analysis using a KQL queryset, and build a Power BI report that refreshes automatically.

Creating a Kusto Query Language (KQL) database

Like other databases, a KQL database organizes tables, materialized views, and functions. It is also the entry point where a user will go to access the data, whether that is by using the Fabric UX, Azure Data Explorer, or even Azure Data Studio. A Fabric workspace can hold multiple KQL databases. The KQL database that is created in this section will be used to store the stock exchange data generated later in this chapter.

Fabric has a core concept of storing a single copy of the data, which can then be used across all the compute engines. By default, the data in a KQL database is only accessible from the RTA experience. To allow the other Fabric experiences access to the data, it is necessary to enable the OneLake folder policy at the database level, which we will do later in this chapter. After enabling, all new tables created and populated are visible in OneLake and accessible through other Fabric experiences. This policy will be enabled as part of the database creation in this section.

To get started, follow these steps:

1. Open your web browser, navigate to Microsoft Fabric (`https://app.fabric.microsoft.com`), and sign in.

2. From the list of experiences, select **Synapse Real-Time Analytics**:

Figure 5.2 – Microsoft Fabric landing page and experience list

3. Select **Workspaces** from the left-hand navigation bar. Go to the workspace created in *Chapter 2, Understanding Different Workloads and Getting Started with Microsoft Fabric*, by typing its name in the search textbox at the top, then click on the workspace to open it. You can also pin it so that it always appears at the top of the list.

4. Select **New | KQL Database** in the top-left corner of the screen:

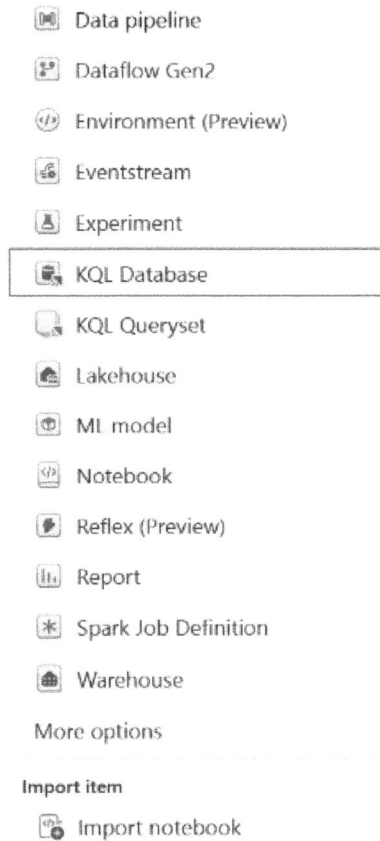

⬚ Data pipeline

⬚ Dataflow Gen2

⬚ Environment (Preview)

⬚ Eventstream

⬚ Experiment

⬚ KQL Database

⬚ KQL Queryset

⬚ Lakehouse

⬚ ML model

⬚ Notebook

⬚ Reflex (Preview)

⬚ Report

⬚ Spark Job Definition

⬚ Warehouse

More options

Import item

⬚ Import notebook

Figure 5.3 – New item list highlighting how to create a new KQL database

5. Enter `StockMarket` in the KQL database name box.

6. Ensure the dropdown for **Type** is set to **New database**.

7. Click on **Create**.

8. In the **Database details** section, click on the pencil icon next to the OneLake availability option.

9. Change the toggle to **Active** to enable the OneLake folder.

10. Click on **Done**.

With the KQL database created and the OneLake folder policy enabled, it is time to generate and populate some sample stock ticker data.

Capturing and delivering data using eventstreams

In this section, you will create an eventstream, which is designed to capture events from a variety of sources such as Azure Event Hubs or Kafka clients. There are built-in sample datasets such as the New York City taxi trips and the focus of this chapter, stock ticker data.

To get started, follow these steps:

1. Return to the workspace item list by clicking on the workspace name in the left-hand navigation bar.

2. Select **New** | **Eventstream** in the top-left corner of the screen.

3. In the **New Eventstream** dialog box, enter `StockMarket` for **Name** and select **Create**.

4. Click on the **New source** dropdown from the ribbon and select **Sample data**:

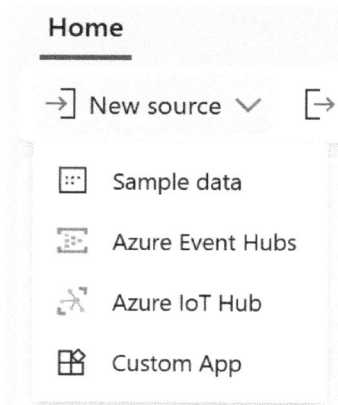

Figure 5.4 – The New source menu in the eventstream editor

5. Enter `SRC_StockMarket` in the **Source name** box.

6. Select **Stock Market** from the **Sample data** drop-down menu.

7. Click on **Add**.

8. From the ribbon, select **New destination** | **KQL Database**.

9. On the **KQL Database** screen, configure the following settings:

    *   **Data ingestion mode: Direct ingestion**

    *   **Destination name**: `KQL_StockMarket`

    *   **Workspace**: Select your workspace from the drop-down menu

    *   **KQL Database**: Select **StockMarket** from the drop-down menu

    Click on **Add and configure**.

10. In the **Select or create a destination table** section, click on **New table** located below the **StockMarket** database name.

11. Enter `StockMarket` for the table name and click the check mark.

12. Click on **Next**.

13. On the **Inspect the data** screen, change the **Format** dropdown to **JSON**.

14. Click on **Edit columns** from the options in the top-right corner of the screen.

15. Locate the **lastUpdated** field in the column list.

16. Change the **Type** to **datetime** and **Mapping transformation** to **DateTimeFromUnixMilliseconds**.

17. Locate the **lastSaleTime** field, change the **Type** to **datetime**, and set **Mapping transformation** to **DateTimeFromUnixMilliseconds**.

18. Click on **Create and configure** and do the following:

   · **KQL Database**: Select **StockMarket** from the drop-down menu

   · Below the **Destination table** box, select **Create new**

   · On the **Create new table** dialog, enter `StockMarket` and click **Done**

   · **Input data format: Json**

   Click on **Add**.

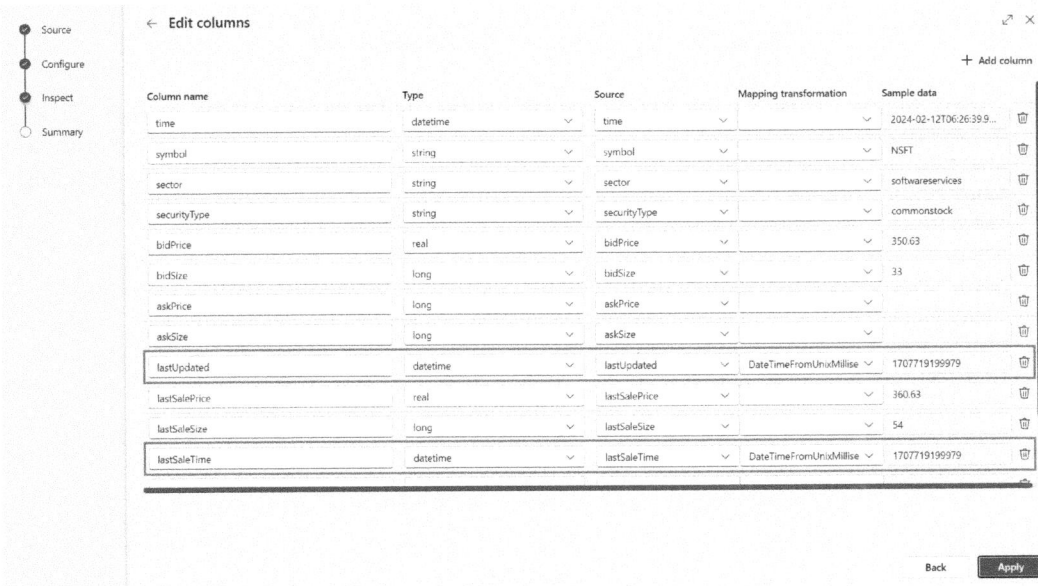

Column name	Type		Source		Mapping transformation	Sample data	
time	datetime	∨	time	∨		2024-02-12T06:26:39.9...	
symbol	string	∨	symbol	∨	∨	NSFT	
sector	string	∨	sector	∨	∨	softwareservices	
securityType	string	∨	securityType	∨	∨	commonstock	
bidPrice	real	∨	bidPrice	∨	∨	350.63	
bidSize	long	∨	bidSize	∨	∨	33	
askPrice	long	∨	askPrice	∨	∨		
askSize	long	∨	askSize	∨			
lastUpdated	datetime	∨	lastUpdated	∨	DateTimeFromUnixMillise ∨	1707719199979	
lastSalePrice	real	∨	lastSalePrice	∨	∨	360.63	
lastSaleSize	long	∨	lastSaleSize	∨	∨	54	
lastSaleTime	datetime	∨	lastSaleTime	∨	DateTimeFromUnixMillise ∨	1707719199979	

Figure 5.5 – The column configuration page of the eventstream KQL destination

19. Click on **Apply** to close the column editor.
20. Click on **Finish**.
21. On the **Summary** page, click on **Close**.

After a few seconds, the status on the **KQL_StockMarket** destination will change to **Ingesting**. A preview of the incoming data can be seen by clicking on the **StockMarket** eventstream in the middle of the canvas:

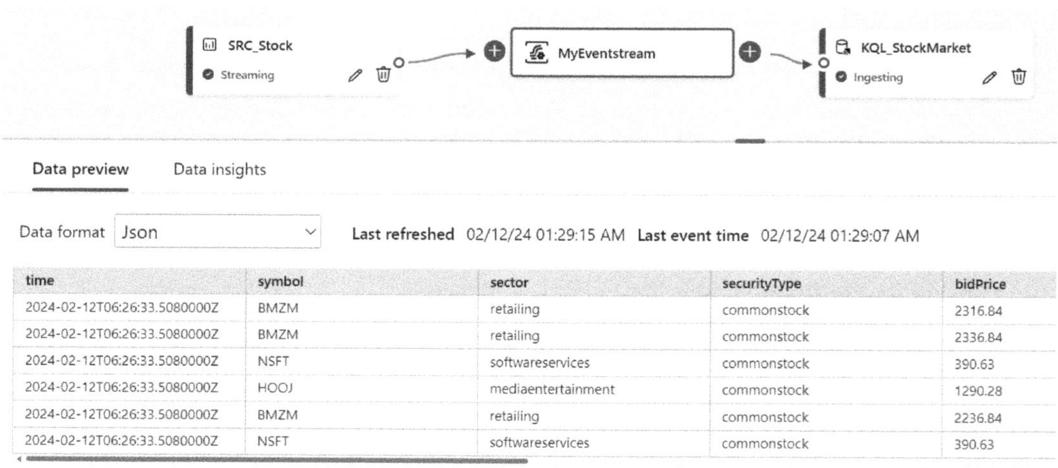
SRC_Stock
Streaming
MyEventstream
KQL_StockMarket
Ingesting
Data preview
Data insights
Data format
Json
Last refreshed 02/12/24 01:29:15 AM
Last event time 02/12/24 01:29:07 AM
time
symbol
sector
securityType
bidPrice
2024-02-12T06:26:33.5080000Z BMZM retailing commonstock 2316.84
2024-02-12T06:26:33.5080000Z BMZM retailing commonstock 2336.84
2024-02-12T06:26:33.5080000Z NSFT softwareservices commonstock 390.63
2024-02-12T06:26:33.5080000Z HOOJ mediaentertainment commonstock 1290.28
2024-02-12T06:26:33.5080000Z BMZM retailing commonstock 2236.84
2024-02-12T06:26:33.5080000Z NSFT softwareservices commonstock 390.63

Figure 5.6 – The eventstream data preview page

Switching to the **Data insights** tab will display metrics related to the data flowing through the eventstream, including the number of messages and the size of the messages. This information is useful for monitoring the activity and performance of the eventstream. Data insights, along with slightly different metrics, are also available on event hub sources and lakehouse destinations.

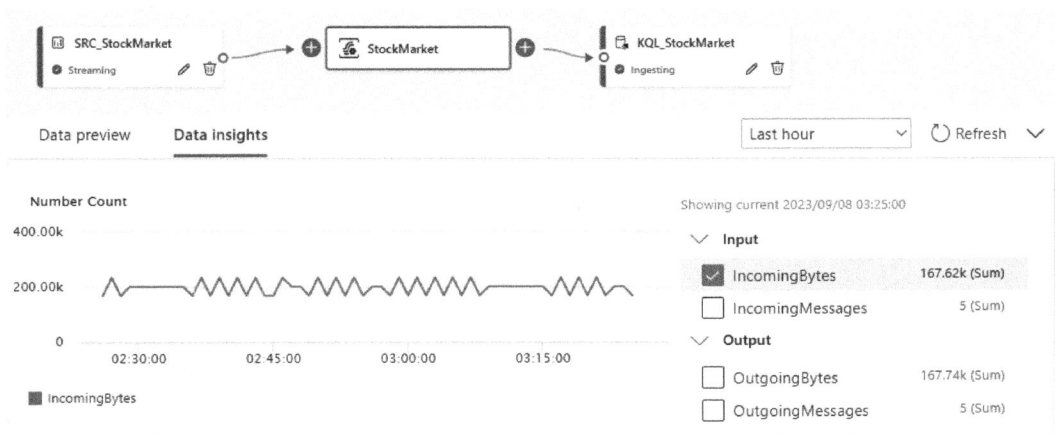

Figure 5.7 – The Data insights page for a Real-Time Analytics eventstream

Now that the data is flowing into the KQL database, let's explore how to query and analyze the data using KQL and querysets.

Analyzing data with KQL

With SQL Server, a user will interact with data using T-SQL; with Spark, they will use Scala, PySpark, or SparkSQL, and with a KQL database, they will use KQL. This is an extremely powerful yet straightforward and easy-to-learn language that will allow you to explore data. Just like other query languages, KQL uses a database context along with tables and columns to identify the data to query.

The structure of a query is slightly different from many of the common SQL languages because it starts with a table followed by operators that accept a tabular input and return a tabular output, which can then be returned to the user or passed to the next operator for further refinement. A few examples of operators are where, summarize, union, and join.

> **Note**
> The entirety of the KQL language is case-sensitive, including table names, column names, and operators.

With a few basics about query structure out of the way, let's dive into analyzing the stock exchange data using KQL by following these steps:

1. Return to the workspace item list by clicking on the workspace name in the left-hand navigation bar.

2. Select **New | KQL Queryset** in the top-left corner of the screen.

3. Enter `StockMarketExploration` in the name box.

4. Click on **Create**.

5. From the list of available databases, select the **StockMarket** KQL database from your workspace. This should be the first item on the list. Use the filters or **Explorer** if necessary to locate your database:

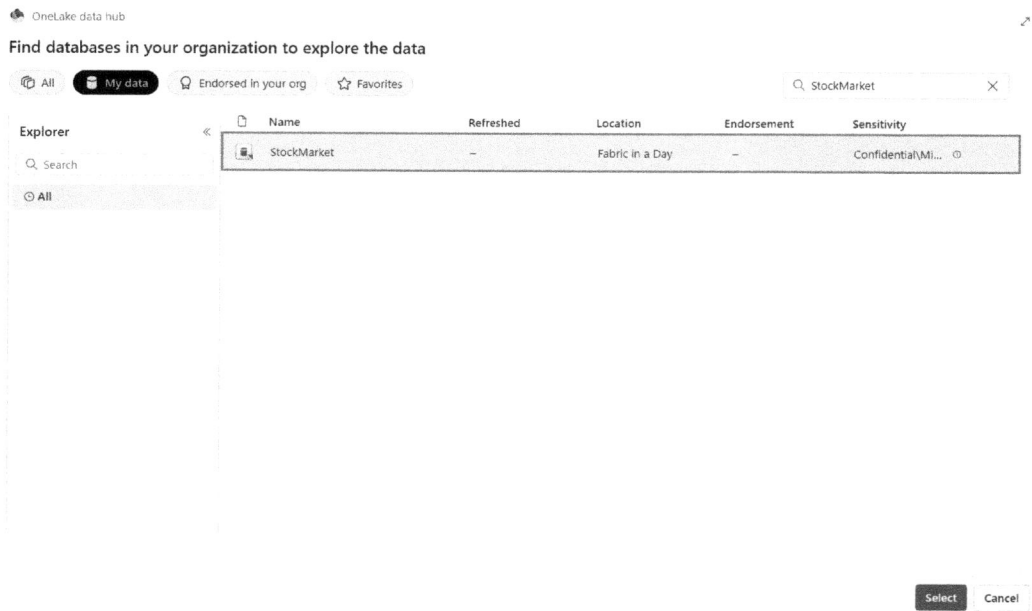

Figure 5.8 – List of KQL databases a user has access to associated with the KQL queryset

6. Click on **Select**.

7. Delete all the code snippets from the script so the query editor is blank.

8. To see how many records have been ingested so far and review the results, type the following query into the editor and click on **Run** on the ribbon:

```
StockMarket
| count
```

Your record count will likely be different than those shown in *Figure 5.9* as data streams in:

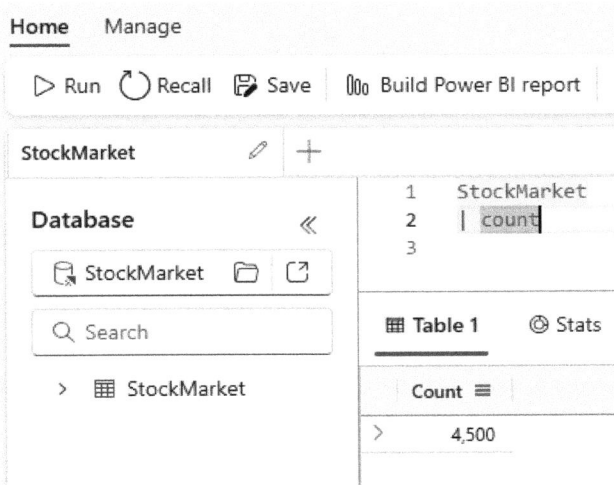

Figure 5.9 – The results showing the count of records in the StockMarket table

9. Run the following code to see 10 random records:

```
StockMarket
| limit 10
```

10. Use KQL to build a simple line chart showing the average bid price for the NSFT stock using the following code:

```
StockMarket
| where symbol == "NSFT"
| summarize avg(bidPrice) by lastUpdated
| render timechart
```

```
1    StockMarket
2    | where symbol == "NSFT"
3    | summarize avg(bidPrice) by lastUpdated
4    | render timechart
```

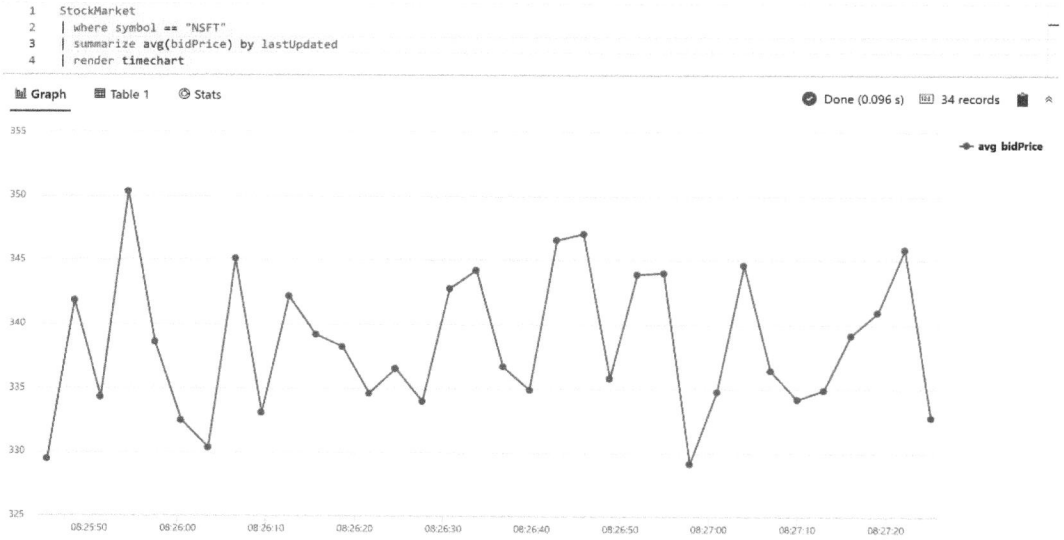

Figure 5.10 – A KQL query showing the average bidPrice for a stock rendered as a timechart

11. Run the following SQL command to display the total bid size and average bid price by ticker symbol:

```
SELECT
      symbol,
      SUM(bidSize) AS TotalBidSize,
      AVG(bidPrice) AS AverageBidPrice
      FROM StockMarket
   GROUP BY symbol
```

The KQL engine will convert this code to KQL automatically and return the result:

```
13    SELECT
14       symbol,
15       SUM(bidSize) AS TotalBidSize,
16       AVG(bidPrice) AS AverageBidPrice
17       FROM StockMarket
18    GROUP BY symbol
19
```

symbol	TotalBidSize	AverageBidPrice
> HOOJ	153,737	1,319.8827563842958
> NSFT	149,273	341.0110295905996
> BMZM	153,508	2,286.3290510948796

Figure 5.11 – Running a SQL query against a KQL database

12. The KQL queryset will save automatically as changes are made, but you can click on the **Save** button on the ribbon to ensure the most recent changes are saved should an error occur with the autosave while editing.

This only scratches the surface of what can be done with KQL and eventstreams. There is a whole world of analytical possibilities including geospatial analysis, window functions, missing data inference, graphs, functions, and so much more.

Now that we know a little bit about the dataset from running some exploratory queries, let's see how to build a Power BI report using this real-time dataset.

Reporting with Power BI

As with all the experiences in Fabric, real-time analytics integrates seamlessly with Power BI to create stunning visuals and actionable reporting. You can start creating a Power BI report directly from a KQL database or a KQL queryset. This will automatically create a dataset so you can get to work building the report quickly.

While not covered in this book, you can author reports in Power BI Desktop as well, as you are not restricted to the web browser report development experience. This is accomplished by copying the query URI from the KQL database in Fabric and entering it in Power BI Desktop's Azure Data Explorer (Kusto) connector.

Creating a new Power BI report

Before we can add any visualizations to a Power BI report, we first need to create a blank report that is connected to a KQL database. This can be accomplished in a variety of ways from the web browser and Power BI Desktop. In this chapter, we will start building the report from within the web browser.

Let's get started building a report with Power BI by following these steps:

1. Return to the workspace item list by clicking on the workspace name in the left-hand navigation bar.

2. From the item list, click on the **StockMarket** KQL database.

3. From the ribbon, click on **Refresh**.

4. In **Data tree**, click on the **StockMarket** table.

5. From the ribbon, click on **Build Power BI report**:

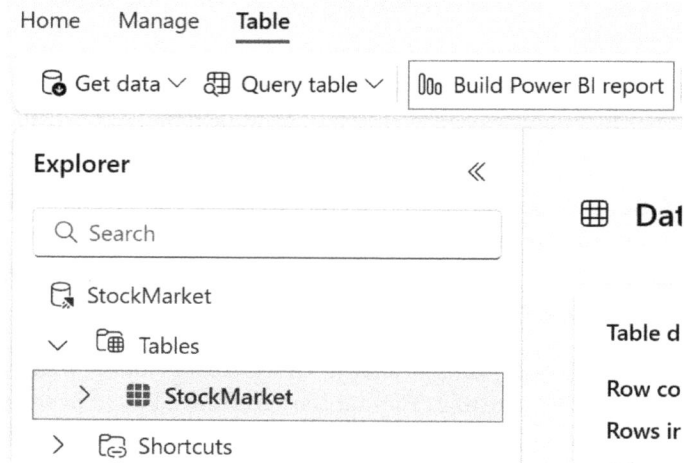

Figure 5.12 – The KQL database overview and data tree

6. From the ribbon, click on the **Text box** button.

7. Make the following changes to the text box:

- Enter the text `Stock Market - Bid Analysis`

- Change the font size to 44

- Center-align the text

- Resize the text box to span the full width of the report canvas

- Reposition the text box to the top edge of the report canvas

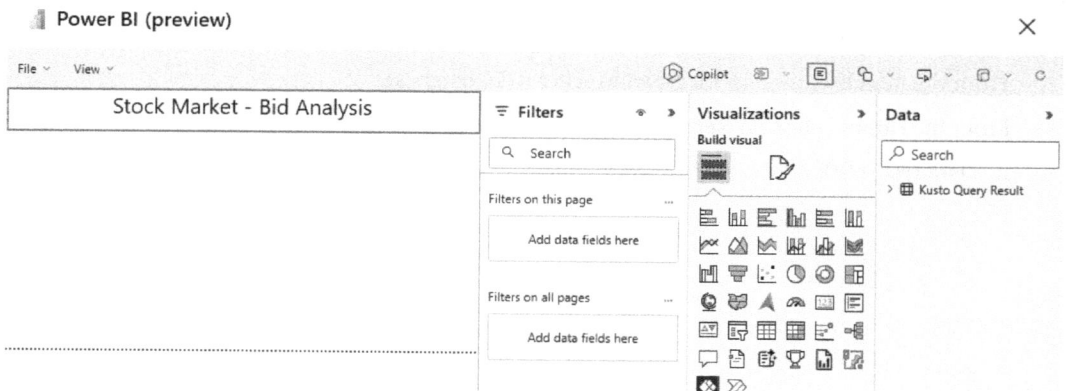

Figure 5.13 – Power BI report with a title text box configured

Up to this point, a few key steps have been performed, the most important being connecting the Power BI report to the KQL database. There are several ways to accomplish this task, but launching the report from the KQL database directly is the most straightforward and simple method.

Adding visualizations to the Power BI report

Now that the Power BI report has been created, a title has been added, and it is connected to your KQL database, it is time to build visualizations that will help tell a story about the stock market data that is flowing in.

Start building visualizations into the report by following these steps:

1. Click anywhere on a blank portion of the report canvas to ensure nothing is selected.
2. In the **Visualizations** pane, click on the card visual:

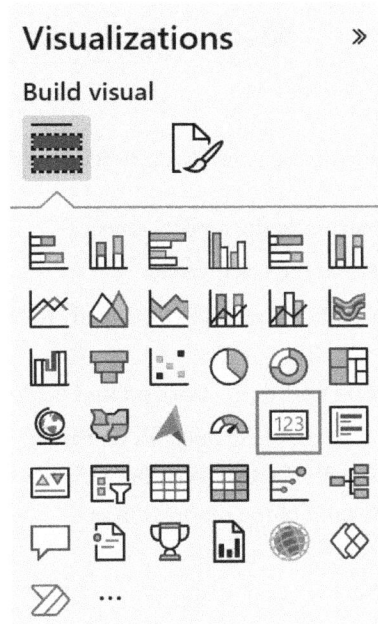

Figure 5.14 – The Visualizations pane with the card visual highlighted

3. Change the width to be approximately half the width of the report canvas and positioned on the left side of the canvas. If necessary, reposition the card to be just under the text box created earlier in this exercise.

4. In the **Data** pane, check the box next to the **symbol** field.

5. In the **Visualizations** pane, locate the **symbol** field in the **Fields** section. Click on the dropdown on the right side of the field and select **Count** to change the display to be a count of the records in the table:

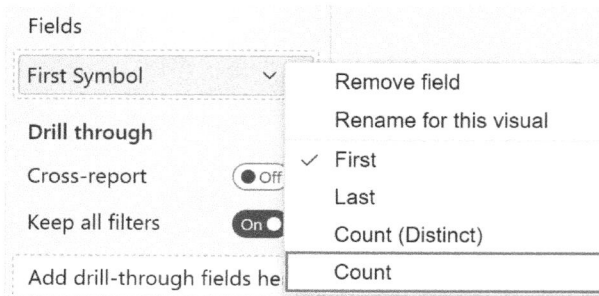

Figure 5.15 – Changing the symbol field to display a record count

6. Click anywhere on a blank portion of the report canvas.

7. In the **Visualizations** pane, select the **Card** visual.

8. Resize and reposition the card on the canvas to be directly to the right of the count of records card that was just created.

9. In the **Data** pane, check the box next to the **lastUpdated** field.

10. In the **Visualizations** pane, click on the dropdown on the right side of the **lastUpdated** field and change the aggregation to **Latest** so the card reflects the most recent record update date.

11. Click anywhere on a blank portion of the report canvas.

12. In the **Visualizations** pane, click on **line chart**:

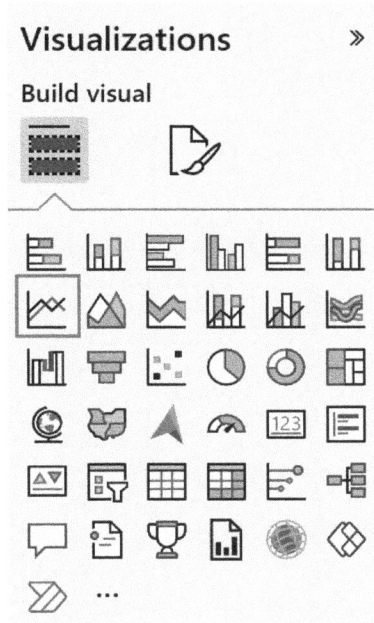

Figure 5.16 – The Visualizations pane with the line chart visual highlighted

13. Resize and reposition the visual to take up the remaining empty space on the left half of the report canvas.

14. In the **Data** pane, check the box next to **bidSize** to add it to the **Y-axis**.

15. In the **Data** pane, check the box next to **lastUpdated** to add it to the **X-axis**.

16. In the **Data** pane, check the box next to **symbol** to add it to **Legend**.

17. In the **Filters** pane, expand the **lastUpdated** field in the **Filters on this visual** section.

18. Change the **Filter type** from **Basic filtering** to **Relative time**.

19. Enter 5 in the box below the **Show items when the value is in the last** setting.

20. Change the **hours** setting to **minutes**.

21. Click on **Apply filter**.

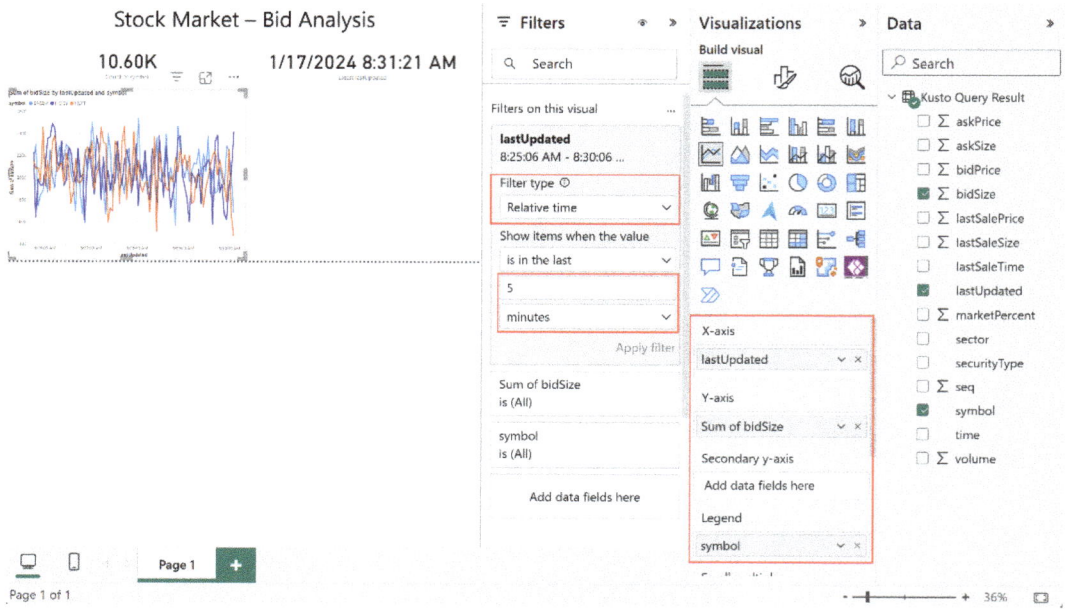

Figure 5.17 – Fully configured line chart including field choices and filter settings

22. Click anywhere on a blank portion of the report canvas.

23. In the **Visualizations** pane, click on **line chart**.

24. If necessary, resize and reposition the visual to take up the remaining empty space on the report canvas.

25. In the **Data** pane, check the box next to **lastUpdated** to add it to the **X-axis**.

26. In the **Data** pane, check the box next to **bidPrice** to add it to the **Y-axis**.

27. In the **Visualizations** pane, locate the **Sum of bidPrice** field, click the dropdown on the right side of the field name, and change the aggregation to **Average**.

28. Apply the same date filter from the bidSize line chart by locating the **lastUpdated** field in the **Filters** pane, changing the filter type to **Relative time** to show values in the last **5 minutes**, and clicking on **Apply filter**:

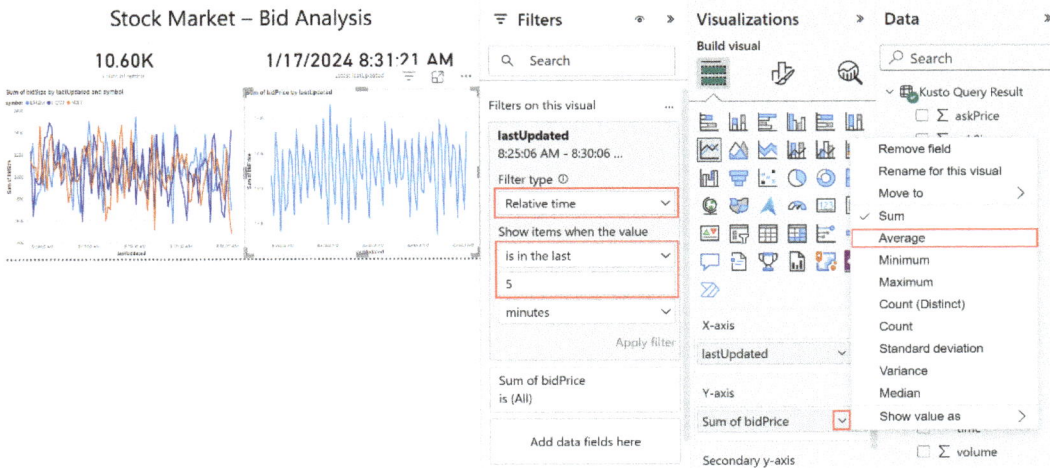

Figure 5.18 – Line chart showing the bidPrice aggregation change from Sum to Average

With all the report visualizations built, it is time to shift the focus to enabling near real-time data refresh.

Configure page refresh on the Power BI report

The eventstream and KQL database will handle consuming all the stock market data but there is still a need to display the data in near real-time on the Power BI report. While the report will not have data pushed to it and automatically displayed, it can be configured to refresh the visuals on a regular basis. This refresh can be as frequent as a few seconds, but the tenant administrators do have the ability to restrict what refresh frequencies are available.

Let's look at how to enable page refresh:

1. Click anywhere on a blank portion of the report canvas.

2. In the **Visualizations** pane, switch to the **Format** page.

3. Toggle the **Page refresh** setting to **On**.

4. Expand the **Page refresh** setting and set it to refresh every 10 seconds:

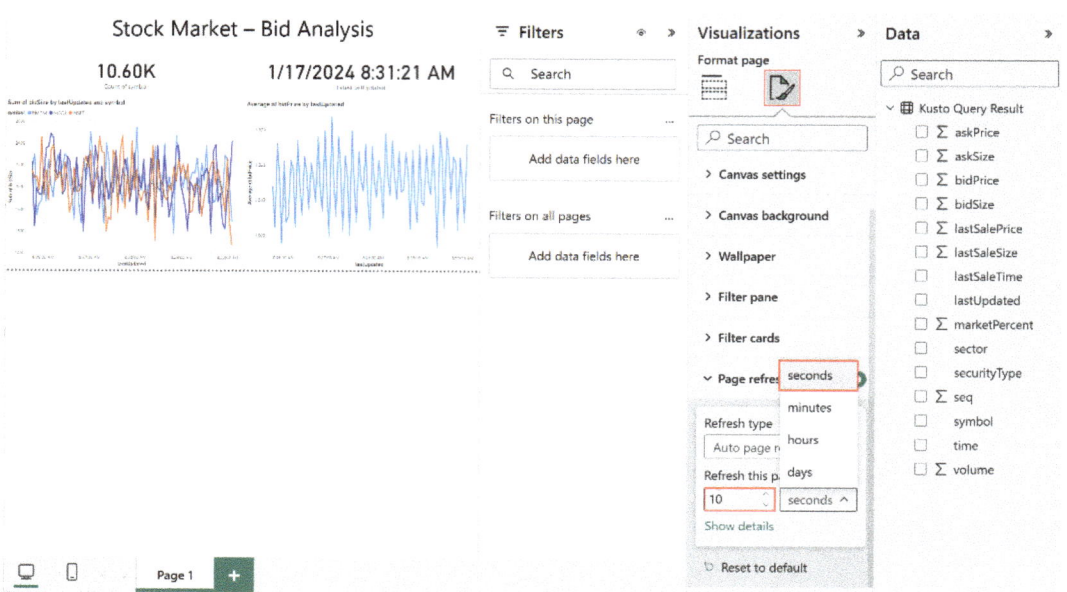

Figure 5.19 – Power BI page refresh configuration settings

5. From the ribbon, click **File | Save**.

6. Enter Bid Analysis for the name.

7. Select the workspace where all your items from this exercise are located.

8. Click on **Continue**.

9. Click on the link with the text **Open the file in Power BI to view, edit, and get a shareable link** to open the report:

Figure 5.20 – The report saved page with a link to open the report in a new browser window

After the report opens, it will automatically refresh the page and show updated data every 10 seconds. If the page does not refresh after 10 seconds, note that admins can set minimum refresh intervals that override the page refresh value configured on the report page, causing the refresh to not occur for several minutes.

Power BI, eventstreams, and KQL databases come together to create compelling analytics. Best of all, this entire end-to-end experience is done without ever leaving Fabric. When a Power BI report is set to automatically refresh, the data is always kept up-to-date as new data is streamed in.

Summary

The importance of real-time data cannot be overstated. It can mean a more reliable business function, a competitive edge, or an experience not previously possible. Fabric's Real-Time Analytics enables organizations to collect data from sources such as IoT devices and telemetry through eventstreams or land large datasets using tools such as Data Factory.

The RTA experience is the perfect solution for analyzing billions or even trillions of records in seconds. With seamless integration to expose data in OneLake, you can take the same data from a KQL database and consume it through shortcuts in a lakehouse to create new data products and extend the analytics using Spark.

In this chapter, you learned how to create an end-to-end real-time analytics solution. You learned how to create a KQL database, use an eventstream to load real-time stock ticker data into the database, use the Kusto Query Language to explore and analyze the data, and use this data stream in a Power BI report. There are many other capabilities that were not discussed, but this represents a few of the core capabilities of Real-Time Analytics in Fabric.

In the next chapter, you will learn how to build an end-to-end solution using Fabric Data Science, in which you will explore the power of artificial intelligence and machine learning.

6

Building an End-to-End Analytics System – Data Science

Almost every organization on the planet is on its journey of taking advantage of innovation and the advancements of **artificial intelligence (AI)** and **machine learning (ML)**. However, the challenge is that there are so many products and libraries to consider that you will spend most of your time trying to figure out ways of doing it right and promptly.

Microsoft Fabric has been designed from the ground up for the era of ML and AI to drive business value for your organization.

In this chapter, you will learn about the data science capabilities in Fabric by following the end-to-end data science life cycle and building an ML model, all the way from data ingestion to cleansing, feature engineering, training, and operationalizing models. We will cover the following topics:

- Understanding the data science project development life cycle and how Fabric's capabilities help in each of the stages
- Data and storage – creating a lakehouse and ingesting data using Apache Spark
- Problem formulation/ideation (business understanding)
- Data acquisition, discovery, and preprocessing
- Experimenting and modeling
- Enriching and operationalizing
- Analyzing and getting insights

Let's get started!

Technical requirements

This chapter assumes you have followed the instructions mentioned in the *Getting started with Microsoft Fabric* section of *Chapter 2, Understanding Different Workloads and Getting Started with Microsoft Fabric*, to create/enable Fabric in your tenant and have created a Fabric workspace to work in.

The code files for this chapter are available on GitHub at `https://github.com/PacktPublishing/Learn-Microsoft-Fabric/tree/main/ch6`.

End-to-end data science scenario

A typical data analytics system for data science in Fabric would consist of the components and layers shown in *Figure 6.1*:

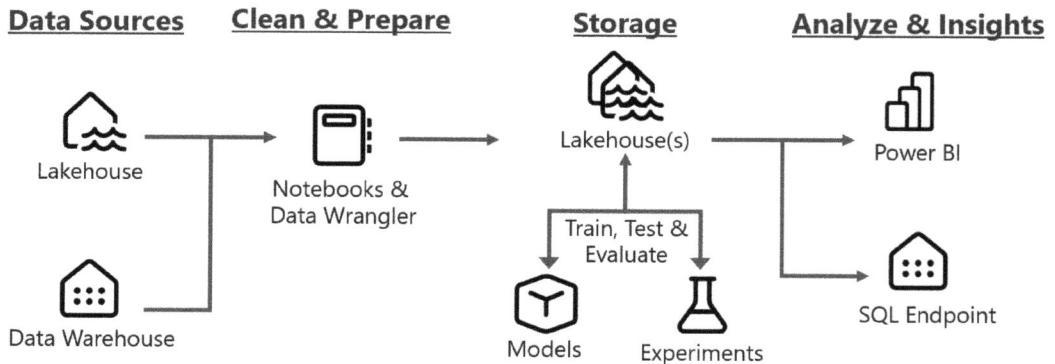

Figure 6.1 – Reference architecture for data science in Fabric

Let's review these components in detail:

- **Data sources**: To ingest data into the lakehouse either from Azure data services or from other cloud platforms or on-premise sources, Fabric provides native or built-in ready-to-use connectors to make use of it, which makes building a data ingestion flow quick and easy. In Fabric, you might also use the data from the lakehouse and data warehouse, which you have brought in and transformed, to train your model.

- **Data cleansing and preparation**: Fabric offers different options for you to prepare, clean, and transform your data before you train your model efficiently. For example, if you prefer a user interface experience, you can use Data Wrangler, with its intuitive interface for data preparation, and then use the code generated by Data Wrangler to make it operational. Alternatively, if you are a code-first user and prefer writing code, you can use a notebook with Apache Spark, which provides more flexibility and control. Additionally, the Fabric runtime comes pre-installed with popular libraries so that you can quickly make use of it without any additional installation and setup. Furthermore, if you require any additional libraries, you can install them (custom libraries or public libraries from `https://pypi.org/` or `https://conda.io/`) either in your Spark session or at the workspace level for all Spark sessions.

- **Experiments and models**: Fabric natively supports creating an **experiment** and a **model** to train, evaluate, and score ML models. These experiments and model artifacts have native integration with MLflow (`https://mlflow.org/`) for tracking, logging, registration, and operationalization.

  You can create an experiment using a user interface that's available as part of the Data Science experience in Fabric or programmatically in a notebook. An experiment allows you to train a model and track its execution. For each of the model training steps, you create a *run* in the experience, which tracks model execution, the dataset and parameters used, and so on. An experiment consists of multiple *runs*, and you can compare these runs to determine the best-performing model among them. Once you have trained the model, you can register and save it as a **model**. Later, this model can be used to score new incoming data. This model supports saving multiple versions of the trained model; you can compare these versions and choose the best-performing model version so that you can generate predictions and insights on your new incoming data.

- **Storage**: Fabric standardizes on Delta Lake (`https://delta.io/`), which means all the engines of Fabric can read and work on the same dataset stored in Fabric – there's no need for data duplicity. For this chapter, we will ingest an open dataset into the lakehouse and use it to prepare and transform the data so that we can train an ML model.

- **Analyze and insights**: Data from a lakehouse can be visualized in a notebook with Apache Spark for **exploratory data analysis** (**EDA**) or can be consumed by Power BI, the industry-leading BI tool for reporting and visualization. Power BI in Fabric now supports Direct Lake mode, which improves performance significantly while still accessing the data directly from the lakehouse to maintain its freshness. When doing EDA in a notebook, you can make use of several popular libraries, such as `seaborn`, `matplotlib`, `plotly`, and many more. Fabric also includes the Semantic Link (`SemPy`) library so that you can query, access, and visualize the data from a Power BI semantic model.

Data science projects are experimental and have an iterative flow that consists of the stages shown in *Figure 6.2*:

> **Note**
>
> *Figure 6.2* shows a simplified example of the different stages of the data science project life cycle. You can learn more about these industry-standard data science project life cycles at the following links:
>
> - *The Team Data Science Process lifecycle*: `https://learn.microsoft.com/en-us/azure/architecture/data-science-process/lifecycle`
> - *CRISP-DM*: `https://www.datascience-pm.com/crisp-dm-2/`

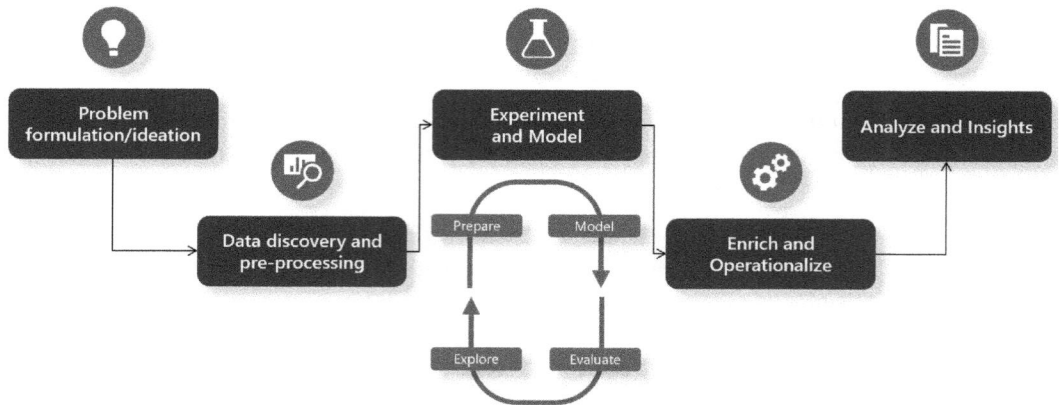

Figure 6.2 – Data science project life cycle and its stages

Let's review these stages in detail:

- **Problem formulation/ideation**: In this first stage, you clearly define your problem by answering why you are undertaking this project, what its impact will be, how it's going to drive business value, and so on. Often, it takes several attempts to get a clear problem statement. Likewise, it may be necessary to revise the problem formulation after some time due to the changing landscape or evolution of the problem itself. You can learn more about this here: https://www.datascience-pm.com/crisp-dm-2/.

- **Data discovery and preprocessing**: In this stage, in collaboration with the data engineering team, you discover your data (internal or external) and integrate it into one location to further cleanse it from any erroneous or missing data, normalize it, or join it with other data so that it's ready to train your model.

- **Experiment and model:** In this stage, you iteratively train your model by using different datasets, different ML algorithms, different sets of hyperparameters, and so on, and then evaluate its accuracy.

- **Enrich and operationalize**: Once you are satisfied with your model and its accuracy level, you need to put it into operation so that you can start scoring or making predictions on the new incoming data.

- **Analyze and insights**: In this stage, you can run prediction or scoring on your data and analyze it further to get actional insights. Furthermore, you can analyze predicted data from the lakehouse in Power BI using Direct Lake mode, which makes this possible without the need to load the data.

The Data Science experience in Microsoft Fabric includes tools and technologies to empower you at every stage of the data science project life cycle, all the way from helping you understand and define the problem to data cleansing, feature engineering, model training and evaluation, operationalizing, and gathering actional insights.

Now that we understand the data science project life cycle and its stages, we'll implement it by creating a lakehouse to store the data.

Data and storage – creating a lakehouse and ingesting data using Apache Spark

To ingest data into the lakehouse, you can use an existing lakehouse or create a new one. Follow these steps to create a new lakehouse for this chapter:

1. After logging into your Fabric tenant, select the **Workspaces** flyout from the left hand.

2. Search for the workspace (`Learn Microsoft Fabric`) that you created in *Chapter 2, Understanding Different Workloads and Getting Started with Microsoft Fabric*, by typing its name into the search box at the top and clicking on your workspace to open it. You can also pin it so that it always appears at the top of the list.

3. From the workload switcher located at the bottom left of the screen, select **Data Engineering**.

4. In the **Data Engineering** experience, under + **New**, select **Lakehouse** to create a lakehouse.

5. Enter `nyctaxilake` in the **Name** box and click **Create**. The new lakehouse will be created and opened automatically.

Importing notebooks

Let's import the sample notebooks that have been provided as part of this chapter:

1. Download the notebooks in the `ch6` folder of this book's GitHub repository (at `https://github.com/PacktPublishing/Learn-Microsoft-Fabric`) to your local machine. If required, unzip or uncompress it.

2. From the workload switcher located at the bottom left of the screen, select **Data Science**. As shown in *Figure 6.3*, select **Import notebook** from the **New** section at the top of the landing page of the **Data Science** experience:

New

Current workspace: 🐝 **Learn Microsoft Fabric**

Items will be saved to this workspace.

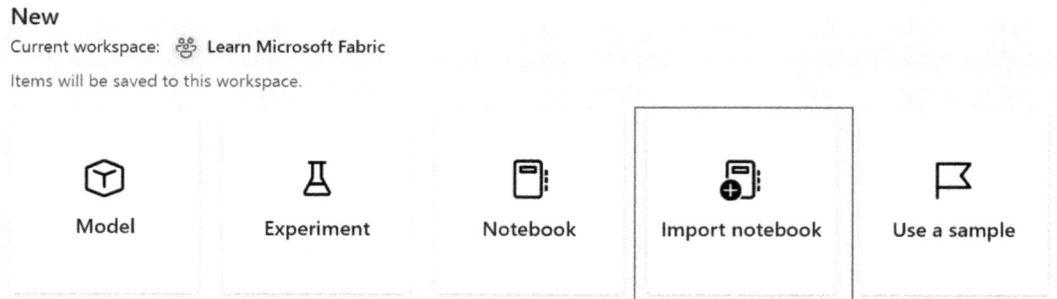

Figure 6.3 – Importing notebooks

3. Select **Upload** from the **Import status** pane that opens on the right-hand side of the screen. Select all notebooks that were downloaded and/or unzipped in *step 1* and hit **Open**. A notification indicating the status of the imports will appear in the top-right corner of the browser window after the import process is completed.

4. Once you've imported the notebooks, you can go to the items view of the workspace, where you will see these newly imported notebooks. This can be seen in *Figure 6.4*:

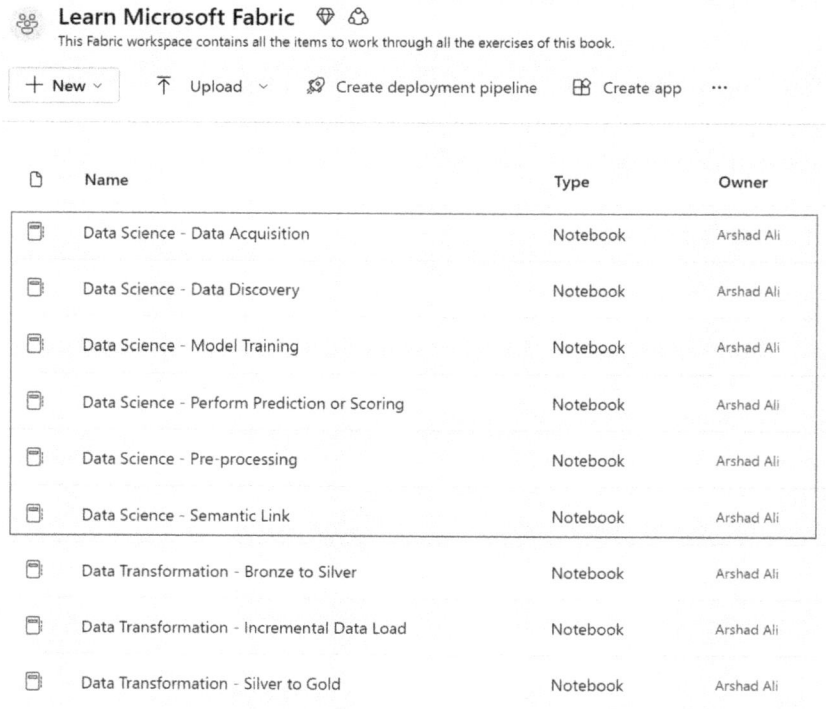

🐝 **Learn Microsoft Fabric** ⬦ ♻
This Fabric workspace contains all the items to work through all the exercises of this book.

+ New ⌄   ⊼ Upload ⌄   🔊 Create deployment pipeline   ⊞ Create app   ⋯

▢	Name	Type	Owner
▢	Data Science - Data Acquisition	Notebook	Arshad Ali
▢	Data Science - Data Discovery	Notebook	Arshad Ali
▢	Data Science - Model Training	Notebook	Arshad Ali
▢	Data Science - Perform Prediction or Scoring	Notebook	Arshad Ali
▢	Data Science - Pre-processing	Notebook	Arshad Ali
▢	Data Science - Semantic Link	Notebook	Arshad Ali
▢	Data Transformation - Bronze to Silver	Notebook	Arshad Ali
▢	Data Transformation - Incremental Data Load	Notebook	Arshad Ali
▢	Data Transformation - Silver to Gold	Notebook	Arshad Ali

Figure 6.4 – Verifying the imported notebooks

Now that we have created a lakehouse and imported the sample notebooks, let's move on to the next stage of understanding the business problem we wish to solve.

Problem formulation/ideation (business understanding)

In this stage, as a data scientist, you primarily work with different stakeholders to understand the business problem you are trying to solve. You work with business leaders to define the problem and the expected outcome of the project and then work with the data engineering team to get access to data for building and training ML models to solve the defined business problem.

To learn how to conduct an end-to-end data science implementation with Fabric, we will be using the *NYC Taxi & Limousine Commission – yellow taxi trip records* dataset (`https://learn.microsoft.com/en-us/azure/open-datasets/dataset-taxi-yellow`) from Azure Open datasets. The records in this dataset contain fields such as pickup and drop-off dates/times, pickup and drop-off locations, trip distances, payment types, itemized fares (fair amount, tax amount, and tip amount), rate types, and driver-reported passenger counts. This dataset contains 1.5 billion rows accumulated from 2009 to 2018 and can be used for various types of analysis and predictions, such as analyzing traffic patterns, demand trends, pricing strategies, driver behavior, and trip duration. In this chapter, you will focus on building an ML model that predicts trip duration using a regression model.

To help you ideate and formulate business problems, Fabric provides the Semantic Link feature, which lets you access your semantic data model in a notebook using Python and Spark. We'll discuss this in more detail before we dive into the next stage of the data science journey.

Semantic Link

Your business teams (leaders and analysts) might have mined lots of business and domain knowledge in the semantic model that they would have built and been using for reporting over the years. With the Semantic Link feature in Fabric, as a data scientist, you can tap into and leverage this hard-earned knowledge quickly and easily, all with a notebook using Python. This allows you to list and access all Power BI datasets, the tables within a dataset, relationships among tables within a dataset, and all the key measures and business logic. This collaboration facilitates building on existing knowledge, removing friction, and avoiding any duplication of efforts. Additionally, Semantic Link helps detect data quality issues.

Figure 6.5 shows an example of listing all Power BI datasets in the workspace using Semantic Link:

```
1   import sempy.fabric as fabric
2
3   df_datasets = fabric.list_datasets()
4   df_datasets
```
✓ 28 sec -Command executed in 23 sec 206 ms by Arshad Ali on 1:04:06 PM, 9/16/23

	Dataset Name	Dataset ID	Cre
0	wwi_bronze	0e19bb2e-e965-4d9f-9327-1fd54c81e1fd	20:
1	wwi_silver	6d06488b-6c06-4ecd-ba28-a38d8406ebbf	20:
2	wwi_gold	f40429e3-e7ef-4d1e-8eb9-af98652fc943	20:
3	wwi_business_aggregates_by_city	9801df3d-3acc-4833-a001-259bf3d44755	20:
4	nyclake	5ba3ae2c-26b6-4b13-a233-0c44e1d6d3f7	20:

Figure 6.5 – Listing Power BI datasets in the workspace

Figure 6.6 shows the relationship among tables from the specified dataset (this is the dataset we created in *Chapter 3, Building an End-to-End Analytics System – Lakehouse*):

```
1   dataset = "wwi_gold"
2   relationships = fabric.list_relationships(dataset)
3   relationships
```
✓ 3 sec -Command executed in 3 sec 236 ms by Arshad Ali on 1:05:27 PM, 9/16/23

› ▤ Log

	Multiplicity	From Table	From Column	To Table	To Column
0	m:1	fact_sale	CityKey	dimension_city	CityKey
1	m:1	fact_sale	StockItemKey	dimension_stock_item	StockItemKey
2	m:1	fact_sale	InvoiceDateKey	dimension_date	Date
3	m:1	fact_sale	SalespersonKey	dimension_employee	EmployeeKey
4	m:1	fact_sale	CustomerKey	dimension_customer	CustomerKey

Figure 6.6 – Identifying the relationship among tables of the specified dataset

Figure 6.7 shows how to plot the relationship between tables from the specified dataset for better readability and understanding:

```
1    from sempy.relationships import plot_relationship_metadata
2    plot_relationship_metadata(relationships)
```
✓ 3 sec -Command executed in 3 sec 94 ms by Arshad Ali on 1:10:05 PM, 9/16/23

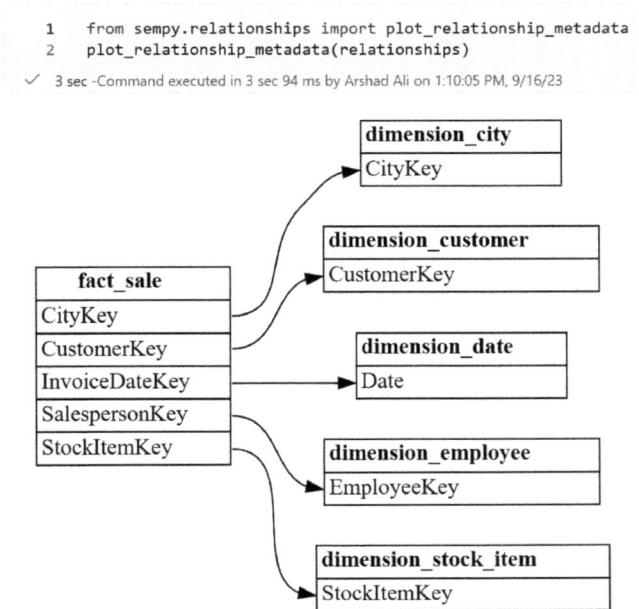

Figure 6.7 – Plotting the relationship among tables of the specified dataset

There are many more capabilities of Semantic Link than what's mentioned here. You can learn about those capabilities at https://sempypreviewdocs.azureedge.net/stable/semantic-link-overview.html and https://pypi.org/project/semantic-link/.

> **Note**
> The code that will be discussed in this section can be found in the Data Science – Semantic Link notebook.

Data acquisition, discovery, and preprocessing

Often, data for building and training ML models is provided by the data engineering team and given to the data science team. In our case, data engineers might have already brought data into either the lakehouse, data warehouse, or both. However, for simplicity's sake, in this example, we will ingest data from Azure Open Datasets (https://learn.microsoft.com/en-us/azure/open-datasets/overview-what-are-open-datasets) into the lakehouse that we created earlier in this chapter.

Data acquisition

In *Chapter 3, Building an End-to-End Analytics System – Lakehouse,* we learned how to open an imported notebook and how to attach a lakehouse as a default lakehouse for the opened notebook. Please ensure you attach the lakehouse (nyctaxilake) you created in the *Data and storage – creating a lakehouse and ingesting data using Apache Spark* section of this chapter. Once you've done that, you can import the data you will be working on:

> **Note**
>
> The code discussed in this section can be found in the Data Science - Data Acquisition notebook.

1. Azure Open Datasets provides a public storage account container that you can retrieve data from. The following code block specifies the names of the storage account and container as part of the source configuration to read the data from. Then, it specifies different filters – in this case, data for yellow taxi for the first 6 months of 2016 – to create a Spark dataframe:

```
# Azure storage access info for open datasets NYC yellow taxi
storage_account_name = "azureopendatastorage"
container_name = "nyctlc"
sas_token = r"" # Specify blank since container is public with
anonymous access
# Set Spark configuration to access blob storage
spark.conf.set("fs.azure.sas.%s.%s.blob.core.windows.net" %
(container_name, storage_account_name),sas_token)

directory = "yellow"
year = 2016
months = "1,2,3,4,5,6"
wasbs_path = f"wasbs://{container_name}@{storage_account_name}.
blob.core.windows.net/{directory}"
nyc_yellowtaxi_df = spark.read.parquet(wasbs_path)
# Filter data by year 2016 and months 1-6
filtered_nyc_yellowtaxi_df = nyc_yellowtaxi_df.filter(f"puYear =
{year} AND puMonth IN ({months})")
```

2. To persist the data of the dataframe to a delta table, you must call the saveAsTable function in Delta format:

```
table_name = "nyc_yellowtaxi_raw"
filtered_nyc_yellowtaxi_df.write.mode("overwrite").
format("delta").saveAsTable(f"{table_name}")
print(f"Spark dataframe (filtered_nyc_yellowtaxi_df) saved to a
delta table: {table_name}")
```

3. You can validate the existence of the table and its data by running the following query:

```
%%sql
select puYear, puMonth, count(*) from nyc_yellowtaxi_raw group
by puYear, puMonth order by puYear, puMonth
```

You will get the result shown in *Figure 6.8*:

Table   Chart |→ Export results ⌄

Index	puYear	puMonth	count(1)
1	2016	1	10906427
2	2016	2	11382005
3	2016	3	12208463
4	2016	4	11932723
5	2016	5	11840525
6	2016	6	11132795

Figure 6.8 – Validating the data for the newly created raw Delta table

4. Once the dataframe has been persisted to a Delta table, you can right-click on **Tables** under **Lakehouse explorer** and click on **Refresh** to see the table, as shown in *Figure 6.9*:

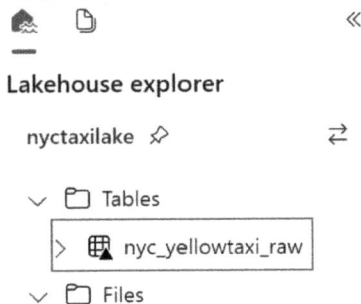

Figure 6.9 – Validating the existence of the raw Delta table in Lakehouse explorer

Data discovery

In Fabric, the Spark runtime comes preinstalled and preconfigured with popular open source data visualization libraries such as matplotlib, seaborn, plotly, and more, as well as ML libraries such as SparkML, SynapseML, scikit-learn, and others.

In this section, we will perform EDA to understand the data and patterns better. To do so, we will use the matplotlib and seaborn libraries.

> **Note**
>
> seaborn is a Python data visualization library that provides a high-level interface for building attractive data visuals and statistical graphics on dataframe and arrays. You can learn more about seaborn here: https://seaborn.pydata.org/.
>
> The code that will be discussed in this section can be found in the Data Science - Data Discovery notebook. Please make sure you attach the lakehouse (nyctaxilake) you created in the *Data and storage – creating a lakehouse and ingesting data using Apache Spark* section of this chapter to this notebook.

Let's start the EDA process:

1. First, you need to import the required libraries into your Spark session for data visualization and statistical insights. You may also wish to change the seaborn library's theme parameters so that you can control the aesthetics of the visuals, such as style, color palette, and size of the visual:

    ```
    import matplotlib.pyplot as plt
    import matplotlib.ticker as mticker
    import seaborn as sns
    sns.set_theme(style="darkgrid", palette="deep", rc = {'figure.figsize':(9,6)})
    ```

2. Now, let's read data from the Delta table from the lakehouse and then create a random sample of this data by randomly picking one record for every 1,000 records. We can use a complete dataset to do EDA or train a model. However, to minimize the overall execution time, we will work on a sample dataset. In this table, there are over 100 million rows, so the sample will have over 100,000 rows – which is still significant for understanding the data and the patterns within it. Finally, we can generate summary statistics for the columns in the dataset:

> **Note**
>
> A random seed is used to ensure that results are reproducible – that is, when you specify the same seed value, the sample data is deterministic so that you get the same results. Although a detailed discussion of random sampling and seed values is outside the scope of this book, you can learn more about choosing an effective seed value here: https://towardsdatascience.com/how-to-use-random-seeds-effectively-54a4cd855a79.

```
SEED = 1234
nyc_yellowtaxi_raw_df = spark.read.table("nyc_yellowtaxi_raw")
nyc_yellowtaxi_sampled_df = nyc_yellowtaxi_raw_df.sample(True,
0.001, seed=SEED)
display(nyc_yellowtaxi_sampled_df.summary())
```

The generated statistics can be seen in *Figure 6.10*:

Table   Chart |→ Export results ∨

Index	summary	vendorID	passengerCount	tripDistance	puLocatic
1	count	69511	69511	69511	1
2	mean	1.5324337155270389	1.6619240120268735	2.9477003639711645	68.0
3	stddev	0.4989505341896946	1.3093359878738489	3.631461068325874	NULL
4	min	1	0	0.0	68
5	25%	1.0	1	1.0	68.0
6	50%	2.0	1	1.7	68.0
7	75%	2.0	2	3.17	68.0
8	max	2	6	69.28	68

Figure 6.10 – Summary statistics of the columns of the raw Delta table

3.   Next, let's add some computed or derived columns and filter out rows for the various conditions.

Computed columns:

- **Trip duration**: By subtracting the pickup date/time from the drop-off date/time
- **Day of week**: By using the date of week function on the drop-off date/time
- **Pickup hour**: By using the hour function on the pickup date/time

Filters:

- **Trip duration**: Only consider rows where the trip duration is greater than zero. If this is zero, it's likely a canceled trip.
- **Fare amount**: Only consider rows where the fare amount is greater than zero. If this is zero, it's likely a canceled trip.

The code is as follows:

```
nyc_yellowtaxi_sampled_pd_df = nyc_yellowtaxi_sampled_
df.toPandas()
nyc_yellowtaxi_sampled_pd_df['tripDuration'] = (nyc_yellowtaxi_
sampled_pd_df['tpepDropoffDateTime'] - nyc_yellowtaxi_sampled_
pd_df['tpepPickupDateTime']).astype('timedelta64[m]')
nyc_yellowtaxi_sampled_pd_df['pickupHour'] = nyc_yellowtaxi_
sampled_pd_df['tpepPickupDateTime'].dt.hour
nyc_yellowtaxi_sampled_pd_df['dayOfWeek'] = nyc_yellowtaxi_
sampled_pd_df['tpepDropoffDateTime'].dt.dayofweek
```

```
nyc_yellowtaxi_sampled_pd_df = nyc_yellowtaxi_sampled_pd_df[nyc_
yellowtaxi_sampled_pd_df["tripDuration"] > 0]
nyc_yellowtaxi_sampled_pd_df = nyc_yellowtaxi_sampled_pd_df[nyc_
yellowtaxi_sampled_pd_df["fareAmount"] > 0]
```

4. With the following code, we are creating a histogram that shows the count of taxi trips by hour of the day:

```
sns.histplot(data=nyc_yellowtaxi_sampled_pd_df, x="pickupHour",
stat="count", discrete=True, kde=True)
plt.title("Distribution by Hour of the day")
plt.xlabel('Hours')
plt.ylabel('Count of trips')
```

As shown in *Figure 6.11*, the number of trips starts dropping after midnight and picks up again in the early morning. Also, the total number of trips peaked during the evening:

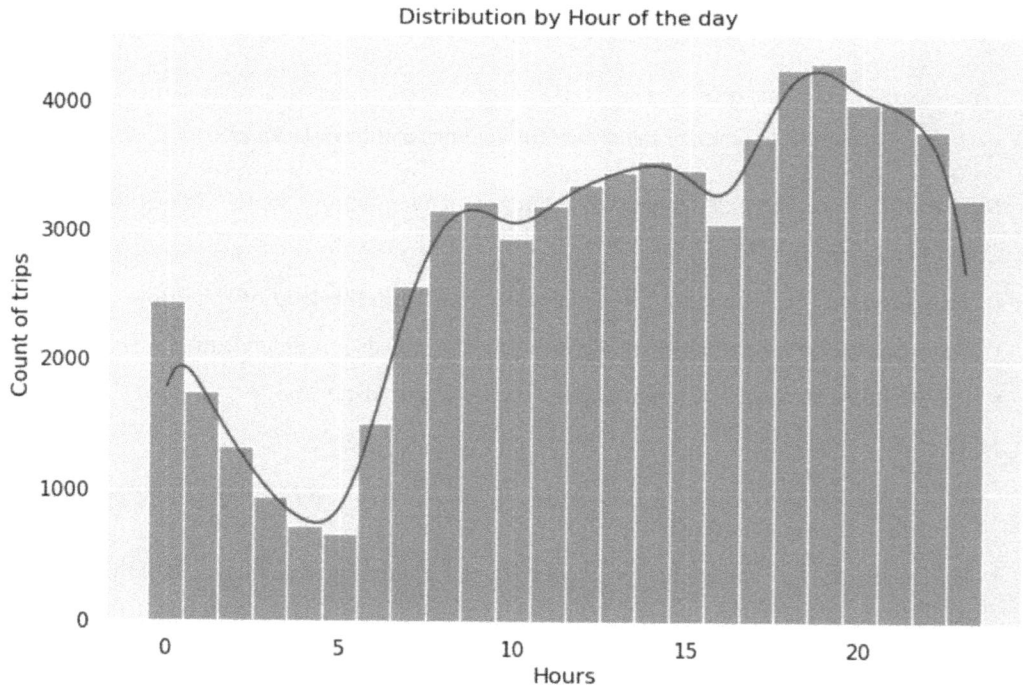

Figure 6.11 – Histogram showing trip counts by hour of the day

5. Next, we'll create a scatterplot that shows trip duration, trip distance, and passenger count:

```
sns.scatterplot(data=nyc_yellowtaxi_sampled_pd_df,
x="tripDistance", y="tripDuration", hue="passengerCount")
```

The results can be seen in *Figure 6.12*:

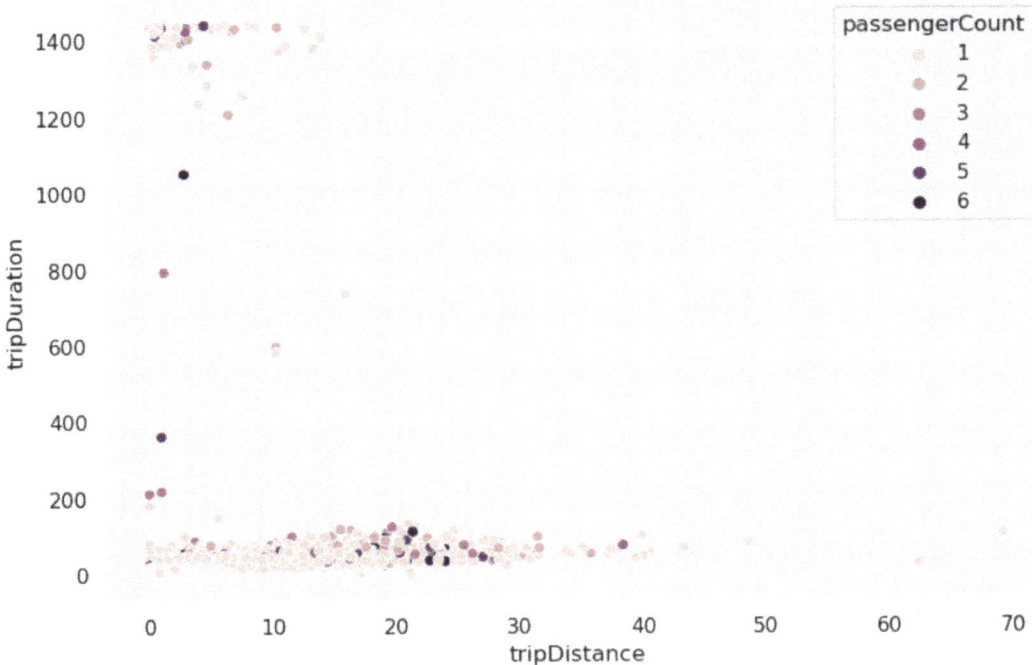

Figure 6.12 – Scatterplot showing trip distance, trip duration, and passenger count

There are a few interesting things to observe regarding *Figure 6.12*:

- There are a couple of trips with a passenger count of zero. These seem to be data quality issues and need to be removed. As a data scientist, you need to maintain a balance between what needs to be part of the dataset on which you train your model and what needs to be removed from it. Keeping too many observations with outliers might influence the outcome in a different direction while removing most of the rows (so that you don't have a true representation of your population) might cause data skew and generalize your model.

- There are a few trips with extremely high trip durations; these could be intercity trips. For this chapter, we will remove all the trips that took over 3 hours since they are outliers. This 3-hour threshold is based on the mean of the trip duration and then adding three standard deviations to the mean.

6. Now, create two box plots:

```
fig, axes = plt.subplots(1, 2, figsize=(12, 6))
sns.boxplot(ax=axes[0], data=nyc_yellowtaxi_sampled_pd_df,
x="passengerCount", y="tripDuration").set(title='Distribution of
Trip duration by passengerCount')
```

```
nyc_yellowtaxi_sampled_clean_pd_df = nyc_yellowtaxi_sampled_pd_
df[(nyc_yellowtaxi_sampled_pd_df["passengerCount"] > 0) & (nyc_
yellowtaxi_sampled_pd_df["tripDuration"] <= 180)]
sns.boxplot(ax=axes[1], data=nyc_yellowtaxi_sampled_clean_pd_df,
x="passengerCount", y="tripDuration").set(title='Distribution of
Trip duration by passengerCount (outliers removed)')
```

Here's the output:

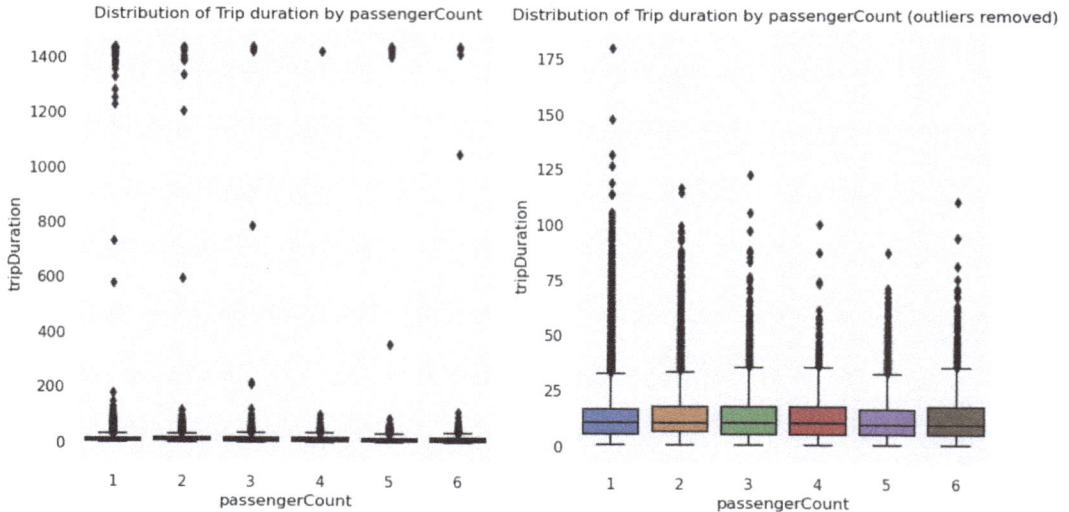

Figure 6.13 – Two boxplots showing passenger count and trip duration – the first one
shows data as-is, whereas the second one shows data when outliers are removed

Both charts in *Figure 6.13* show the distribution of trip duration by passenger count. However, the first one shows the data as-is, whereas the second one removes the outliers. We will use the second one, with outliers removed, for further analysis. As shown in the first boxplot, there are a few trips with a passenger count of zero and extremely high trip duration. The second boxplot shows the same distribution after the outliers have been removed.

7. Now, we will create two scatter plots:

```
F, axes = plt.subplots(1, 2, figsize=(12, 5))
sns.scatterplot(ax =axes[0], data=nyc_yellowtaxi_sampled_pd_df,
x="fareAmount", y="tripDuration",  hue="paymentType")
sns.scatterplot(ax =axes[1],data=nyc_yellowtaxi_sampled_pd_df,
x="fareAmount", y="tripDuration",  hue="vendorID")
```

Here's the output:

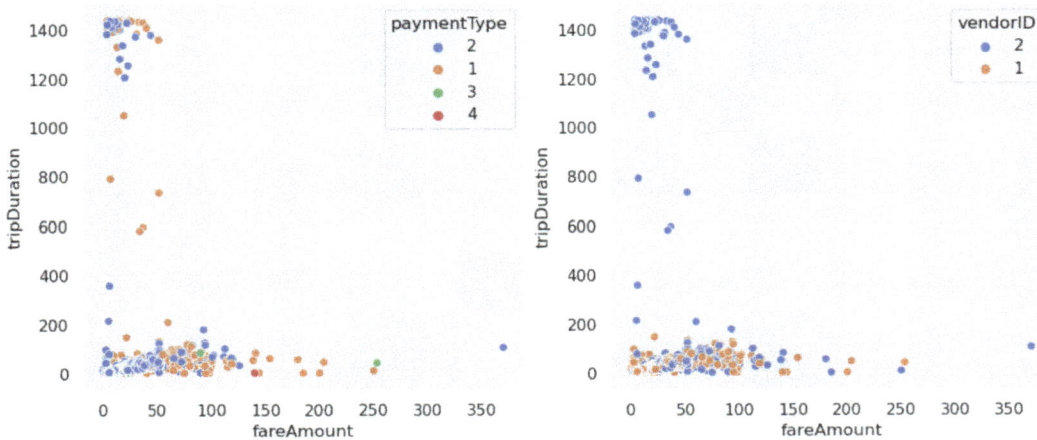

Figure 6.14 – Scatterplots showing fare amount and trip duration – the first one
shows it by payment types, whereas the second one shows it by vendors

Both charts in *Figure 6.14* show the distribution of trip duration by fare amount; however, the first one shows distribution based on payment method whereas the second one shows distribution based on vendors – you will notice a large number of trips were done by vendorID 2.

8. Now that we've explored and analyzed the data from different perspectives and know how to fix data quality issues, let's take this one step further and understand the correlation between the different numerical variables of the datasets. For our analysis, we will create a correlation plot, as shown in *Figure 6.15*, for a small subset of numerical variables in the dataset, which should show the correlation coefficient for each pair of variables:

```
cols_to_corr = ['tripDuration','fareAmount', 'passengerCount',
'tripDistance', 'extra', 'mtaTax', 'tollsAmount',
        'improvementSurcharge', 'tipAmount',
'pickupHour','dayOfWeek']
sns.heatmap(data = nyc_yellowtaxi_sampled_pd_df[cols_to_corr].
corr(),annot=True,fmt='.3f', cmap="Greens")
```

Here's the output:

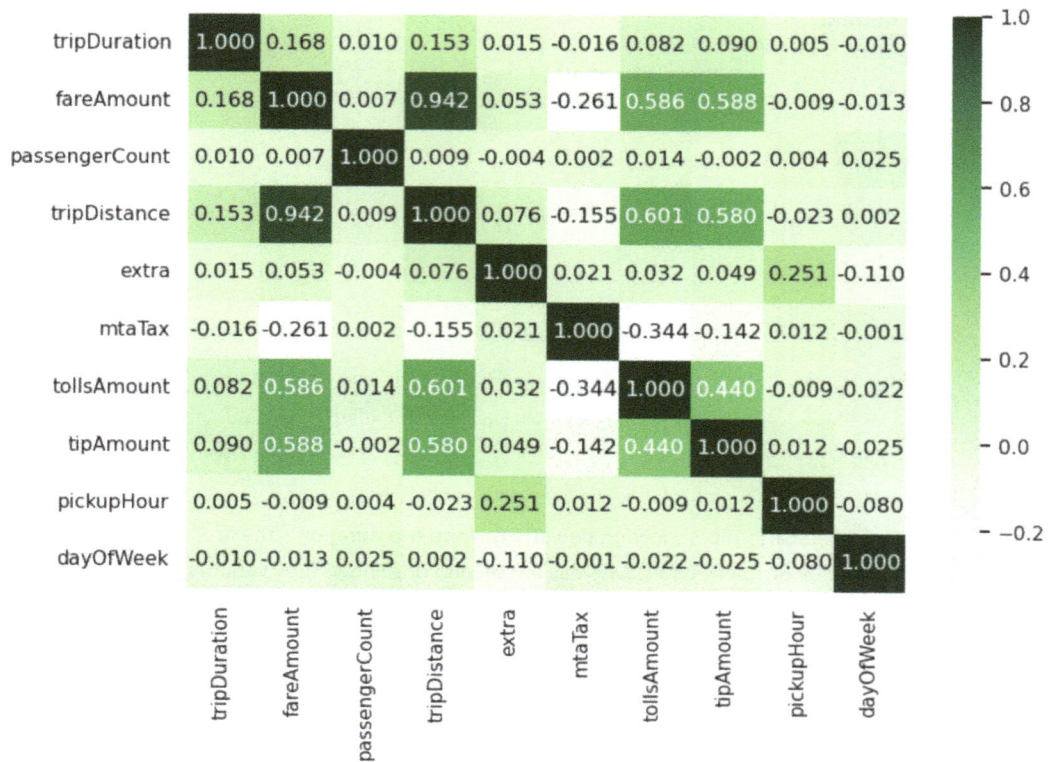

	tripDuration	fareAmount	passengerCount	tripDistance	extra	mtaTax	tollsAmount	tipAmount	pickupHour	dayOfWeek
tripDuration	1.000	0.168	0.010	0.153	0.015	-0.016	0.082	0.090	0.005	-0.010
fareAmount	0.168	1.000	0.007	0.942	0.053	-0.261	0.586	0.588	-0.009	-0.013
passengerCount	0.010	0.007	1.000	0.009	-0.004	0.002	0.014	-0.002	0.004	0.025
tripDistance	0.153	0.942	0.009	1.000	0.076	-0.155	0.601	0.580	-0.023	0.002
extra	0.015	0.053	-0.004	0.076	1.000	0.021	0.032	0.049	0.251	-0.110
mtaTax	-0.016	-0.261	0.002	-0.155	0.021	1.000	-0.344	-0.142	0.012	-0.001
tollsAmount	0.082	0.586	0.014	0.601	0.032	-0.344	1.000	0.440	-0.009	-0.022
tipAmount	0.090	0.588	-0.002	0.580	0.049	-0.142	0.440	1.000	0.012	-0.025
pickupHour	0.005	-0.009	0.004	-0.023	0.251	0.012	-0.009	0.012	1.000	-0.080
dayOfWeek	-0.010	-0.013	0.025	0.002	-0.110	-0.001	-0.022	-0.025	-0.080	1.000

Figure 6.15 – Correlation graph showing the correlation among different variables in the dataset

The correlation coefficient shows in what direction and how strongly two numerical variables are correlated. It can go from -1 to 1. A negative correlation indicates that with the increase in one variable, the other variable decreases – that is, they move in the opposite direction. Likewise, a positive correlation indicates that both variables move in the same direction – that is, if one variable increases, the other variable increases too. As an example, as shown in *Figure 6.15*, the darker the field is, the stronger the correlation is. For example, the fare amount has a strong positive correlation (0.942) with the trip distance – that is, if the trip distance increases, so does the fare amount.

> **Note**
>
> As a data scientist, you might know this already, but it's worth emphasizing here that correlation doesn't imply causation.

Now that we've learned how to perform EDA and understood the data better, it's time to cleanse and prepare this dataset before we start training our ML model with it.

Data preprocessing

In the previous section, we explored data and understood different data quality issues, as summarized here:

- The passenger count is zero for some trips; this seems to be a data quality issue and these records need to be removed.

- The trip duration is zero for some trips. This could be because of the canceled trips and should be removed from further consideration.

- There are a few trips with a high trip duration, which likely indicates intercity travel. These can be removed. We can choose the threshold based on the mean plus a standard deviation of three, which will be roughly 3 hours.

- The fare amount is zero or negative for some trips. This is another case of a data quality issue or canceled trips that should be removed.

- Some of the records have starting and ending location information (latitude and longitude) missing and can be removed from the dataset.

> **Note**
>
> The code that will be discussed in this section can be found in the Data Science – Pre-processing notebook. Please make sure you attach the lakehouse (nyctaxilake) you created in the *Data and storage – creating a lakehouse and ingesting data using Apache Spark* section of this chapter to this notebook.

Now that we know about a few of the data quality issues in our dataset, let's write some code to fix these issues before we use this dataset to train the ML model:

1. We will start by creating a couple of derived or computed columns based on data from other columns in the same dataset:

```
From pyspark.sql.functions import *
nyc_yellowtaxi_raw_df = spark.read.table("nyc_yellowtaxi_raw")
nytaxi_yellowtaxi_prep_df = nyc_yellowtaxi_raw_
df.withColumn('pickupDate', col('tpepPickupDateTime').
cast('date'))\
   .withColumn("weekDay", dayofweek(col("tpepPickupDateTime")))\
   .withColumn("weekDayName", date_
format(col("tpepPickupDateTime"), "EEEE"))\
   .withColumn("dayofMonth",
dayofweek(col("tpepPickupDateTime")))\
   .withColumn("pickupHour", hour(col("tpepPickupDateTime")))\
   .withColumn("tripDuration", (unix_
timestamp(col("tpepDropoffDateTime")) - unix_
timestamp(col("tpepPickupDateTime")))/60)\
   .withColumn("timeBins", when((col("pickupHour") >=7) &
```

```
(col("pickupHour")<=10) ,"MorningRush")\
    .when((col("pickupHour") >=11) & (col("pickupHour")<=15)
,"Afternoon")\
    .when((col("pickupHour") >=16) & (col("pickupHour")<=19)
,"EveningRush")\
    .when((col("pickupHour") <=6) | (col("pickupHour")>=20)
,"Night"))
```

2. Next, we'll write a code block that applies filters, as discussed earlier in this section, to remove records with data quality issues and save the cleansed or prepared dataframe to a new Delta table:

```
Nytaxi_yellowtaxi_clean_df = nytaxi_yellowtaxi_prep_
df.filter("""
    fareAmount > 0 AND fareAmount < 100
    AND tripDuration > 0 AND tripDuration <= 180
    AND passengerCount > 0 AND passengerCount <= 8
    AND tripDistance > 0 AND tripDistance < 100
    AND startLat IS NOT NULL AND startLon IS NOT NULL
    AND endLat IS NOT NULL AND endLon IS NOT NULL
    """)
table_name = "nyc_yellowtaxi_clean"
nytaxi_yellowtaxi_clean_df.write.mode("overwrite").
format("delta").saveAsTable(f"{table_name}")
print(f"Spark dataframe (nytaxi_yellowtaxi_clean_df) saved to a
delta table: {table_name}")
```

3. Once the dataframe has been persisted to a Delta table, you can right-click on **Tables** under **Lakehouse explorer**, as shown in *Figure 6.16*, and click on **Refresh** to see the newly created table:

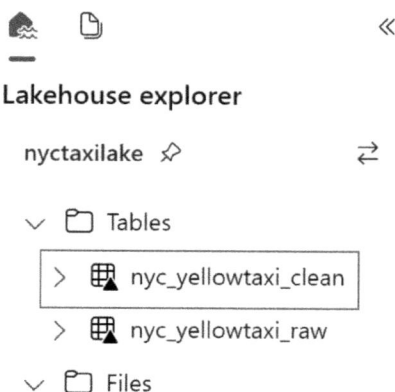

Figure 6.16 – Validating the existence of the new Delta table with
the cleansed dataset in Lakehouse explorer

Data Wrangler

For citizen developers, Fabric offers a low-code yet powerful and intuitive tool called Data Wrangler for EDA. The Data Wrangler tool makes data cleansing and preparation easier than ever before by providing you with a built-in dynamic data display, built-in statistics, and nice and intuitive chart-rendering capabilities. You, as a developer, an engineer, or a business user, can use its intuitive interface to apply a variety of data cleansing and data preparation operations in a matter of clicks, update the data that's displayed in real time, and generate code that can be saved back to the notebook as a reusable function for future. This generated code can be enhanced further, when necessary, to suit your changing needs. You can learn about this capability at `https://learn.microsoft.com/en-us/fabric/data-science/data-wrangler`.

Now that we've cleansed and prepared our dataset, it's time to build and train the ML model.

Experimenting and modeling

In this section, we will use a regression ML algorithm to train an ML model to predict trip duration based on several features in the dataset, such as date, time, pickup and drop-off locations, distance, and so on. To learn about the capabilities related to the Data Science experience in Fabric, we will create two versions of the trained model with different sets of hyperparameters and then register each of them in the model registry. While doing this, we will log all the hyperparameters and evaluation metrics by taking advantage of the native integration of MLflow in Fabric.

> **Note**
>
> MLflow is an open source platform for managing the end-to-end ML life cycle. You can read more about it at `https://mlflow.org/docs/latest/index.html`.
>
> The code that will be discussed in this section can be found in the `Data Science - Model Training` notebook. Please make sure you attach the lakehouse (`nyctaxilake`) you created in the *Data and storage – creating a lakehouse and ingesting data using Apache Spark* section of this chapter to this notebook.

Now, let's start building our regression ML model:

1. Due to the native integration of MLflow in Fabric, the MLflow library is already included in the Fabric Spark runtime and no manual installation or configuration is required. We need to import this library into our notebook to make use of it in our Spark session. Next, we need to specify the name for the experiment and ML model we are going to create, and then call the `set_experiment` method to create or set the specified experiment in our session so that we can work on it:

    ```
    # Create an experiment to track and register model with mlflow
    import mlflow
    ```

```
# Specify names for experiment and model
mlexperiment_name = "nyc_yellowtaxi_predict_tripduration"
mlalgorithm_name = "lightgbm"
mlmodel_name = f"{mlexperiment_name}_{mlalgorithm_name}"
mlflow.set_experiment(mlexperiment_name)
```

2. Previously, we created a cleansed and prepared dataset and stored it as a Delta table. We are going to read it and take a random sample of 50% of the dataset to speed up its execution:

```
SEED = 1234 # Specify a random seed to use with random sampling
# we are randomly sampling training data to speed up overall
execution time - 50% of the total data
nyc_yellowtaxi_clean_sampled_df = spark.read.table("nyc_
yellowtaxi_clean").sample(fraction = 0.5, seed = SEED)
nyc_yellowtaxi_clean_sampled_df.count()
```

3. For the random sample, we are going to randomly split it into two datasets: a **training dataset** that consists of 75% of the sample and a **test dataset** that consists of 25% of the sample. We will cache these datasets in memory to improve the speed of subsequent reads of this data. Note that this initial execution might take some time to complete:

```
nyc_yellowtaxi_predict_tripduration_train_df, nyc_yellowtaxi_
predict_tripduration_test_df = nyc_yellowtaxi_clean_sampled_
df.randomSplit([0.75, 0.25], seed=SEED)
# Cache these dataframes in memory to improve the speed of
subsequent reads
nyc_yellowtaxi_predict_tripduration_train_df.cache()
nyc_yellowtaxi_predict_tripduration_test_df.cache()
print(f"train set count:{nyc_yellowtaxi_predict_tripduration_
train_df.count()}")
print(f"test set count:{nyc_yellowtaxi_predict_tripduration_
test_df.count()}")
```

4. For all the features we are going to use to build and train the ML model, we are going to identify and create lists of categorical and numerical features:

```
categorical_features =
["storeAndFwdFlag","timeBins","vendorID","weekDayName",
"pickupHour","rateCodeId","paymentType"]
numerical_features = ['passengerCount', "tripDistance"]
```

5. Next, we will create a function that will create an ML pipeline based on the LightGBM regressor algorithm for the specified categorical and numerical features and set of hyperparameters after we apply different feature engineering techniques, such as one-hot encoding. As mentioned previously, we're using the LightGBM regressor framework, a distributed and high-performance gradient-boosting algorithm based on the decision tree model; it's available as part of the

SynapseML (`https://microsoft.github.io/SynapseML/`) library. SynapseML is an open source project that's developed by Microsoft for distributed ML. If you are interested in this, you can learn more about it at `https://microsoft.github.io/SynapseML/docs/Explore%20Algorithms/LightGBM/Overview/`:

```
from pyspark.ml import Pipeline
from synapse.ml.core.platform import *
from pyspark.ml.feature import OneHotEncoder, VectorAssembler,
StringIndexer
from synapse.ml.lightgbm import LightGBMRegressor
# Define a machine learning pipeline steps for training a
LightGBMRegressor regressor model
def create_lgbmr_pipeline(categorical_features,numerical_
features, hyperparameters):
    # Create string indexer
    strindx = StringIndexer(inputCols=categorical_features,
            outputCols=[f"{feat}StrIdx" for feat in
categorical_features]).setHandleInvalid("keep")
    # Apply one hot encoding for categorical/indexed columns
    ohe = OneHotEncoder(inputCols= strindx.getOutputCols(),
            outputCols=[f"{feat}OHEnc" for feat in categorical_
features])
    # convert all feature of the dataset into a vector
    featurizer_vector = VectorAssembler(inputCols=ohe.
getOutputCols() + numerical_features, outputCol="features")
    # Define the LightGBM regressor hyperparameters
    lgbmr_hyperparameters = LightGBMRegressor(
        objective = hyperparameters["objective"],
        alpha = hyperparameters["alpha"],
        learningRate = hyperparameters["learning_rate"],
        numLeaves = hyperparameters["num_leaves"],
        labelCol="tripDuration",
        numIterations = hyperparameters["iterations"],
    )
    # Define the steps and sequence of the Spark ML pipeline
    spark_ml_pipeline = Pipeline(stages=[strindx, ohe,
featurizer_vector, lgbmr_hyperparameters])
    return spark_ml_pipeline
```

6. The following code block creates a function that registers your trained ML model in the model registry, along with its specified hyperparameters and evaluation metrics:

```
from mlflow.models.signature import ModelSignature
from mlflow.types.utils import _infer_schema

# Define a function to register a spark model
```

```
def register_spark_ml_model(mlflow_active_run, mlmodel,
mlmodel_name, mlmodel_signature, mlmodel_metrics, mlmodel_
hyperparameters):
        # log the model, parameters and metrics
        mlflow.spark.log_model(mlmodel, artifact_path = mlmodel_
name, signature=mlmodel_signature, registered_model_name =
mlmodel_name, dfs_tmpdir="Files/mlflow/tmp/")
        mlflow.log_params(mlmodel_hyperparameters)
        mlflow.log_metrics(mlmodel_metrics)
        mlmodel_uri = f"runs:/{mlflow_active_run.info.run_id}/
{mlmodel_name}"
        print(f"Model saved in run{mlflow_active_run.info.run_
id}")
        print(f"Model URI: {mlmodel_uri}")
        return mlmodel_uri
```

Now that we've done all the basic configuration and created some reusable functions, it's time to train our ML model. We will train and register two versions of the ML model that have been trained with different sets of hyperparameters to show the different capabilities and how easy it is to train and compare models with different sets of hyperparameters (https://en.wikipedia.org/wiki/Hyperparameter_(machine_learning)).

Training – version 1

Now, we will train two versions of the ML model. Version 1 will have a set of hyperparameters, while version 2 will have the same set of parameters, but those parameters will be tuned for optimal performance. Let's start with version 1:

1. Specify the hyperparameters as a Python dictionary that will be used while training the model with the LightGBM algorithm:

    ```
    # Default hyperparameters for LightGBM regressor
    lgbmr_hyperparameters = {"objective":"regression",
        "alpha":0.09,
        "learning_rate":0.01,
        "num_leaves":92,
        "iterations":200}
    ```

2. With the MLflow object we created earlier in our session, we will start a run and call the create_ lgbmr_pipeline function to create an ML pipeline based on the set of hyperparameters we defined previously. Next, we will call the fit method by passing the training dataset to

train the model and then call the `transform` method to get predictions on the test dataset. Finally, we will cache this predicted data to memory so that when we evaluate the result later, it runs faster:

```
if mlflow.active_run() is None:
    mlflow.start_run()
mlflow_active_run = mlflow.active_run()
print(f"Active experiment run_id: {mlflow_active_run.info.run_
id}")
lgbmr_pipeline = create_lgbmr_pipeline(categorical_
features,numerical_features,lgbmr_hyperparameters)
lgbmr_model = lgbmr_pipeline.fit(nyc_yellowtaxi_predict_
tripduration_train_df)
# Get Predictions on test dataset
lgbmr_predictions = lgbmr_model.transform(nyc_yellowtaxi_
predict_tripduration_test_df)
## Caching scored predictions so that when running model
evaluation it runs faster
lgbmr_predictions.cache()
print(f"Prediction run for {lgbmr_predictions.count()} samples")
```

3.   Now that the model has been trained and a prediction has been generated on the test dataset, it's time to evaluate the performance of this trained model. For this, we are going to use the `ComputeModelStatistics` module from SynapseML:

```
from synapse.ml.train import ComputeModelStatistics
import json
# compute model statistics to evaluate its performance
lgbmr_metrics = ComputeModelStatistics(
    evaluationMetric="regression", labelCol="tripDuration",
scoresCol="prediction"
).transform(lgbmr_predictions)
lgbmr_metrics_dict = json.loads(lgbmr_metrics.toJSON().first())
lgbmr_metrics_dict
```

Figure 6.17 shows some of the statistics regarding the accuracy of the model, such as the **mean squared error (MSE)**, **root mean squared error (RMSE)**, **R squared (R^2)**, and **mean absolute error (MAE)**:

```
{'mean_squared_error': 31.32707418869297,
 'root_mean_squared_error': 5.597059423366253,
 'R^2': 0.7369768686952491,
 'mean_absolute_error': 3.6737069472412704}
```

Figure 6.17 – Evaluation metrics for version 1

> **Note**
>
> There are different evaluation metrics, such as MSE, RMSE, R^2, and MAE, for regression models. You can learn about them here: `https://machinelearningmastery.com/regression-metrics-for-machine-learning/`.

4. Finally, we want to register this model in the model registry. For that, we will create the model signature and call the `register_spark_model` function we created earlier to register it and then end the currently active MLflow run:

```
# Define model signature object
mlmodel_signature = ModelSignature(inputs=_infer_schema(nyc_
yellowtaxi_predict_tripduration_train_df.select(categorical_
features + numerical_features)),
outputs=_infer_schema(nyc_yellowtaxi_predict_tripduration_train_
df.select("tripDuration")))
# Call model register function
model_uri = register_spark_ml_model(
            mlflow_active_run = mlflow_active_run,
            mlmodel = lgbmr_model,
            mlmodel_name = mlmodel_name,
            mlmodel_signature = mlmodel_signature,
            mlmodel_metrics = lgbmr_metrics_dict,
            mlmodel_hyperparameters = lgbmr_hyperparameters)
mlflow.end_run()
```

Training – version 2

Let's train version 2 of this model but this time with a tuned set of hyperparameters:

1. This time, we'll specify a different set of hyperparameters as a Python dictionary that will be used while training this second version of the model:

> **Note**
>
> Hyperparameters can affect the speed, quality, and accuracy of model training and hence identifying the right set of hyperparameters is important. There are different technics for identifying and tuning hyperparameters, such as random search, grid search, and others. You can also use AutoML to identify tuned hyperparameters. Discussing hyperparameter tuning is outside the scope of this book to keep it simple; however, if you are interested, you can learn more about it at the following links:
>
> *   `https://en.wikipedia.org/wiki/Hyperparameter_optimization`
> *   `https://www.analyticsvidhya.com/blog/2022/02/a-comprehensive-guide-on-hyperparameter-tuning-and-its-techniques/`

```
# Tuned hyperparameters for LightGBM regressor
lgbmr_tuned_hyperparameters = {"objective":"regression",
    "alpha":0.9,
    "learning_rate":0.1,
    "num_leaves":31,
    "iterations":100}
# Remove paymentType
categorical_features.remove("paymentType")
```

2. This time, with the MLflow object we created earlier, we will start a run and call the `create_lgbmr_pipeline` function to create an ML pipeline based on the set of hyperparameters we defined previously. Next, we will call the `fit` method by passing the training dataset to train the model and then call the `transform` method to get predictions on the test dataset. Finally, we will cache this predicted data to memory so that when we evaluate the result later, it runs faster:

```
if mlflow.active_run() is None:
    mlflow.start_run()
mlflow_active_run = mlflow.active_run()
print(f"Active experiment run_id: {mlflow_active_run.info.run_
id}")
lgbmr_tuned_pipeline = create_lgbmr_pipeline(categorical_
features, numerical_features, lgbmr_tuned_hyperparameters)
lgbmr_tuned_model = lgbmr_tuned_pipeline.fit(nyc_yellowtaxi_
predict_tripduration_train_df)
# Get predictions on test dataset
lgbmr_tuned_predictions = lgbmr_tuned_model.transform(nyc_
yellowtaxi_predict_tripduration_test_df)
# Caching predictions so that when running model evaluation, it
runs faster
lgbmr_tuned_predictions.cache()
print(f"Prediction run for {lgbmr_tuned_predictions.count()}
samples")
```

3. Now that the model has been trained and a prediction has been generated on the test dataset, it's time to evaluate the performance of this trained model. For that, we are going to use the `ComputeModelStatistics` module from SynapseML:

```
from synapse.ml.train import ComputeModelStatistics
import json
# compute model statistics to evaluate its performance
lgbmr_tuned_metrics = ComputeModelStatistics(
    evaluationMetric="regression", labelCol="tripDuration",
scoresCol="prediction"
).transform(lgbmr_tuned_predictions)
lgbmr_tuned_metrics_dict = json.loads(lgbmr_tuned_metrics.
```

```
toJSON().first())
lgbmr_tuned_metrics_dict
```

The evaluation metrics are shown in *Figure 6.18*:

```
{'mean_squared_error': 28.54970506348561,
 'root_mean_squared_error': 5.34319240374943,
 'R^2': 0.7602957499830791,
 'mean_absolute_error': 3.425641443239282}
```

Figure 6.18 – Evaluation metrics for version 2

4. Finally, as we want to register this model in the model registry, we will create the model signature and call the `register_spark_model` function to register it, and then end the currently active MLflow run:

```
# Define model signature object
mlmodel_signature = ModelSignature(inputs=_infer_schema(nyc_
yellowtaxi_predict_tripduration_train_df.select(categorical_
features + numerical_features)),
outputs=_infer_schema(nyc_yellowtaxi_predict_tripduration_train_
df.select("tripDuration")))
model_uri = register_spark_ml_model(
    mlflow_active_run = mlflow_active_run,
    mlmodel = lgbmr_tuned_model,
    mlmodel_name = mlmodel_name,
    mlmodel_signature = mlmodel_signature,
    mlmodel_metrics = lgbmr_tuned_metrics_dict,
    mlmodel_hyperparameters = lgbmr_tuned_hyperparameters)
mlflow.end_run()
```

The following code block, which contains a `for` loop, lists all the experiments you have in the current workspace. The next two lines of code return different runs of the specified experiment:

```
import mlflow
experiments = mlflow.search_experiments()
for exp in experiments:
    print(exp.name)
exp = mlflow.get_experiment_by_name(mlexperiment_name)
mlflow.search_runs(exp.experiment_id, order_by=["start_time DESC"],
max_results=10)
```

Alternatively, you can go to the workspace item view and open the experiment (name = nyc_yellowtaxi_predict_tripduration), as shown in *Figure 6.19*. As you can see, it shows two runs of the experiment that we executed earlier:

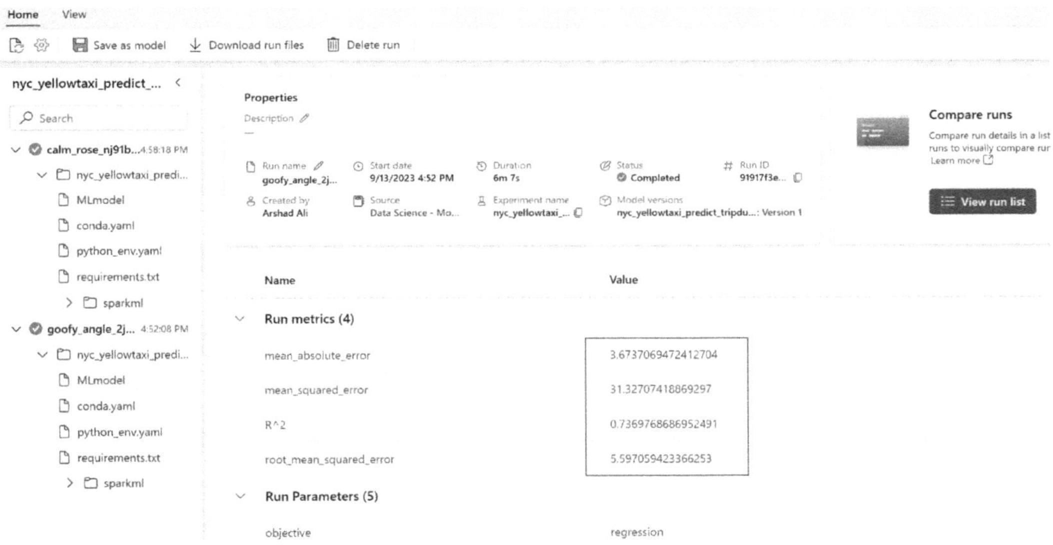

Figure 6.19 – The experiment view in the user interface showing different runs

As shown in *Figure 6.20*, from here, we can compare multiple runs to see the difference in performance, as well as compare its evaluation metrics, pick the best-performing one, and save it as a model for future predictions:

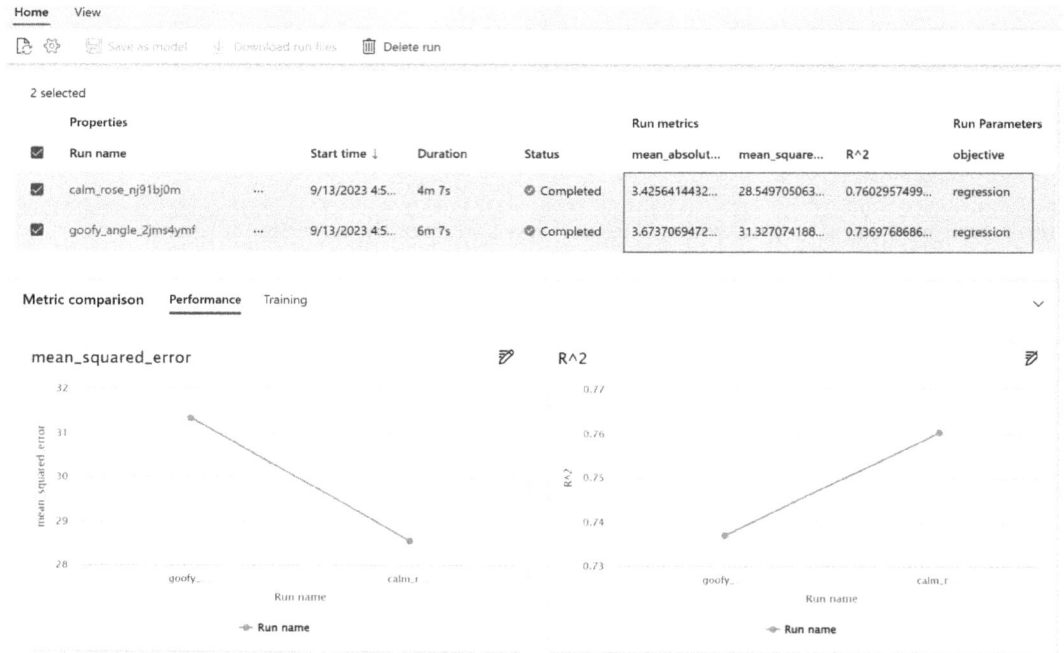

Figure 6.20 – Comparing evaluation metrics for different runs of the experiment in the user interface

Likewise, you can go to the workspace item view and open the model (name = nyc_yellowtaxi_predict_tripduration_lightgbm), as shown in *Figure 6.21*, to see different versions of the model registered in the model registry, different runs, and check/uncheck each run you want to include/exclude for comparison (please note that the run name is random). Once again, you can pick the model version that suits your business requirements by comparing its different aspects and applying it to generate future predictions:

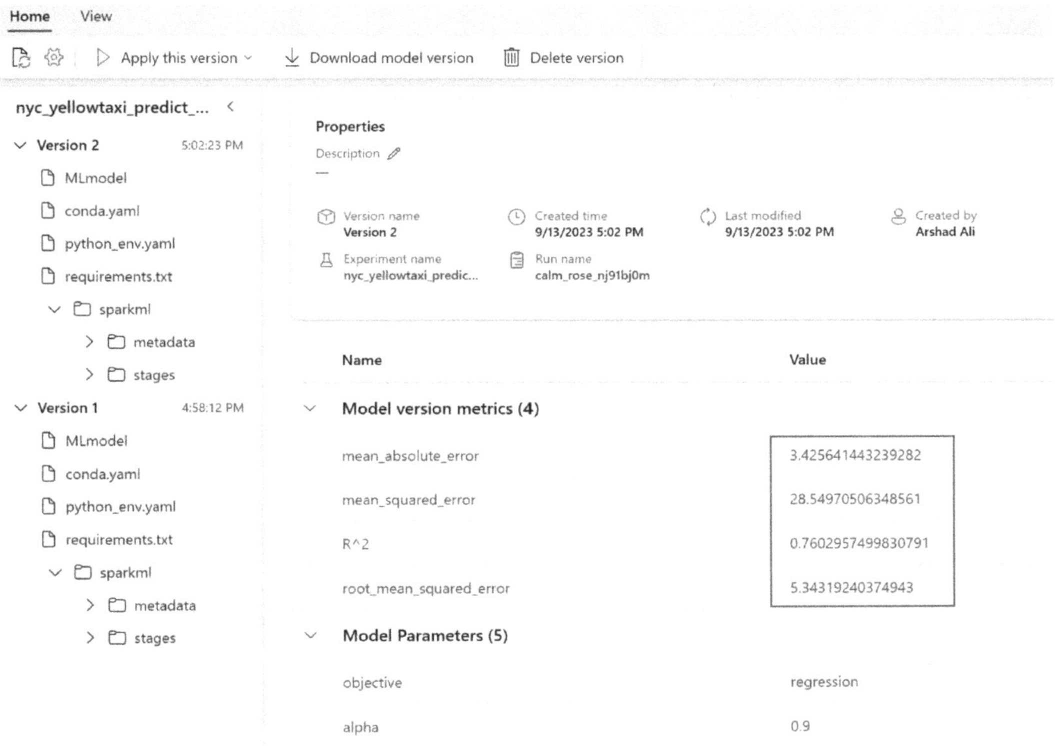

Figure 6.21 – Model view with different versions in the user interface

AutoML with FLAML

The native integration of FLAML (`https://microsoft.github.io/FLAML/`) in Fabric's Data Science experience offers the automated process of optimizing ML models and hyperparameter tuning. This process can also be easily tuned so that it can be used with SparkML and SynapseML models and is further supported by code-first integration to parallelize **AutoML** trials with Spark. Additionally, costs can be reduced by parallelizing hyperparameter trials with Spark.

As demonstrated earlier, MLflow can be used to automatically track hyperparameter metrics and parameters, making it easier to build and evaluate ML models quickly and efficiently.

> **Note**
>
> FLAML is a fast library for AutoML and parameter tuning. FLAML finds accurate models or configurations with low computational resources for common ML/AI tasks. It frees users from selecting models and hyperparameters for training or inference, with smooth customizability. You can learn more at `https://microsoft.github.io/FLAML/`.

Now that we've trained the model, let's see how we can use it to generate predictions on a new set of data.

Enriching and operationalizing

In this section, we will look at loading an already trained ML model from the model registry and generate predictions on new incoming data. Once these predictions have been generated, we will save this data in another Delta table so that we can create a report on it.

> **Note**
>
> The code that will be discussed in this section can be found in the `Data Science - Perform Prediction or Scoring` notebook. Please make sure you attach the lakehouse (`nyctaxilake`) you created in the *Data and storage – creating a lakehouse and ingesting data using Apache Spark* section of this chapter to this notebook.

The steps are as follows:

1. The first step is to import the required libraries into the current Spark session. Next, we must load the trained ML model from the MLflow-based model registry. While specifying the model's name, we also need to specify the version of the model – in this case, it's `version = 2`:

```
import mlflow
from pyspark.ml import Pipeline
from synapse.ml.core.platform import *
from synapse.ml.lightgbm import LightGBMRegressor
## Define model_uri to load the model with its specified version
mlexperiment_name = "nyc_yellowtaxi_predict_tripduration"
mlalgorithm_name = "lightgbm"
mlmodel_name = f"{mlexperiment_name}_{mlalgorithm_name}"
mlmodel_uri = f"models:/{mlmodel_name}/2"
loaded_model = mlflow.spark.load_model(mlmodel_uri, dfs_
tmpdir="Files/mlflow/tmp/")
```

2. Next, we must write a code block that specifies a random seed to randomly sample the data and then read cleansed data from June 2016 so that it takes a 25% random sample of it:

```
SEED = 1234 # Specify a random seed to use with random sampling
# Read cleansed data for the month of June and take 25% random
sample of it
nyc_yellowtaxi_prediction_input_df = spark.read.table("nyc_
yellowtaxi_clean")\
    .filter("puYear = 2016 AND puMonth = 6")\
    .sample(True, 0.25, seed=SEED)
```

3. The following code block generates predictions on the sample dataset by calling the `transform` function and leveraging the loaded ML model. While generating predictions, the model creates a feature vector and adds additional columns to the dataset. We will remove these additional columns to keep it simple:

```
# Generate predictions by applying model transform on the input
dataframe
nyc_yellowtaxi_prediction_output_df = loaded_model.
transform(nyc_yellowtaxi_prediction_input_df)
# Remove unnecessary columns added during prediction generation
cols_toremove = ['storeAndFwdFlagStrIdx', 'timeBinsStrIdx',
'vendorIDStrIdx', 'paymentTypeStrIdx', 'vendorIDOHEnc',
 'rateCodeIdOHEnc', 'paymentTypeOHEnc', 'weekDayOHEnc',
'pickupHourOHEnc', 'storeAndFwdFlagOHEnc', 'timeBinsOHEnc',
'features','weekDayNameStrIdx',
 'pickupHourStrIdx', 'rateCodeIdStrIdx', 'weekDayNameOHEnc']
nyc_yellowtaxi_prediction_output_df = nyc_yellowtaxi_
prediction_output_df.withColumnRenamed("prediction",
"predictedtripDuration").drop(*cols_toremove)
```

4. The following code block writes the dataset, along with its generated predictions, in a new Delta table:

```
table_name = "nyc_yellowtaxi_prediction"
nyc_yellowtaxi_prediction_output_df.write.mode("overwrite").
format("delta").saveAsTable(f"{table_name}")
print(f"Trip duration batch predictions saved to the delta
table: {table_name}")
```

5. When you query the newly created Delta table, you will see the original trip duration, as well as the predicted trip duration, in the dataset, as shown in *Figure 6.22*. Note that your result or output might be different than what's shown here:

```
1   %%sql
2   SELECT tripDuration, predictedtripDuration, *
3   FROM nyc_yellowtaxi_prediction LIMIT 20
```

✓ 3 sec -Command executed in 2 sec 602 ms by Arshad Ali on 5:46:20 PM, 9/13/23

> ☰ Spark jobs (3 of 3 succeeded)

> ⚕ Diagnostics   ⚠ 1

Table   Chart |→ Export results ⌄

Index	tripDuration	predictedtripDuration	vendorID	tpepPickupDateTime
4	56.833333333333336	54.78106080785214	1	2016-06-21T18:07:42Z
5	63.65	63.827310670153715	1	2016-06-27T17:51:25Z
6	60.61666666666667	65.44402928301034	2	2016-06-30T17:54:18Z
7	36.31666666666667	38.516358912519685	1	2016-06-07T19:19:46Z
8	42.63333333333333	24.514911726464515	2	2016-06-10T16:17:09Z
9	56.75	45.86565221519733	1	2016-06-14T19:16:19Z
10	79.18333333333334	58.86541266416315	2	2016-06-09T18:00:40Z
11	71.03333333333333	52.20628944418497	2	2016-06-08T18:37:31Z
12	72.36666666666666	48.85277231511892	1	2016-06-07T18:02:46Z
13	40.43333333333333	38.188235670935	1	2016-06-10T19:10:40Z

Figure 6.22 – Exploring the dataset with the original trip duration
and predicted trip duration for validation purposes

Now that we have a Delta table with generated predictions, let's create a report for it.

Analyzing and getting insights

In this section, we will use Power BI to create a report by connecting it to the lakehouse table we created in the previous section. Power BI is natively integrated into the whole Fabric experience. This provides a unique mode of accessing the data, called Direct Lake, which we discussed in earlier chapters, from the lakehouse to provide the most performant query and reporting experience. Let's create a report based on the data from the nyctaxilake lakehouse:

1. Open the nyctaxilake lakehouse and click on **SQL endpoint** under mode selection at the top right of the screen to switch to SQL endpoint mode for the selected lakehouse.

2. Once you are in SQL endpoint mode, you should be able to see all the tables you've created. If you don't see them, please click on the **Refresh** icon at the top. Next, click on the **New report** icon at the top to create a Power BI report.

3. On the Power BI report canvas, you can add a title for your report. In the ribbon, click on the text box icon (available at the top right of the screen) and drag it to the top left, type in Trip

`Duration Prediction Analysis`, and then select the typed text and increase its font size to 24.

4. Next, we will add the average trip duration and predicted trip duration to the report as another card. From the **Data** pane, expand **nyc_yellowtaxi_prediction**, drag **tripDuration** onto the canvas, and drop it. Next, change the visualization type to **Card** (when you hover over the visual, it shows the type). Under **Fields**, you can rename this measure if you wish. Also, make sure the aggregation method is set to **Average**, as shown in *Figure 6.23*. Click anywhere in the canvas, drag **predictedtripDuration** onto the canvas, and drop it. Next, change the visualization type to **Card**. Under **Fields**, you can rename this measure if you wish. As mentioned previously, make sure the aggregation method is set to **Average**:

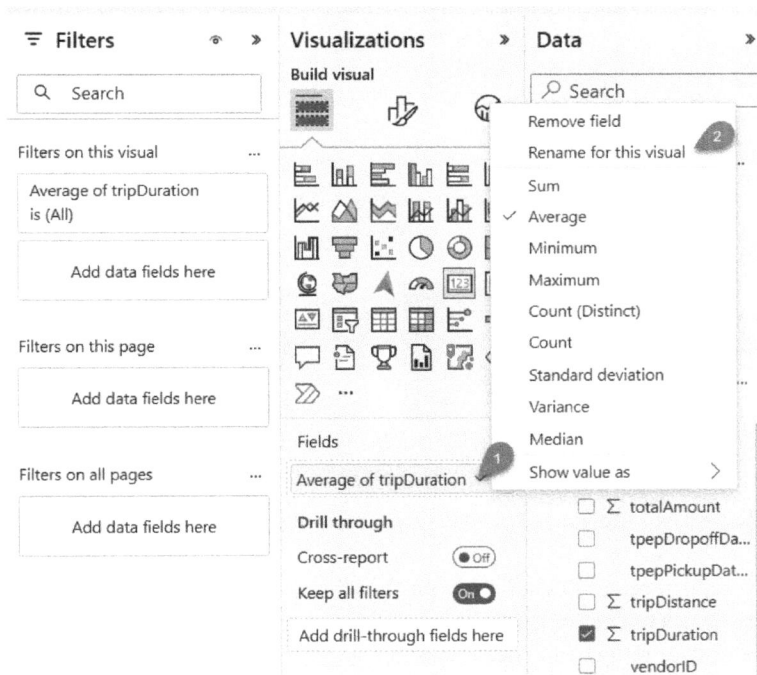

Figure 6.23 – Renaming a field and changing the aggregation type

5. Next, we'll create a line chart – make sure nothing is selected on the canvas, drag **tripDuration** (from the **nyc_yellowtaxi_prediction** table) onto the canvas, and drop it. Next, drag **predictedtripDuration** onto the canvas and drop it. Both these columns should appear in the **Y-axis** area. Now, set the aggregation method to **Average** for both. Once you've done that, drag **weekDayName** onto the canvas and drop it. Finally, change the chart type to **Line Chart**.

6. Next, let's create a clustered column chart – make sure nothing is selected on the canvas, drag **tripDuration** (from the **nyc_yellowtaxi_prediction** table) onto the canvas, and drop it. Then, drag **predictedtripDuration** onto the canvas and drop it. Both these columns should appear

in the **Y-axis** area. Now, set the aggregation method to **Average** for both. Once you've done that, drag **timeBins** onto the canvas and drop it. Finally, change the chart type to **Clustered Column Chart**.

7.   After adding these visuals and organizing them on the canvas, your report should look like what's shown in *Figure 6.24*:

Trip Duration Prediction Analysis

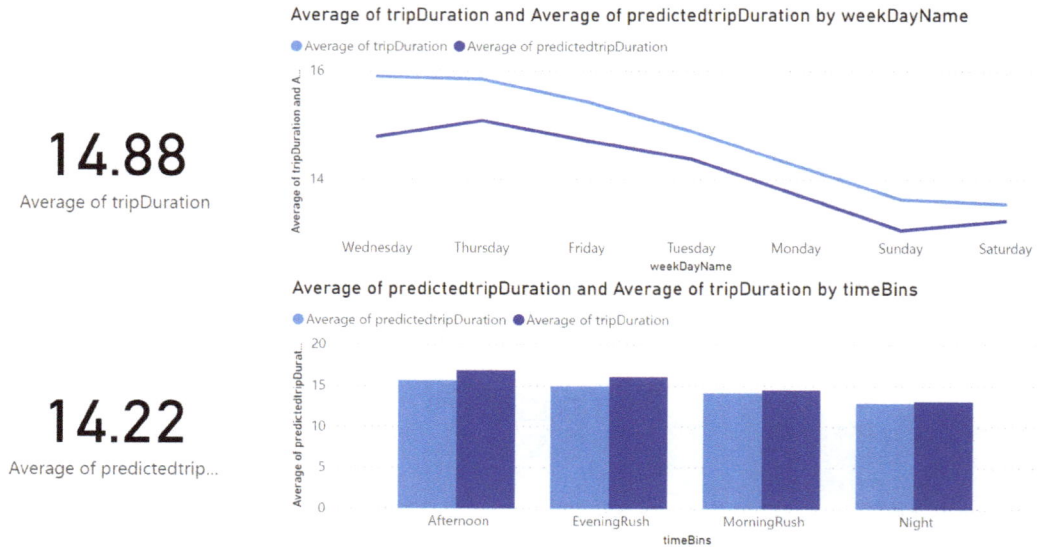

Figure 6.24 – Creating a Power BI report to analyze the predicted results

8.   To save this report, select **File** | **Save** from the ribbon or click *Ctrl + S* while on the canvas. Enter `Trip Duration Prediction Analysis` (or whatever name you want to give) as the name of your report and click on **Save**.

These saved predictions can be analyzed further in reports and dashboards. In this section, we used Power BI to do that.

Summary

In this chapter, you learned about the data science process and data science project development life cycle, after which you learned about different capabilities in Microsoft Fabric that empower you at each step in this journey. You learned about all these capabilities by implementing an end-to-end data science project in Microsoft Fabric based on the regression model and also learned how to leverage advanced capabilities, such as using the model registry and tracking with MLflow, Semantic Link, AutoML, and SynapseML.

This whole experience is natively integrated and built into Fabric, giving you the power and flexibility to build end-to-end data science projects without having to switch to or learn about other technologies. This includes capabilities for data ingestion, data transformation, and feature engineering with Notebooks/Spark to training ML models in a distributed manner with SynapseML. Furthermore, it allows you to leverage different open source libraries such as MLflow for model registry and tracking, Semantic Link to leverage the knowledge harvested in semantic business models, FLAML for automated ML, and more. Finally, you learned how to run model scoring on new incoming data and then use Power BI, with its new Direct Lake mode, to create reports and dashboards.

In the next chapter, you will learn about monitoring capabilities in Microsoft Fabric for different types of workloads – Data Factory, Data engineering, Data Science, Data Warehouse, Real-Time Analytics, and more.

Part 3:
Administration and Monitoring

This part of the book covers monitoring different aspects of Microsoft Fabric using **Monitoring hub**, including Data Factory pipelines, Spark jobs for both the data science and data engineering workloads, DMVs and query insights to monitor the data warehouse, and the KQL database activity for real-time analytics. Further, it covers the administration aspect of Microsoft Fabric to enable, manage, and work with it.

This part contains the following chapters:

- *Chapter 7, Monitoring Overview and Monitoring Different Workloads*
- *Chapter 8, Administering Fabric*

7

Monitoring Overview and Monitoring Different Workloads

While Fabric has been designed with built-in auto-optimization for optimal performance, there are times when you would like to look into currently running jobs (for auditing and control) and/or learn to monitor, troubleshoot, and optimize it even further than what is natively provided. In this chapter, you will learn about how to monitor different Fabric workloads, gain an understanding of what's going on under the hood, and learn how to perform troubleshooting for your jobs.

The topics covered in this chapter are as follows:

- Overview of monitoring capabilities in Fabric
- Monitoring Data Factory pipelines and dataflows
- Monitoring Spark jobs (data engineering and data science)
- Monitoring data warehouse activity
- Monitoring Real-Time Analytics activity
- Monitoring capacity usage with the Capacity Metrics app

With the help of these topics, you will learn about monitoring different aspects of Fabric and its workloads.

Technical requirements

This chapter builds on *Chapters 3, 4, 5,* and *6,* and you should have completed these chapters to monitor the execution of the jobs from those chapters.

Overview of monitoring capabilities in Fabric

Monitoring hub in Fabric is a central, single entry point for you to monitor and track every aspect of jobs' progress from different Fabric workloads. You can launch **Monitoring hub** from the left pane by clicking on the **Monitoring hub** icon, as shown in *Figure 7.1*. By default, it shows logged job execution data (**In progress**, **Completed**, **Failed**, **Cancelled**, **Not started**, and so on) for the last seven days; however, you can change the time range based on your needs.

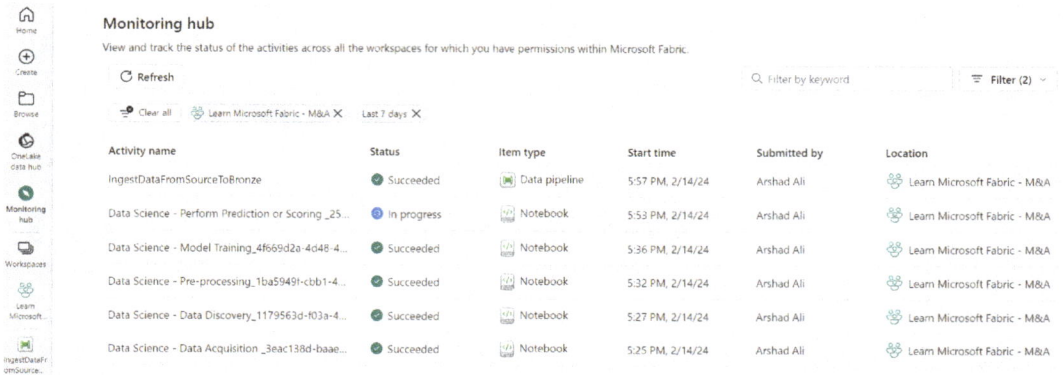

Figure 7.1 – Monitoring hub

On the top- right side of the **Monitoring hub** page, you will find options to choose columns you want to see as part of the table, as shown in *Figure 7.2*. There are some default columns already included; however, you can include additional columns with additional information to learn more about what's going on. Likewise, you can also apply filters to the tracked monitoring information. For example, you can choose the time range, the submitter of the jobs, workspaces where these logs come from, and so on, as shown in *Figure 7.2*:

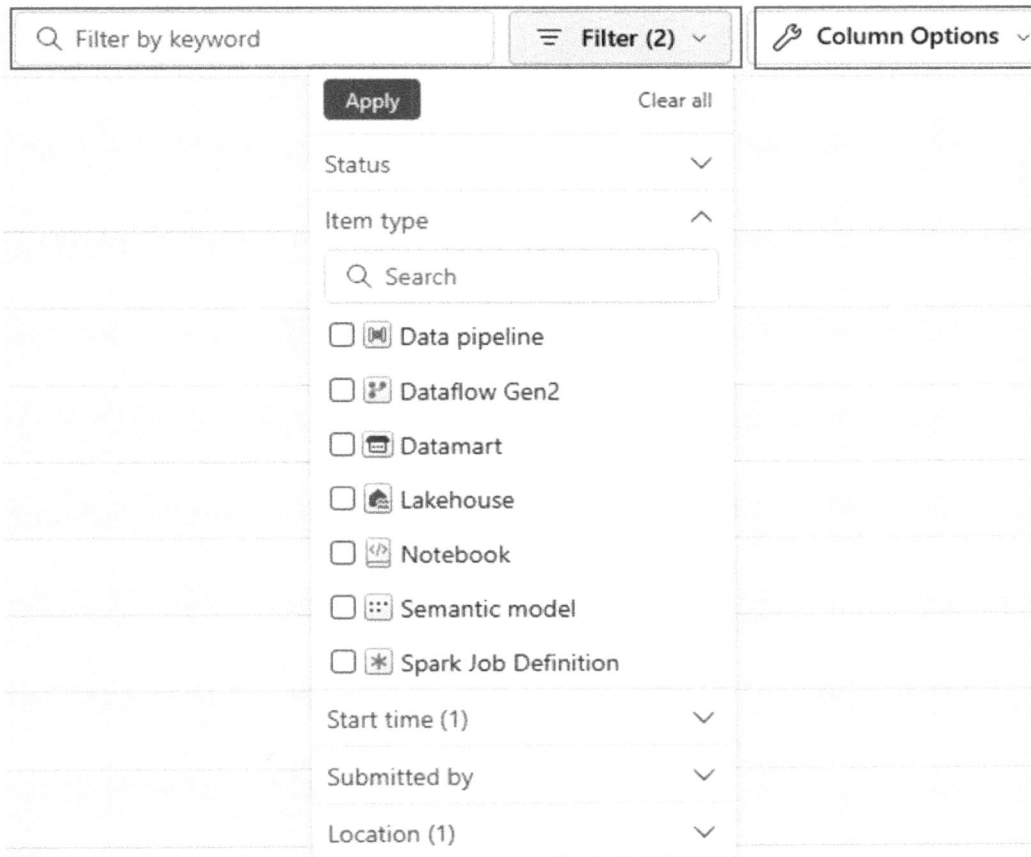

Figure 7.2 – Options to choose columns and apply filters in the Monitoring hub view

Additionally, when you are in the workspace view, you can hover over an item and then click on the
... button to get an option to see all its recent runs, as shown in *Figure 7.3*:

🗋	Name	Type
📊	Customer Analysis	Report
🏠	LH_WideWorldImporters	Lakehouse
⠿	LH_WideWorldImporters	Semantic model (...
🌐	LH_WideWorldImporters	SQL analytics end...
📼	Load DimEmployee	
📼	Load DimEmployee Table	
🏠	MyLakehouse	
⠿	MyLakehouse	
🌐	MyLakehouse	
</>	NB_BronzeToSilver	
📄	Operational Sales Report	
📼	PL_BronzeToSilver	
📼	PL_SilverToGold	Data pipeline
📼	PL_SourceToBronze	Data pipeline

Menu overlay:
- ⧉ Open
- 🗑 Delete
- ⚙ Settings
- ☆ Add to Favorites
- ⚬ View lineage
- ▤ View details
- 📥 Move to
- 🕐 Schedule
- 🕔 Recent runs
- 💾 Save as

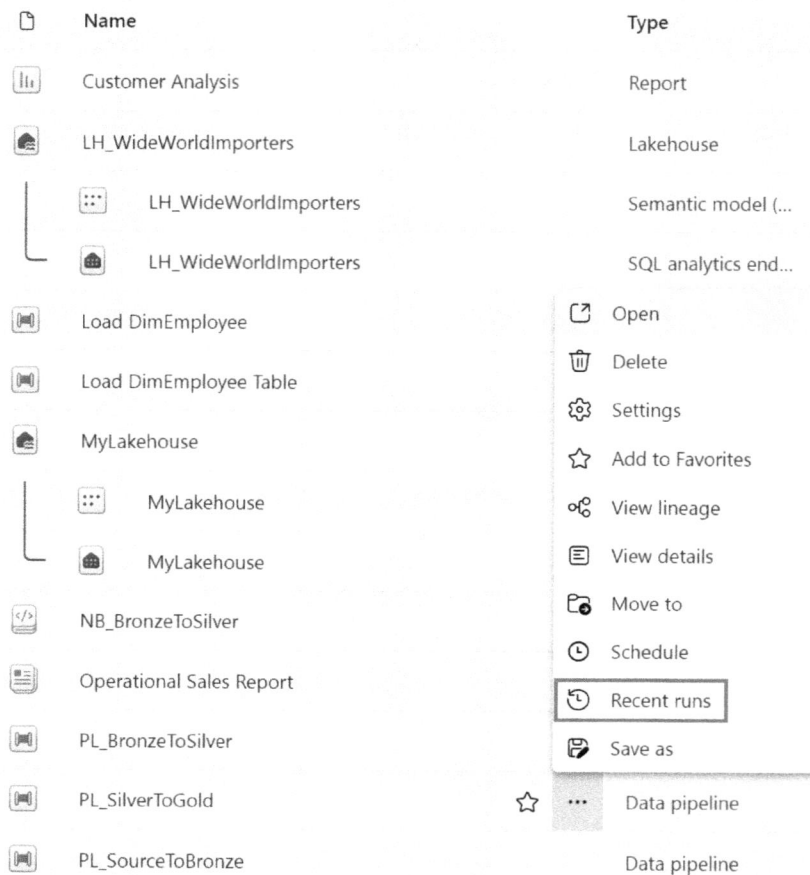

Figure 7.3 – Recent runs of the selection item in the workspace view

The **Monitoring Hub** page will be the default location for viewing activity in Fabric. Let's dive deeper into monitoring individual Fabric workloads, starting with Data Factory pipelines.

Monitoring Data Factory pipelines and dataflows

A Data Factory workload in Fabric brings together the ease of use of Power Query and the scale and power of Azure Data Factory for you to build the data integration component of your analytics system. It offers **pipelines**, which are groupings of one or more activities that are executed together (either serially or parallelly based on how you have designed it) to perform a specific task, and **dataflows**, which are transformation engines of Microsoft Fabric that use Power Query to deliver a low- to no-code data transformation experience. You can monitor the execution of pipelines and dataflows in **Monitoring hub**.

You can scroll through the list of tracked information or you can use the filter available at the top of the **Monitoring hub** page to filter tracked information for pipelines or dataflows. As shown in *Figure 7.4*, you can also use text-based search to filter out information to easily locate the pipeline or dataflow execution instance to get more details about it.

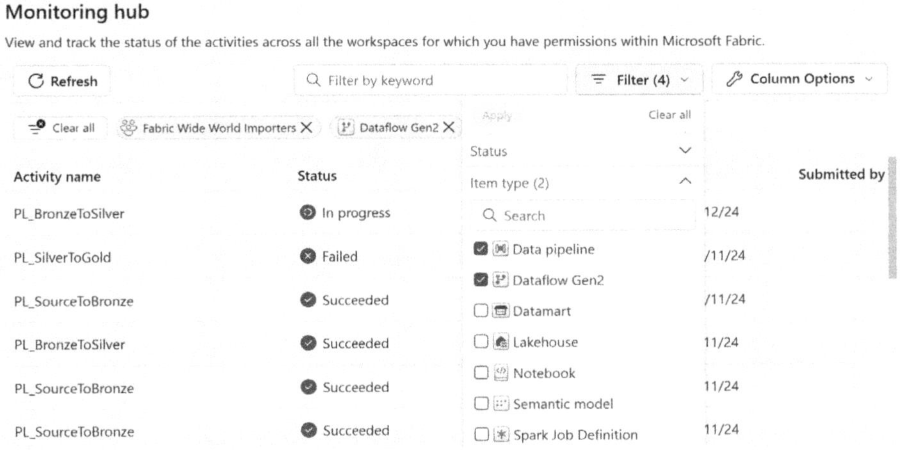

Figure 7.4 – Filtering information for Data Factory in Monitoring hub

When you hover over or select a specific activity in the table in the **Monitoring hub** window, it shows you options to retry or to get more details about it. When you click to view more details, it takes you to a detail page where you can see the execution status of the pipeline with all of its activities. *Figure 7.5* shows an example of the pipeline with just one data copy activity. It shows the execution status, start time, total duration, input, output, and so on.

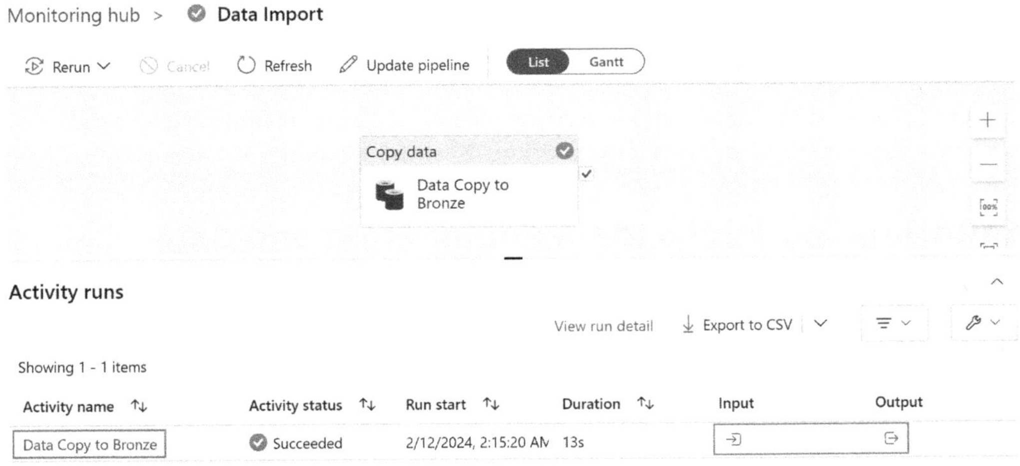

Figure 7.5 – Tracking execution of the pipeline

You can click on the activity name as shown in *Figure 7.5*, and it takes you to a details page as shown in *Figure 7.6*. As this is a data copy activity, it shows source and destination information, data read and written, files read and written, the overall time it took, data transfer throughput, and so on.

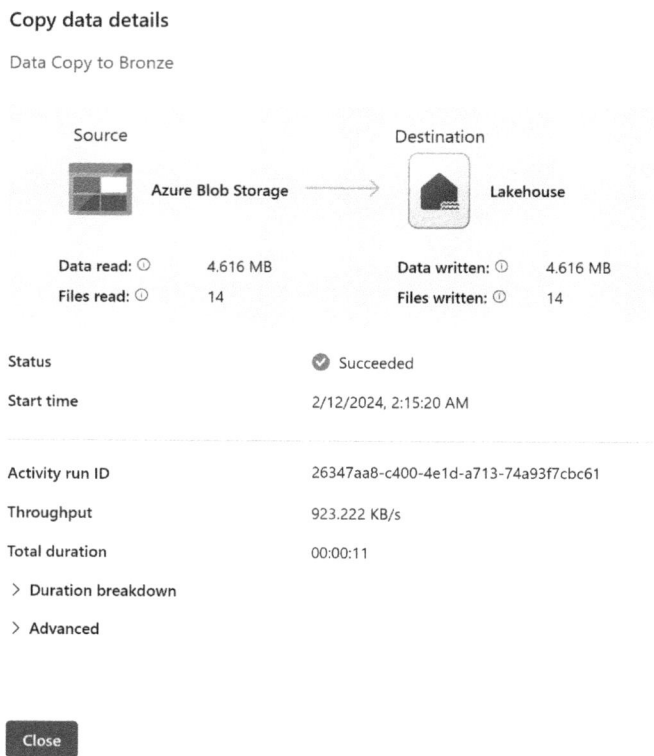

Copy data details

Data Copy to Bronze

Source   Destination

Azure Blob Storage   →   Lakehouse

Data read: ⓘ	4.616 MB	
Files read: ⓘ	14	

Data written: ⓘ	4.616 MB	
Files written: ⓘ	14	

Status   ✓ Succeeded

Start time   2/12/2024, 2:15:20 AM

Activity run ID   26347aa8-c400-4e1d-a713-74a93f7cbc61

Throughput   923.222 KB/s

Total duration   00:00:11

> Duration breakdown

> Advanced

[Close]

Figure 7.6 – Monitoring execution of a data copy activity execution

Monitoring ETL is an important activity in every organization. If data is not loaded into the lakehouse or warehouse, then the business cannot make decisions. Next, let's explore how to monitor Spark jobs.

Monitoring Spark jobs (data engineering and data science)

Data engineering and data science workloads are powered by **Fabric Spark Runtime** (based on Apache Spark). With the flexibility Fabric provides, you can either choose Notebook for interactive development, use a Spark job definition for batch execution, or use REST APIs for programmatically submitting and executing these jobs. In all these cases, these jobs will be executed by Fabric Spark Runtime and telemetry will be captured for you to look into.

You can monitor these jobs while they're still executing or when they have completed their execution in **Monitoring hub**. You can scroll through the list of tracked activity or you can use a filter at the top to search logged information of a specific type. *Figure 7.7* shows an example where it uses text-based search to search for all the logs for notebook execution. You can hover over each row to get its details or you can click on it to get more granular details for the Spark application or session execution.

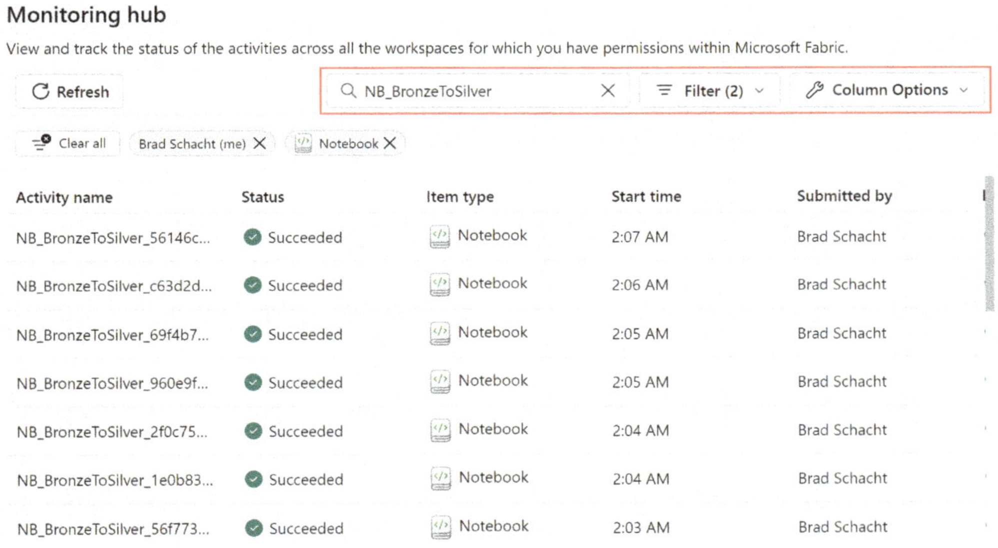
Monitoring hub
View and track the status of the activities across all the workspaces for which you have permissions within Microsoft Fabric.
Refresh
NB_BronzeToSilver
Filter (2)
Column Options
Clear all
Brad Schacht (me)
Notebook
Activity name
Status
Item type
Start time
Submitted by
NB_BronzeToSilver_56146c...
Succeeded
Notebook
2:07 AM
Brad Schacht
NB_BronzeToSilver_c63d2d...
Succeeded
Notebook
2:06 AM
Brad Schacht
NB_BronzeToSilver_69f4b7...
Succeeded
Notebook
2:05 AM
Brad Schacht
NB_BronzeToSilver_960e9f...
Succeeded
Notebook
2:05 AM
Brad Schacht
NB_BronzeToSilver_2f0c75...
Succeeded
Notebook
2:04 AM
Brad Schacht
NB_BronzeToSilver_1e0b83...
Succeeded
Notebook
2:04 AM
Brad Schacht
NB_BronzeToSilver_56f773...
Succeeded
Notebook
2:03 AM
Brad Schacht

Figure 7.7 – Filtering information for notebook executions in Monitoring hub

Figure 7.8 shows details about a Spark application or session execution. As you can see, there were several jobs submitted or triggered when executing Spark action commands. Additionally, you would see lots of other useful information that can help you in your troubleshooting or debugging, such as total duration, Livy ID, and diagnostic information (data or time skewness). In *Figure 7.8*, you can also switch to the **Logs** tab to see and analyze *Driver or Livy logs*.

> **Note**
>
> The Spark driver negotiates resources with the cluster manager and schedules Spark job execution. Driver logs provide information about how a Spark job is scheduled and run, and how resources were used. Livy provides REST API access to submit Spark jobs.

⚙ Data Science - Perform Prediction or Scoring _e218e056-af66-4582-95bf-a032e00ff8f5

↻ Refresh   ⊘ Stop application   ⊏ Spark History Server

Jobs   Resources (Preview)   Logs   Data   Item snapshots

	ID ↑	Description		Status	Stages	Tasks	
>	Job 40	take at SQLInterpreter.scala:155		✅ Succeeded	1/1	4/4 succeec	
>	Job 39	take at SQLInterpreter.scala:155		✅ Succeeded	1/1	1/1 succeec	
>	Job 38	$anonfun$recordDeltaOperationInternal$1 at SynapseLoggingShim.scala:95		✅ Succeeded	1/1	50/50 succe	
>	Job 37	toString at String.java:2994		✅ Succeeded	1/1	1/1 succeec	
>	Job 36	toString at String.java:2994		✅ Succeeded	1/1	50/50 succe	
>	Job 35	toString at String.java:2994		✅ Succeeded	1/1	2/2 succeec	
>	Job 34	$anonfun$recordDeltaOperationInternal$1 at SynapseLoggingShim.scala:95		✅ Succeeded	1/1	50/50 succe	

Details

Status
⊘ Stopped

Application ID
application_170

Total duration
7 min 41 sec

Running duration
7 min 41 sec

Queued duration
0 sec

Livy ID
e218e056-af66-4582-95bf-a032e

Submitter
ara

Submit time
2/14/24 6:15:21 PM

Runtime information
Runtime 1.1 (Spark 3.3, Delta 2.2)

Number of executors
1

Diagnostics ⚠ 1   ⌄

> ⚠ Data and time skew

Figure 7.8 – Analyzing job execution in a Spark application/session

If you scroll to the right of the table, you will see additional details about each job such as duration, total rows processed, data read or written, and code snippet as shown in *Figure 7.9*:

Jobs   Logs   Data   Item snapshots

Status	Stages	Tasks	Duration	Processed	Data read	Data written	Code snippet
✅ Succeeded	1/1	1/1 succeeded	35 ms	50 rows	4.47 KB	0 B	</>
✅ Succeeded	1/1	50/50 succeeded	629 ms	117 rows	28.1 KB	4.47 KB	</>
✅ Succeeded	1/1	8/8 succeeded	305 ms	134 rows	11.87 KB	28.1 KB	</>
✅ Succeeded	1/1	1/1 succeeded	836 ms	28 rows	337 B	2.28 KB	</>
✅ Succeeded	1/1	1/1 succeeded	401 ms	42 rows	3.25 KB	337 B	</>
✅ Succeeded	1/1	1/1 succeeded	1 sec 429 ms	14 rows	2.78 KB	787 B	</>
✅ Succeeded	1/1	1/1 succeeded	543 ms	28 rows	615 B	1.29 KB	</>

Figure 7.9 – Analyzing details about Spark job executions

For each of the jobs, where applicable, you can click on the **Code snippet** link to get the code, as shown in the last column in *Figure 7.9*, which triggered the execution of that specific job. *Figure 7.10* shows an example of a job that was triggered when writing a data frame to a delta table:

Figure 7.10 – Analyzing code that triggered a Spark job execution

As shown in *Figure 7.8*, you can click on the **Spark history server** or **Spark Web UI** link to get to the Spark UI for monitoring further details. Spark Web UI or Spark history server is a web interface that comes as part of the open source Apache Spark, however, Fabric includes more information in addition to that. As shown in *Figure 7.11*, the **Graph** tab shows a graph view of all the jobs submitted in that session, which you can analyze by using different filters or using playback capabilities and so on, and the **Diagnostic** tab shows diagnostic information such as data skewness and time skewness. You can learn more about it here: `https://learn.microsoft.com/en-us/fabric/data-engineering/apache-spark-history-server`.

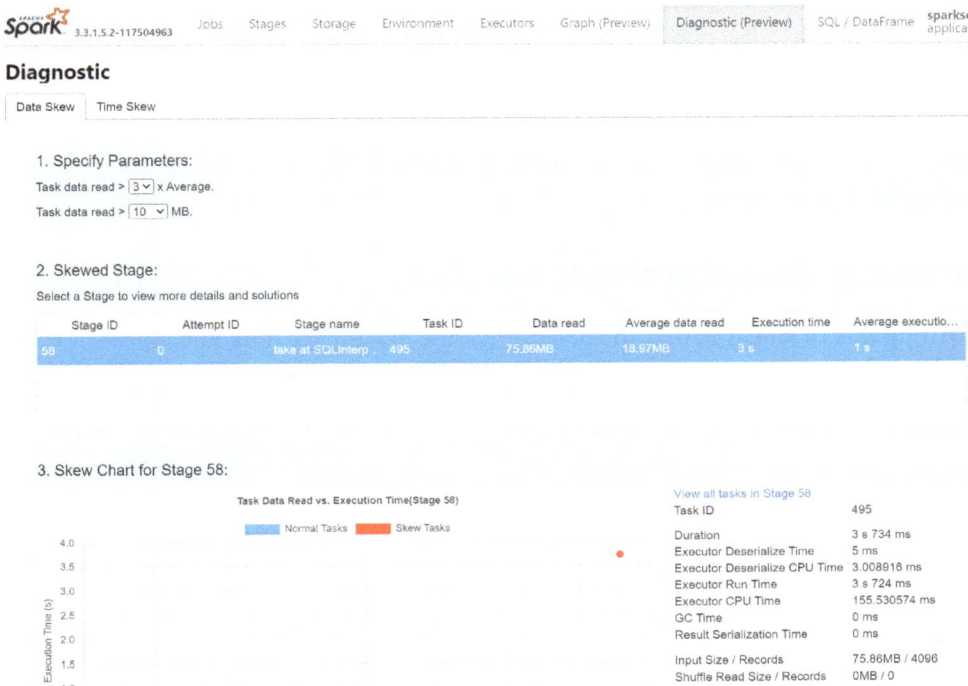

Figure 7.11 – Spark history server – the Diagnostic tab

While monitoring Spark applications and jobs through **Monitoring hub** is always an option, Fabric also makes it easy to do contextual monitoring when you are working interactively in the notebook at the cell level, as shown in *Figure 7.12*. When you execute a cell in the notebook interactively, it shows the execution status and other details such as all the jobs submitted from the code in that specific cell, total tasks for each job, data read and written, diagnostic information (data and time skewness), if any, and an option to navigate to the Spark Web UI directly from here, as well as quick and easy access to the logs.

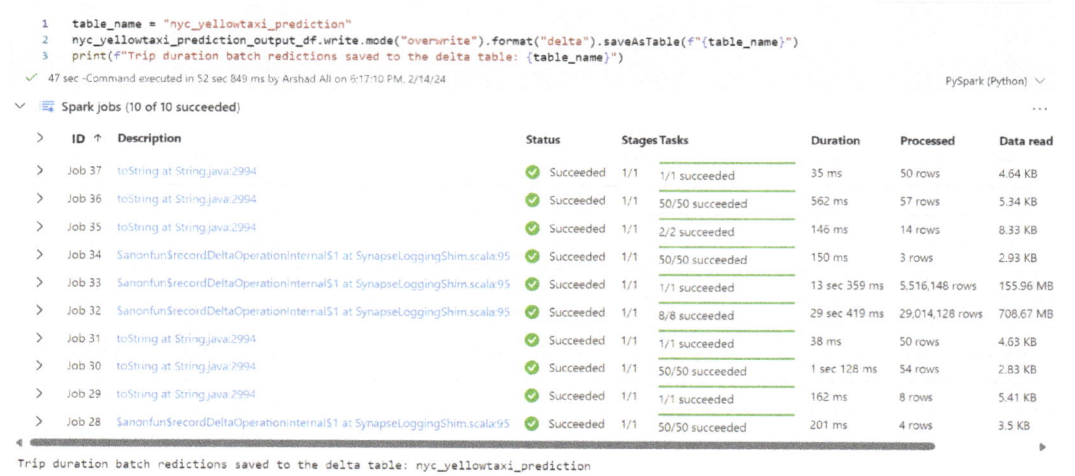

```
1    table_name = "nyc_yellowtaxi_prediction"
2    nyc_yellowtaxi_prediction_output_df.write.mode("overwrite").format("delta").saveAsTable(f"{table_name}")
3    print(f"Trip duration batch redictions saved to the delta table: {table_name}")
```

✓ 47 sec -Command executed in 52 sec 849 ms by Arshad Ali on 6:17:10 PM, 2/14/24   PySpark (Python) ∨

Spark jobs (10 of 10 succeeded)   ...

	ID ↑	Description	Status	Stages	Tasks	Duration	Processed	Data read
>	Job 37	toString at String.java:2994	Succeeded	1/1	1/1 succeeded	35 ms	50 rows	4.64 KB
>	Job 36	toString at String.java:2994	Succeeded	1/1	50/50 succeeded	562 ms	57 rows	5.34 KB
>	Job 35	toString at String.java:2994	Succeeded	1/1	2/2 succeeded	146 ms	14 rows	8.33 KB
>	Job 34	$anonfun$recordDeltaOperationInternal$1 at SynapseLoggingShim.scala:95	Succeeded	1/1	50/50 succeeded	150 ms	3 rows	2.93 KB
>	Job 33	$anonfun$recordDeltaOperationInternal$1 at SynapseLoggingShim.scala:95	Succeeded	1/1	1/1 succeeded	13 sec 359 ms	5,516,148 rows	155.96 MB
>	Job 32	$anonfun$recordDeltaOperationInternal$1 at SynapseLoggingShim.scala:95	Succeeded	1/1	8/8 succeeded	29 sec 419 ms	29,014,128 rows	708.67 MB
>	Job 31	toString at String.java:2994	Succeeded	1/1	1/1 succeeded	38 ms	50 rows	4.63 KB
>	Job 30	toString at String.java:2994	Succeeded	1/1	50/50 succeeded	1 sec 128 ms	54 rows	2.83 KB
>	Job 29	toString at String.java:2994	Succeeded	1/1	1/1 succeeded	162 ms	8 rows	5.41 KB
>	Job 28	$anonfun$recordDeltaOperationInternal$1 at SynapseLoggingShim.scala:95	Succeeded	1/1	50/50 succeeded	201 ms	4 rows	3.5 KB

Trip duration batch redictions saved to the delta table: nyc_yellowtaxi_prediction

Figure 7.12 – Inline monitoring while executing code in the notebook interactively

Now that we have seen how to view the summary and detail logs for all Spark jobs, let's look at monitoring the data warehouse.

Monitoring data warehouse activity

As of writing this in January 2024, the data warehouse experience does not appear in Fabric's **Monitoring hub**. Instead, administrators will rely on **Dynamic Management Views** (**DMVs**) to gain insight into warehouse and SQL endpoint activity. Combined, the DMVs provide a view into server connections (sys.dm_exec_connections), sessions (sys.dm_exec_sessions), and active queries (sys.dm_exec_requests).

Looking at the data in these can answer a few key questions:

- Who is connected to the warehouse and from where?
- What queries are executing right now?

- Who is executing queries right now?

- How long have queries been executing?

Using a script available in the Fabric toolbox (`https://aka.ms/FabricToolbox`), these DMVs can be joined together to provide a look at all the current database activity.

```
▷ Run    🔖 Save as view
                   LEFT(t.TEXT, (r.[statement_end_offset]/2) +1)
29          END
30          END
31          AS [executing_statement]
32          ,t.[text] AS [parent_batch]
33          , s.program_name
34          , r.query_hash
35          , r.query_plan_hash
36          , r.dist_statement_id
37          , r.label
38          , s.client_interface_name
39          ,r.sql_handle
40          ,c.client_net_address
41          ,c.connection_id
42     FROM sys.dm_exec_requests r
43     CROSS APPLY sys.[dm_exec_sql_text](r.[sql_handle]) t
44     JOIN sys.dm_exec_sessions s
45          ON r.session_id = s.session_id
46     JOIN sys.dm_exec_connections c
47          ON s.session_id = c.session_id
48     JOIN sys.databases d
49          ON d.database_id = r.database_id
50     WHERE r.dist_statement_id != '00000000-0000-0000-0000-000000000000'
51     AND r.session_id <> @@SPID
```

Messages   **Results**   ⊞ Save as table   ⌧ Open in Excel   ⨝ Explore this data (preview) ∨   🔍 Search   ≫

	ABC database_name ↓	ABC login_name	12S session_id	start_time	ABC status	123 total_elapsed_time
2	master	DB00000B\WF-NIXoQPADddISfil	131	2024-02-12T06:39:41.8000000	running	712004
1	WH_WideWorldImporters		55	2024-02-12T06:49:10.0770000	running	143731
3	WH_WideWorldImporters		156	2024-02-12T06:51:33.1230000	running	679

Figure 7.13 – An example output from the Fabric SQL DMVs

DMVs provide valuable information but only show a single point in time view of database activity. This leaves organizations with a decision on how to gather and store query history, which can be useful for a variety of reasons such as troubleshooting, auditing, and performance tracking. The query insights store continuously collects key pieces of information on the system and stores them for up to 30 days.

Three views are provided that deliver important points of analysis:

- `queryinsights.exec_requests_history` stores a full history of every query executed, including start time, end time, and query text

	UID distributed_statement_id	start_time	end_time	ABC command
1	4D03151B-617C-4C56-90C4-A60A9A384B5A	2024-02-12 06:46:45.000000	2024-02-12 06:46:45.000000	SELECT d.name as "database_name" , s.login_name , r
2	ADACB107-ECB4-4EC8-AEEF-9991EB81EECE	2024-02-12 06:47:58.000000	2024-02-12 06:47:58.000000	SELECT * FROM dbo.DimCity CROSS APPLY dbo.FactS
3	24303DD2-0651-479E-8658-C7491CDA7D45	2024-02-12 06:48:17.000000	2024-02-12 06:48:43.000000	SELECT * FROM dbo.DimEmployee CROSS APPLY dbo
4	E68BB1D2-4652-4C64-AB56-D4A5AF138C25	2024-02-12 06:48:20.000000	2024-02-12 06:48:20.000000	SELECT d.name as "database_name" , s.login_name , r
5	0EB5927E-6213-4381-AECD-4750CAC3AB85	2024-02-12 06:48:27.000000	2024-02-12 06:48:27.000000	SELECT d.name as "database_name" , s.login_name , r
6	9CA594AC-F333-4DC0-9A5F-005964933B08	2024-02-12 06:49:04.000000	2024-02-12 06:49:04.000000	SELECT * FROM sys.dm_exec_requests WHERE status
7	75B6F097-D6D6-44FE-928B-D3E21F26FBF5	2024-02-12 06:43:07.000000	2024-02-12 06:43:08.000000	SELECT TOP (1000) * FROM [WH_WideWorldImporter
8	03A08485-6F81-4A2A-9EB4-C3F1352A5D76	2024-02-12 06:43:47.000000	2024-02-12 06:43:47.000000	SELECT 79 as XLOrdinal, HAS_PERMS_BY_NAME("[dbc
9	A8F6C3BB-BD60-4CBF-8248-86E239098C77	2024-02-12 06:43:48.000000	2024-02-12 06:43:48.000000	SELECT 6 as XLOrdinal, COUNT(*) as RLSPolicyCnt FRC
10	DEAC57E0-D17C-4E1C-8153-D092317DA60D	2024-02-12 06:43:49.000000	2024-02-12 06:43:49.000000	SELECT TOP (1000) * FROM [WH_WideWorldImporter

Figure 7.14 – The output from queryinsights.exex_requests_history, which holds the last 30 days of queries

- `queryinsights.long_running_queries` helps users analyze the execution time of each query to identify opportunities for tuning and optimization
- `queryinsights.frequently_run_queries` returns a list of queries with a few stats around execution, including the number of runs, the most recent run's duration, the maximum run duration, and the average duration

DMVs show current activity while query insights provide historical information. This gives administrators the ability to review database activity and developers the tools to optimize queries for future use. Next, let's explore how to monitor the Real-Time Analytics workload.

Monitoring Real-Time Analytics activity

With Fabric Real-Time Analytics, there are two main areas that need to be monitored: eventstreams and KQL database activity. While there is no centralized report to see activity across all eventstreams and KQL databases inside a workspace, the relevant information can be found by navigating to each item individually. Because the experience is slightly different for each of these two items, let's look at them individually.

Monitoring eventstreams

Recall from *Chapter 5, Building an End-to-End Analytics System – Real-Time Analytics*, that an eventstream captures, transforms, and routes events to destinations such as KQL databases or Fabric lakehouses. There are two options for monitoring the health and performance of an eventstream, and both are available from the eventstream editor.

The first option, **Data insights**, displays a variety of metrics related to performance and health. This chart allows you to easily determine if there are issues with the eventstream by checking the number of messages and the size of data coming into and leaving the eventstream.

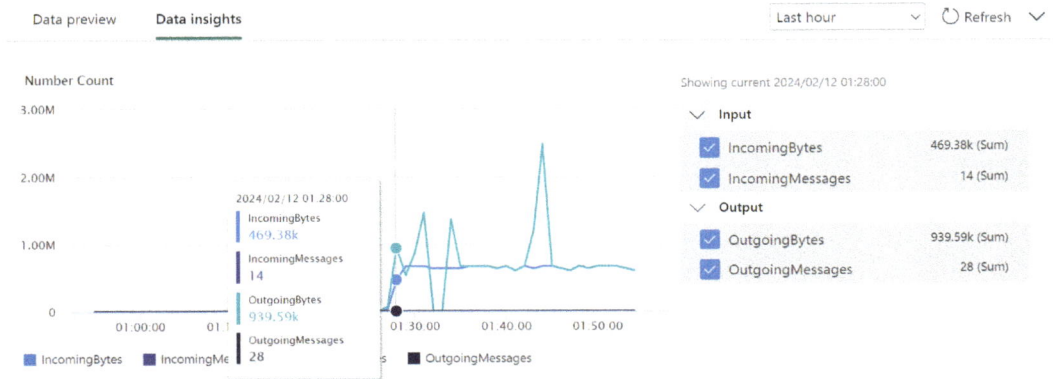

Figure 7.15 – The Data insights section of an eventstream

Metrics don't always provide the full picture though. Additional metrics are available for event hub sources and lakehouse destinations, including backlogged input events, runtime errors, data conversion errors, and deserialization errors. These can be found in **Runtime logs** when selecting an event hub or lakehouse in the eventstream editor.

Monitoring eventstreams provides insight into the data being collected. Now let's look at the consumption side of Real-Time Analytics in the KQL database.

Monitoring KQL databases

As with any database or analytics tool, it will be important to understand the overall database consumption in addition to the activity that is taking place. How large is the database, what queries have been executed, at what time were they executed, who executed them, and what was the performance of the queries are common questions asked by administrators and developers alike.

From the dashboard shown in *Figure 7.16*, when opening a KQL database in Fabric, we see many important metrics at a glance. This includes the overall database size, a list of the largest tables, the most active users, and the last time data was ingested.

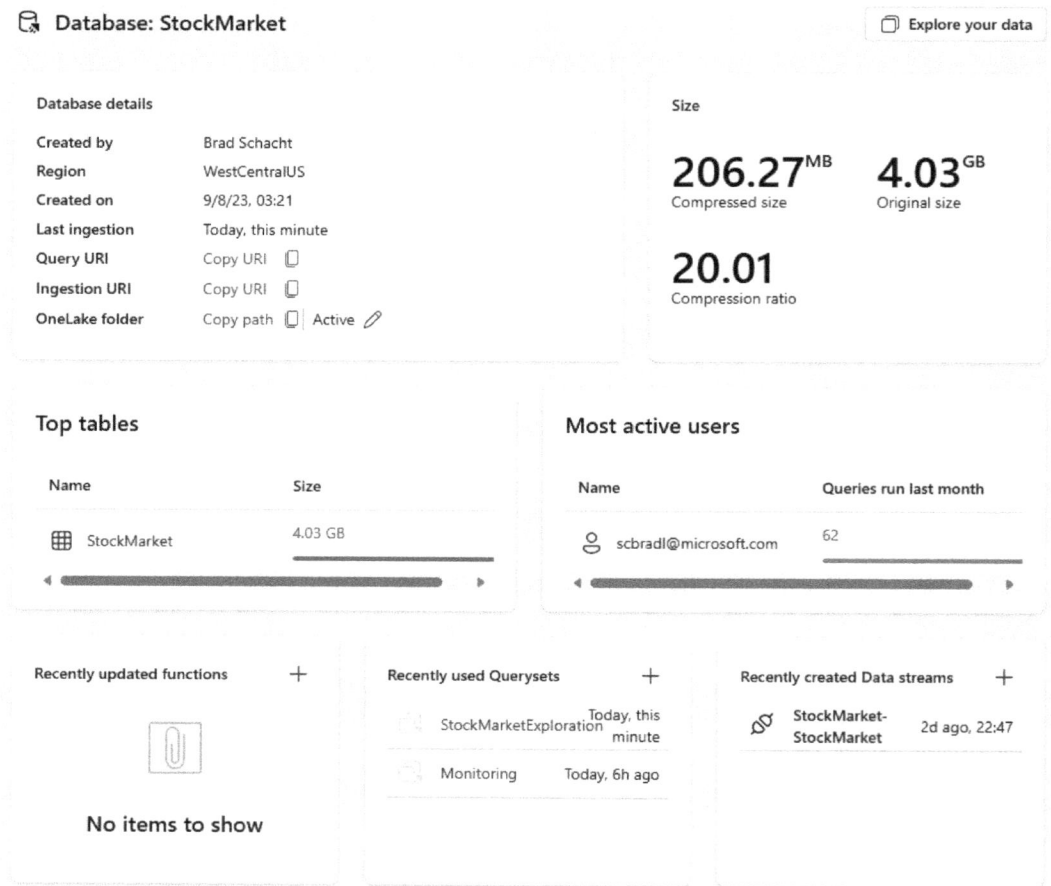

Figure 7.16 – The dashboard displaying important information about a KQL database

KQL databases also have several built-in commands, which display system information that can be used for many of the purposes previously mentioned:

- `.show queries` provides a list of all the queries executed in the last 30 days. By default, this command returns only the completed queries and includes information such as CPU used, cache usage, start and end times, the user running the query, and failure details, if applicable.

- `.show journal` includes metadata-related operations such as table creation, table mappings, and dropping extents.

- `.show table details` displays a list of tables, compressed size, estimated uncompressed size, row counts, retention policy, caching policies, and more.

These commands, such as the one shown in *Figure 7.17*, operate like any table in a KQL database when queried. The data can be filtered and joined to create custom monitoring solutions that can be referenced as part of normal database administration or when troubleshooting a slow or failed query.

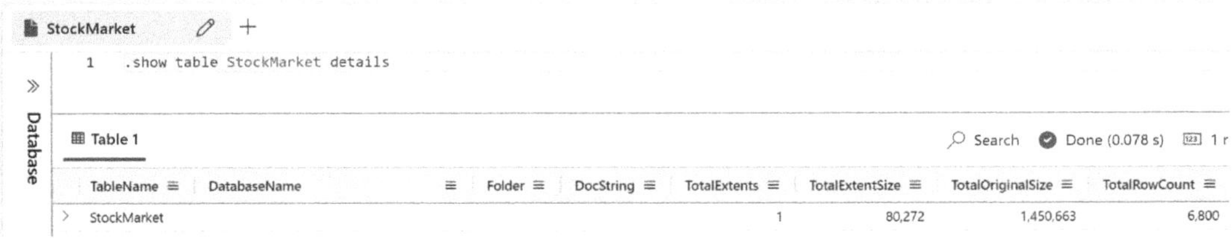

Figure 7.17 – One of the commands, .show table details, used to monitor a KQL database

The show commands can provide valuable information for monitoring and troubleshooting a KQL database. Next, let's explore how to monitor usage across all of Fabric with the Capacity Metrics app.

Monitoring capacity usage with the Microsoft Fabric Capacity Metrics app

Microsoft Fabric is based on a unified business model that uses the **capacity units** (distinct pool of resources allocated) across all its engines or capabilities and simplifies your whole experience of how you purchase and use computing resources.

Further, Microsoft Fabric provides a **Capacity Metrics app**, which you can use to monitor capacity units and their usage across different engines/workloads/capabilities.

Follow the instructions provided at `https://learn.microsoft.com/en-us/fabric/enterprise/metrics-app-install` to install the Fabric Capacity Metrics app.

Once you have installed the app, you can click on **Apps** on the left flyout and click on **Microsoft Fabric Capacity Metrics** (this will be followed by the date it was installed) as shown in *Figure 7.18* to launch it.

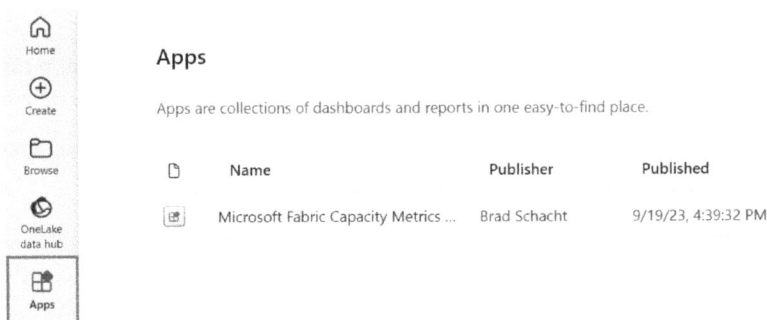

Figure 7.18 – Launching the Fabric Capacity Metrics app

For the first time, you will have to connect this app to the capacity you want to monitor. You will need to be an administrator in this capacity. Once you are connected, you should be able to see the usage of capacity – an example of this is shown in *Figure 7.19*. You can learn more about these different charts and different metrics here: `https://learn.microsoft.com/en-us/fabric/enterprise/metrics-app`.

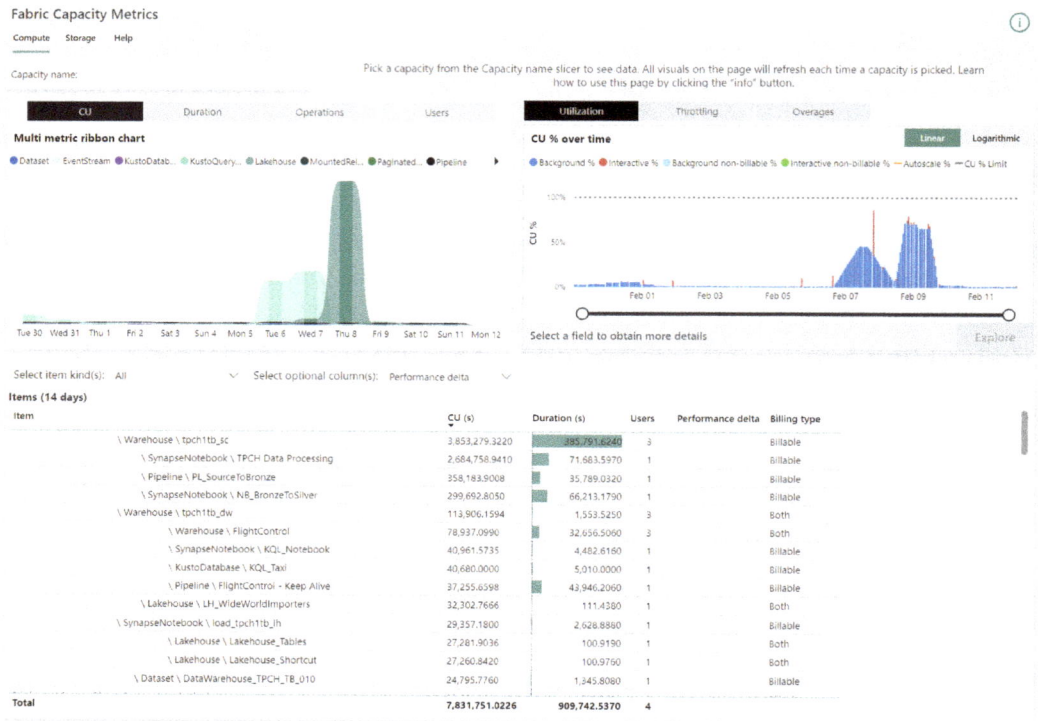

Figure 7.19 – An example of capacity units usage shown in the Fabric Capacity Metrics app

This app also captures current and billed storage information and, for that, you will have to switch to the **OneLake** tab of this app. You can learn more about how the Capacity Metrics app shows storage information here: `https://learn.microsoft.com/en-us/fabric/enterprise/metrics-app-storage-page`.

Summary

Microsoft Fabric provides built-in rich capabilities for monitoring every aspect of all the jobs submitted from any of the workloads to track its progress over time and its outcome. With **Monitoring hub**, it provides a central and single entry point to track all the jobs submitted in one place while still providing the ability and flexibility to contextually monitor an individual item while developing or working on it, such as a pipeline or notebook.

In this chapter, we learned about different ways of monitoring Data Factory, Spark jobs, data warehouse queries, Real-Time Analytics, and capacity usage in Fabric to troubleshoot any performance issues and optimize its performance. In the next chapter, we will get into the details of Fabric administration.

8
Administering Fabric

In this chapter, we will cover how to enable Fabric for a tenant, the options for overwriting the tenant-level settings at a capacity level, and how to associate a capacity with a workspace. We will also cover the different types of capacities and how tenants, capacities, and workspaces are all tied together. This information is vital to being able to administer Fabric effectively across teams and capacities.

We will go through the following topics in this chapter:

- Enabling Microsoft Fabric in your tenant
- What are capacities?
- Managing Spark job configurations

Before diving into capacities and capacity management, it is important to understand the tenant-level settings that are available for tenant administrators of Microsoft Fabric.

Enabling Microsoft Fabric in your tenant

Fabric is governed at two levels: tenant and capacity. By default, Fabric is enabled on all capacities and for all users in a tenant. *Figure 8.1* shows the granular controls that allow admins to select specific security groups that will have access to Fabric rather than every individual in the organization. This can be useful if you are not ready to make Fabric widely available but instead would like to have smaller groups or departments evaluate the functionality and perform reviews before rolling out to the larger enterprise. To modify the tenant-level setting, navigate to **Admin portal** | **Tenant settings** | **Microsoft Fabric**, where you will be presented with the following options:

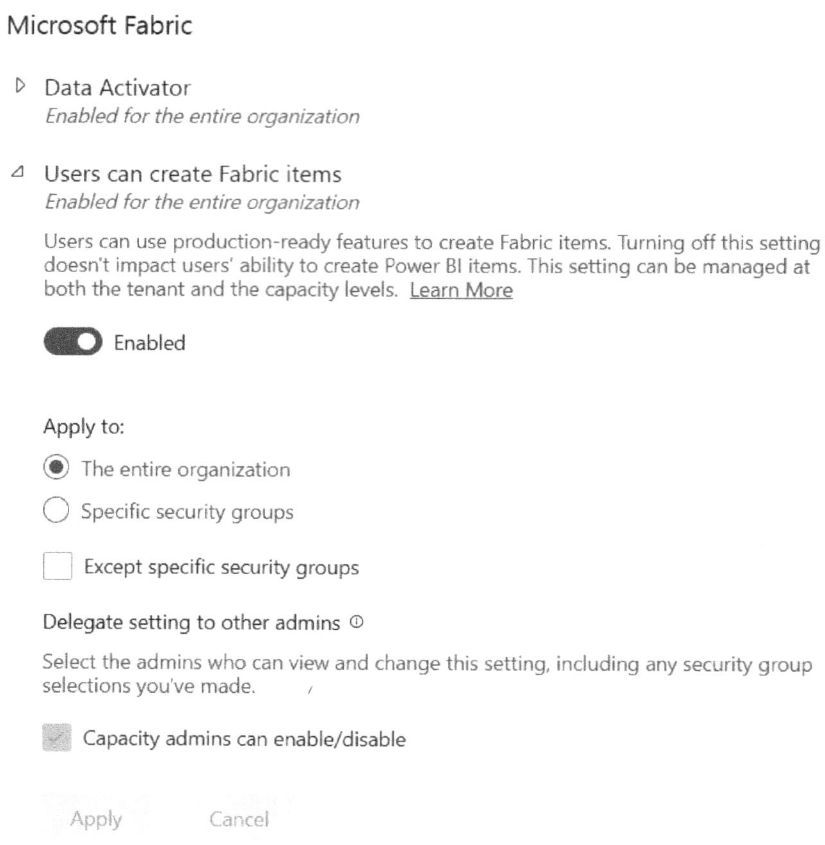

Microsoft Fabric

▷ Data Activator
Enabled for the entire organization

◁ Users can create Fabric items
Enabled for the entire organization

Users can use production-ready features to create Fabric items. Turning off this setting doesn't impact users' ability to create Power BI items. This setting can be managed at both the tenant and the capacity levels. Learn More

⬤ Enabled

Apply to:

◉ The entire organization

◯ Specific security groups

☐ Except specific security groups

Delegate setting to other admins ⓘ

Select the admins who can view and change this setting, including any security group selections you've made.

☑ Capacity admins can enable/disable

Apply   Cancel

Figure 8.1 – Tenant-level settings for enabling Microsoft Fabric

Some organizations will want to manage Fabric more granularly at the capacity level. Capacity-level settings allow you to disable Fabric at the tenant level while selectively enabling it at the capacity level. This can prevent business units from creating unauthorized or ungoverned data products within their capacity. In Fabric, a workspace is tied to a single capacity, but a single capacity can back multiple workspaces. It is important to understand that there is no option to enable or disable Fabric at the workspace level, so all workspaces backed by a capacity will share the same Fabric setting. The capacity-level setting, which overrides the tenant-level setting, for enabling Fabric can be found by going to **Fabric Admin portal** (https://app.fabric.microsoft.com/admin-portal) | **Capacity settings** | **Select a capacity from the list** | **Delegated tenant settings** | **Microsoft Fabric**.

What are capacities?

Every operation needs compute power. For each workload in Fabric, the optimal type of compute may look slightly different. Where SQL runs best on CPUs, Spark will be better on GPUs. Some workloads, such as Power BI, require large amounts of memory, while others such as Data Factory may just need small amounts of CPU for orchestrating activities. Fabric capacities remove the complexity of choosing the right type and size compute for each operation that is run by providing a single, blended compute metric called a capacity unit that is delivered through Fabric capacities, often referred to as a **Fabric SKU** or simply an **F SKU**.

Therefore, Fabric capacity is simply a pool of available resources that is shared by all the workspaces assigned to a capacity and is shared by all the workloads running in those workspaces. Based on the type of operation running, the appropriate blend of compute and memory will be allocated and torn down after the operation is complete because Fabric leverages a serverless compute architecture.

Fabric capacities are provisioned through the Azure portal and assigned to workspaces using the Fabric workspace settings UI. Because the resources behind a capacity are serverless, there is very little latency associated with scaling a capacity up or down and there is no downtime associated with a scaling operation.

While not covered in depth in this book, if an organization has an existing investment in Power BI Premium capacities, those can also be used for all Fabric workloads. This means that Power BI Premium will not be limited to running just the Power BI workload. The non-Power BI workloads are only available on Power BI Premium per capacity or Fabric capacity.

Managing Fabric capacities

As mentioned previously, Fabric capacities are provisioned through the Azure portal. However, much of the administration is performed inside the Fabric UI. The only administration activity that requires the Azure portal is performing a scaling or pause operation. To provision an Azure capacity, you should navigate to `https://portal.azure.com` and create a new Microsoft Fabric resource. After providing a subscription, resource group, region, capacity size, and administrator, the resource will be created. From the Azure portal, you can pause/resume the capacity, change its size, and add/remove administrators, as shown in *Figure 8.2*:

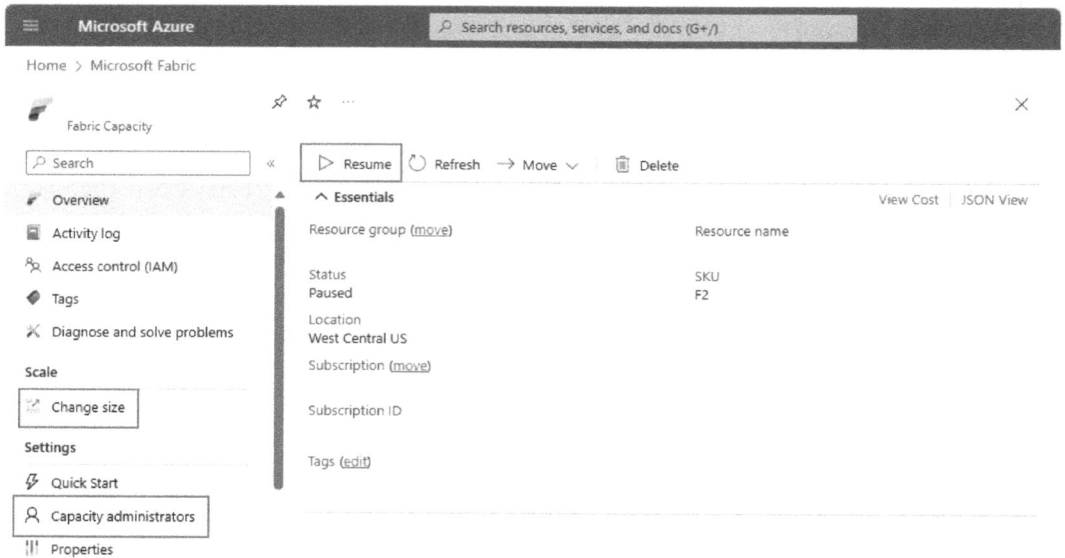

Figure 8.2 – The Fabric capacity overview and important settings in the Azure portal

Purchasing Fabric capacity through an Azure subscription will be a major change for those familiar with purchasing Power BI Premium per capacity.

Power BI Premium per capacity is billed monthly, and Fabric capacities are billed hourly. This means that if a capacity is running for 1 minute, then 1 hour of usage will be charged. However, pausing a Fabric capacity means no billing is taking place. This effectively means a Fabric capacity can be turned on for business hours to do development work and paused at night to save on cost, whereas Premium capacity requires reserving the compute 24 hours a day for an entire month, regardless of usage.

Fabric capacity can also be scaled as low as an F2, which is effectively $1/32^{nd}$ the size of a P1, the smallest Premium capacity. Having such a wide range of available Fabric capacity sizes means organizations can separate workloads more easily and at a more granular level than ever before. The flexibility of capacity size combined with pause/resume functionality means more control over cost than ever before.

The remaining administration settings will match what can be found in the Power BI Premium capacity. They can be accessed by navigating to **Fabric Admin portal** | **Capacity settings** | **Fabric capacity** | **Select a capacity from the list**. You will see the options shown in *Figure 8.3*.

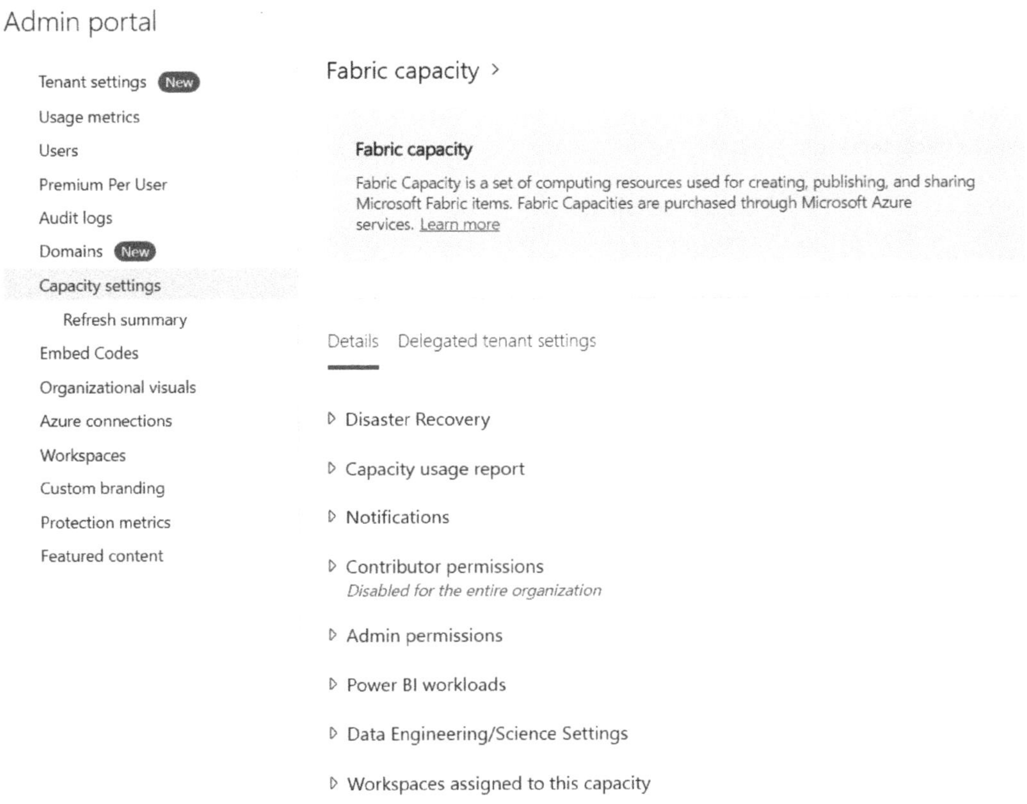

Admin portal

Tenant settings [New]
Usage metrics
Users
Premium Per User
Audit logs
Domains [New]
Capacity settings
    Refresh summary
Embed Codes
Organizational visuals
Azure connections
Workspaces
Custom branding
Protection metrics
Featured content

Fabric capacity >

Fabric capacity

Fabric Capacity is a set of computing resources used for creating, publishing, and sharing Microsoft Fabric items. Fabric Capacities are purchased through Microsoft Azure services. Learn more

Details   Delegated tenant settings
_____

▷ Disaster Recovery

▷ Capacity usage report

▷ Notifications

▷ Contributor permissions
   Disabled for the entire organization

▷ Admin permissions

▷ Power BI workloads

▷ Data Engineering/Science Settings

▷ Workspaces assigned to this capacity

Figure 8.3 – The Fabric capacity settings in the admin portal

Now that you are familiar with managing Fabric at the tenant and capacity level, let's look at the configuration options that are available for Spark.

Managing Spark job configurations

Microsoft Fabric is based on the **Software-as-a-Service (SaaS)** model, which provides features such as auto-integration, auto-optimization, and auto-tuning for all the workloads, including the fully managed Spark runtime, which powers data engineering and data science experiences. While the default configuration will work fine in most cases, empowering you to do more with less, there are times when you'll need more control. For these types of scenarios, you can control several aspects of the Fabric Spark runtime and Spark jobs to suit your business needs.

Open any Fabric workspace, click on the **Workspace settings** icon at the top, and then, under **Data Engineering/Science**, select **Spark compute**. You will find various options to make changes, as shown in *Figure 8.4*:

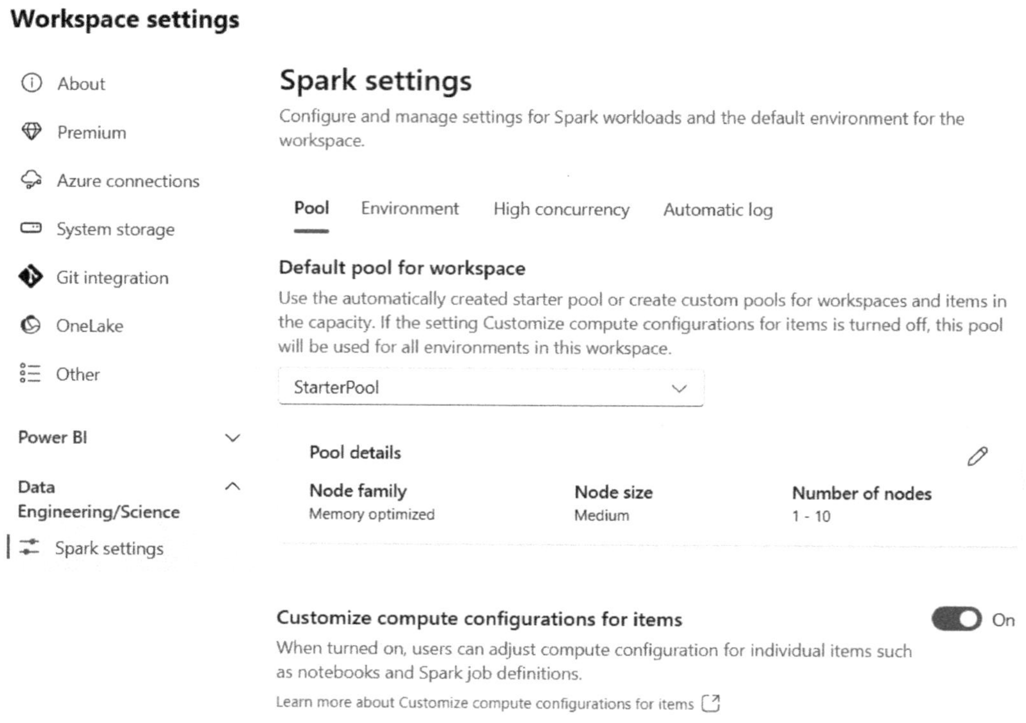

Workspace settings

ⓘ About	
♙ Premium	
☁ Azure connections	
▭ System storage	
◆ Git integration	
◉ OneLake	
☰ Other	

Power BI ⌄

Data
Engineering/Science ⌃

| ⇄ Spark settings

Spark settings

Configure and manage settings for Spark workloads and the default environment for the workspace.

Pool   Environment   High concurrency   Automatic log

Default pool for workspace

Use the automatically created starter pool or create custom pools for workspaces and items in the capacity. If the setting Customize compute configurations for items is turned off, this pool will be used for all environments in this workspace.

StarterPool   ⌄

Pool details   🖉

Node family	Node size	Number of nodes
Memory optimized	Medium	1 - 10

Customize compute configurations for items   🔘 On

When turned on, users can adjust compute configuration for individual items such as notebooks and Spark job definitions.

Learn more about Customize compute configurations for items ⌕

Figure 8.4 – Spark compute settings

In the next few sections, we will look at Spark configurations, including starter and custom Spark pools, configuring the environment for high-concurrency mode, library management, and more. These settings govern the experience end users will have each time they develop, run a notebook, or run a Spark job within a workspace.

Starter pools

Each Fabric workspace comes pre-configured with a **Starter pool**, and no manual setup or configuration is needed for running Spark jobs. A Starter pool is a set of live or warm computing resources in a pool to create a Spark cluster/session when you submit your Spark jobs either interactively through *Notebooks* or in batch mode using *Spark job definition*. This means your session is up and running in a few seconds – and you no longer need to wait to acquire machines and set up clusters, which usually takes several minutes. The best part is that we only pay for its usage while our jobs are running and do not keep these computing resources live in the pool. You can learn more about starter pools here: `https://learn.microsoft.com/en-us/fabric/data-engineering/spark-compute#starter-pools`.

Custom Spark pools

While the starter pool will be sufficient for most of your Spark jobs, if there is a need, you can also create a **custom Spark pool** with your own configuration (node type, size, number, auto-scaling, and so on). For example, if you have a long-running job that runs on several terabytes of data and you need more nodes than what's available with the starter pool, you can create a custom Spark pool, as shown in *Figure 8.5*, and use it with that specific job:

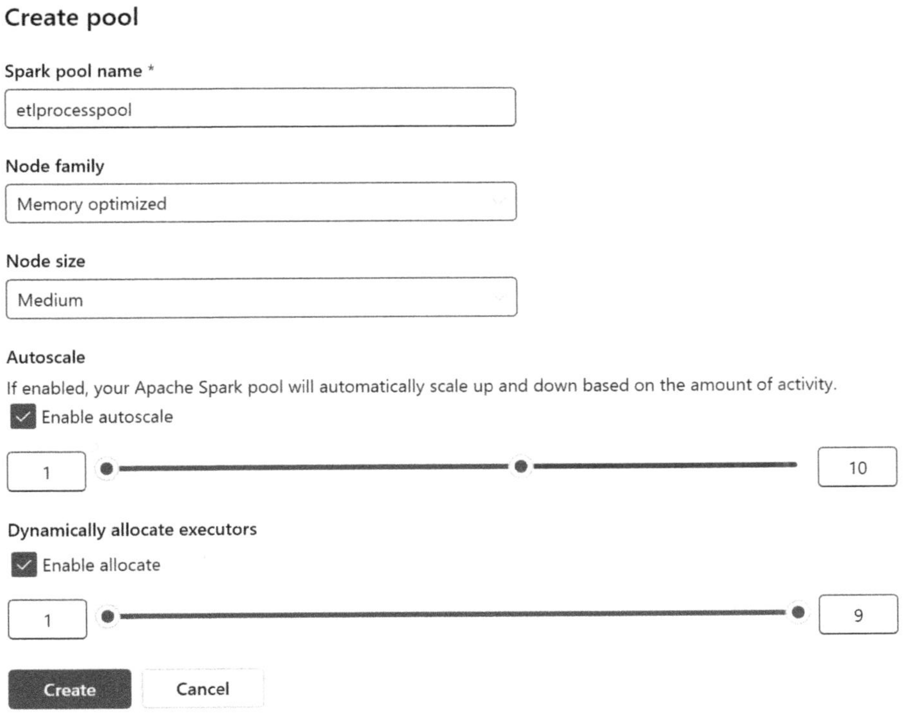

Create pool

Spark pool name *

    etlprocesspool

Node family

    Memory optimized

Node size

    Medium

Autoscale

If enabled, your Apache Spark pool will automatically scale up and down based on the amount of activity.

☑ Enable autoscale

    1 ●————————————————●———————————————— 10

Dynamically allocate executors

☑ Enable allocate

    1 ●————————————————————————————● 9

    [Create]   Cancel

Figure 8.5 – Creating a custom Spark pool

You can learn more about custom Spark pools and how to create them here: `https://learn.microsoft.com/en-us/fabric/data-engineering/create-custom-spark-pools`.

Spark runtime

As new versions of Apache Spark and Delta Lake are released, Spark runtime brings in a new runtime with these newer versions for you to take advantage of – all without any additional cost. This Fabric Spark runtime includes Apache Spark and Delta Lake added with Microsoft optimization in the engine. Additionally, it includes several industry standard or popular libraries (for Java/Scala, Python, and R) preinstalled so that we, as data engineers and data scientists, can make use of it immediately without worrying about its installation and solving its dependencies. You can learn more about Spark runtime here: `https://learn.microsoft.com/en-us/fabric/data-engineering/runtime`.

High concurrency

By default, when you start executing a notebook, a **standard session** is created, which is tied to the notebook you are executing. Then, if you start executing another notebook in parallel, another standard session gets created, which is tied to this other notebook. This provides complete isolation and there is no resource contention; however, you are paying for multiple sets of computing resources based on how many standard sessions you are using or notebooks you are executing. To optimize the cost in this scenario, you can take advantage of the newly introduced **high-concurrency session**. High-concurrency mode allows you to share the same session (and its underlying computing resources) to run multiple notebooks in parallel within a single user boundary when these notebooks share the same default lakehouse, matching Spark configuration, and libraries while sharing the high-concurrency session across. A high-concurrency session provides isolation for each notebook within the same session and prevents overwriting of local variables with the same name declared in multiple notebooks.

By default, a notebook gets executed in a standard session. So, if you want to execute it in a high-concurrency session, before you start executing it, as shown in *Figure 8.6*, go to the **Run** tab at the top and click on **New high-concurrency session** if you are running the notebook for the first time and no high-concurrency session is available yet. When you have a high-concurrency session already available, you will get the option to choose to run this notebook in this existing high-concurrency session or start a new session:

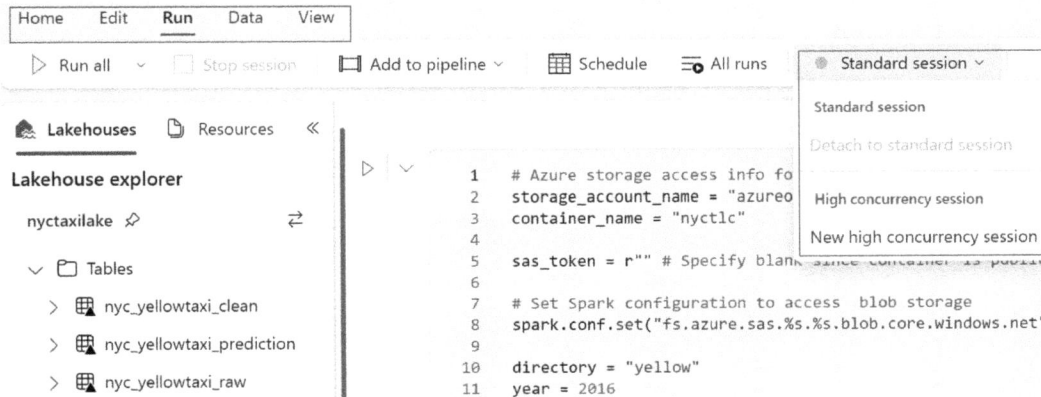

Figure 8.6 – Using a high-concurrency session

The default behavior when selecting any run button (ribbon or next to a cell) is to start a standard session. Following these steps is only necessary if you want to start a high-concurrency session.

Automatically tracking machine learning experiments and models

The Data Science experience in Microsoft Fabric makes it easier for data scientists to enable automatic logging of their machine learning models and experiments (such as metrics, input and output parameters, and models) without requiring them to write code explicitly. By default, this feature is enabled at the workspace level, as shown in *Figure 8.7*, and applies to all the sessions that are created in the workspace. However, if you want to disable it, you can do so by toggling this option; in that case, you will have to manually log your parameters and metrics using MLflow APIs. Additionally, it makes it easy to enable or disable this feature at the session level:

Workspace settings

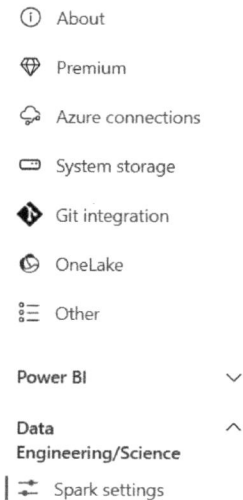

ⓘ About	
⬥ Premium	
☁ Azure connections	
▭ System storage	
◆ Git integration	
◉ OneLake	
☰ Other	

Power BI   ⌄

Data   ⌃
Engineering/Science

⇄ Spark settings

Spark settings

Configure and manage settings for Spark workloads and the default environment for the workspace.

Pool   Environment   High concurrency   **Automatic log**

Automatically track machine learning experiments and models   ⬤ On

Automatically log metrics, parameters, and models without coding explicit statements in your notebook.

Learn more about Automatically track machine learning experiments and models ⬀

Figure 8.7 – Enabling or disabling automatic model and experiment tracking

You can learn more about this here: `https://learn.microsoft.com/en-us/fabric/data-science/mlflow-autologging`.

Spark properties/configuration

The Fabric Spark runtime has an optimized default configuration for Spark properties that should work in most cases. However, if you want to change it in some specific case or to meet a specific job requirement, you can change it both at the workspace level and the session level. Navigate to **Workspace Settings | Spark Settings | Environment**, then enable **Set default environment**, and, if necessary, select **New Environment** from the drop-down menu. On the **Spark properties** page shown in *Figure 8.8*, click on + **Add** from the ribbon, and then select the property from the available combo box. The value text box next to the selected property/configuration will show the default value in Fabric for the selected specific property, which you can change to meet your needs. To save the configuration without applying the configurations, select **Save**. To apply the configurations, select **Publish**:

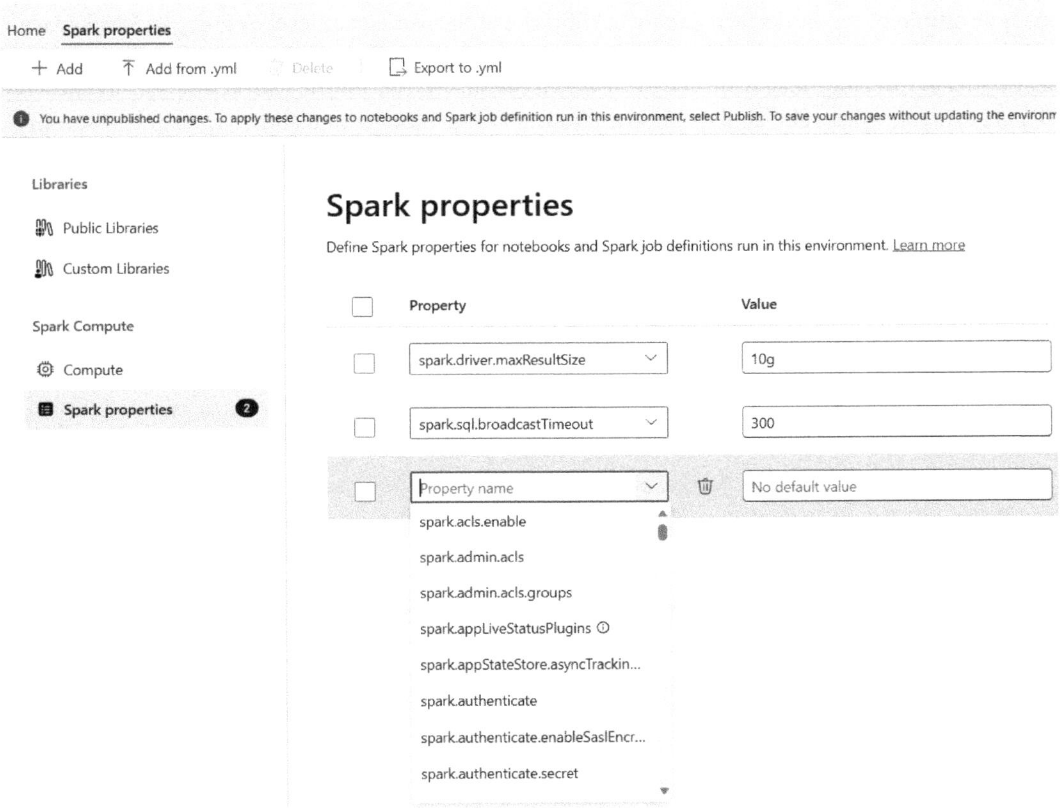

Home   **Spark properties**

+ Add   ⊤ Add from .yml   🗑 Delete   ⬚ Export to .yml

ℹ You have unpublished changes. To apply these changes to notebooks and Spark job definition run in this environment, select Publish. To save your changes without updating the environm

Libraries

📚 Public Libraries

📚 Custom Libraries

Spark Compute

⚙ Compute

▦ Spark properties   ②

Spark properties

Define Spark properties for notebooks and Spark job definitions run in this environment. Learn more

	Property	Value
☐	spark.driver.maxResultSize ⌄	10g
☐	spark.sql.broadcastTimeout ⌄	300
☐	Property name ⌄ 🗑	No default value

spark.acls.enable

spark.admin.acls

spark.admin.acls.groups

spark.appLiveStatusPlugins ⓘ

spark.appStateStore.asyncTrackin...

spark.authenticate

spark.authenticate.enableSaslEncr...

spark.authenticate.secret

Figure 8.8 – Spark properties configurations

Library management

The Fabric Spark runtime comes with several industry-standard or popular libraries (for Java/Scala, Python, and R) preinstalled as built-in libraries, so that we, as data engineers and data scientists, can make use of them immediately without worrying about their installation and solving their dependencies. However, if you want to bring in additional libraries from public repositories (such as PyPI or Conda) or want to use your own custom libraries, you can do so either at the workspace level, which applies to all the sessions that get created in the workspace (either via a notebook or Spark job definition), or at the session level to have session-specific libraries.

You, as an admin of the workspace, can install libraries at the workspace level by going to **Workspace Settings | Spark Settings | Environment**, then enabling **Set default environment**, and, if necessary, selecting **New Environment** from the drop-down menu. On the **Public Libraries** page, as shown in *Figure 8.9*, you will be able to feed libraries from `PyPI` or `Conda` and add your custom libraries:

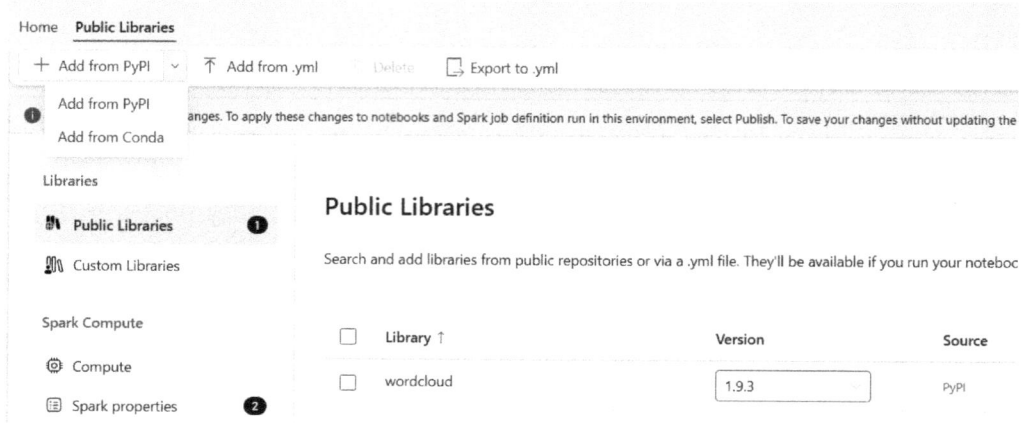

Figure 8.9 – Library management – installation options and an example

For inline or session-specific installation of libraries, you can use `%pip install` or `%conda install`. You can learn more about this here: `https://learn.microsoft.com/en-us/fabric/data-engineering/library-management`.

Auto-tune

The auto-tune feature in the Fabric Spark runtime is designed to automatically tune session-specific Spark configurations to minimize overall execution time for subsequent executions. This helps you save time when running multiple iterations so that you can learn optimal configurations for your Spark workloads by running a machine learning algorithm internally. This helps you learn patterns and automatically tune Spark session-level configurations as necessary for optimized performance. You can enable and disable this feature using these configurations:

```
# To enable auto-tune
spark.conf.set('spark.ms.autotune.enabled', 'true') # global switch
spark.conf.set('spark.ms.autotune.queryTuning.enabled', 'true')

# To disable auto-tune
spark.conf.set('spark.ms.autotune.enabled', 'false') # global switch
spark.conf.set('spark.ms.autotune.queryTuning.enabled', 'false')
```

You can learn more about this here: `https://learn.microsoft.com/en-us/fabric/data-engineering/autotune`.

Spark utility (MSSparkUtils)

The Fabric Spark runtime includes a utility called **MSSparkUtils** that you can use in the following scenario – the example shown in *Figure 8.10*:

- Filesystem utilities such as reading a file, writing a file, and so on

- Notebook utilities such as calling a notebook from another notebook

- Credential utilities such as getting a secret key or token from Azure Key Vault

- Lakehouse utilities for managing and working with Lakehouse

- Mounting utilities such as an external storage account in your Spark session:

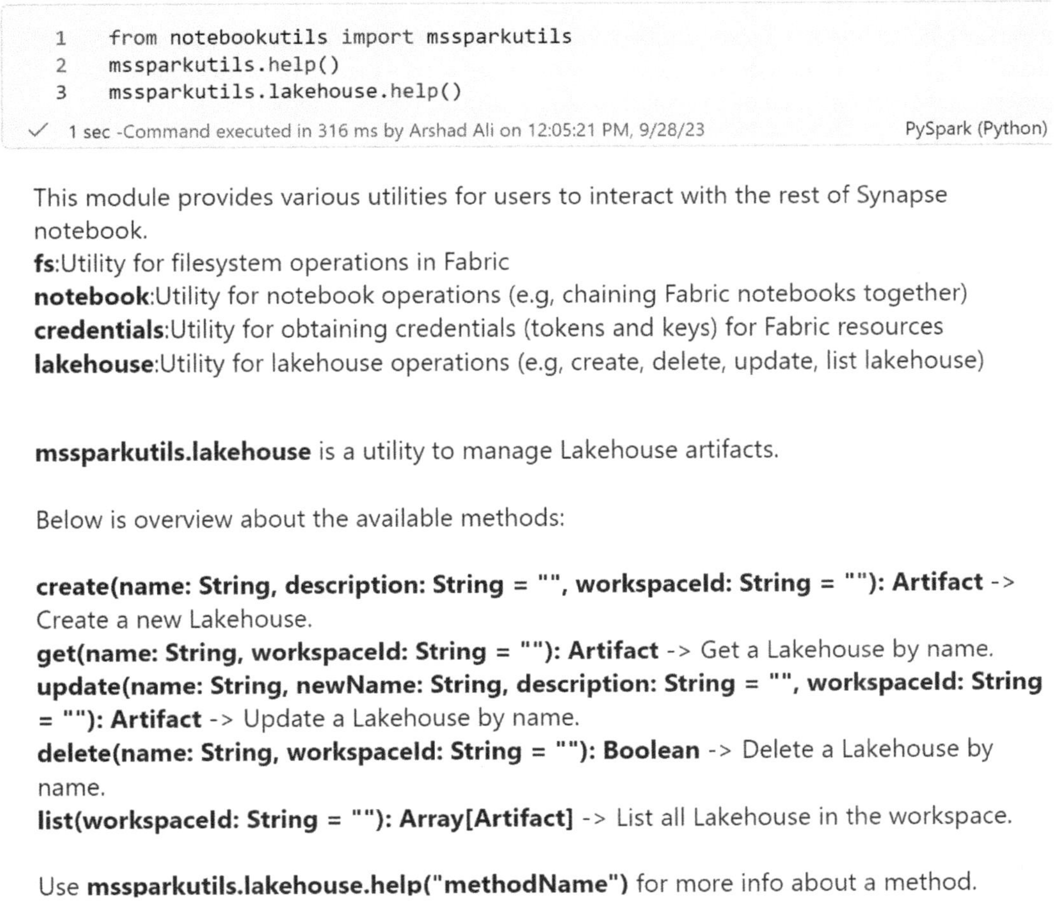

```
1    from notebookutils import mssparkutils
2    mssparkutils.help()
3    mssparkutils.lakehouse.help()
```

✓ 1 sec -Command executed in 316 ms by Arshad Ali on 12:05:21 PM, 9/28/23   PySpark (Python)

This module provides various utilities for users to interact with the rest of Synapse notebook.
fs:Utility for filesystem operations in Fabric
notebook:Utility for notebook operations (e.g, chaining Fabric notebooks together)
credentials:Utility for obtaining credentials (tokens and keys) for Fabric resources
lakehouse:Utility for lakehouse operations (e.g, create, delete, update, list lakehouse)

mssparkutils.lakehouse is a utility to manage Lakehouse artifacts.

Below is overview about the available methods:

create(name: String, description: String = "", workspaceId: String = ""): Artifact -> Create a new Lakehouse.
get(name: String, workspaceId: String = ""): Artifact -> Get a Lakehouse by name.
update(name: String, newName: String, description: String = "", workspaceId: String = ""): Artifact -> Update a Lakehouse by name.
delete(name: String, workspaceId: String = ""): Boolean -> Delete a Lakehouse by name.
list(workspaceId: String = ""): Array[Artifact] -> List all Lakehouse in the workspace.

Use **mssparkutils.lakehouse.help("methodName")** for more info about a method.

Figure 8.10 – MSSparkUtils capabilities and help

You can learn more about this utility here: `https://learn.microsoft.com/en-us/fabric/data-engineering/microsoft-spark-utilities`.

Whether the need arises to manage the size of a Spark cluster, you need a set of default libraries to be installed, or you want Fabric to automatically tune your Spark configurations, there are extensive options available to customize the session exactly as you need.

Summary

In this chapter, you learned how to enable Fabric in your tenant, what capacities are, how to manage capacities, how to override tenant settings at the capacity level, and how to manage Spark settings for workspaces. The flexibility provided by the Fabric capacity model allows organizations to decide how much capacity is needed, when it is needed, and which workspaces need it. The added benefit of the Fabric SaaS model is that it removes the need to complicate capacity planning by assigning the right kind of compute at runtime through a serverless infrastructure that delivers the right CPU/GPU/memory configuration based on the workload requesting the compute resources.

In the next chapter, we will discuss the importance of security and governance in Fabric and how to apply best practices across the entire tenant.

Part 4:
Security and Developer Experience

This part of the book explores tenant-level Fabric security settings, how Entra ID is used to allow external users access to Fabric, and how to secure workspaces and items. It also demonstrates how to use Purview for data cataloging and governance, and domains for data organization. Additionally, it covers the DevOps process and teaches you how to implement CI/CD to move your code items from one environment (such as development) to another (such as test or production).

This part contains the following chapters:

- *Chapter 9, Security and Governance Overview*
- *Chapter 10, Continuous Integration and Continuous Deployment (CI/CD)*

9

Security and Governance Overview

As we have explored throughout this book, Microsoft Fabric is all about driving insights through data. There is another side of analytics that must be carefully considered: security and governance. These topics don't have eye-catching dashboards that will be displayed during board meetings or often land as the main topic of a keynote at major international conferences, but they are vital to the success of any organization. If data loss is the worst thing that can happen, a data leak is the second. No one wants to be responsible for drafting the communication telling customers that their data was part of a breach, that it could end up being sold online, and that they should change their passwords just to be safe any more than they want to have to answer to leadership about how the sales numbers were accessed or that an analyst somehow was given access to modify data that drives the annual report sent to investors.

As data architectures and platforms change over time, so do the security, governance, and discoverability challenges. The shift from on-premises to the cloud, from an office-centric to an always connected, geographically distributed user base, and departmental solutions to enterprise data lake and data mesh architectures has forced many organizations to completely rethink their approach to security and governance.

In this chapter, you will see the different functionalities that make up the security and governance structure of Microsoft Fabric:

- Securing the Microsoft Fabric platform
- Securing Microsoft Fabric workspaces and items
- Understanding governance and compliance in Microsoft Fabric

Before diving into securing specific data assets, let's explore what it means to secure the Microsoft Fabric platform as a whole.

Securing the Microsoft Fabric platform

Security starts at the front door. No one would consider their home secure if they were sitting in their bedroom with the door locked but their front or back door was just wide open for anyone to walk in and take a look around. Cloud data solutions are no different. No DBA would consider their database secure if anyone could connect, even though they may be locked out of the individual tables storing the data. And no systems administrator would be satisfied with a solution that allowed anyone to see a list of their workspaces even though the workspace itself could not be accessed.

Ensuring that the first layer of security is in place, the layer that prevents anyone from accessing your organization's confidential information, including metadata such as the names of workspaces, users, capacities, and more, is vital to getting new data platforms approved for use. Because Fabric is delivered as **Software as a Service (SaaS)**, it looks a little different than it would for a traditional on-premises solution or even pure PaaS services in Azure.

To start, let's discuss how external users are granted access to Fabric.

Guest users

Content within Fabric can be shared with individuals outside your organization, but only if you choose to allow guest user access. These users are called guest users or external users. A guest's identity resides in their organization's Entra ID directory and is invited as a guest user to your organization's Entra ID directory. After accepting the invitation, the guest user will appear in the directory so that they can be managed like any other user. For the most part, they are treated just like any other local user. Guests can be added to groups, given access to PaaS or SaaS services that leverage Entra ID for security, and in the case of Fabric be granted access to workspaces to view and interact with items.

> **Note**
> Except for dashboards, reports, and semantic models, specific items cannot be shared with guest users. They must be granted access to the workspace to view and interact with Fabric items.

Before inviting a guest either through Entra ID or directly from the Fabric user interface, there are two administration settings to be aware of that govern whether external users can use Fabric and if external users can be invited through the Power BI item-sharing functionality outlined later in this section:

- **Allow Azure Active Directory guest users to access Microsoft Fabric**: This governs whether **business-to-business (B2B)** – that is, guests – can access Fabric. Even if a guest is granted permissions within Fabric, if this setting is disabled, they will not be able to access the shared content.

- **Invite external users to your organization**: This governs whether external users can be invited from the sharing and permissions settings on reports and dashboards.

To modify these and other settings that control how guests can interact with Fabric content, execute the following steps:

1. Navigate to the Fabric **Admin portal** area.

2. Select **Tenant settings**.

3. Locate the **Export and sharing settings** section.

4. Expand either **Allow Azure Active Directory guest users to access Microsoft Fabric** or **Invite external users to your organization** and change the settings as appropriate. Notice that these settings can also be filtered to a specific set of security groups in Entra ID:

Admin portal

Tenant settings

Usage metrics	Export and sharing settings
Users	
Premium Per User	▷ External data sharing (preview)
	Disabled for the entire organization
Audit logs	
Domains	▷ Users can accept external data shares (preview)
	Disabled for the entire organization
Capacity settings	
Refresh summary	▷ Allow Azure Active Directory guest users to access Microsoft Fabric
	Enabled for the entire organization
Embed Codes	
Organizational visuals	▷ Invite external users to your organization
	Enabled for the entire organization
Azure connections	

Figure 9.1 – External user settings in the Fabric Admin portal area

5. Select **Apply** if any modifications are made.

With the settings in place for guests to be invited and allowed to access Fabric, let's look at the two ways to invite guests.

To invite a guest to your Entra ID directory from the Azure portal, follow these steps:

1. In a web browser, navigate to the Azure portal (`https://portal.azure.com`).

2. Go to the Microsoft Entra ID service.

3. In the **Manage** section of the left-hand side navigation menu, select **Users**.

4. If necessary, from the left-hand side navigation menu, select **All users**.

5. From the ribbon, select **New user | Invite external user**, as shown here:

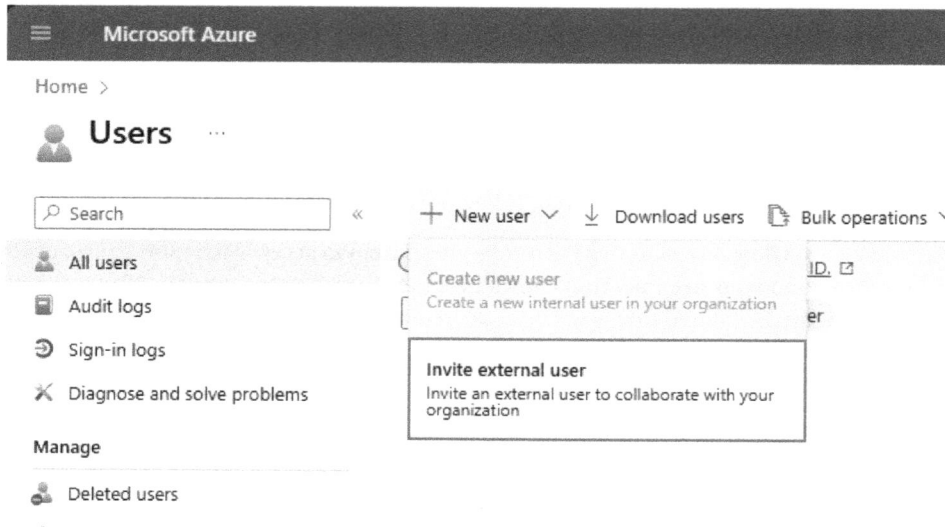

Figure 9.2 – The Invite external user button in the Entra ID settings of the Azure portal

6.   Fill in the user details on the **Invite external user** form.

7.   On the final page, click **Review + invite** and select **Invite**.

The guest will need to accept the invitation that's sent to them by email. Once they've done that, they will be ready to be added to workspaces or specific items in Fabric.

Guests can also be invited from several locations within Fabric, including reports, dashboards, and semantic models. The experience is slightly different based on where sharing is initiated from, but generally, this is found on the **Manage permissions** page in the **Direct access** section by selecting **Add user**, as shown here:

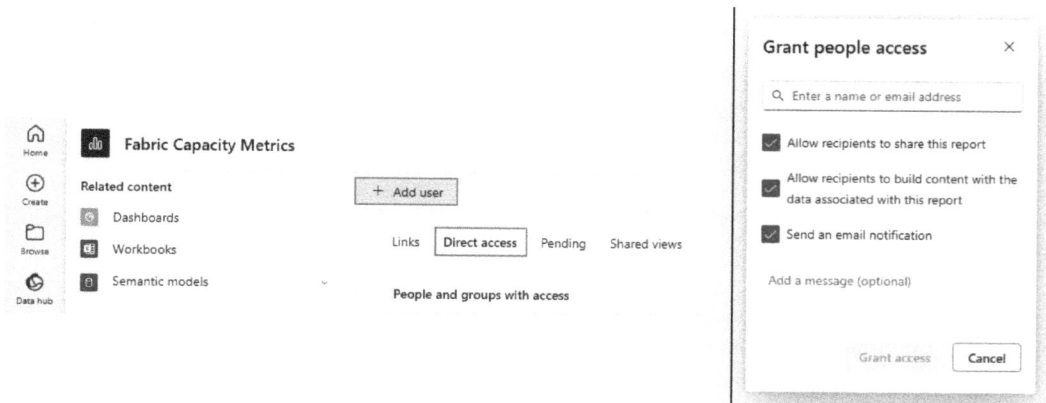

Figure 9.3 – The steps for initiating a sharing invitation from inside the Fabric environment

With guest user access to Fabric items enabled or disabled as appropriate and invite settings changed to meet your security needs, it's time to look at conditional access for securing Fabric's entry points.

Conditional access

Conditional access is not a Fabric concept or feature, such as the ability to invite guest users. It is handled through Microsoft Entra ID. Conditional access is the driving force behind Microsoft's Zero Trust security model, which relies on the core principles of verification, least privileged access, and assuming breach to protect data no matter where it is being accessed from.

With conditional access policies, administrators can define a policy that contains a series of conditions, which can then be combined to determine whether a user will be allowed into the environment at any given time.

Let's assume that a user, Rob, has been given access to some data in Microsoft Fabric but the organization wants to ensure Rob is not accessing company data from any unmanaged devices and that users are only accessing data from their home country to comply with local regulations. A policy must be created that defines the location from where requests originate combined with Intune's device-based conditional access policies to ensure access is controlled by the company's security standards.

Conditional access extends beyond just the device and location. Policies can be created with a variety of conditions, including device platform (Windows, Mac OS, Android, iOS, or Linux) or the client application being used. Sign-in and user risk are also taken into account to evaluate if a given sign-in request was or was not made by the identity being used or whether a user's identity has been compromised.

Now that we understand how to secure the Fabric platform through Entra ID and Fabric administrator settings, let's look at securing our data with workspaces and item-level security.

Securing Microsoft Fabric workspaces and items

For this chapter, we will be looking at security in the context of access to data stored in OneLake. There is a broader security story as it relates to Power BI reports, semantic models, SQL row-level security and dynamic data masking, SQL object-level security, and more. Additionally, Fabric's OneSecurity model is not available at the time of writing and will serve as an extension, not a replacement, to the foundational topics covered in this section.

To begin, let's look at how different workspace-level permissions affect data access.

Workspace-level permissions

The most common method for granting access to data in Fabric will be through workspace-level permissions. This gives blanket access to the items within the workspace and the data within OneLake that is associated with the items within the workspace.

Four roles can be assigned to a user at the workspace level:

- An **Admin** can perform all actions within a workspace, including deleting the workspace, adding users (including adding/removing other admins), creating/deleting/viewing all items, modifying gateway connection settings, and more.

- A **Member** can perform all the same functionality as an admin except they cannot update/delete workspaces or add/remove admins. They can, however, add/remove other members and anyone with lower permissions.

- A **Contributor** has the same permissions as a member except they cannot manage other user permissions.

- A **Viewer** can view items such as pipelines, Spark notebooks, and real-time dashboards, and connect to the workspace's SQL endpoint. Importantly, a Viewer cannot execute a Spark notebook but they can execute data pipelines.

Because each user type is given some level of data access, it is important to know what each user can and cannot see or modify by default within a workspace. Of course, not all of these items will be used in a workspace but because there is no ability to disable specific item types, there is always the possibility that an item of any type could be created in the future.

The following table summarizes the permissions provided to each role when accessing data through various methods within Fabric:

Data Stored In	Can Read	Can Write
OneLake	Admin, Member, Contributor	Admin, Member, Contributor
Data Warehouse	Admin, Member, Contributor	Admin, Member, Contributor
SQL Analytics Endpoint	Admin, Member, Contributor	N/A
KQL Databases	All roles	Admin, Member, Contributor

Table 9.1 – Default permissions granted by each role to data in Fabric

As we discussed in *Chapter 1, Overview of Microsoft Fabric and Understanding Its Different Concepts*, shortcuts are used to deliver on the promise of one copy of data. Like item-level access, which is granted by each workspace role, some level shortcut access is also granted by default to each workspace role. Admins, Members, and Contributors can all create shortcuts, read files/folders within a shortcut, and write to the shortcut's target location. All roles, including the Viewer role, can read data from shortcuts in the tables section of the lakehouse through SQL Analytics Endpoint.

> **Note**
> When shortcuts reference other OneLake locations, additional permissions may be needed on the shortcut target location (source) to read or write data depending on the action being taken.

With an understanding of how each role relates to data within various Fabric items and how those roles affect shortcuts, you can decide which role each user should be assigned on a given workspace. Roles are assigned when a user is added to a workspace through the **Manage access** page. If changes need to be made to a user's role assignment later, that can also be done from the **Manage access** page.

To manage workspace-level permissions, follow these steps:

1. Open the Fabric portal in a web browser and navigate to a workspace.

2. From the options across the top of the screen, select **Manage access**:

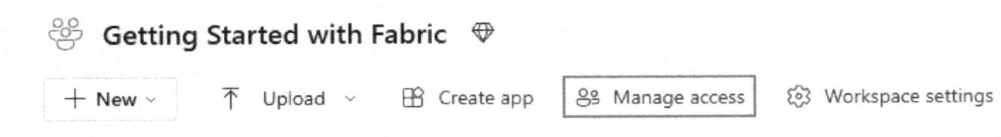

👥 Getting Started with Fabric ⬦

| + New ⌄ | ⬆ Upload ⌄ | ⊞ Create app | 👥 Manage access | ⚙ Workspace settings |

Figure 9.4 – The Manage access button in a Fabric workspace

3. On the **Manage access** flyout, you can view and modify existing permissions using the dropdown next to the user or group's name.

4. To add new users, select + **Add people or groups**:

Manage access   ✕
Getting Started with Fabric

[+ Add people or groups]

Figure 9.5 – The Add people or groups button on the Manage access flyout in Microsoft Fabric

5. In the search box, type a user's name or email address.

6. From the drop-down menu next to the **Add** button, select the permissions this user should be given:

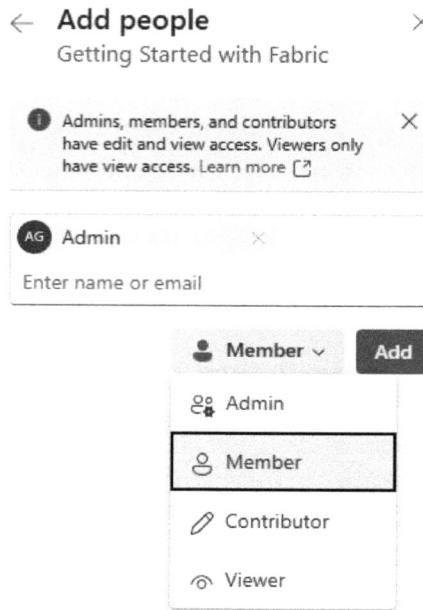

Figure 9.6 – The role selection list when managing workspace access

7.   Select **Add**.

Workspaces serve as the first major boundary for permissions in Fabric and there are varying levels of access granted to each workspace role. Next, let's look at item-level permissions.

Item-level permissions

Often, it is necessary to limit access to individual items within a workspace or to provide more granular access to data. Item-level permissions allow for a greater level of flexibility than workspace permissions because they do not require access to all items within a workspace and in some cases, such as data warehouses, you can even provide granular permissions down to the individual row of data in the database.

While you can share Power BI items such as reports and dashboards, we will focus on the non-Power BI items.

Regardless of the permissions that are granted during sharing items, which will be covered later in this section, the process of sharing is the same for all of them:

1.   Open the Fabric portal in a web browser and navigate to a workspace. Locate the item you would like to share and click on the ellipsis (...) next to the item.

2. Select **Manage permissions**:

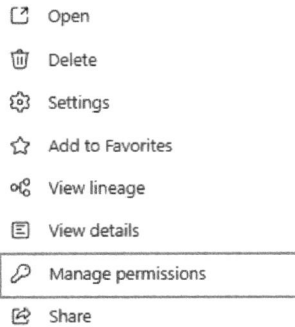

- Open
- Delete
- Settings
- Add to Favorites
- View lineage
- View details
- Manage permissions
- Share

Figure 9.7 – List of settings found on items within a Fabric workspace

3. Go to the **Direct access** section and select **Add user**.

4. Search for the user by entering their name or email address.

5. Select the permissions you want to grant and click on **Grant**:

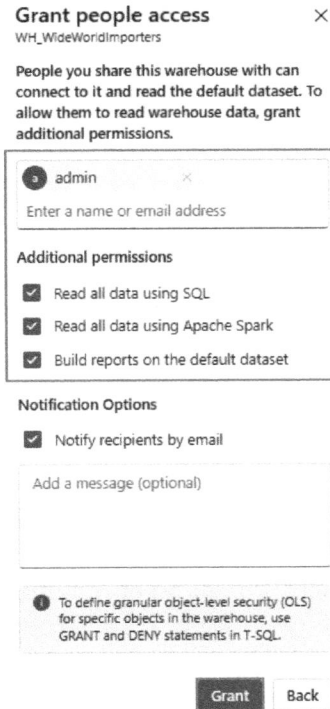

Grant people access   ×
WH_WideWorldImporters

People you share this warehouse with can connect to it and read the default dataset. To allow them to read warehouse data, grant additional permissions.

- admin

Enter a name or email address

Additional permissions

☑ Read all data using SQL
☑ Read all data using Apache Spark
☑ Build reports on the default dataset

Notification Options

☑ Notify recipients by email

Add a message (optional)

ⓘ To define granular object-level security (OLS) for specific objects in the warehouse, use GRANT and DENY statements in T-SQL.

Grant   Back

Figure 9.8 – The additional permissions that are available when sharing a data warehouse

An alternative method for sharing is to click the ellipsis (...) next to an item in the workspace and select **Share**. However, this option does not exist on all items.

The following items have custom permissions that can be set when sharing, with more granular sharing options being added over time:

- A **KQL database** can be shared with read permissions. Optionally, a user can also be granted edit permissions.

- A **KQL queryset** can be shared with view permissions. Optionally, a user can also be granted edit permissions.

- A **lakehouse** can be shared with open and read the default dataset permissions. Optionally, extend read permissions on SQL Analytics Endpoint, read from Apache Spark, and build reports on the default dataset permission.

- A **Spark notebook** can be shared with view permissions. Optionally, extend edit and run permissions.

- A **data warehouse** can be shared with connect (which does not provide data access) and read on the default dataset permissions. Optionally, extend read data from SQL, read data using Apache Spark, and build reports on the default dataset permissions. Additional granular permissions can be granted through T-SQL, even if the **Read all data using SQL** box is not checked.

Together with workspace roles, item sharing provides a solid foundation for granting access to Fabric items. Next, let's look at the governance options available in Fabric.

Understanding governance and compliance in Microsoft Fabric

Governance and compliance functionality help ensure data is managed and protected within Microsoft Fabric. There are a variety of smaller features available within Fabric to help administrators with governance and users with discoverability, as well as two major features, domains and Microsoft Purview, which we will explore in more detail.

Let's look at the major functionality that's included with Fabric for data governance:

- **Endorsements**, which help users identify the "gold standard" items within Fabric and allow a path for dataset promotion and increased rank in search results.

- **Metadata scanning** functionality. This is a set of APIs that enable metadata retrieval from items within Fabric.

- **Lineage**, which provides a visual representation of how items in Fabric are connected, allowing users to see what the upstream and downstream impacts of potential changes are.

Next, let's discuss how domains help to reduce governance challenges.

Domains

Due to the potentially large number of workspaces and data assets in a Fabric environment, it is important to be able to group related data quickly and easily. In Fabric, these are called domains. There is no hard rule about how domains need to be used for grouping. A domain could align with a business unit, a department, or an enterprise-wide initiative that has specific regulatory requirements.

Subdomains can be created to provide an even more granular grouping of workspaces. Workspaces are assigned to domains or subdomains. Administrative permissions are delegated at the domain level and inherited by the subdomains.

Managing domains is simple:

- To create a new domain, go to the Fabric **Admin portal** area, then **Domains**, and select **Create new domain**.
- To create a new subdomain, go to the Fabric **Admin portal** area, then **Domains**. Then, select a domain, and then **New subdomain**.
- To assign a workspace to a domain, go to the **Fabric Admin** portal area, then **Domains**. From here, select a domain, then **Assign workspaces**, and follow the resulting prompts.

Today, domains mainly facilitate searching through the Fabric Data Hub, but more functionality will be added to domain governance in the future. Finally, let's look at the Microsoft Purview integration.

Microsoft Purview

Microsoft Purview has grown from a simple data catalog to a set of governance and compliance tools that can be used to manage data across a variety of on-premises and cloud data stores.

In addition to the governance tooling already discussed, Purview adds the following:

- **Information protection**: This allows for data classification using sensitivity labels, which remain in place even when data is exported through supported paths (currently only supported by Power BI scenarios)
- **Data loss prevention**: This scans and determines if sensitive data points such as credit card numbers are added to semantic models (currently only supported by Power BI semantic models)
- **Data catalog**: This contains metadata related to various Fabric items without the need to configure any scanner APIs; all the items are scanned automatically, in real time
- **Audit**: This logs user activities within the Fabric environment to the Purview audit log so that you always know when and who is interacting with items, including create, delete, and read operations

To browse Fabric items within Microsoft Purview, follow these steps:

1. In a web browser, navigate to `https://purview.microsoft.com`.

2. From the main page, select **Data Catalog**:

Figure 9.9 – The Data Catalog button found on the Purview home page

3. In the **Explore your data** section, select **Microsoft Fabric**.

4. On the **Browse by source type** page, select **Fabric workspaces**.

5. From the list, select a Fabric workspace.

6. Select any item within the workspace to view its associated metadata:

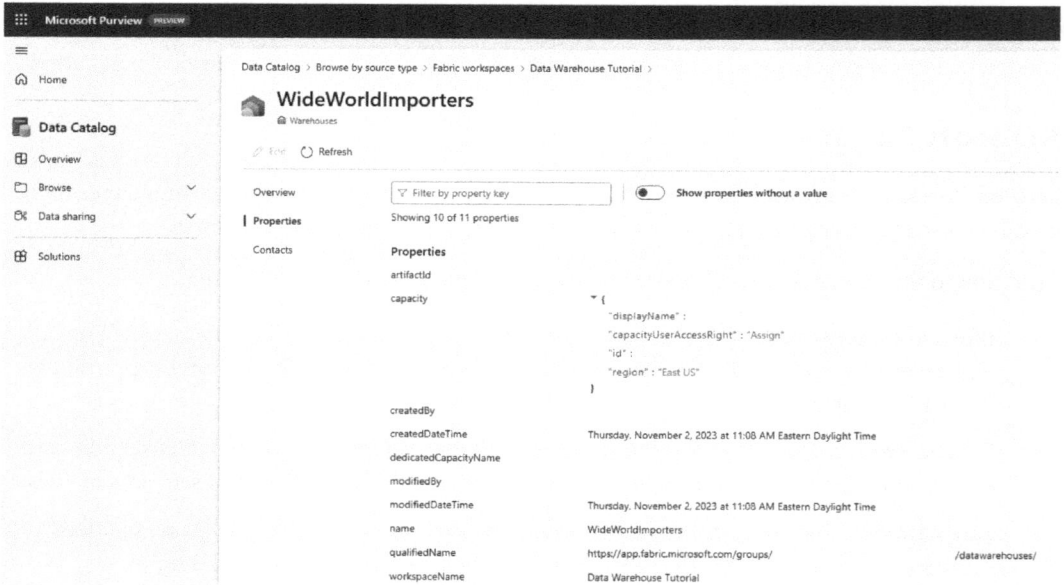

Figure 9.10 – The Properties page for a data warehouse in Microsoft Purview

Lastly, the Purview hub, which is embedded directly in the Fabric UI, provides an overview of important information related to your Fabric environment, such as the number of workspaces, the number of items overall, the type and number of items by workspaces, and details around certified and promoted items. This data can be accessed by selecting the icon in the top-right corner of the Fabric UI and selecting **Microsoft Purview hub**. The view will be different if a user is a Fabric admin or a general user:

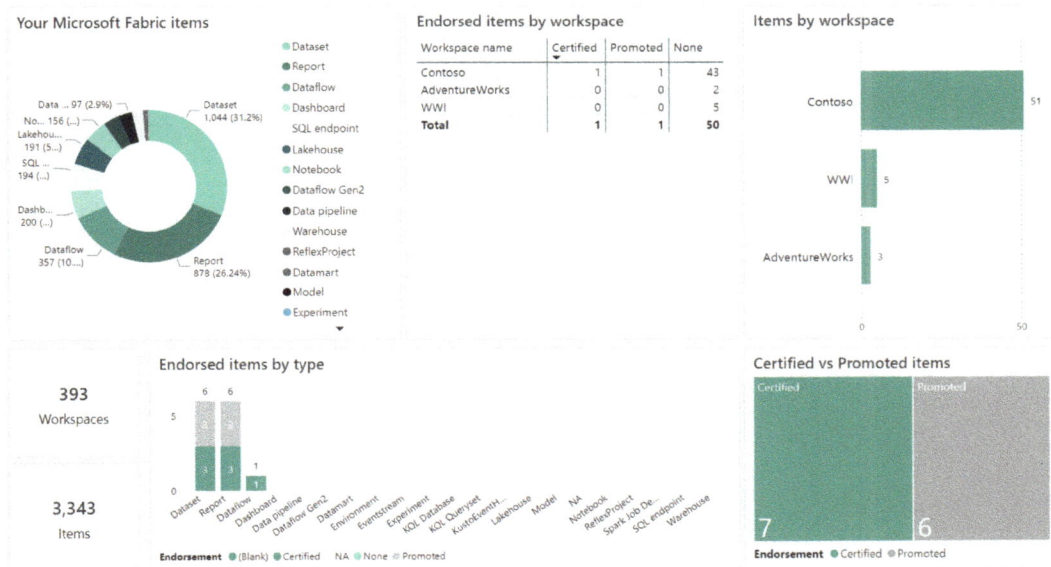

Figure 9.11 – The Purview hub, as seen by an administrator in Fabric

Microsoft Purview is the centerpiece of Microsoft's data governance solution and we've seen how those features can allow organizations to secure, discover, and audit the Fabric data landscape. The integration between Fabric and Purview will continue to deepen over time.

Summary

As you have seen, authentication for Fabric is handled through Microsoft Entra ID for internal and external users. External, also known as guests, can be invited from the Azure portal to the Entra ID directory or from select locations within Fabric. There are additional settings in the Fabric **Admin portal** area that govern how external users can operate beyond what was covered in this chapter. First, we saw how conditional access can be used to secure the front door of the Fabric environment. Next, we looked at the roles and permissions available for securing workspaces, as well as more granular item-level sharing and security. Finally, we explored a suite of governance tools, such as Microsoft Purview, to take cataloging and discovery to the next level. When combined, these concepts will help you design and implement a secure and compliant analytics environment.

In the next chapter, we will operationalize the Fabric environment with **continuous integration and continuous deployment (CI/CD)**.

10

Continuous Integration and Continuous Deployment (CI/CD)

Continuous integration (**CI**) is a part of the DevOps process that allows you to automate the building and testing of code every time a team member commits and approves a code change to source code version control such as a GitHub repository. On the other hand, **continuous deployment** (**CD**) is the process of building, testing, configuring, and deploying code items/artifacts from the lower environment (such as development) to higher environments (such as test or production). In this chapter, we will learn about **application lifecycle management** (**ALM**) or **DevOps** processes support in Fabric and implement CI/CD to move our code items from lower environments to higher environments. When combined, this provides an effective and robust process for delivering new changes, features, or bug fixes quicker to your end users.

Specifically, we will cover the following topics:

- Understanding the end-to-end flow
- Connecting to a Git repo with Azure DevOps
- Working on a new feature or release
- Creating and executing a deployment pipeline
- Managing database code for a Fabric data warehouse

Before diving into the details, let's understand the prerequisites and technical requirements.

Technical requirements

Azure DevOps is a project management and DevOps tool, and out of the many features it provides, the ability to set up a CI/CD pipeline along with version control is at the heart of it. We will be focusing on these features in this chapter. You can learn more about Azure DevOps and the whole gamut of features it provides here: https://azure.microsoft.com/en-us/products/devops.

Before we get into the details, please create an Azure DevOps project and Git repository by following the instructions at `https://learn.microsoft.com/en-us/azure/devops/repos/git/create-new-repo` and name it `Learn Microsoft Fabric`. At this time, your GitHub repository will be empty.

> **What is Git?**
>
> Git is a distributed **version control system** (**VCS**) that allows you to back up and version your work, revert to the previous version if needed, collaborate with other developers, and so on. You can learn more about Git and its benefits here: `https://learn.microsoft.com/en-us/devops/develop/git/what-is-git`.

In this chapter, we will take the Fabric workspace that we created in *Chapter 3, Building an End-to-End Analytics System – Lakehouse*, as a source, link it to the Azure DevOps GitHub repository, and commit all our changes or code items that we have developed so far.

Understanding the end-to-end flow

When we create a **Git repository**, it gets created with a `collaboration` or `main` branch. You commit all your reviewed or approved code items in this branch. Next, whenever a developer or team is going to work on a new feature or release, you create a `feature` or `working` branch by using the `main` branch as the source. The team works in this `feature` branch during development, and once they have completed their work, they create a *pull request* to request merging changes from the `feature` branch to the `main` branch. This typically goes through review, and when it gets approved, these changes are merged into the `main` branch, as shown in *Figure 10.1*. This flow represents the CI part of the DevOps process. Based on the approach an organization has taken, this process repeats for a single feature or a single release with multiple features:

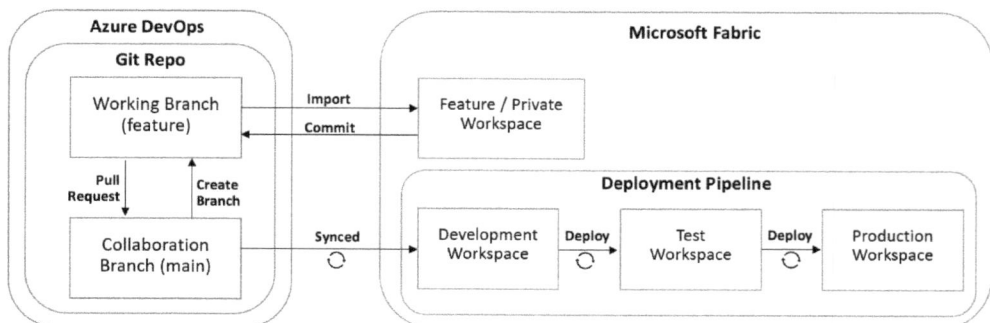

Figure 10.1 – End-to-end DevOps for Microsoft Fabric

For the CD part of the DevOps process, you create a **deployment pipeline** in Fabric to automate the deployment of code items from one environment/workspace to another environment/workspace, as shown in *Figure 10.1*.

Now that we understand the end-to-end CI/CD flow, let's move on to implement it for Fabric code items.

Connecting to a Git repo with Azure DevOps

Native Git integration capability in Fabric makes it easy for developers to collaborate and release changes quickly and continuously. Let's set this up and get started.

Open the Fabric workspace we created in *Chapter 3, Building an End-to-End Analytics System – Lakehouse*, click on the ellipsis (…), and then click on **Workspace settings**, as shown in *Figure 10.2*:

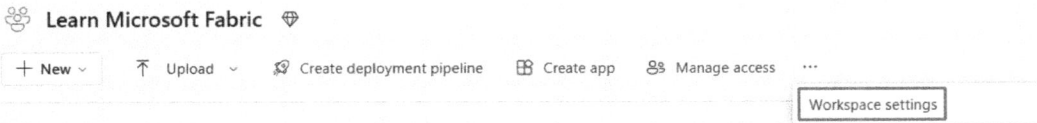

Figure 10.2 – Reviewing workspace settings

On the **Workspace settings** pane, click on **Git integration** on the left and connect the Azure DevOps account. Next, select the organization, DevOps project, and repository you created earlier, specify the `main` branch, and then click on **Connect and sync**, as shown in *Figure 10.3*:

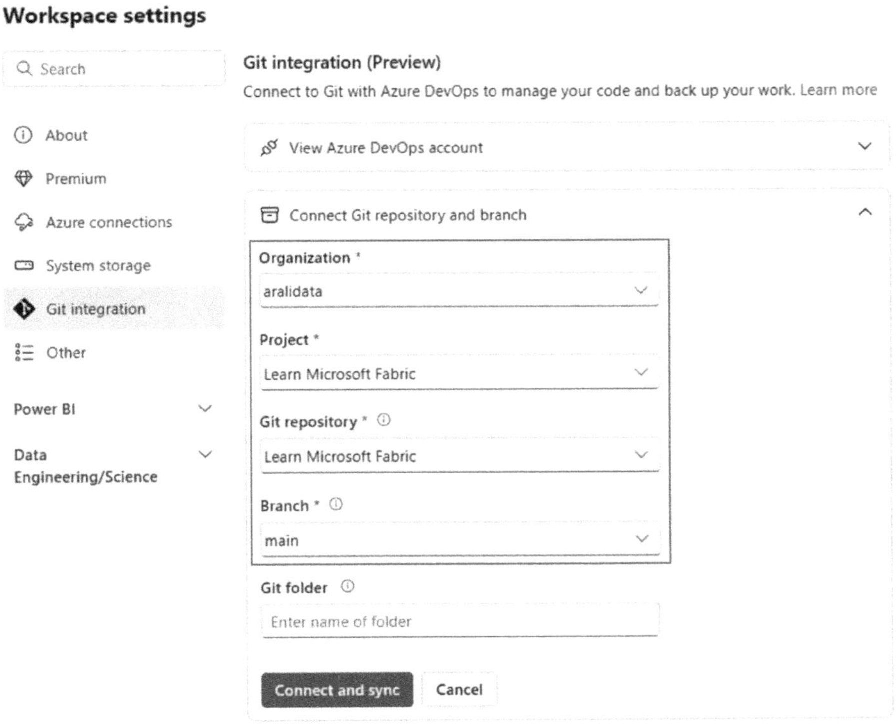

Figure 10.3 – Connecting your workspace to a Git repository

Clicking on **Connect and sync** in *Figure 10.3* will start syncing your code items (such as notebook, lakehouse, and so on) to the specified Git repository. Once the syncing is completed, you will see the Git status of these code items as **Synced**, as shown in *Figure 10.4*:

> **Note**
> As of this writing in January 2024, lakehouses, notebooks, paginated reports, reports, and semantic models are synced; however, the list of supported items is growing fast.

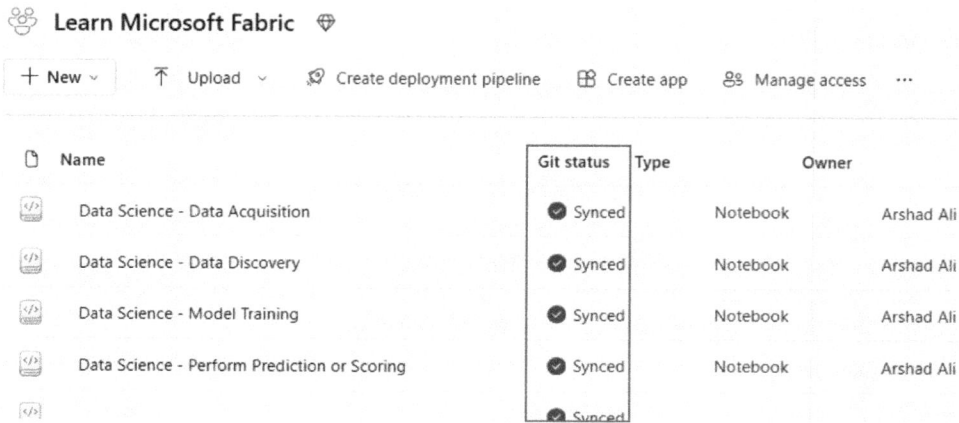

Figure 10.4 – Code items synced with Git repository when connected

You can also go to the Git repository, and you will see the code items from the Fabric workspace are synced to it, as shown in *Figure 10.5*:

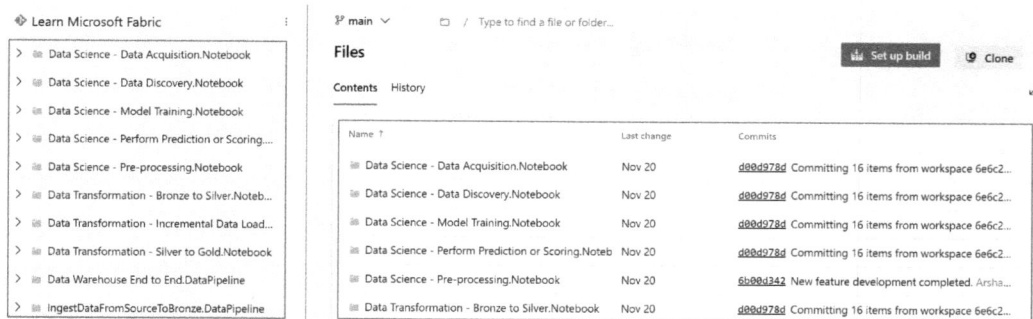

Figure 10.5 – Committed code items in Git repository from workspace

As you will notice in *Figure 10.5*, code items from Fabric are stored in a folder structure in Git where each item in the folder is represented in its own subdirectory with the same name as the item followed by the item type.

Now that you have connected your workspace to the Git repository, let's look at how to make changes in the code for new features or releases.

Working on a new feature or release

Now, suppose you are going to work on a new feature or a release, and for that, you want to create a `feature` branch. In the current workspace, you can do that by clicking on **Source control** and then clicking on **Checkout new branch**, as shown in *Figure 10.6*:

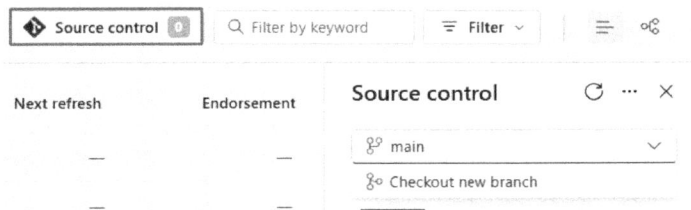

Figure 10.6 – Managing source control in workspace

Specify the name of the branch and click on **Checkout branch**, as shown in *Figure 10.7*. This will create a new branch from your `main` branch as the source and connect your workspace to the newly created branch:

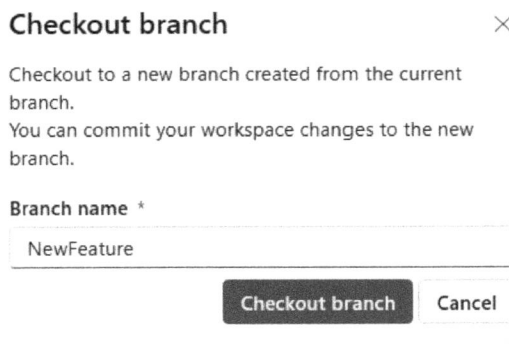

Figure 10.7 – Creating a new branch and checking out

If you have a workspace already created but not connected to the Git repository yet, you can create a new branch while connecting to the Git repository, as shown in *Figure 10.8*, and connect this workspace to this newly created branch:

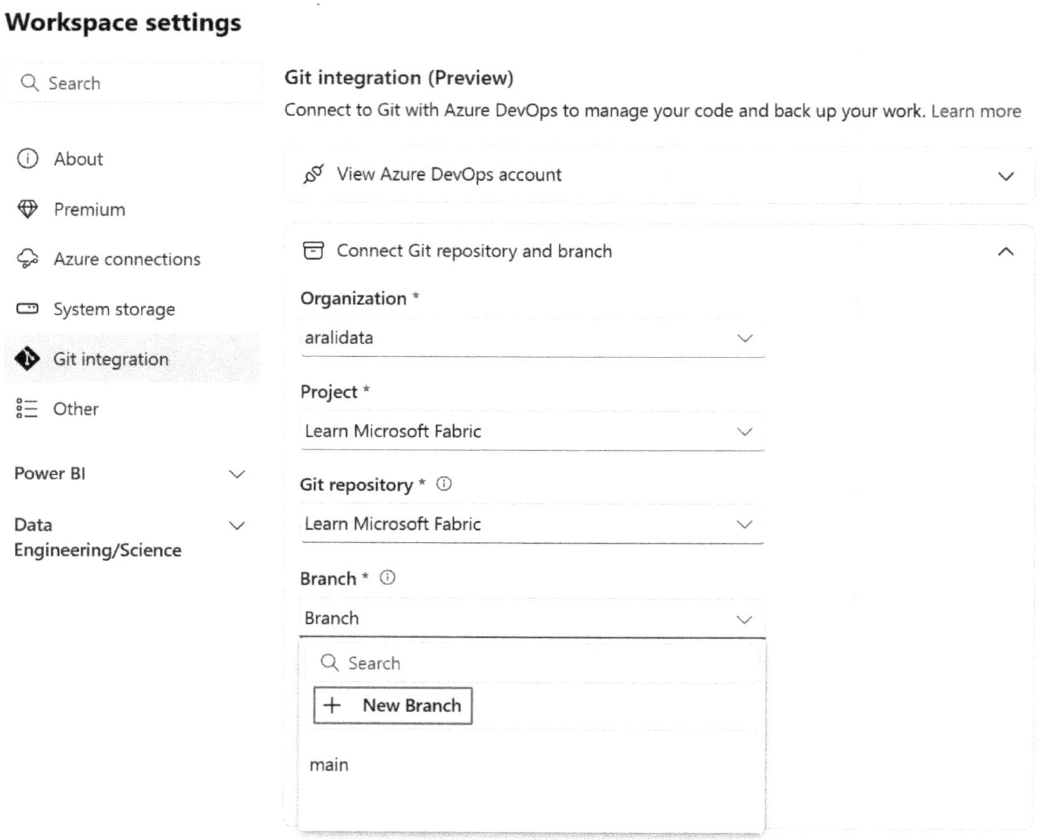

Workspace settings

🔍 Search	**Git integration (Preview)**
	Connect to Git with Azure DevOps to manage your code and back up your work. Learn more
ⓘ About	
	⚙️ View Azure DevOps account ⌄
🏵️ Premium	
☁️ Azure connections	▭ Connect Git repository and branch ⌃
▭ System storage	**Organization ***
◆ Git integration	aralidata ⌄
☰ Other	**Project ***
	Learn Microsoft Fabric ⌄
Power BI ⌄	
	Git repository * ⓘ
Data Engineering/Science ⌄	Learn Microsoft Fabric ⌄
	Branch * ⓘ
	Branch ⌄
	🔍 Search
	＋ New Branch
	main

Figure 10.8 – Creating a new branch from Workspace settings

At this time, you can work on your feature by modifying existing code items or creating new ones. In my case, I created a new notebook and modified an existing one, which gets highlighted, as shown in *Figure 10.9*, as **Uncommitted** under **Git status** as you work through it:

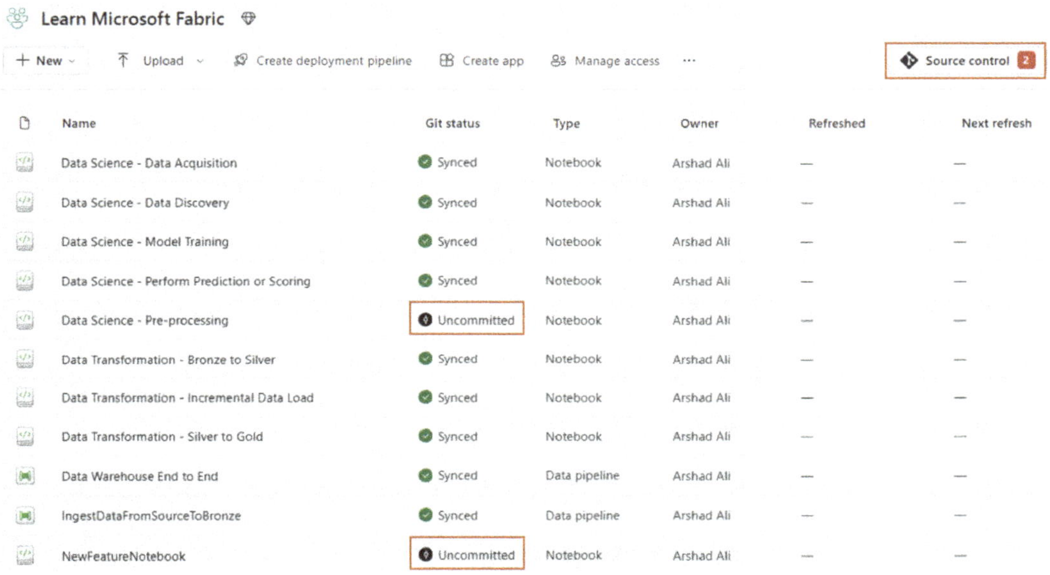

Name	Git status	Type	Owner	Refreshed	Next refresh
Data Science - Data Acquisition	✓ Synced	Notebook	Arshad Ali	—	—
Data Science - Data Discovery	✓ Synced	Notebook	Arshad Ali	—	—
Data Science - Model Training	✓ Synced	Notebook	Arshad Ali	—	—
Data Science - Perform Prediction or Scoring	✓ Synced	Notebook	Arshad Ali	—	—
Data Science - Pre-processing	⊘ Uncommitted	Notebook	Arshad Ali	—	—
Data Transformation - Bronze to Silver	✓ Synced	Notebook	Arshad Ali	—	—
Data Transformation - Incremental Data Load	✓ Synced	Notebook	Arshad Ali	—	—
Data Transformation - Silver to Gold	✓ Synced	Notebook	Arshad Ali	—	—
Data Warehouse End to End	✓ Synced	Data pipeline	Arshad Ali	—	—
IngestDataFromSourceToBronze	✓ Synced	Data pipeline	Arshad Ali	—	—
NewFeatureNotebook	⊘ Uncommitted	Notebook	Arshad Ali	—	—

Figure 10.9 – Reviewing the difference between workspace contents and Git repository

While you work through your features and their related changes, all these changes are saved in the workspace; however, you might want to commit those changes to the Git repository. To do that, click on **Source control**, as shown in *Figure 10.9*, then select changes that you are ready to commit to the Git repository and click on the **Commit** button, as shown in *Figure 10.10*. As you will notice, all changes are marked as new or modified under the **Status** column:

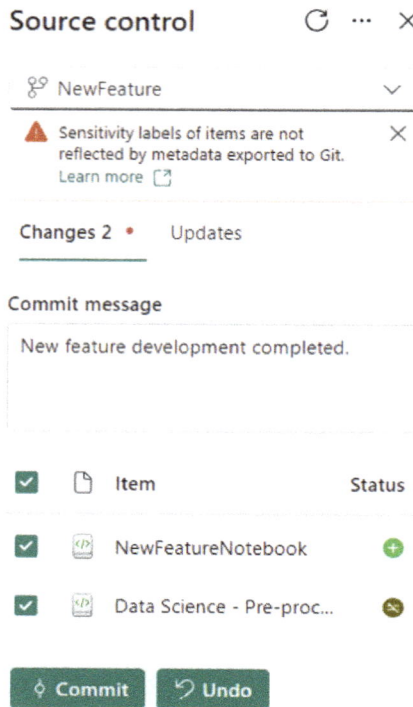

Figure 10.10 – Committing new changes to the Git repository

Typically, you would commit all your changes as they reach a reasonable state, and once these changes are committed after hitting the **Commit** button, you will see a confirmation status in the top-right corner, as shown in *Figure 10.11*:

Figure 10.11 – Confirmation of code items committed to the Git repository

At this time, let's assume that all changes for the new feature are completed and committed to the newly created `feature` branch. Next, we can create a *pull request* to merge changes from the `feature` branch to the main branch. To do that, go to the Git repository, switch to the `feature` branch, and then click on the **Create a pull request** button, as shown in *Figure 10.12*, to update the changes of the new feature and see the code files impacted:

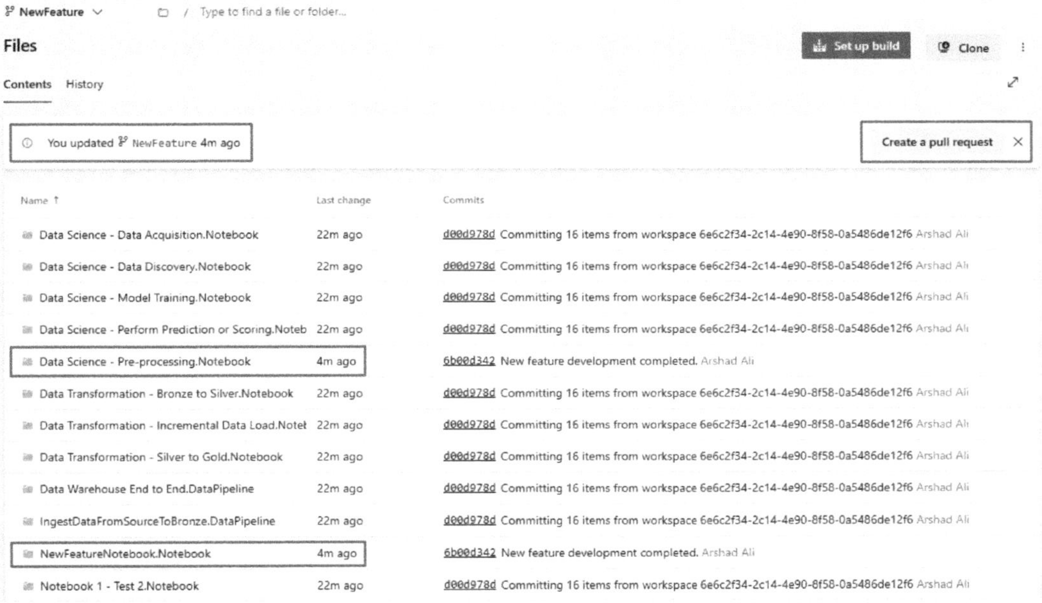

Figure 10.12 – Reviewing newly committed changes in the feature branch

In the **New pull request** wizard, specify a title and description, and click on the **Create** button, as shown in *Figure 10.13*. On this screen, you can also review changes included in the pull request, such as the number of files changed, commits submitted, and so on. You can add extra reviewers as well:

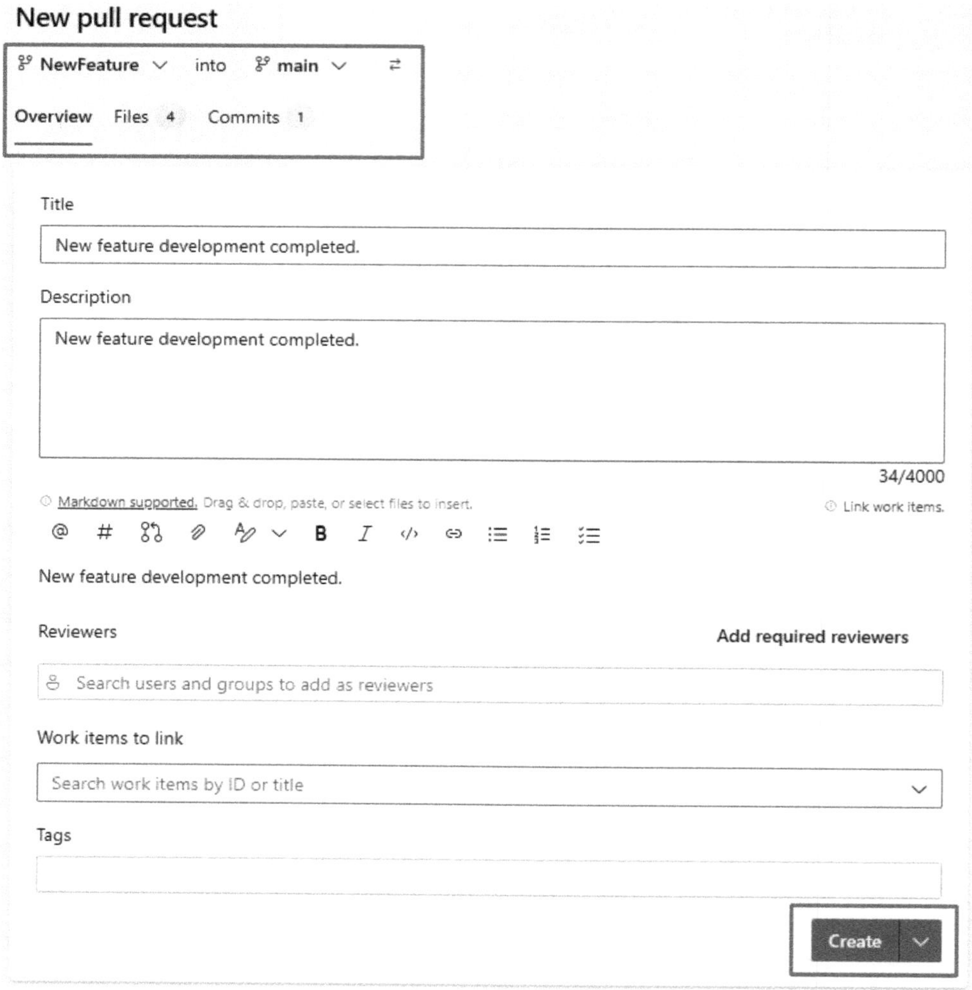

New pull request

⅄ NewFeature ∨   into   ⅄ main ∨   ⇄
Overview   Files 4   Commits 1

Title

New feature development completed.

Description

New feature development completed.

34/4000

ⓘ Markdown supported. Drag & drop, paste, or select files to insert.   ⓘ Link work items.

@ # ⅄⅄ ⌀ A̷ ∨ **B** *I* </> ⌗ ☰ ☷ ☰

New feature development completed.

Reviewers   **Add required reviewers**

👤 Search users and groups to add as reviewers

Work items to link

Search work items by ID or title   ∨

Tags

Create ∨

Figure 10.13 – Creating a pull request to merge changes from the feature branch

Once a pull request is created by a developer, the reviewer can review all these changes, reject/approve them, and complete the merge process, as shown in *Figure 10.14*:

New feature development completed.

Active 113   Arshad Ali proposer to merge NewFeature into main

Overview Files Updates Commits **Synapse diff**

4 changed files: 3 adds. 1 edits.

/Data Science - Pre-processing.Notebook/notebook-content.py

Figure 10.14 – Reviewing changes of the pull request and merging it

Now that all changes have been merged into the main branch and the feature branch is deleted after that, you can go to **Workspace settings** again and switch to the main branch, as shown in *Figure 10.15*:

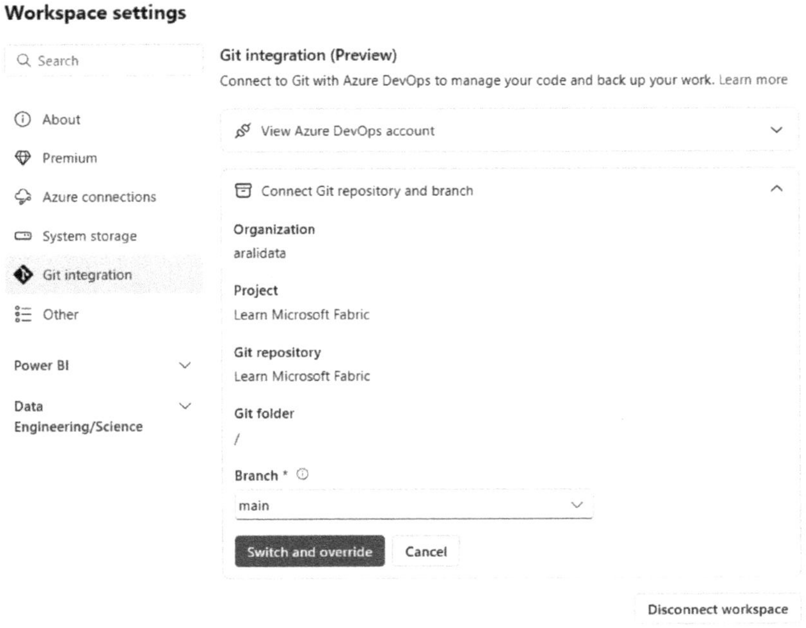

Figure 10.15 – Switching back to the main branch in the workspace

Now, let's move on to creating a deployment pipeline to deploy changes to the next environment, such as test and production.

Creating and executing a deployment pipeline

Now that you have learned about how CI works in Fabric, it's time to switch gears and look at the CD of your code items from a lower environment such as *development* to higher environments such as *test* and *production*.

When you are in the workspace view, you will notice a **Create deployment pipeline** option at the top of the screen, as shown in *Figure 10.16*:

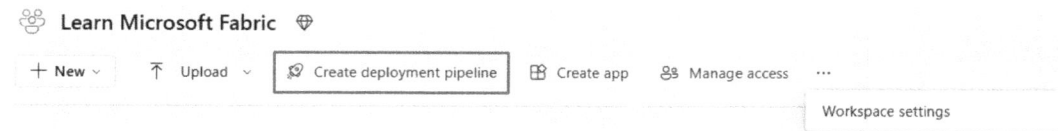

Figure 10.16 – Creating a deployment pipeline

Click on it to create a deployment pipeline, specify a name and optional description for it, as shown in *Figure 10.17*, and then click on the **Next** button:

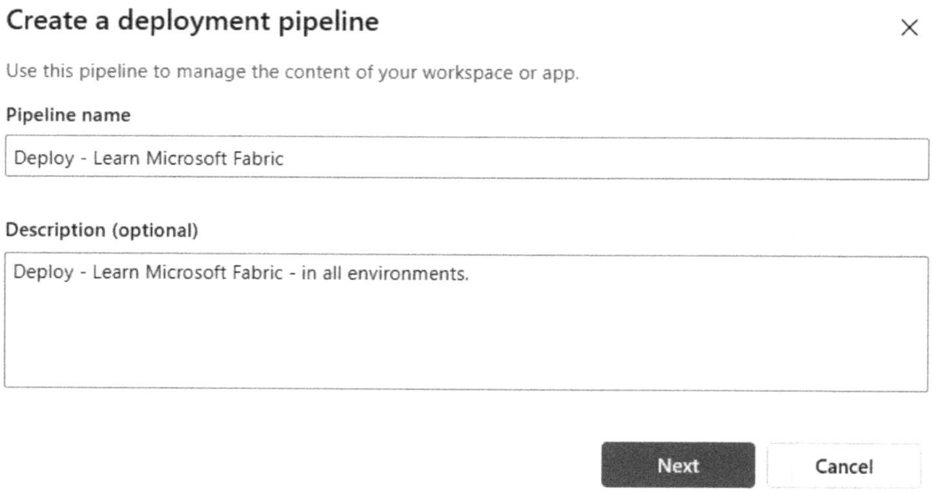

Figure 10.17 – Specifying a name and providing an optional description for the deployment pipeline

On the next screen of the wizard, you specify deployment stages, as shown in *Figure 10.18*. Typically, you will have **Development**, **Test**, and **Production**; however, if you need to, you can add additional stages or remove any that are not needed from the default proposed deployment stages:

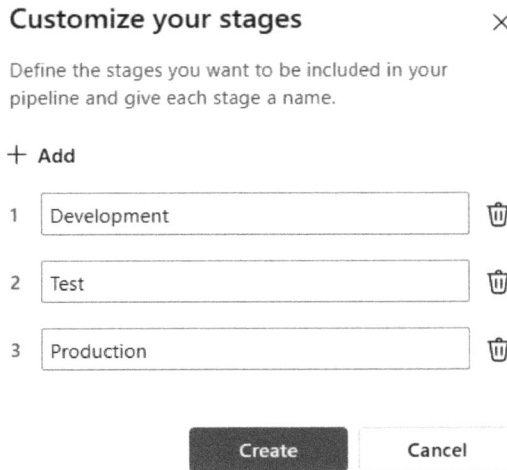

Figure 10.18 – Customizing deployment stages

When you click on the **Create** button, as shown in *Figure 10.18*, it asks you to specify a workspace for the **Development** environment. You can choose the current workspace, as this workspace is connected to the main branch and is expected to serve as a source for deployment to the other environments. As you will notice, *Figure 10.19* shows code items that are candidates for deployment to the next environment:

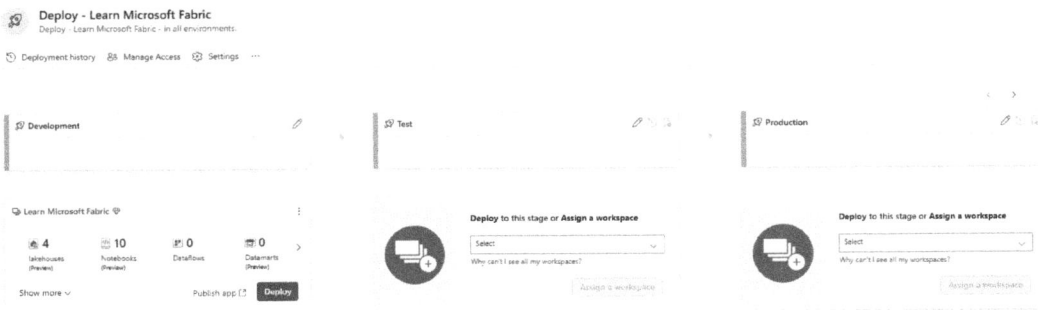

Figure 10.19 – Viewing the deployment pipeline with default deployment stages

For higher environments, you can choose to use existing workspaces, if available, or create new ones. For this example, let's say we want to create new workspaces for both **Test** and **Production** environments, and hence leave combo boxes for each of these as blank or with a **Select** value, as shown in *Figure 10.19*.

On the screen shown in *Figure 10.19*, click on the **Deploy** button under the **Development** tile to start deployment. This will bring in a detail page that shows all changes that will be deployed, as shown in *Figure 10.20*. You can also specify a description or note here:

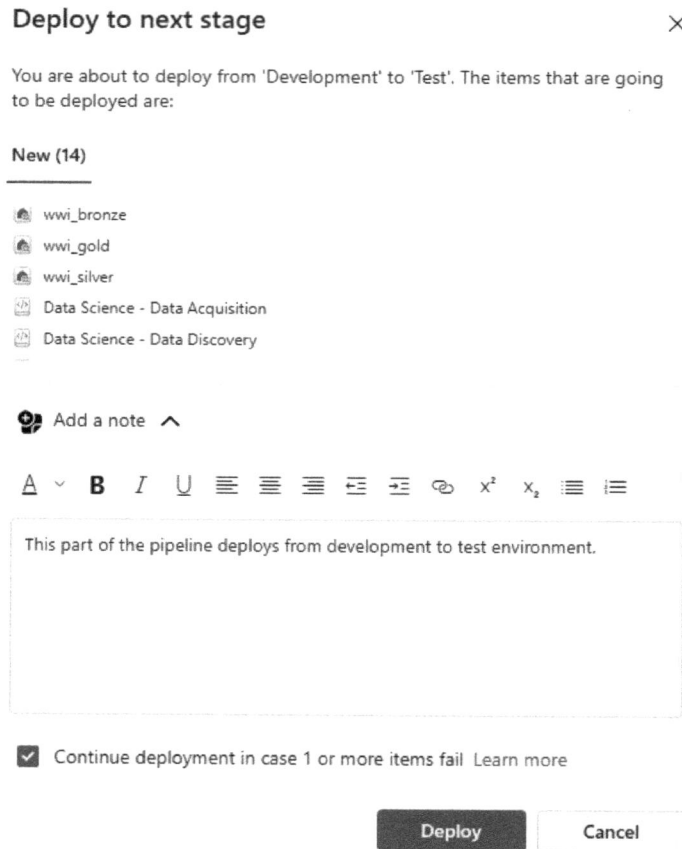

Deploy to next stage   ✕

You are about to deploy from 'Development' to 'Test'. The items that are going to be deployed are:

New (14)

   📄 wwi_bronze
   📄 wwi_gold
   📄 wwi_silver
   📄 Data Science - Data Acquisition
   📄 Data Science - Data Discovery

   📝 Add a note ⋀

A ⌄ **B** *I* U̲ ≡ ≡ ≡ ⇥ ⇤ ⊘ x² x₂ ≡ ≡

> This part of the pipeline deploys from development to test environment.

☑ Continue deployment in case 1 or more items fail Learn more

Deploy   Cancel

Figure 10.20 – Reviewing code items ready for deployment to the test environment

Once you hit the **Deploy** button, as shown in *Figure 10.20*, the deployment process starts and shows progress as it continues. Once the deployment is completed, you will be able to see all changes have been synced or deployed from the **Development** to the **Test** environment, as shown in *Figure 10.21*:

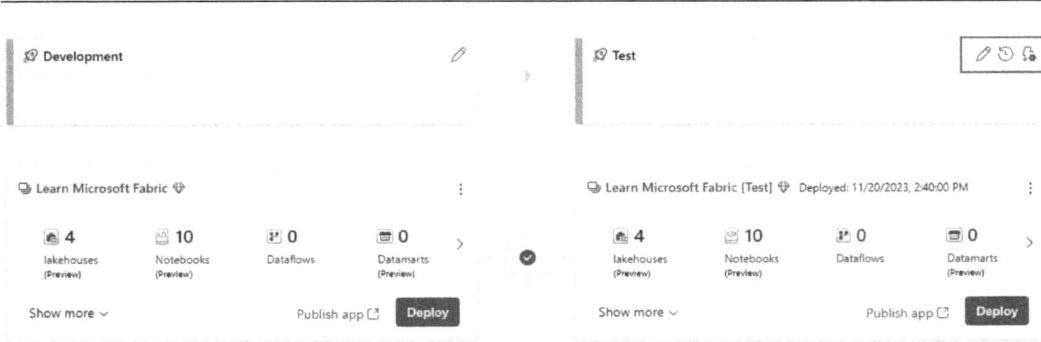

Figure 10.21 – Deployment status review

By clicking on the *deployment history* icon next to **Test**, you will be able to see the history of all deployments in this stage – an example is shown in *Figure 10.22*:

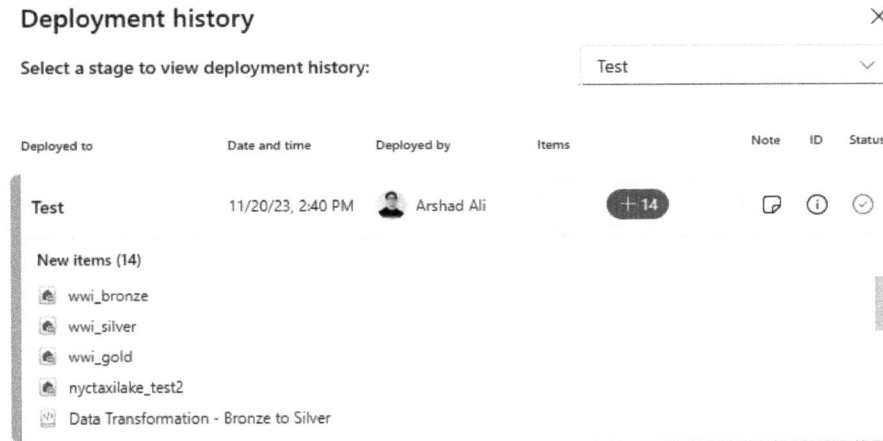

Figure 10.22 – Reviewing the deployment history for a stage

There are times when you need to define *deployment rules*. For example, a notebook has a default lakehouse, and this default lakehouse might be different from **Development** to **Test** to **Production** environments, and you would like to create a deployment rule that changes this default setting during deployment. This is possible by creating deployment rules.

To create deployment rules, click on the *deployment rules* icon shown in *Figure 10.21* (at the top right) and choose a notebook for which you want to change the default lakehouse, as shown in *Figure 10.23*:

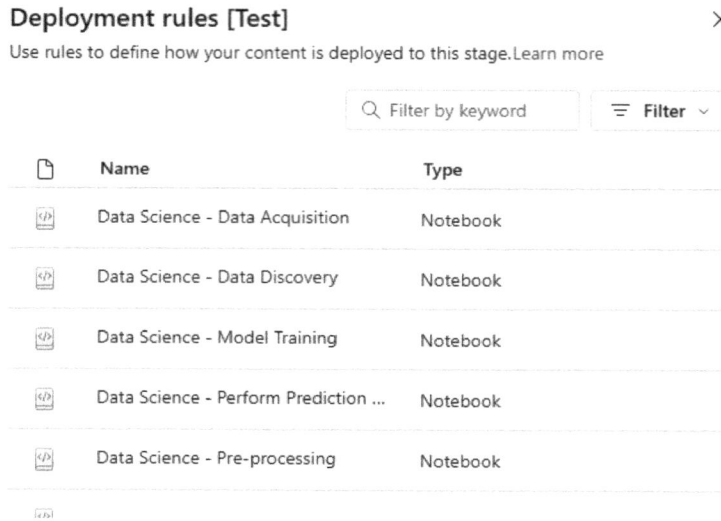

Deployment rules [Test]   ✕

Use rules to define how your content is deployed to this stage. Learn more

Q Filter by keyword		☰ Filter ˅

🗋	Name	Type
	Data Science - Data Acquisition	Notebook
	Data Science - Data Discovery	Notebook
	Data Science - Model Training	Notebook
	Data Science - Perform Prediction ...	Notebook
	Data Science - Pre-processing	Notebook

Figure 10.23 – Defining a deployment rule

On the **Set deployment rules** page, as shown in *Figure 10.24*, click on + **Add rule**:

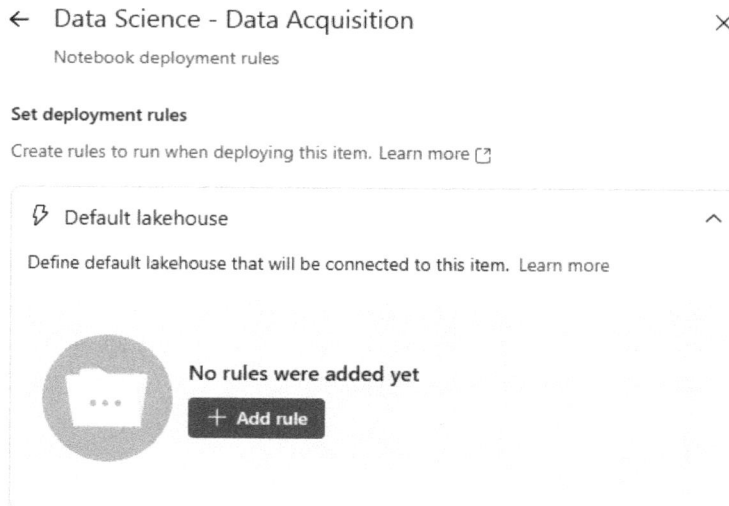

← Data Science - Data Acquisition   ✕

Notebook deployment rules

Set deployment rules

Create rules to run when deploying this item. Learn more ⬀

⑂ Default lakehouse   ∧

Define default lakehouse that will be connected to this item. Learn more

No rules were added yet

+ Add rule

Figure 10.24 – Adding a new rule to change the default lakehouse

Next, change the default lakehouse for the selected notebook to the target environment, as shown in *Figure 10.25*:

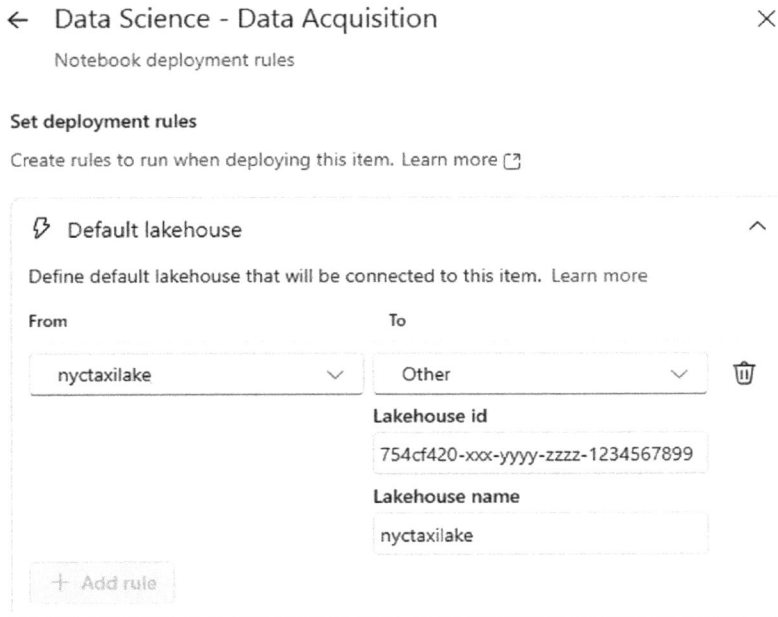

Figure 10.25 – Specifying new lakehouse details to change the default

Now that you have completed deployment in the **Test** environment, you will run all your test cases, and when ready, you will start deployment to your **Production** environment. To do that, click on **Deploy** under the **Test** tile, as shown in *Figure 10.26*. Also, you can choose to deploy in an existing workspace or let the deployment process create a new workspace for you:

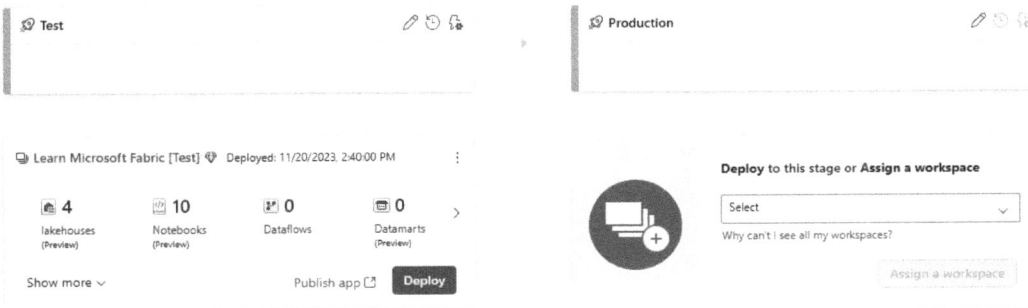

Figure 10.26 – Deploying from a test environment to a production environment

Next, you can review all code items that will get deployed to your target stage and specify the deployment notes if applicable. Once you are ready, click on the **Deploy** button, as shown in *Figure 10.27*, to kick off the deployment:

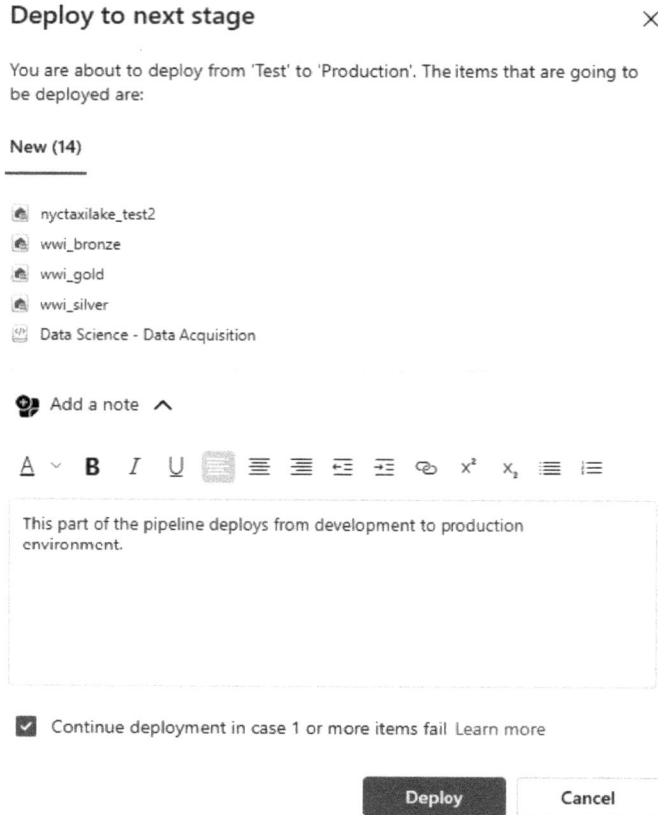

Deploy to next stage ✕

You are about to deploy from 'Test' to 'Production'. The items that are going to be deployed are:

New (14)

- nyctaxilake_test2
- wwi_bronze
- wwi_gold
- wwi_silver
- Data Science - Data Acquisition

Add a note ∧

A ∨   **B**   *I*   U̲   ▤   ≡   ≡   ≡   ≡   ⊘   x²   x₂   ☰   ☷

This part of the pipeline deploys from development to production environment.

☑ Continue deployment in case 1 or more items fail Learn more

Deploy   Cancel

Figure 10.27 – Reviewing the code items to be deployed before deployment to production

Once the deployment process completes, you can see the status, as shown in *Figure 10.28*. In this case, since deployment was successful, it shows a green check mark; however, if there is any failure or if any difference is identified between the two environments, it will show all these details here:

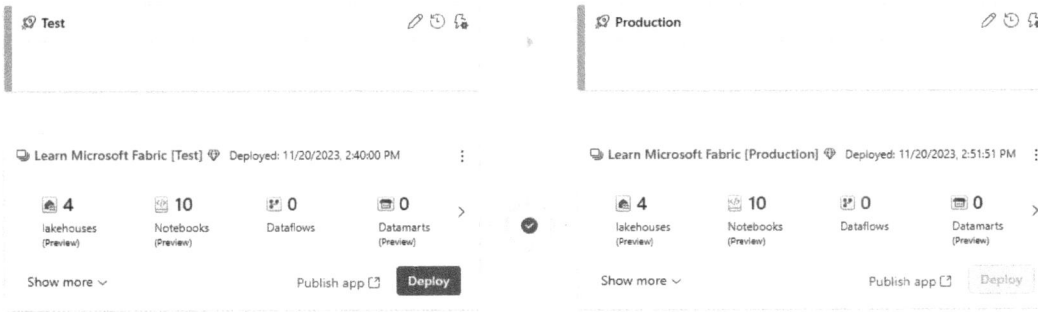

Figure 10.28 – Reviewing production deployment status

You can review existing deployment pipelines or create new ones by clicking on the **Deployment pipelines** link right above + **New workspace** when you click on **Workspaces** from the left navigation bar, as shown in *Figure 10.29*:

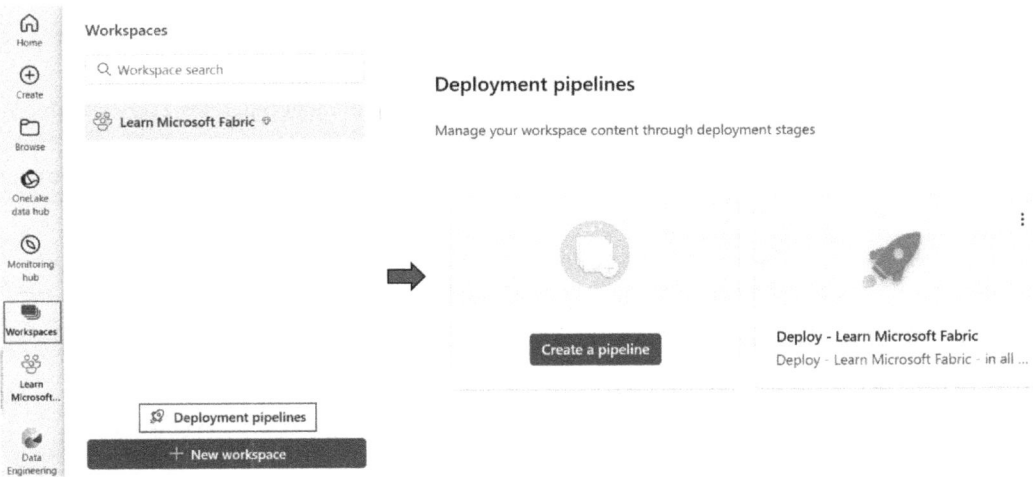

Figure 10.29 – Switching to Deployment pipelines view

When you click on the existing deployment pipeline, you can find options to modify its properties, such as changing access, deleting the pipeline, and so on, as shown in *Figure 10.30*:

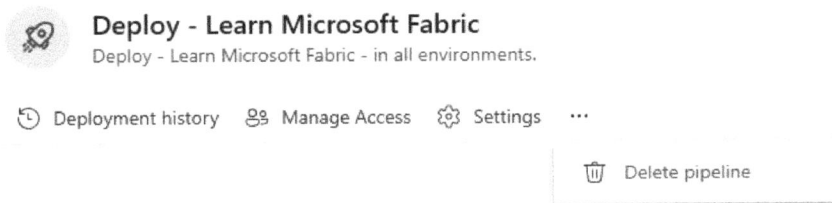

Figure 10.30 – Reviewing an existing deployment pipeline

You can also review the deployment history for your deployment pipeline (for all stages), as shown in *Figure 10.31*:

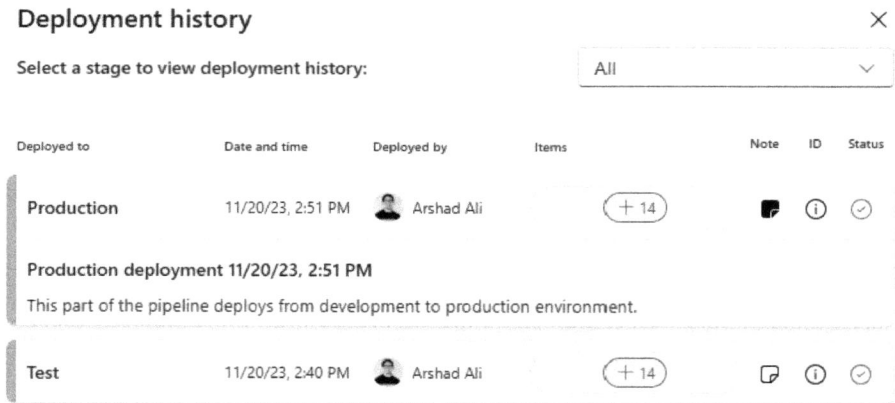

Figure 10.31 – Reviewing the deployment history for all stages in one place

While we looked at user interface experience to create and run deployment pipelines, there are times when you want to automate this process to run it programmatically. Instructions on how to do that are accessible at https://learn.microsoft.com/en-us/fabric/cicd/deployment-pipelines/pipeline-automation.

Additionally, you can learn more about lifecycle management best practices here: https://learn.microsoft.com/en-us/fabric/cicd/best-practices-cicd.

Now, let's move on to understanding how to manage database code.

Managing database code for a Fabric data warehouse

Putting items in a Fabric workspace in source control is important for being able to deploy changes between workspaces, but what about code within your data warehouse? A warehouse itself is of no use if changes to the table definitions, stored procedures, and views don't move as well. A Fabric data warehouse is integrated with several industry-standard tools and will be adding more native support for database objects in the future.

Among the ways to interact with and manage database code are the following:

- **Data built tool (dbt)**: This is an open source framework that creates `dbt` projects that can then be deployed to different Fabric data warehouses

- **SqlPackage**: This is a command-line utility for automating database deployment tasks, including extraction of schema, scripting schema updates, and publishing project updates to databases

- **SQL Database Projects**: This extension gives a project-based approach to development in Azure Data Studio, allowing for development, project build, project deployment, schema comparison, and more

Let's dive into the most common method for managing database code: the SQL Database Projects extension in Azure Data Studio.

Managing database code with the SQL Database Projects extension

Support for SQL database projects is delivered through a free extension, developed by Microsoft, in Azure Data Studio. Support for Microsoft Fabric Data Warehouse was added in the extension's November 2023 release. After installing the extension, a **Database Projects** option will appear on the primary sidebar.

To get started with the **Database Projects** extension, the steps are as follows:

1. From the primary sidebar, select **Database Projects**.
2. Select **Create new**.
3. On the **Create a new project** screen, select the **SQL Server Database** option, enter a name and location for the project, and select **Synapse Data Warehouse in Microsoft Fabric** from the **Target Platform** drop-down list.
4. Select **Create**.

After the project is created, you can begin developing code by right-clicking on the project name and selecting **Add Table** | **View** | **Stored procedure** to open a script template. You can also add existing code and create blank scripts, as shown in *Figure 10.32*:

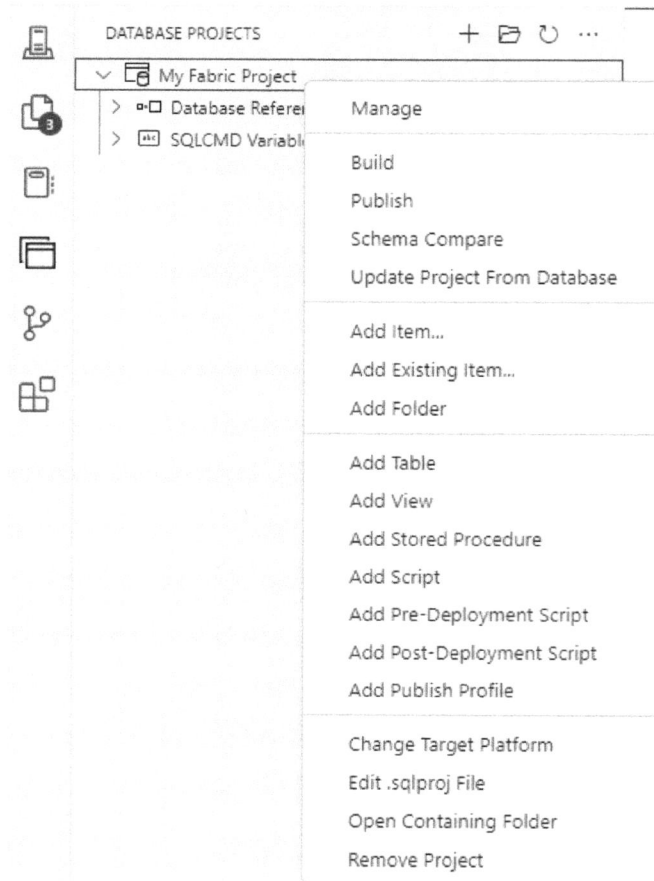

Figure 10.32 – Menu of options displayed when right-clicking on a database project

Many database projects don't start from ground zero, though. Often, a small database will be stood up, some development for a POC will take place, and then the project will need to become more managed. In this case, we will use the **Update Project From Database** option found on the right-click menu shown in *Figure 10.32*. Simply fill in the form providing the server, using the SQL endpoint (we covered SQL endpoints in the *SQL endpoint* section of *Chapter 3, Building an End-to-End Analytics System – Lakehouse*) from the Fabric workspace, select a database for the project and some details around structure, and then select **Update**:

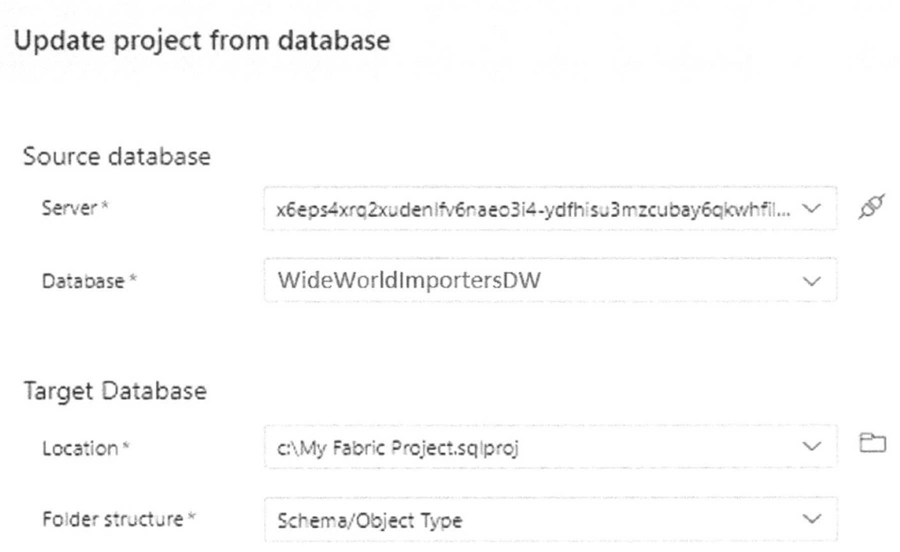

Update project from database

Source database

Server *	x6eps4xrq2xudenlfv6naeo3i4-ydfhisu3mzcubay6qkwhfil... ∨
Database *	WideWorldImportersDW ∨

Target Database

Location *	c:\My Fabric Project.sqlproj ∨
Folder structure *	Schema/Object Type ∨

Figure 10.33 – The update project form used to import an existing
database's objects into a SQL database project

After confirming the project changes, this database project can be managed and deployed just like any other deployment you have as part of your DevOps that fits into your organization's processes, such as performing manual builds, schema comparisons, and deployments from inside Azure Data Studio. The code can also then be put under source control management with Git or Azure DevOps, where deployment pipelines can be used for automated database build and deployment.

As shown, many options exist for managing code within a Fabric data warehouse, and even more options will be added in the future with the goal of creating maximum flexibility to fit every organization's management and deployment needs.

Summary

Almost every organization nowadays follows DevOps processes to offer a collaborative platform for its developers to work together and for its ALM. In this chapter, you learned how you can leverage native integration of Git with Fabric for CI and build deployment pipelines for CD as part of your ALM – for delivering new changes, features, or bug fixes quicker to your end users. You now know how to move your code items from a lower environment (development) to a higher environment (test and/or production).

In the next chapter, we will discuss a wide range of AI experiences, called Copilots, in Fabric that help accelerate each step of the analytics journey.

Part 5:
AI Assistance with
Copilot Integration

This part of the book explores how AI is used to extend the developer experience and provide deeper insights into your data, with the Copilot experiences built into each workload. This includes an overview of the Copilots for data science, data engineering, Data Factory, and Power BI, as well as the tenant-level settings required to enable the capabilities in the Fabric tenant.

This part contains the following chapter:

- *Chapter 11, Overview of AI Assistance and Copilot Integration*

11

Overview of AI Assistance and Copilot Integration

Microsoft Fabric has introduced a wide range of generative **artificial intelligence** (**AI**) experiences, called **Copilot**, that help accelerate each step of the analytics journey by potentially increasing overall developer productivity. This chapter explores the Copilot experiences built into different Fabric workloads:

- What is Copilot in Fabric?
- Copilot in data engineering and data science
- Copilot in Data Factory
- Copilot in Power BI

By the end of the chapter, you will have learned about Copilot and how you can leverage it to unlock new insights into your data.

Before diving into details, let's take a step back and look at some technical requirements to get started with using Copilot.

Technical requirements

As of this writing in January 2024, the Microsoft Fabric Copilot feature is in preview, and you need P1, F64, or higher capacity to use Copilot.

> **Note**
> A capacity is a distinct pool of computing resources allocated to Microsoft Fabric and assigned to one or more Fabric workspaces. This capacity is available in multiple tiers, can be scaled up and down, and can be paused and resumed when needed. You can learn more about it here: `https://learn.microsoft.com/en-us/fabric/enterprise/licenses#capacity-license`.

By default, this feature is disabled, and your Fabric tenant admin needs to enable it by going to **Admin portal | Tenant settings** and then, in the **Copilot and Azure OpenAI Service** section, toggle the slider to enable this feature, as shown in *Figure 11.1*. The important point to note, however, is that Copilot sends customer data such as prompts, augmented data with prompts, and AI outputs to **Azure OpenAI Service** for processing, where it is temporarily stored; hence, you need to consent to it.

> **Note**
>
> Azure OpenAI Service offers advanced large language AI models such as GPT-4 and GPT-3.5-Turbo. You can learn more about Azure OpenAI Service here: `https://learn.microsoft.com/en-us/azure/ai-services/openai/overview`.

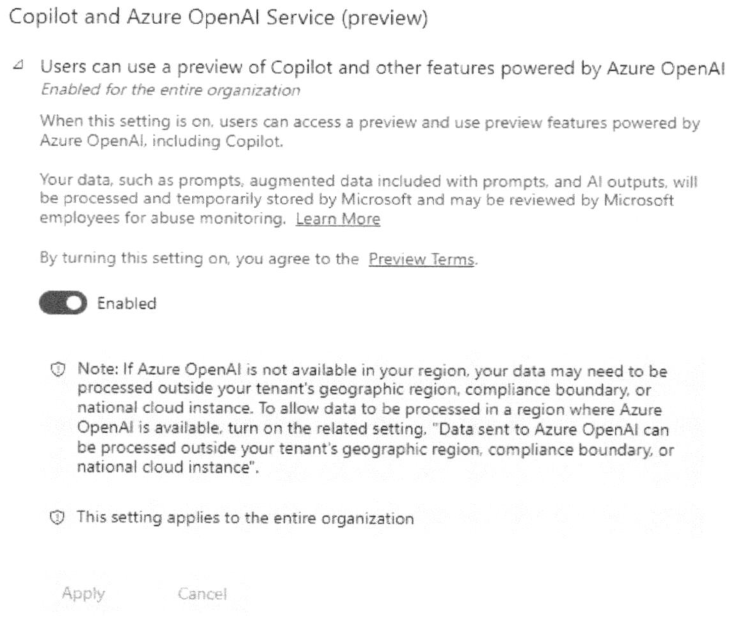

Copilot and Azure OpenAI Service (preview)

⊿ Users can use a preview of Copilot and other features powered by Azure OpenAI
Enabled for the entire organization

When this setting is on, users can access a preview and use preview features powered by
Azure OpenAI, including Copilot.

Your data, such as prompts, augmented data included with prompts, and AI outputs, will
be processed and temporarily stored by Microsoft and may be reviewed by Microsoft
employees for abuse monitoring. Learn More

By turning this setting on, you agree to the Preview Terms.

🔵⚪ Enabled

ⓘ Note: If Azure OpenAI is not available in your region, your data may need to be
processed outside your tenant's geographic region, compliance boundary, or
national cloud instance. To allow data to be processed in a region where Azure
OpenAI is available, turn on the related setting, "Data sent to Azure OpenAI can
be processed outside your tenant's geographic region, compliance boundary, or
national cloud instance".

ⓘ This setting applies to the entire organization

Apply   Cancel

Figure 11.1 – Enable Copilot in Microsoft Fabric

When Azure OpenAI Service is not available in your Microsoft Fabric tenant region and you want to use Copilot, you need to consent to that by changing the toggle as shown in *Figure 11.2*:

◁ Data sent to Azure OpenAI can be processed outside your tenant's geographic region, compliance boundary, or national cloud instance
Enabled for the entire organization

Azure OpenAI is currently available in a limited number of regions and geographies.
When this setting is on, data sent to Azure OpenAI can be processed in a region where
the service is available, which might be outside your tenant's geographic region,
compliance boundary, or national cloud instance. Learn More

By turning this setting on, you agree to the Preview Terms.

⬤▬ Enabled

ⓘ Note: Even if this setting is on, you will also need to turn on the related setting
    "Users can use a preview of Copilot and other features powered by Azure
    OpenAI" for these features to work.

ⓘ This setting applies to the entire organization

Apply   Cancel

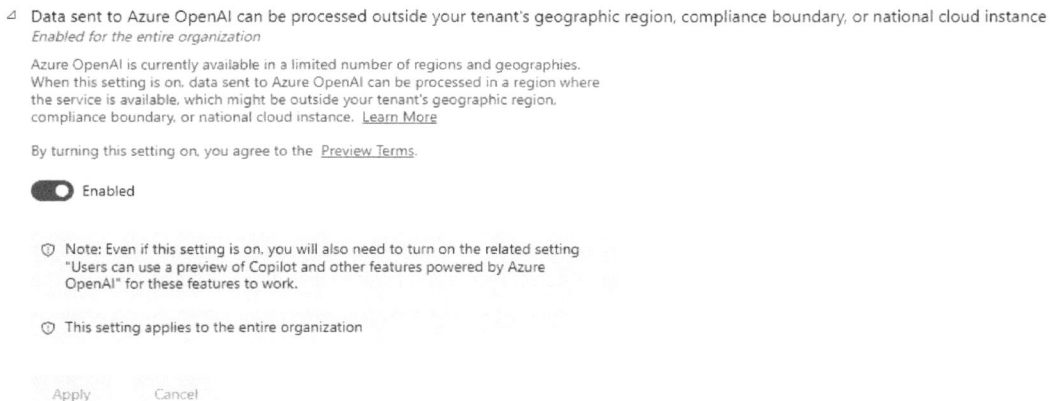

Figure 11.2 – Required consent for enabling Copilot in Microsoft Fabric

Now, let's learn more about what Copilot is and what are its capabilities to improve our productivity.

What is Copilot in Fabric?

With the native integration of Copilot, a generative AI service in Microsoft Fabric, you can elevate your team's productivity by leveraging these AI-assisted capabilities. While Copilot in different Fabric workloads provides different capabilities, in general, it aims to enhance developers' productivity by offering a newer and quicker way for data integration, data transformation, building and training machine learning models, generating insights, and creating visualizations and reports. We will explore some of these capabilities in the next few sections.

Please note that Copilot is based on a probabilistic model and is still evolving; hence, you need to consider these points before you decide to use it:

- The output might vary from one execution to another or over time given its probabilistic nature. Likewise, the output shown in the following examples might be different from what you see; however, the goal remains the same – that is, accelerating your analytics journey by improving productivity.

- The output and responses might be inaccurate; hence, it's recommended to review and validate its accuracy, appropriateness, and completeness before using it for your work.

- Copilot sends customer data such as prompts, augmented data with prompts, and AI outputs to Azure OpenAI Service where it is temporarily stored for 30 days; hence, it's recommended to check your company policy to ensure its compliance. However, Azure OpenAI Service is fully controlled by Microsoft and Microsoft assures that customer data is not used to train models and isn't available to other customers. Also, you, as a customer, can control where your data is processed and stored. You can learn more about it here: `https://learn.microsoft.com/en-us/fabric/get-started/copilot-privacy-security`.

Now that we know about Copilot and its capabilities, let's learn how to use it in data engineering and data science workloads in Fabric.

Copilot in data engineering and data science

Copilot for data engineering and data science workloads provides features to analyze and visualize your data to give you data insights with different types of visualizations, and it offers code-generation capability to improve productivity for data transformation and building and training machine learning models.

Copilot offers context-based automatic code generation, intelligent code completion, code documentation, fixing coding issues, automating routine tasks, providing standard coding templates, and so on. Further, it also allows you to visualize and analyze your data, which either comes from lakehouse or Power BI datasets or the dataframe you have created in your session, quicker and intuitively.

You can use the **Copilot chat panel** as a user interface or **chat magic** commands in notebook cells when taking advantage of this AI assistant. For our demonstration, we will first start using chat panels and then look into a few examples of using chat magic commands at the end of this section.

For our scenario in this chapter, we will take the same New York taxi data as in *Chapter 6, Building an End-to-End Analytics System – Data Science,* and will have a similar data discovery process and preprocessing of data to cleanse it for further analysis as in the *Data discovery* and *Data preprocessing* sections of *Chapter 6*. We will carry out all these exercises with the help of Copilot (the AI assistant) and without writing code on our own.

When you are in the **Workspace** view, use the experience switcher in the bottom left corner and select **Data engineering**. Then click on +**New** at the top and select **Notebook** to create a new notebook, and then attach this notebook to the `nyctaxilake` lakehouse that you created in the *Data and storage – creating a lakehouse and ingesting data using Apache Spark* section of *Chapter 6, Building End-to-End Analytics System – Data Science*. You will notice these two tables, as highlighted in *Figure 11.3*, are already available from our exercises from *Chapter 9, Security and Governance Overview*. Further, on the notebook ribbon interface, you will notice the **Copilot** button as well.

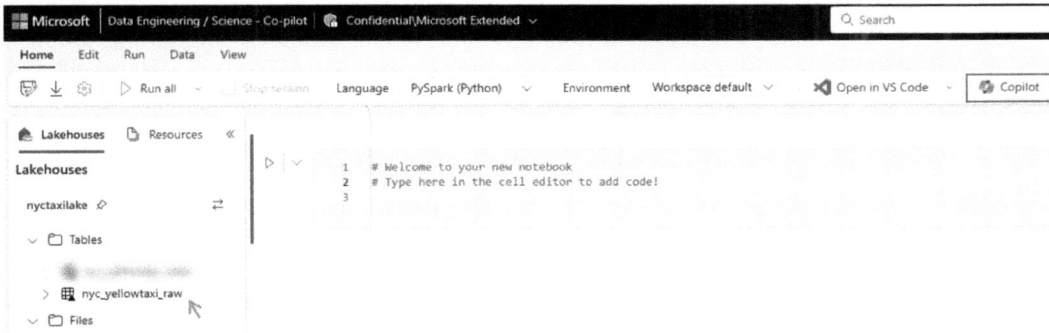

Figure 11.3 – The Copilot button in the notebook

Click on the **Copilot** button as shown in *Figure 11.3* to launch a chat panel, which will appear on the right side of the notebook user interface as shown in *Figure 11.4*:

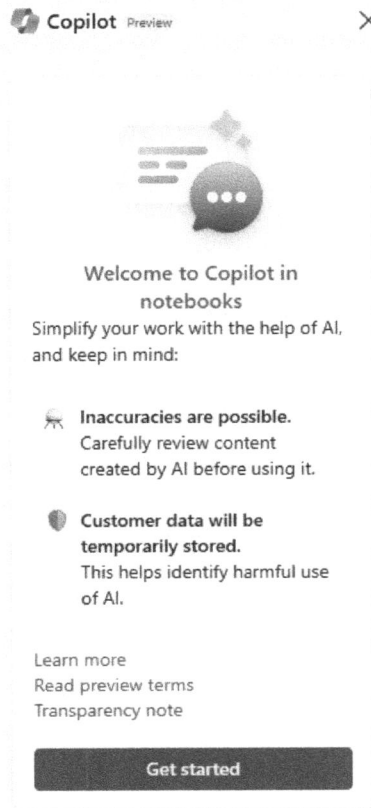

Figure 11.4 – Getting started with Copilot in the notebook

Clicking on the **Get started** button, as shown in *Figure 11.4*, will insert a cell at the top of your notebook with commands as shown in *Figure 11.5* to install the required libraries in your session to take advantage of the Copilot experience.

Run the cell below to install the required packages for Copilot

```
1
2    #Run this cell to install the required packages for Copilot
3    %pip install https://aka.ms/chat-magics-0.0.0-py3-none-any.whl
4    %load_ext chat_magics
5
```

Figure 11.5 – Installing required libraries to use Copilot in the notebook

> **Note**
>
> As of this writing in January 2024, installing libraries as the first cell in the notebook is the requirement and this experience is expected to change in the future. That means these libraries might come pre-installed with Fabric Runtime, and you wouldn't have to do it on your own in the future.

The Copilot chat panel suggests prompts that you can leverage to quickly get started or you can start writing your own prompts. While Copilot works with lakehouse tables and Power BI datasets, the most effective way is to load your data into a Spark dataframe as it understands the schema and metadata as well as has awareness of the data inside of the dataframe. That makes it easier and quicker for Copilot to provide insights into your data and create visualizations.

The left side of *Figure 11.6* shows a prompt to create a dataframe based on sampled data from a lakehouse table and you can see the code generated by the Copilot to do that work on the right side of *Figure 11.6*. Copilot also provides a detailed explanation of the steps it has taken to generate code and changes you can make to this code to suit your changing needs.

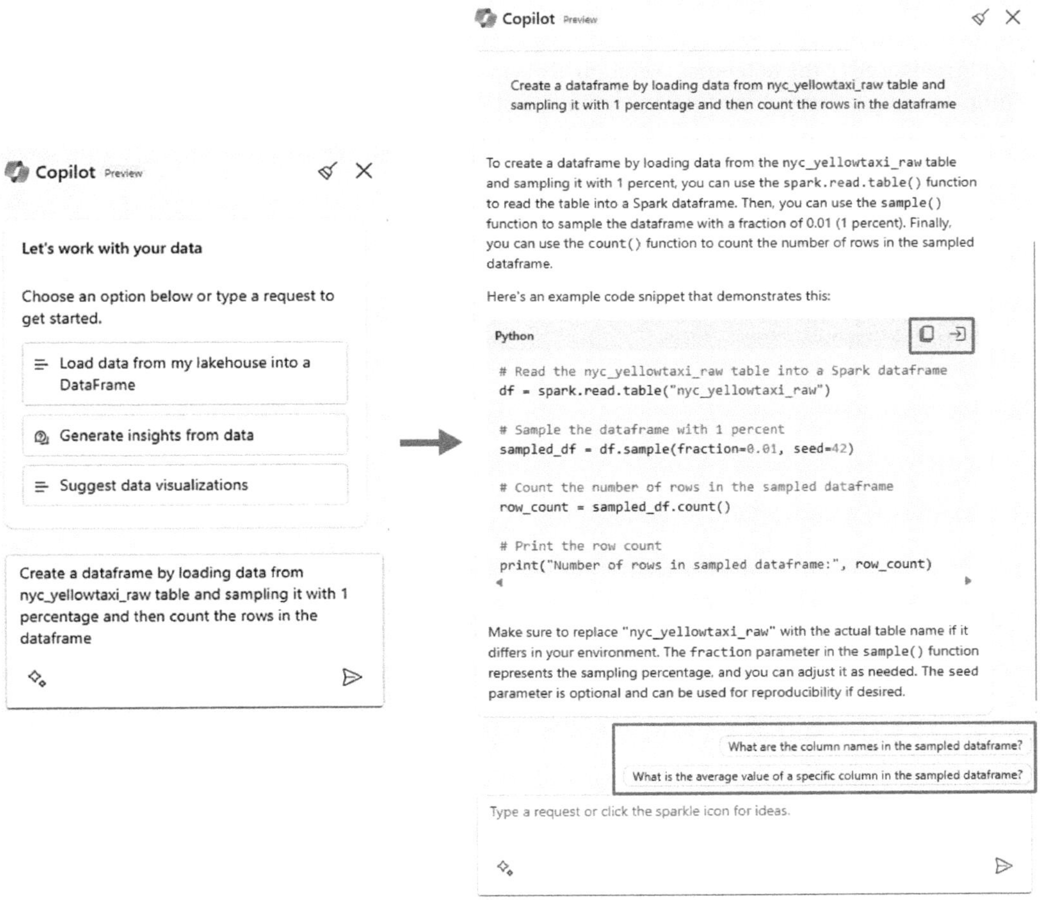

Figure 11.6 – Creating a dataframe with Copilot

Further, as seen highlighted in *Figure 11.6* in the top-right corner of the code box, it offers you the ability to copy this code so that you can paste it into your notebook cell or allows you to directly insert this code into a cell of the notebook. Additionally, based on this current step, Copilot further suggests additional prompts that you can quickly make use of.

Figure 11.7 shows the generated code, copied into a notebook cell, and executed. You can see its result as well.

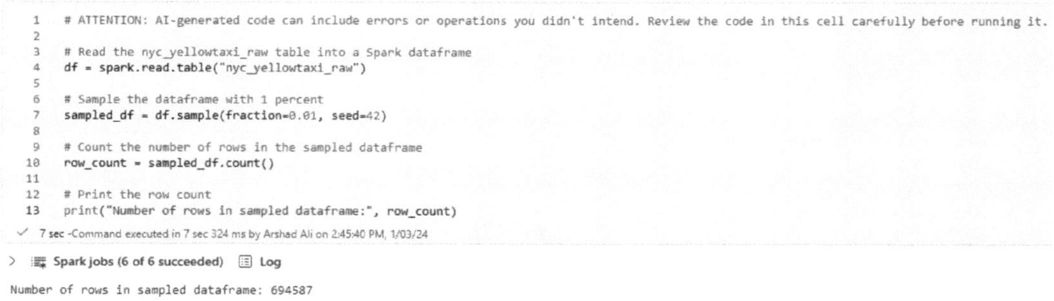

```
1    # ATTENTION: AI-generated code can include errors or operations you didn't intend. Review the code in this cell carefully before running it.
2
3    # Read the nyc_yellowtaxi_raw table into a Spark dataframe
4    df = spark.read.table("nyc_yellowtaxi_raw")
5
6    # Sample the dataframe with 1 percent
7    sampled_df = df.sample(fraction=0.01, seed=42)
8
9    # Count the number of rows in the sampled dataframe
10   row_count = sampled_df.count()
11
12   # Print the row count
13   print("Number of rows in sampled dataframe:", row_count)
```
✓ 7 sec -Command executed in 7 sec 324 ms by Arshad Ali on 2:45:40 PM, 1/03/24

> ☰ Spark jobs (6 of 6 succeeded)   ▤ Log

Number of rows in sampled dataframe: 694587

Figure 11.7 – Creating a dataframe based on the code generated by Copilot

Now that you have a dataframe created, you can ask Copilot to analyze it in different ways. *Figure 11.8* shows an example; we ask Copilot to analyze the data in the dataframe and provide suggestions for different types of visualizations that would make sense for analyzing our data and Copilot responds with all these details. Further, it has modified the list of new prompts based on the current context for you to quickly use it.

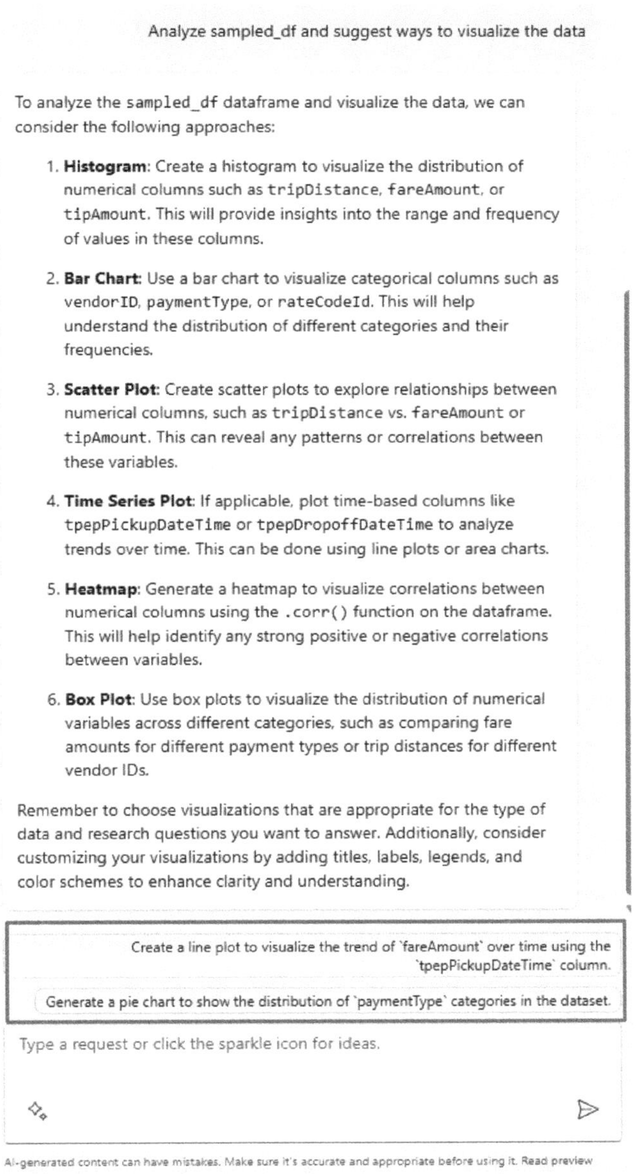

Analyze sampled_df and suggest ways to visualize the data

To analyze the `sampled_df` dataframe and visualize the data, we can consider the following approaches:

1. **Histogram**: Create a histogram to visualize the distribution of numerical columns such as `tripDistance`, `fareAmount`, or `tipAmount`. This will provide insights into the range and frequency of values in these columns.

2. **Bar Chart**: Use a bar chart to visualize categorical columns such as `vendorID`, `paymentType`, or `rateCodeId`. This will help understand the distribution of different categories and their frequencies.

3. **Scatter Plot**: Create scatter plots to explore relationships between numerical columns, such as `tripDistance` vs. `fareAmount` or `tipAmount`. This can reveal any patterns or correlations between these variables.

4. **Time Series Plot**: If applicable, plot time-based columns like `tpepPickupDateTime` or `tpepDropoffDateTime` to analyze trends over time. This can be done using line plots or area charts.

5. **Heatmap**: Generate a heatmap to visualize correlations between numerical columns using the `.corr()` function on the dataframe. This will help identify any strong positive or negative correlations between variables.

6. **Box Plot**: Use box plots to visualize the distribution of numerical variables across different categories, such as comparing fare amounts for different payment types or trip distances for different vendor IDs.

Remember to choose visualizations that are appropriate for the type of data and research questions you want to answer. Additionally, consider customizing your visualizations by adding titles, labels, legends, and color schemes to enhance clarity and understanding.

Create a line plot to visualize the trend of `fareAmount` over time using the `tpepPickupDateTime` column.

Generate a pie chart to show the distribution of `paymentType` categories in the dataset.

Type a request or click the sparkle icon for ideas.

AI-generated content can have mistakes. Make sure it's accurate and appropriate before using it. Read preview

Figure 11.8 – Copilot suggestions for analyzing the data from the loaded dataframe

Now that we have created our dataframe, we would like to understand the structure of the data it refers to. *Figure 11.9* shows an example of asking Copilot to describe the structure of the dataset – it responds with all the details. It shows all the columns and their descriptions, as well as a brief description of the whole dataset itself. Additionally, it also provides new suggested prompts to analyze the structure further.

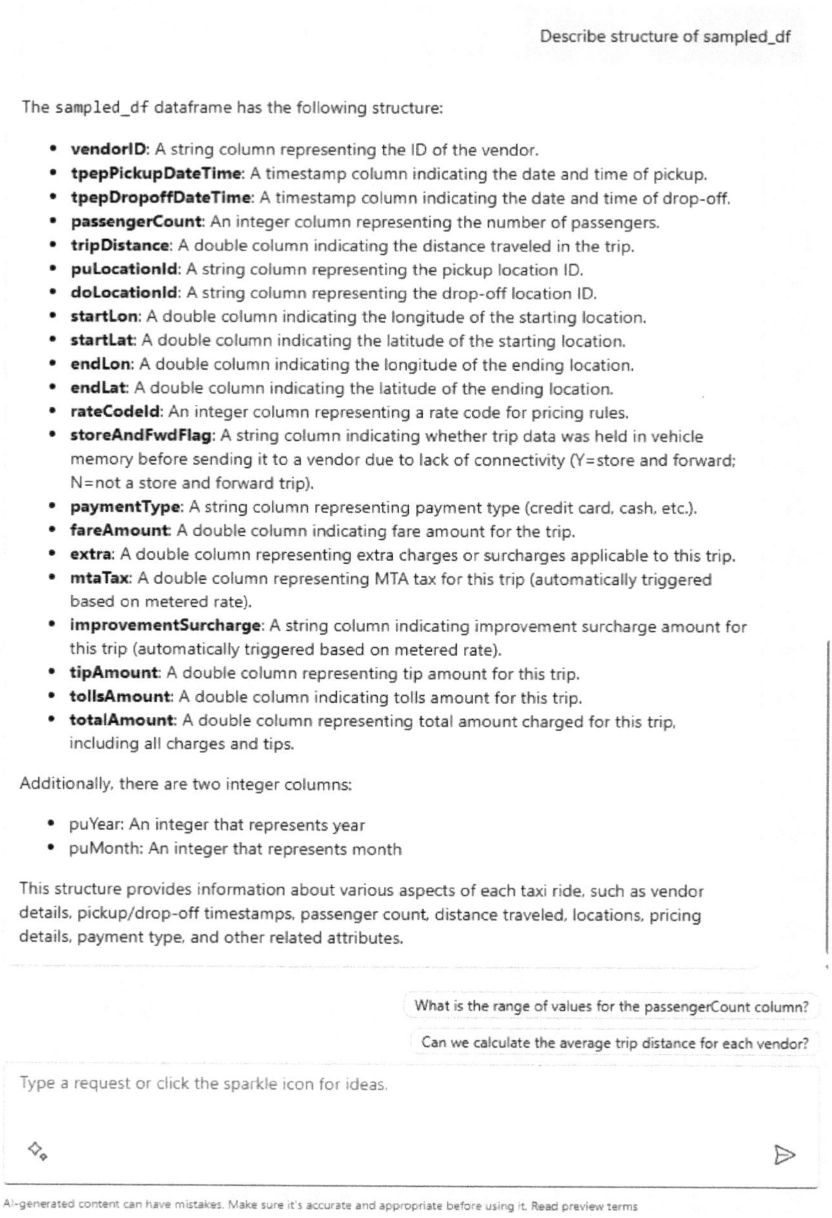

Describe structure of sampled_df

The sampled_df dataframe has the following structure:

- **vendorID**: A string column representing the ID of the vendor.
- **tpepPickupDateTime**: A timestamp column indicating the date and time of pickup.
- **tpepDropoffDateTime**: A timestamp column indicating the date and time of drop-off.
- **passengerCount**: An integer column representing the number of passengers.
- **tripDistance**: A double column indicating the distance traveled in the trip.
- **puLocationId**: A string column representing the pickup location ID.
- **doLocationId**: A string column representing the drop-off location ID.
- **startLon**: A double column indicating the longitude of the starting location.
- **startLat**: A double column indicating the latitude of the starting location.
- **endLon**: A double column indicating the longitude of the ending location.
- **endLat**: A double column indicating the latitude of the ending location.
- **rateCodeId**: An integer column representing a rate code for pricing rules.
- **storeAndFwdFlag**: A string column indicating whether trip data was held in vehicle memory before sending it to a vendor due to lack of connectivity (Y=store and forward; N=not a store and forward trip).
- **paymentType**: A string column representing payment type (credit card, cash, etc.).
- **fareAmount**: A double column indicating fare amount for the trip.
- **extra**: A double column representing extra charges or surcharges applicable to this trip.
- **mtaTax**: A double column representing MTA tax for this trip (automatically triggered based on metered rate).
- **improvementSurcharge**: A string column indicating improvement surcharge amount for this trip (automatically triggered based on metered rate).
- **tipAmount**: A double column representing tip amount for this trip.
- **tollsAmount**: A double column indicating tolls amount for this trip.
- **totalAmount**: A double column representing total amount charged for this trip, including all charges and tips.

Additionally, there are two integer columns:

- puYear: An integer that represents year
- puMonth: An integer that represents month

This structure provides information about various aspects of each taxi ride, such as vendor details, pickup/drop-off timestamps, passenger count, distance traveled, locations, pricing details, payment type, and other related attributes.

What is the range of values for the passengerCount column?

Can we calculate the average trip distance for each vendor?

Type a request or click the sparkle icon for ideas.

✧

▷

AI-generated content can have mistakes. Make sure it's accurate and appropriate before using it. Read preview terms

Figure 11.9 – Copilot describes the structure of the data in the dataframe

As you can see in the structure of the data in *Figure 11.9*, there are a few redundant columns (meaning they contain the same or similar information); hence, you would like to remove them. *Figure 11.10* shows a prompt to remove these redundant or duplicate columns as well as to add a computed column, which would be necessary for our further analysis. Copilot responds to this prompt with the code to achieve it. As you can see, in the generated code the relevant comments have been added already as well and Copilot summarizes the action at the end so that you know what this code does overall.

> Remove the columns startLon, startLat, endLon, and endLat as they are redundant with the pickup and dropoff location IDs and add a column tripDuration in the sampled_df by deducting tpepPickupDateTime from tpepDropoffDateTime in minutes

To remove the redundant columns and add a new column `tripDuration` to the `sampled_df` dataframe, where the duration is calculated in minutes by subtracting `tpepPickupDateTime` from `tpepDropoffDateTime`, you can use the following code:

Python

```python
from pyspark.sql.functions import col, expr

# Remove the redundant columns
sampled_df = sampled_df.drop("startLon", "startLat", "endLon", "endLat")

# Add a new column tripDuration in minutes
sampled_df = sampled_df.withColumn("tripDuration", expr("(unix_timestamp(tp
```

This code will remove the columns `startLon`, `startLat`, `endLon`, and `endLat` from the dataframe and create a new column `tripDuration` in minutes by calculating the difference between `tpepDropoffDateTime` and `tpepPickupDateTime`. The resulting dataframe will have these modifications applied.

Figure 11.10 – Removing redundant columns from the dataframe

Copilot can help you create different types of visualizations for exploratory data analysis. *Figure 11.11* shows an example of asking Copilot to plot a line chart to show trip counts and their patterns throughout different hours of the day. Copilot responds by generating the code to create this line chart to show the different trip counts and usage patterns throughout the day. Additionally, it provides an explanation of the code that it has generated as the documentation for the code.

Plot the trip counts by hour of the day to identify any patterns or trends in taxi usage throughout the day in the sampled_df

1. **Line Plot: Trip Counts by Hour of the Day** This line plot will show the trend of taxi usage throughout the day by plotting the trip counts on the y-axis and the hour of the day on the x-axis. This will help identify any patterns or trends in taxi usage throughout different hours of the day.

Python

```python
import pandas as pd
import plotly.express as px

# Convert PySpark dataframe to pandas dataframe if needed
if isinstance(sampled_df, pyspark.sql.DataFrame):
    sampled_df = sampled_df.toPandas()

# Extract hour from tpepPickupDateTime column
sampled_df['hour'] = sampled_df['tpepPickupDateTime'].dt.hour

# Group by hour and count number of trips
trip_counts = sampled_df.groupby('hour').size().reset_index(name='count')

# Plotting trip counts by hour of the day using Plotly
fig = px.line(trip_counts, x='hour', y='count', title='Trip Counts by Hour
fig.update_layout(template='plotly_dark')
fig.show()
```

Explanation: The code snippet first converts the PySpark dataframe to a pandas dataframe (if needed). Then, it extracts the hour from tpepPickupDateTime column and groups the data by hour to count the number of trips for each hour. The resulting trip counts are then plotted using Plotly's line plot, with hours on the x-axis and trip counts on the y-axis. The plot is displayed with a dark template for better visibility.

Figure 11.11 – Copilot generates code for creating a line chart

When you execute the code generated in *Figure 11.11*, it generates a line chart as shown in *Figure 11.12*. As you can see, in this line chart the number of trips decreases in the early morning time and reaches its highest point in the late evening time.

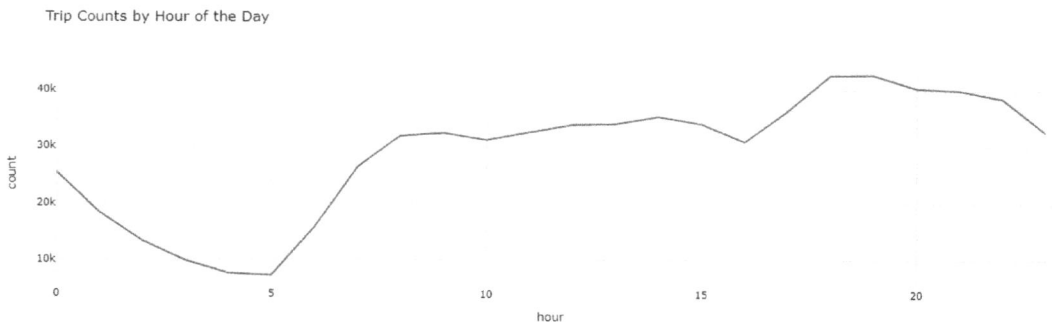

Figure 11.12 – Line chart based on the code generated by Copilot

Now, let's get the help of Copilot again to generate a new visual for exploratory data analysis, and, in this case, we will create a scatter plot to show the relationship between trip duration with fare amount as shown in *Figure 11.13*. Again, Copilot responds by generating the code for creating a scatter plot.

Can you create a scatter plot to visualize the relationship between trip duration and fare amount in the sampled_df?

1. **Scatter Plot: Trip Duration vs Fare Amount** This scatter plot will visualize the relationship between trip duration and fare amount in the sampled_df. Each data point represents a trip, with trip duration on the x-axis and fare amount on the y-axis. This plot helps to understand if there is any correlation or pattern between these two variables.

Python

```python
import pandas as pd
import plotly.express as px

# Convert PySpark dataframe to pandas dataframe if needed
if isinstance(sampled_df, pyspark.sql.DataFrame):
    sampled_df = sampled_df.toPandas()

# Plotting scatter plot of trip duration vs fare amount using Plotly
fig = px.scatter(sampled_df, x='tripDuration', y='fareAmount', title='Trip
fig.update_layout(template='plotly_dark')
fig.show()
```

Explanation: The code snippet first converts the PySpark dataframe to a pandas dataframe (if needed). Then, it uses Plotly's scatter plot to visualize the relationship between trip duration and fare amount. The trip duration is plotted on the x-axis and fare amount on the y-axis. The resulting scatter plot provides insights into any correlation or pattern between these two variables. The plot is displayed with a dark template for better visibility.

Figure 11.13 – Asking Copilot to generate code for creating a scatter plot

When you execute the code generated in *Figure 11.13*, you will see a scatter plot being created, similar to the one in *Figure 11.14*, based on your dataset. When you look at this plot closely, you will notice that there are certain outliers in your data; for example, there are a few records where trip duration is either zero or less than zero; likewise, there are a few records with negative and a very high fare amount.

Trip Duration vs Fare Amount

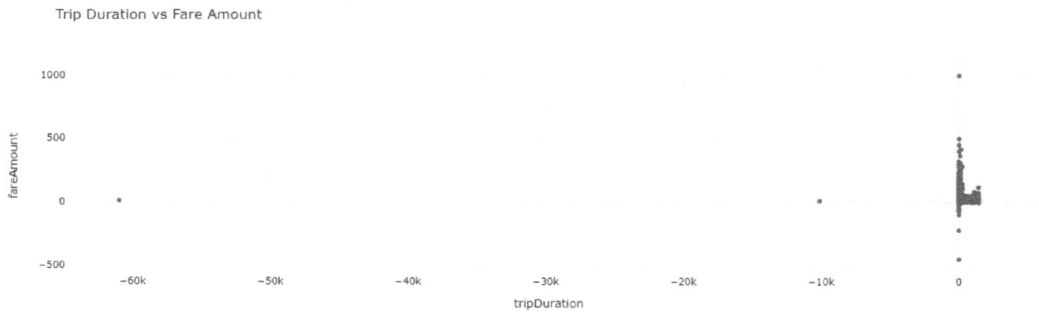

Figure 11.14 – Initial scatter plot which shows outliers

To remove outliers from our dataset, we can get the help of Copilot again. *Figure 11.15* shows a prompt that specifies to remove the rows where trip duration is 0 or less than 0 and more than 180, and Copilot responds with the code to remove this outlier, and it also provides an explanation of this code and what it does at the end.

Remove rows where trip duration is less than zero and more than 180

To remove rows where the trip duration is less than zero and more than 180, you can use the following code:

```Python
# Remove rows where trip duration is less than zero or more than 180
sampled_df = sampled_df[(sampled_df['tripDuration'] >= 0) & (sampled_df['tr
```

Explanation: The code snippet filters the sampled_df dataframe using a boolean condition. It keeps only the rows where the trip duration (tripDuration column) is greater than or equal to zero and less than or equal to 180. This effectively removes any rows with trip durations outside of this range. The filtered dataframe is then assigned back to sampled_df.

Figure 11.15 – Asking Copilot to generate code for removing trip duration outliers

When you execute the code from *Figure 11.15* to remove outliers, you can see the outlier for trip duration has been removed. When you execute the code again from *Figure 11.13* to create a scatter plot, you will notice this time that the outliers have been removed, and now the graph shows the cleansed data, as in *Figure 11.16*.

Trip Duration vs Fare Amount

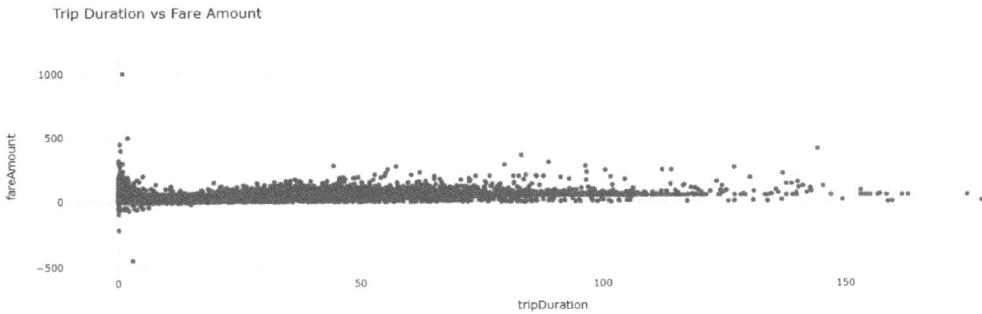

Figure 11.16 – Scatter plot after the trip duration outliers have been removed

Now, let's see if there is an outlier in fare amount as well, and to do that, let's ask Copilot to generate a box plot for the fare amount column from our dataset. As shown in *Figure 11.17*, Copilot responds with the code to create a box plot as requested and provides an explanation of this code and what it does at the end.

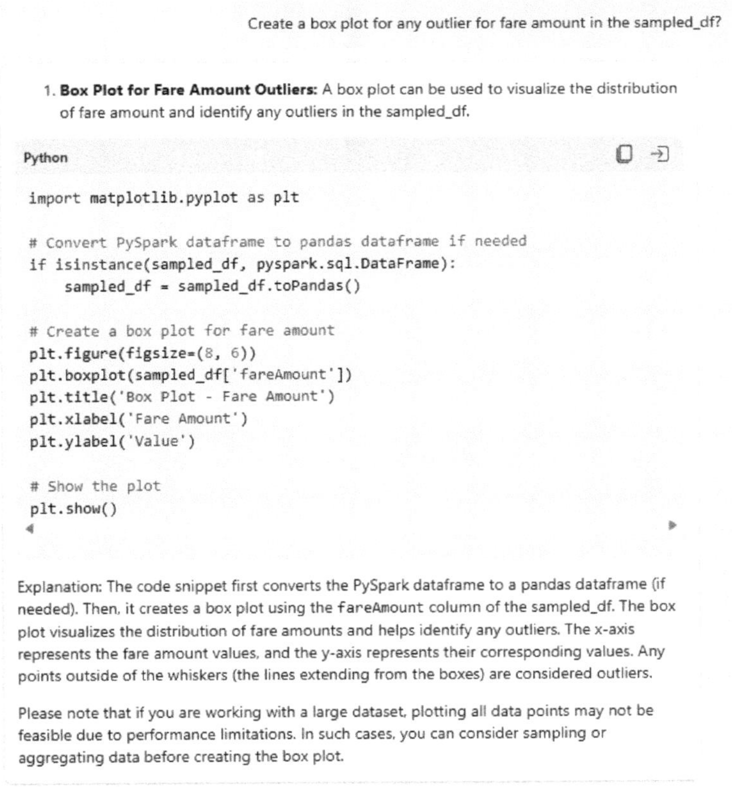

Create a box plot for any outlier for fare amount in the sampled_df?

1. **Box Plot for Fare Amount Outliers:** A box plot can be used to visualize the distribution of fare amount and identify any outliers in the sampled_df.

Python

```python
import matplotlib.pyplot as plt

# Convert PySpark dataframe to pandas dataframe if needed
if isinstance(sampled_df, pyspark.sql.DataFrame):
    sampled_df = sampled_df.toPandas()

# Create a box plot for fare amount
plt.figure(figsize=(8, 6))
plt.boxplot(sampled_df['fareAmount'])
plt.title('Box Plot - Fare Amount')
plt.xlabel('Fare Amount')
plt.ylabel('Value')

# Show the plot
plt.show()
```

Explanation: The code snippet first converts the PySpark dataframe to a pandas dataframe (if needed). Then, it creates a box plot using the fareAmount column of the sampled_df. The box plot visualizes the distribution of fare amounts and helps identify any outliers. The x-axis represents the fare amount values, and the y-axis represents their corresponding values. Any points outside of the whiskers (the lines extending from the boxes) are considered outliers.

Please note that if you are working with a large dataset, plotting all data points may not be feasible due to performance limitations. In such cases, you can consider sampling or aggregating data before creating the box plot.

Figure 11.17 – Asking Copilot to generate a box plot to show any outliers for fare amount

When you execute the code from *Figure 11.17*, you will notice a box plot as shown in *Figure 11.18*. Looking at the plot, you can see that there are certain records with outliers for fare amounts. For example, there are a few records where the fare amount is either zero or less than zero; likewise, there are a few records where the fare amount is a very high number. Before you get into further analysis, you would like to get rid of these outliers from your dataset.

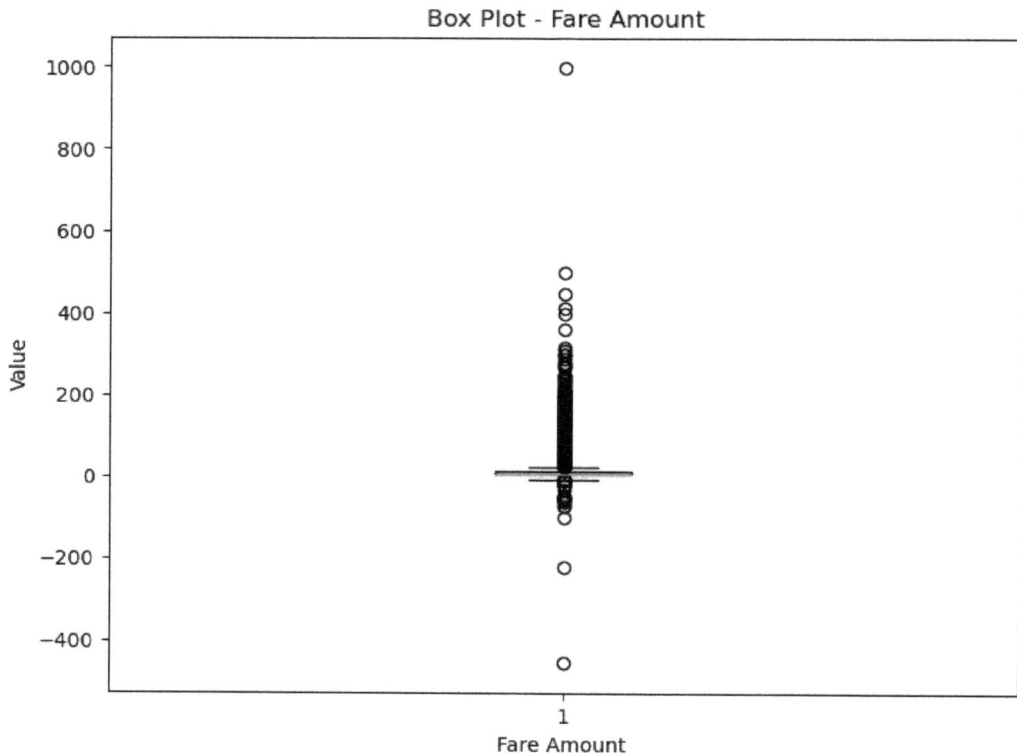

Figure 11.18 – Box plot showing outliers for fare amount

To remove outliers for fare amounts, you can take advantage of Copilot again. *Figure 11.19* shows a prompt asking Copilot to remove rows where the fare amount is 0 or less than 0 and greater than 100. In this case, Copilot responds again with the required code to remove these outliers from our dataset.

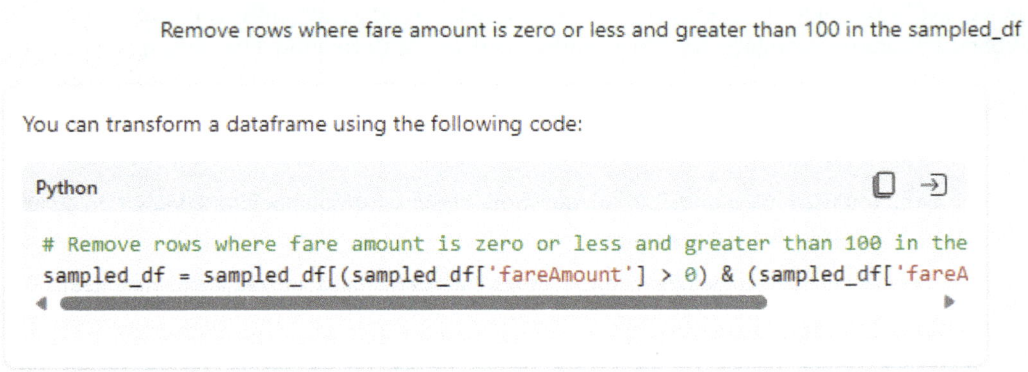

Remove rows where fare amount is zero or less and greater than 100 in the sampled_df
You can transform a dataframe using the following code:
Python
# Remove rows where fare amount is zero or less and greater than 100 in the
sampled_df = sampled_df[(sampled_df['fareAmount'] > 0) & (sampled_df['fareA

Figure 11.19 – Taking the help of Copilot to remove outliers for fare amount

When you execute the code from *Figure 11.19* to remove outliers for fare amount and execute the code from *Figure 11.18* again to create the box plot, you will notice the outliers have been removed from our dataset, as shown in *Figure 11.20*:

Box Plot - Fare Amount
Value
100
80
60
40
20
0
1
Fare Amount

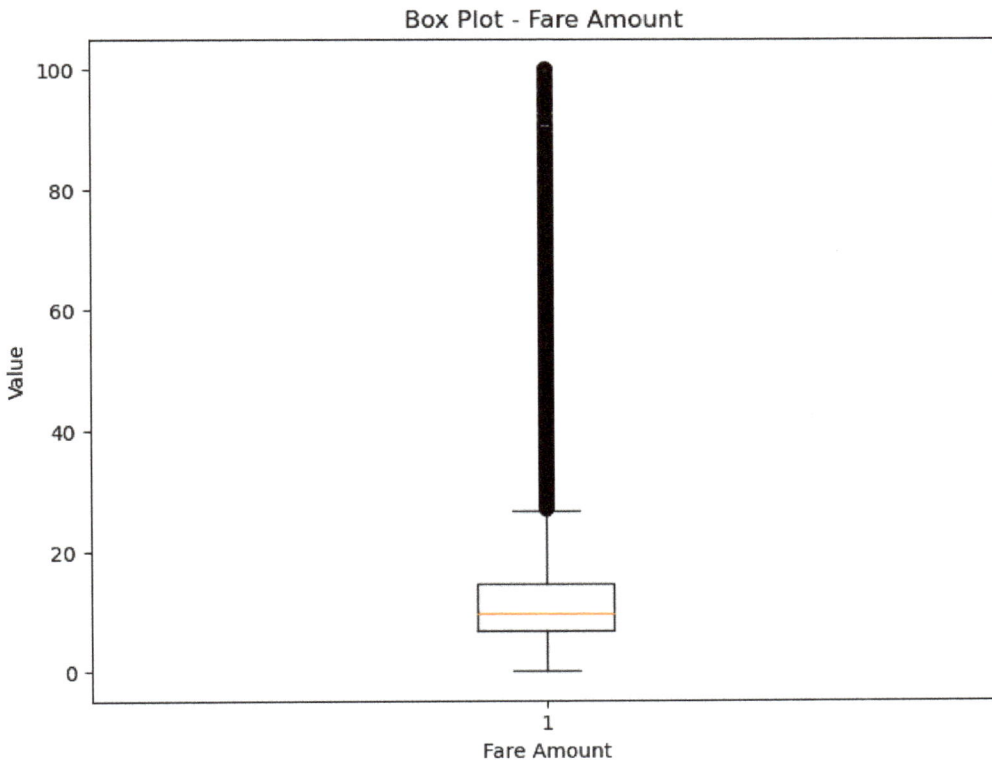

Figure 11.20 – Box plot showing fare amount after removing its outliers

So far, we have looked at the Copilot chat panel to ask questions and got responses for creating different types of visualization for exploratory data analysis and data transformation. However, that is not the only way – data engineering and data science in Fabric also provide magic commands that you can use in notebook cells to take advantage of Copilot as part of your coding experience. Here are these magic commands:

- `%%chat`: You use it in your cell to ask questions about your notebook and dataset, in a very similar way as with the chat panel

- `%%code`: You use this to generate code to work with or visualize or transform your data

- `%%describe`: You can use this magic command to describe a loaded dataframe

- `%%add_comments`: When you have code already and you want to add documentation, you can take advantage of this magic command

- `%%fix_errors`: When you make a code error in a notebook cell, you can take advantage of this magic command to provide suggestions to fix coding errors

- `%%translate`: You can use this magic command to translate code from one language to another

Let's continue our exploratory data analysis; however, this time we will use a magic command instead of the Copilot chat panel. *Figure 11.21* shows an example of asking Copilot to create a code block for creating a heatmap for certain selected columns of the dataframe that we created earlier. As you can see at the bottom of *Figure 11.21*, Copilot responds by generating the code to create a heatmap for the specified columns of the dataframe.

```
1   %%code
2   Create a heatmap for 'tripDuration','fareAmount', 'passengerCount', 'tripDistance', 'extra', 'mtaTax', 'tollsAmount', 'improvementSurcharge', 'tipAmount'.
    Command executed in 7 sec 384 ms by Arshad Ali on 5:54:02 PM, 1/03/24                                                    PySpark (Python)  ∨
```

chat-magics generated the following cell. Tokens: 208

Remember that AI can make mistakes, so carefully review code before executing.

```
                                                                                        Mↄ  ⎘  ▢  🔒  ✳  ⋯  🗑
1   import pandas as pd
2   import seaborn as sns
3   import matplotlib.pyplot as plt
4
5   # Select the columns for the heatmap
6   heatmap_cols = ['tripDuration', 'fareAmount', 'passengerCount', 'tripDistance', 'extra', 'mtaTax', 'tollsAmount', 'improvementSurcharge', 'tipAmount']
7
8   # Create a correlation matrix for the selected columns
9   corr_matrix = sampled_df[heatmap_cols].corr()
10
11  # Create a heatmap using seaborn
12  plt.figure(figsize=(10, 8))
13  sns.heatmap(corr_matrix, annot=True, cmap='coolwarm')
14  plt.title('Heatmap of Selected Columns')
15  plt.show()
                                                                                                            PySpark (Python)  ∨
```

Figure 11.21 – Example of Code chat magic command for creating a heatmap

When you execute the code generated in *Figure 11.21*, you will notice a heatmap similar to the one shown in *Figure 11.22* created for analysis:

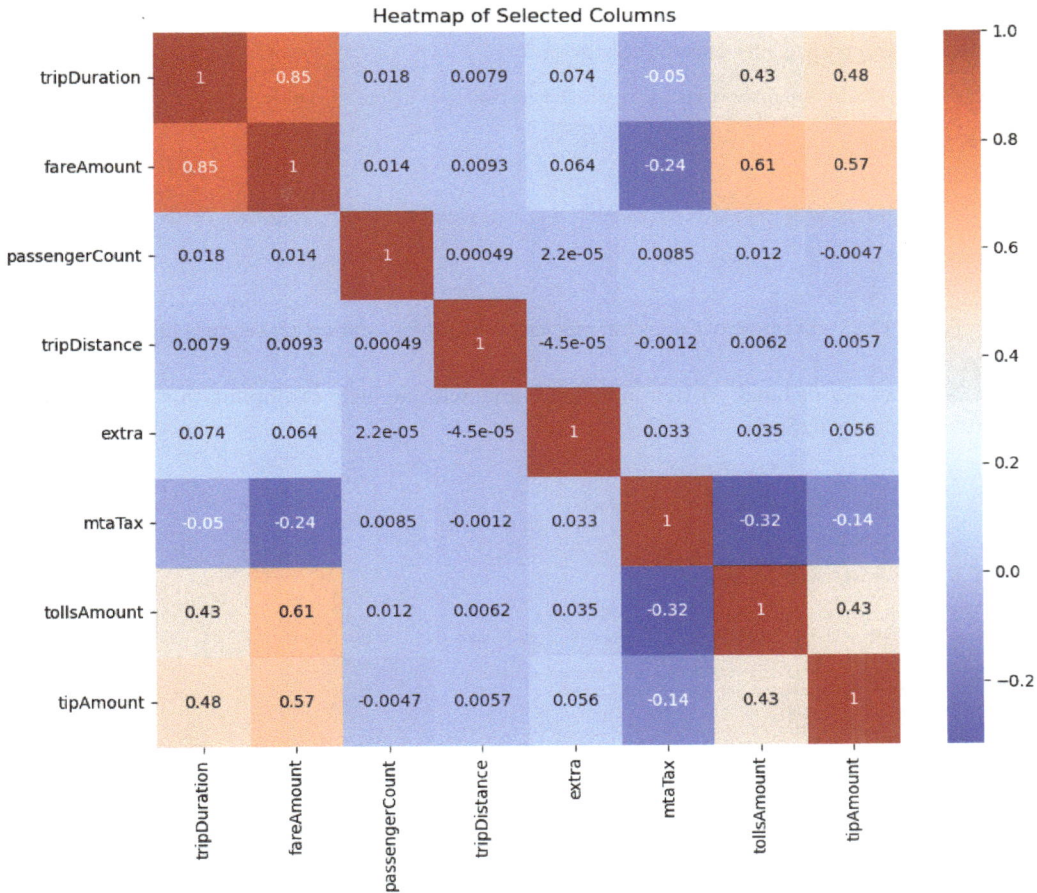

Figure 11.22 – Heatmap showing the relation between different columns of the dataframe

Now that you have cleansed and transformed your data, you would like to write this data into a lakehouse table. Again, you can take advantage of Copilot to generate the code to write this dataframe into a lakehouse table, as shown in *Figure 11.23*:

```
1    %%code
2    write nyc_yellowtaxi_df to a lakehouse table called nyc_yellowtaxi_cleansed
```
-Command executed in 4 sec 167 ms by Arshad Ali on 5:56:47 PM, 1/03/24

chat-magics generated the following cell. Tokens: 24

Remember that AI can make mistakes, so carefully review code before executing.

```
1    df.write.mode("overwrite").format("delta").saveAsTable("nyc_yellowtaxi_cleansed")
```

Figure 11.23 – Example of Code chat magic command for creating a lakehouse table

Figure 11.24 shows a code block written in PySpark and, with the help of Copilot, this code block is translated equivalently to Scala:

```
1    %%translate
2    Translate this code from Python to Scala
3
4    import pandas as pd
5    import seaborn as sns
6    import matplotlib.pyplot as plt
7
8    # Select the columns for the heatmap
9    heatmap_cols = ['tripDuration', 'fareAmount', 'passengerCount', 'tripDistance', 'extra', 'mtaTax', 'to
10
11   # Create a correlation matrix for the selected columns
12   corr_matrix = sampled_df[heatmap_cols].corr()
13
14   # Create a heatmap using seaborn
15   plt.figure(figsize=(10, 8))
16   sns.heatmap(corr_matrix, annot=True, cmap='coolwarm')
17   plt.title('Heatmap of Selected Columns')
18   plt.show()
```
-Running

chat-magics generated the following cell. Tokens: 111

Remember that AI can make mistakes, so carefully review code before executing.

```
1    import org.apache.spark.sql.functions._
2    import org.apache.spark.sql.DataFrame
3
4    // Select the columns for the heatmap
5    val heatmap_cols = Seq("tripDuration", "fareAmount", "passengerCount", "tripDistance", "extra", "mtaTa
6
7    // Create a correlation matrix for the selected columns
8    val corr_matrix = sampled_df.select(heatmap_cols.map(col): _*).toDF.corr()
9
10   // Create a heatmap using seaborn
11   corr_matrix.show()
```

Figure 11.24 – Example of the translate chat magic command

If you have a code block with coding issues, you can get help from Copilot to fix these errors for you. *Figure 11.25* shows an example of code with a few typos at the top, and Copilot responds with the corrected code at the bottom:

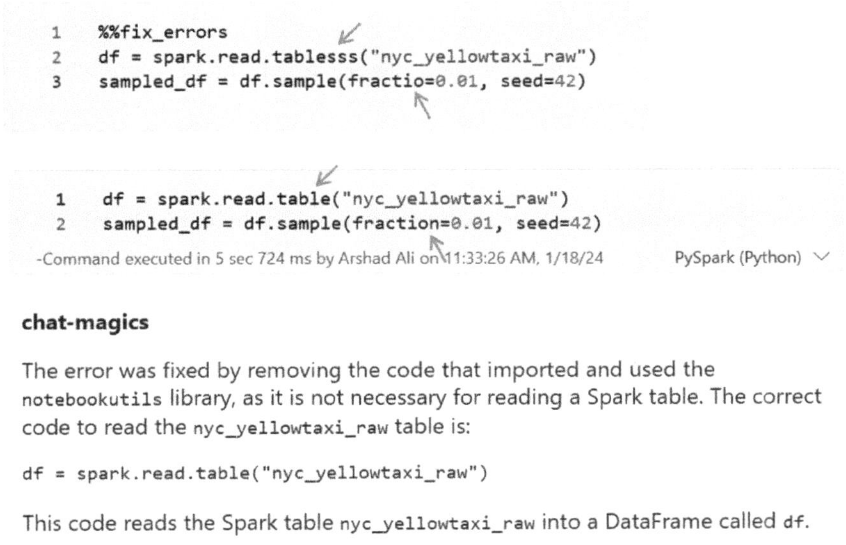

```
1    %%fix_errors
2    df = spark.read.tablesss("nyc_yellowtaxi_raw")
3    sampled_df = df.sample(fractio=0.01, seed=42)
```

```
1    df = spark.read.table("nyc_yellowtaxi_raw")
2    sampled_df = df.sample(fraction=0.01, seed=42)
```
-Command executed in 5 sec 724 ms by Arshad Ali on 11:33:26 AM, 1/18/24   PySpark (Python) ⌄

chat-magics

The error was fixed by removing the code that imported and used the notebookutils library, as it is not necessary for reading a Spark table. The correct code to read the nyc_yellowtaxi_raw table is:

df = spark.read.table("nyc_yellowtaxi_raw")

This code reads the Spark table nyc_yellowtaxi_raw into a DataFrame called df.

Figure 11.25 – Example of the fix errors chat magic command

Furthermore, you can use the chat magic command in your notebook cell to chat with Copilot and ask questions. *Figure 11.26* shows an example of asking Copilot to provide the average trip duration for each hour of the day, and Copilot responds by giving you the code to get this information:

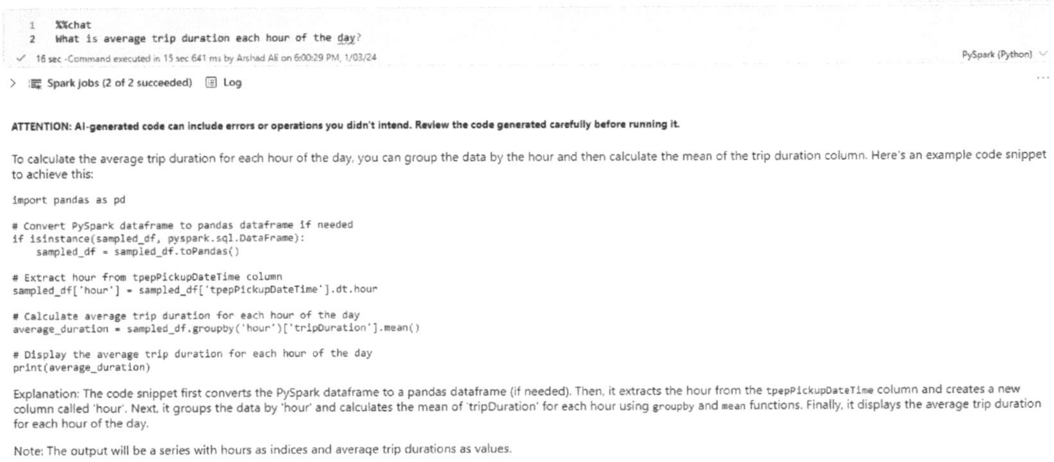

```
1    %%chat
2    What is average trip duration each hour of the day?
```
✓ 16 sec -Command executed in 15 sec 641 ms by Arshad Ali on 6:00:29 PM, 1/03/24   PySpark (Python) ⌄

> ⚡ Spark jobs (2 of 2 succeeded)   ▤ Log   ...

ATTENTION: AI-generated code can include errors or operations you didn't intend. Review the code generated carefully before running it.

To calculate the average trip duration for each hour of the day, you can group the data by the hour and then calculate the mean of the trip duration column. Here's an example code snippet to achieve this:

```
import pandas as pd

# Convert PySpark dataframe to pandas dataframe if needed
if isinstance(sampled_df, pyspark.sql.DataFrame):
    sampled_df = sampled_df.toPandas()

# Extract hour from tpepPickupDateTime column
sampled_df['hour'] = sampled_df['tpepPickupDateTime'].dt.hour

# Calculate average trip duration for each hour of the day
average_duration = sampled_df.groupby('hour')['tripDuration'].mean()

# Display the average trip duration for each hour of the day
print(average_duration)
```

Explanation: The code snippet first converts the PySpark dataframe to a pandas dataframe (if needed). Then, it extracts the hour from the tpepPickupDateTime column and creates a new column called 'hour'. Next, it groups the data by 'hour' and calculates the mean of 'tripDuration' for each hour using groupby and mean functions. Finally, it displays the average trip duration for each hour of the day.

Note: The output will be a series with hours as indices and average trip durations as values.

Figure 11.26 – Example of chat magic command

Now that we have learned about Copilot with data engineering and data science workloads, it's time to switch gears and see how Copilot for Data Factory workloads works.

Copilot in Data Factory

There is currently one Copilot experience for Data Factory, which can be found when building a Dataflow Gen2. Just like the data science experience covered earlier in this chapter, the Data Factory Copilot lets you use natural language to describe the data transformations that you would like to apply to a dataset.

First, you will need to go through the get-data experience to acquire data. Optionally, apply any transformations you may know how to use on your own. Next, launch Copilot by creating a new Dataflow Gen2 and clicking the **Copilot** button on the **Home** tab of the ribbon. At this point, you will be greeted with a message informing you that Copilot can help you transform data or explain how the data is being transformed.

We can perform transformations such as combining all the address fields, in this case, city, state province, and country into a single column, as shown in *Figure 11.27*:

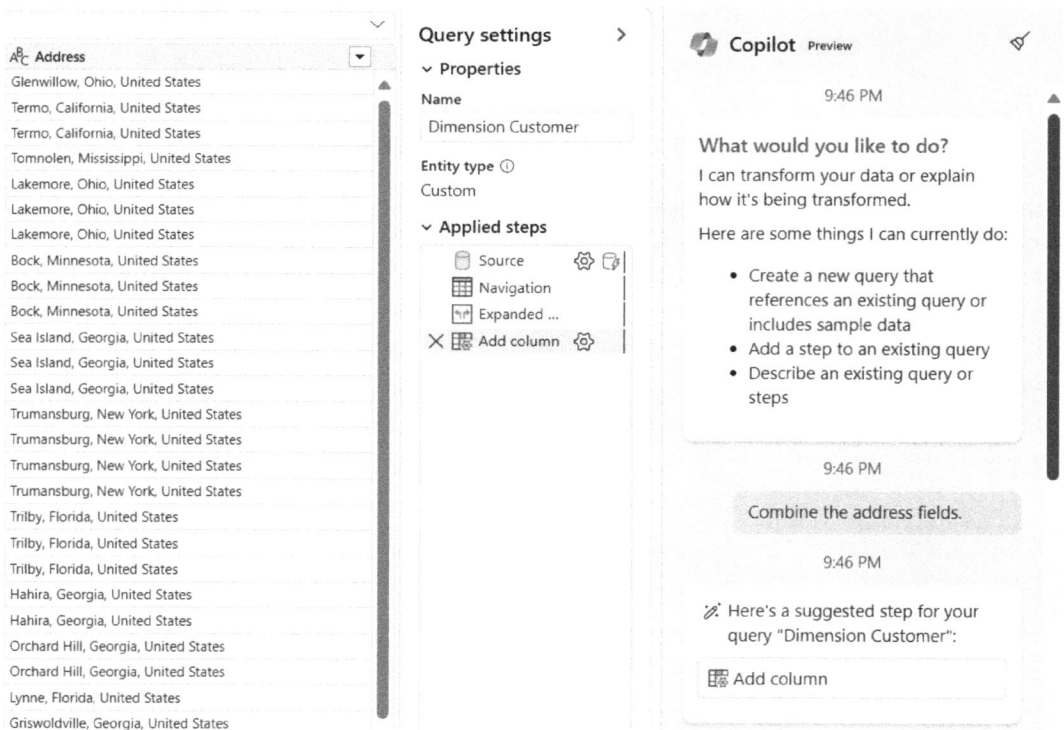

Figure 11.27 – Performing data transformation with the Data Factory Copilot

You can also have Copilot help with more complicated scenarios such as creating aggregated datasets. In this case, we have asked Copilot to summarize our sales data by stock item key and sales territory. We've then gone one step further and created buckets for our profit field classifying each row as having high, medium, or low total profit, as shown in *Figure 11.28*:

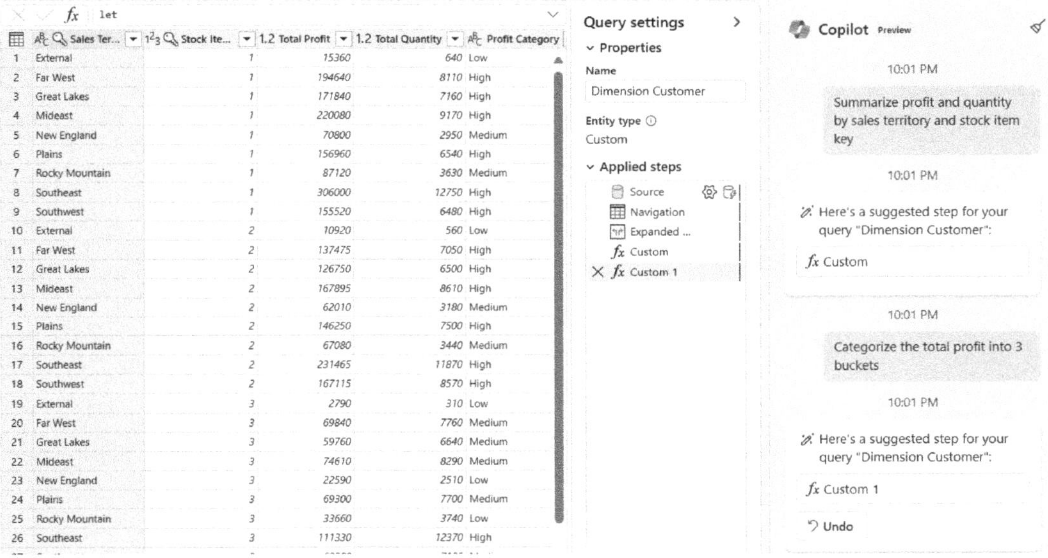

Figure 11.28 – The Data Factory Copilot bucketing results based on total profit

Code documentation is important for developers to pick up where a teammate left off, to troubleshoot an error, to understand something that was built long ago, or just to understand what task is being performed. It can be difficult to open a dataflow and quickly determine what actions are being performed, especially when there are many transformation steps. The Data Factory Copilot simplifies this by describing what a dataflow is doing and providing insights into each step of the query. Simply ask Copilot to "describe the dataflow," "tell me about this dataflow," "what is this query doing," or another prompt with a similar sentiment, and out comes an overall description and details about each step, as shown in *Figure 11.29*:

10:06 PM

Tell me about this dataflow.

10:06 PM

Here's an explanation for **Dimension Customer**: This dataflow connects to the "WideWorldImportersDW" database and performs various transformations on the "Sale" table. It expands the "Sales Territory" column from the "Dimension.City" record, groups the data by "Sales Territory" and "Stock Item Key", computes the total profit and total quantity for each group, and categorizes the profit into "Low", "Medium", or "High".

- **Source**: Connect to the "WideWorldImportersDW" database on server "scbradlsql01.database.windows. net".
- **Navigation**: Select the "Sale" table.
- **Custom**: Group the data by "Sales Territory" and "Stock Item Key" and compute the total profit and total quantity for each group.
- **Custom 1**: Categorize the profit into "Low", "Medium", or "High" based on the total profit.

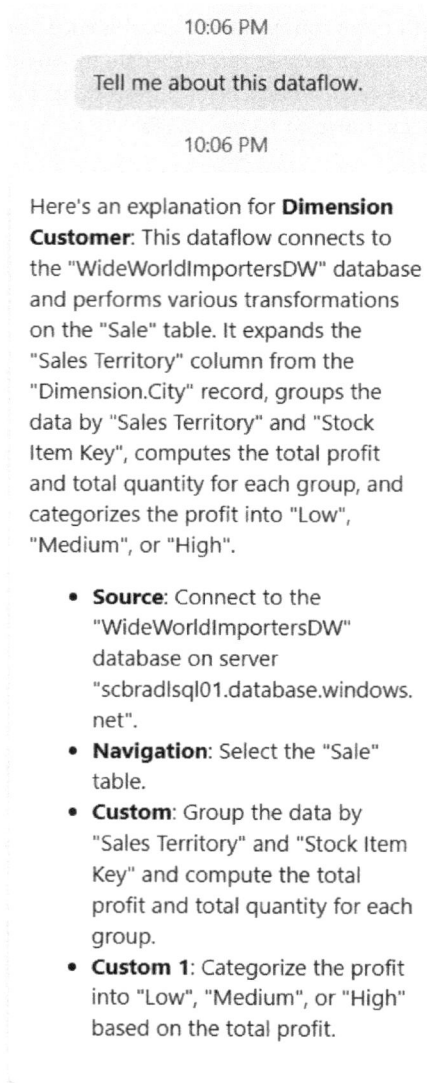

Figure 11.29 – Copilot describing a dataflow

As you can see, the Copilot for Data Factory can be incredibly useful for performing data transformation. It can also perform operations on derived data. For example, if you have a date field, Copilot can generate a day of the week column or even reference data in other queries. Dataflows are powerful because they open data transformation capabilities to low-code and no-code developers. Copilot takes that one step further and truly makes data transformation accessible to anyone in your organization by simply describing what they want to do with the data.

Now that we have seen how Copilot enables transformation with Data Factory, let's look at how it can help shape the data visualization layer with Power BI.

Copilot in Power BI

Power BI has several key components, including data transformation and data modeling, culminating in a visual report that end users will consume. The Copilot experience is centered around the visual storytelling and reporting aspects of Power BI. This materializes in three ways: report page creation, narrative generation, and improving Q&A.

Let's look at each of these Copilot capabilities.

Creating reports with the Power BI Copilot

The most common use for Copilot with Power BI is likely to be for creating reports. There are two features that come together to build reports. The first analyzes the dataset to suggest content for your report by using table relationships and column names, while the second one helps you create intuitive reports quickly. *Figure 11.30* shows an example where Copilot has suggested several report pages, each with a short description of what would be displayed:

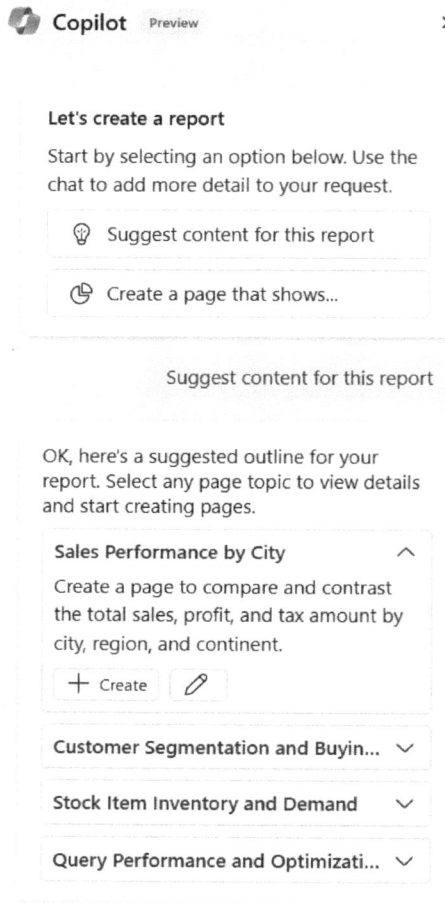

Figure 11.30 – The Power BI Copilot page suggestions

If you like the page suggestions, simply click on the **Create** button and the report page will appear.

While a suggested set of report content is a good starting point, analysts often have a specific need to meet. You can have Copilot create a report from the criteria you provide using prompts as well. These can be as simple as "create a page that shows customer analysis" or more specific, such as "create a page to show the impact of each sales territory on profit and quantity sold."

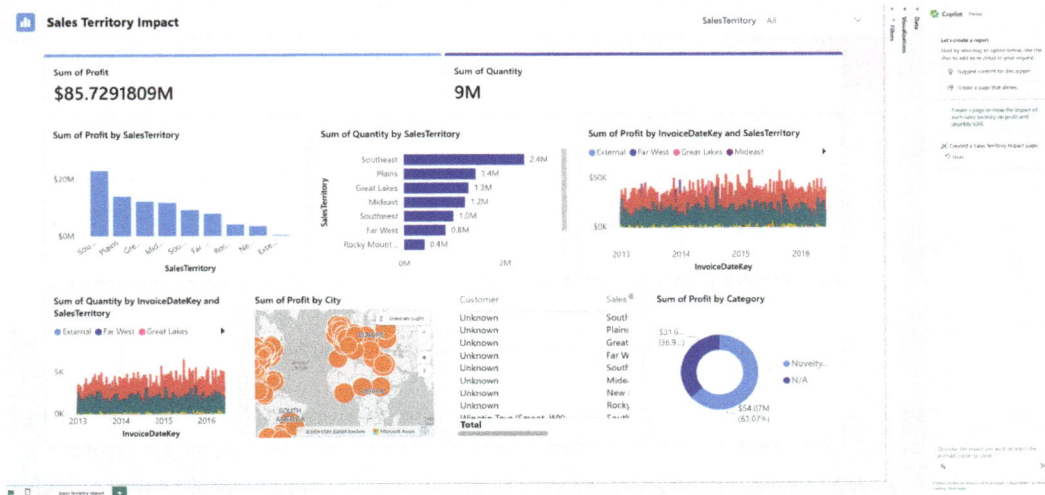

Figure 11.31 – Sales impact report created by Copilot

Once the report page is generated, Copilot cannot update the report, but you can interact with and modify the report as necessary. This is a great way to reduce the time to get started building reports.

A couple of other important things to note are that in addition to not being able to modify reports, Copilot will not allow you to specify specific visual types, apply filters, or change the report layout. All of these can be changed manually after the initial report generation. It is worth noting that users should not expect Copilot to filter results to a specific time period based on their prompt as an example.

Next, let's look at the smart narrative.

Creating a narrative using Copilot

Visuals are a wonderful way to tell a story and give users the ability to explore data on their own. However, sometimes a narrative that summarizes what is being displayed in a report can be useful. It can not only tell a story but also provide some additional context and information for users.

To get started, open a report and add a narrative visualization to the report as shown in *Figure 11.32*. You will see two options; click on **Copilot**. Choose the type of summary you wish to produce and optionally select specific pages or visuals to include in the summary. Then click on **Create**.

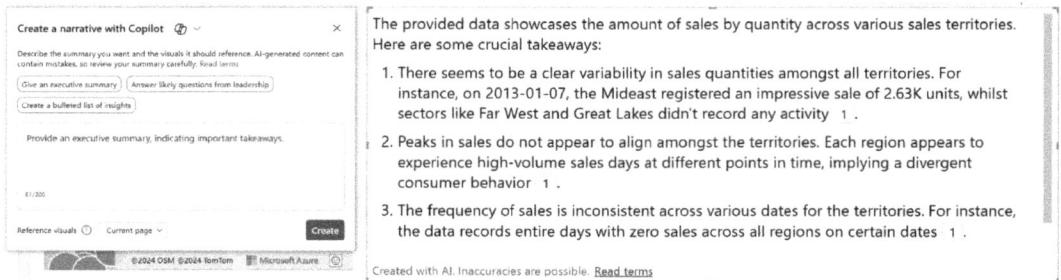

Figure 11.32 – The report narrative generated by Copilot

After the narrative is generated, remember to always review the narrative for accuracy and adjust the prompt, if necessary, to produce more accurate results. In addition to summaries, you can ask it to highlight key information, customize the order in which the data is described to help convey importance, specify specific data points to include in the summary, and even generate impact analysis showing how different factors affect metrics on the report.

Report, page, and visual narratives are a great way to guide users through a report, especially if there isn't a subject matter expert there to explain all the data.

Finally, let's look at using Copilot to improve the Q&A visual.

Generating synonyms with Copilot

The Q&A visual has been dazzling users for years at this point. It is impressive to build a model, walk into the room, and tell users that they can use natural language to query their data without needing to build any visuals. This may not be as impressive as the Copilot functionality that we have today, but it is still a very useful tool in your Power BI visualization toolbelt.

One piece of important information for the success of Q&A is something called a **synonym**. These are end-user-specific ways to reference data. For example, a table in the data model may be called Dim Person, but you know that some report consumers always refer to these as "users." Therefore, you would create a synonym that tells Q&A that when someone asks about users, they are really talking about persons. This can also be done on a column level. A synonym for "postal code" could be "zip code," while a synonym for an "item" could be "product" or "finished good."

Q&A itself may not use Copilot, but Power BI Desktop can leverage Copilot to generate synonyms. This can be done when creating a new Q&A visual by clicking on **Add synonyms** from the ribbon with the label **Improve Q&A with synonyms from Copilot**. They can also be generated from the **Q&A settings** menu by adding Copilot as a source from the **Suggestion settings** list.

The more synonyms that can be used to describe your data, the more likely you are to produce quality Q&A results. It is important to double-check the synonyms generated by Copilot to ensure they line up with your specific business terminology.

With these Copilot experiences for Power BI, you will be able to generate report ideas, report pages and visuals, summaries, and narratives, and improve Q&A.

Summary

Native integration of generative AI in Microsoft Fabric in the form of Copilot aims to accelerate the analytics journey by potentially increasing overall developers' productivity. In this chapter, we learned what Copilot is and what the requirements are to use it in Fabric, and then we looked at different examples for accelerating data integration, data transformation, visualizations, and reports.

The important point to note, however, is that what we covered in this chapter is just the beginning and barely scratched the surface. As this technology is still evolving and underlying models maturing, it is expected to be a game changer in the near future.

Throughout all the chapters of this book, we introduced you to the world of Microsoft Fabric, which opens up tremendous opportunities for you to build an analytics system quickly and derive business insights in this era of AI. We hope you enjoyed reading it as much as we enjoyed writing it. We cannot wait to see the amazing analytical system you build for your organization that creates business values and supports your organization in staying competitive by leveraging the greater insights it provides in a timely manner.

Index

‹packt›

Other Books You May Enjoy

If you enjoyed this book, you may be interested in these other books by Packt:

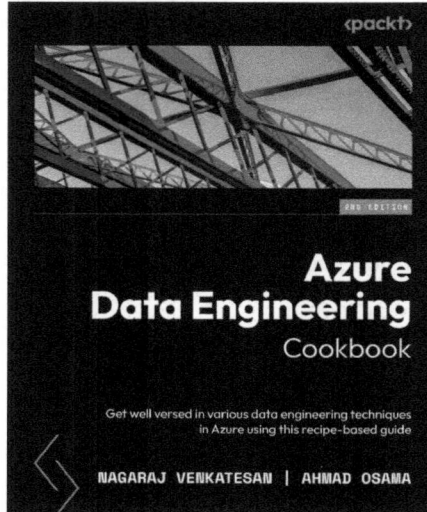

Azure Data Engineering Cookbook

Nagaraj Venkatesan, Ahmad Osama

ISBN: 978-1-80324-678-9

- Process data using Azure Databricks and Azure Synapse Analytics
- Perform data transformation using Azure Synapse data flows
- Perform common administrative tasks in Azure SQL Database
- Build effective Synapse SQL pools which can be consumed by Power BI
- Monitor Synapse SQL and Spark pools using Log Analytics
- Track data lineage using Microsoft Purview integration with pipelines

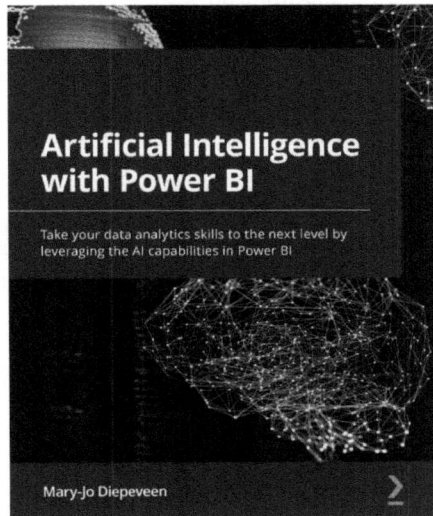

Artificial Intelligence with Power BI

Mary-Jo Diepeveen

ISBN: 978-1-80181-463-8

- Apply techniques to mitigate bias and handle outliers in your data
- Prepare time series data for forecasting in Power BI
- Prepare and shape your data for anomaly detection
- Use text analytics in Power Query Editor
- Integrate QnA Maker with PowerApps and create an app
- Train your own models and identify the best one with AutoML
- Integrate an Azure ML workspace with Power BI and use endpoints to generate predictions

Packt is searching for authors like you

If you're interested in becoming an author for Packt, please visit `authors.packtpub.com` and apply today. We have worked with thousands of developers and tech professionals, just like you, to help them share their insight with the global tech community. You can make a general application, apply for a specific hot topic that we are recruiting an author for, or submit your own idea.

Share Your Thoughts

Now you've finished *Learn Microsoft Fabric*, we'd love to hear your thoughts! Scan the QR code below to go straight to the Amazon review page for this book and share your feedback or leave a review on the site that you purchased it from.

`https://packt.link/r/1-835-08228-9`

Your review is important to us and the tech community and will help us make sure we're delivering excellent quality content.

Download a free PDF copy of this book

Thanks for purchasing this book!

Do you like to read on the go but are unable to carry your print books everywhere?

Is your eBook purchase not compatible with the device of your choice?

Don't worry, now with every Packt book you get a DRM-free PDF version of that book at no cost.

Read anywhere, any place, on any device. Search, copy, and paste code from your favorite technical books directly into your application.

The perks don't stop there, you can get exclusive access to discounts, newsletters, and great free content in your inbox daily

Follow these simple steps to get the benefits:

1. Scan the QR code or visit the link below

https://packt.link/free-ebook/9781835082287

2. Submit your proof of purchase
3. That's it! We'll send your free PDF and other benefits to your email directly

9 781835 082228